Kanawha County Images
Volume II

by Richard A. Andre and Stan B. Cohen

A grand photo of a 1931 Halloween party at the home of Virginia Blair at the corner of California Avenue and Quarrier Street across from the east wing of the state capitol. Tommy Reeves, who provided the photo, is in the second from the top row with the cowboy hat. TOMMY REEVES COLL.

PICTORIAL HISTORIES PUBLISHING CO., INC
Charleston, West Virginia 25301.

LIBRARY OF CONGRESS
CONTROL NUMBER
87-90434

ISBN 1-57510-090-8

First Printing: November 2001

Layout and pre-production by Leslie Maricelli, Donna Elliot, Jan Taylor, Peggy Nesbit, John Cohen, Ken Lockwood and Gateway Printing.

Printed by Jostens Printing and Publishing

PICTORIAL HISTORIES PUBLISHING CO., INC.
1416 Quarrier Street
Charleston, West Virginia 25301
(304) 342-1848
E-Mail-phpc@newwave.net

Introduction

In 1987 the authors, in conjunction with the Kanawha County Bicentennial Commission, produced a 486-page volume – *Kanawha County Images* – containing over 1,000 photographs, drawings and ephemera for the 1988 county bicentennial celebration. The book went through four printings and became the best selling Kanawha County history of all time.

At the time of the publication of the first volume, we knew that there would be more photos and information appearing, partly, we think, in response to the book. Never did we expect to uncover the amount of material that is presented in this–Volume Two.

The purpose of producing these two volumes is to record for future generations the history of our great county. Perhaps 50 years from now some historian will carry on the tradition and produce a third volume portraying the events of the 21st century.

As we enter a new century and a new millenium, we hope this volume, like the first, will cause the reader to reflect on where we were and where we are going.

To all who have read and enjoyed Volume I, we thank you, and hope that you will find Volume II equally interesting.

Richard Andre
Stan Cohen

Alene G. Andre
1910-1982
Photo 1937

Ruth L. Cohen
1910-
Photo 1935

This book is dedicated to our mothers.

Acknowledgments

Thanks to all the good people who helped make this book possible:

Bill Wintz
Terry Lowry
J.W. Williams
Todd Hanson
Gerald Ratliff
Tom Hanshaw
Ed O'Dell
Lawson Hamilton
Capt. Harry White
Hugh Stewart

Raymond Shamblen
Bill Sparkmon
Bob Craigo
Rosalie Earle
Charleston Newspapers
Warren Woomer
Ann Bird
Sam Flournoy
Vince Sodaro
Benny Marshall

Charleston Police Dept.
Charleston Fire Dept.
Howard Cottrell
Jim Barth
Gen. James K.
    McLaughlin
W.Va. State Library
    Staff
Joe Childress
Henry Battle

Bob Deahl
Ken Shock
Phil Goldstein
Sam McCorkle
Charlene Wideman -
    Glenwood
Jerry Smith
Walt Smith
Julius Jones
Tom Blankenship
Bill Kelly

Our apologies to those good people we may have failed to mention.

A special thank you to Chris Parsley, Jerry Waters, Bob Kirk, C.E. "Tank" Turley, Daniel E. Davidson, and Tom Dixon of the C&OHS.

Kanawha County 1873

The Threads of History

The history of the Great Kanawha Valley is woven of threads from nearly every chapter of the American story.

From the ancient mound-builders, most of whom remain cloaked in mystery, to the leading edge technology of the 20th century, the people of our beautiful valley have blazed the trails, tamed the rivers, harvested the timber, packed the salt and mined the coal that has lighted our nation's homes and factories.

The famous pioneer scout, Daniel Boone, lived for five years in the valley, and were he to return today, he would recognize the timeless hills and rivers that he knew so well.

The tragedy of the Civil War left its mark as Blue and Gray contested the strategic valley.

Two future presidents served many months along the Great Kanawha. Union Army officers, Rutherford B. Hayes and William McKinley, praised the beauty and future potential of western Virginia.

Out of the fiery crucible of war, West Virginia was born and Charleston took its place as state capital.

A growing America reached out for the raw materials to build a nation and West Virginia was quick to provide them.

Railroads grew like spreading vines to carry the rich bounty of nature's treasure chest.

Strong hands were in demand as thousands of immigrant Americans joined the trek to mine and factory gates.

The 20th Century has been called "the American Century," and this land along the river played its part in the industrial drama of two world wars and all the way to putting a man on the moon!

The past is important because a sense of continuity is necessary to people, the knowledge that some things have a longer than mortal existence.

It is apparent that human life is not limited to a single lifespan but goes far beyond.

Our children are the living messages we send to a time we will not see and it is crucial that they carry forth our rich heritage.

We must resolve to resist those acts of destruction that would separate us forever from the past.

Our history must be sought out, reawakened and defended!

The Photographs and Photographers

The earliest photographers in the county used the daguerrotype photographic method (1844). Union troops left a record of photographs in the Kanawha Valley during the Civil War. Some photos show up in the 1870s and '80s and several photographers set up shop in Charleston before the turn of the century. Some of the late 19th century and early 20th century photographers were J. Leonard Gates and Gravely and Moore.

One of the most prolific photographers of the 20th century was W.E. Bollinger and his sons, Cramer and Sprague. For almost half a century the Bollingers recorded on film nearly every facet of county life. The family moved to Charleston from Braxton County in 1910. The parents, W.E. and Louisa Bollinger bought a home on Bigley Avenue. Cramer had a keen interest in aviation and the small airport - Bollinger Field - which was located on Route 119 where the Southridge Center is now located, was named for him. Aerial photography was a specialty of Cramer and he often teamed up with local aviator Glenn Clark. Cramer died in 1964.

Bollinger's photographs are always top quality and they were truly artists with their cameras. Their collection of photos is scattered throughout the state, some in private hands and a large portion on deposit at the West Virginia and Regional History Collection in Morgantown.

The Bollinger family on the front porch of their Bigley Avenue home. W.E. on left, Cramer and Louise seated on swing and Sprague on porch rail, circa 1915. The Interstate off ramp is now at this site. The Central Methodist Church in the distance still stands.

W. E. BOLLINGER & SONS
Commercial Photographers
Banquet - Aerial - Press - Color
Photographers
Motion Pictures and Aerial Survey Maps
Photo Copies-Lantern Slides-Photo Murals
Industrial and Progress Photography
Group Photos In Your Home
Fifty Years of Commercial Photography
Experience At Your Service
Competent Operators Available 24 Hours
A Day
128 Delaware Avenue ----- Capitol 26-561
If no answer call ----------- Capitol 22-805
Or --------------------------- Capitol 26-561

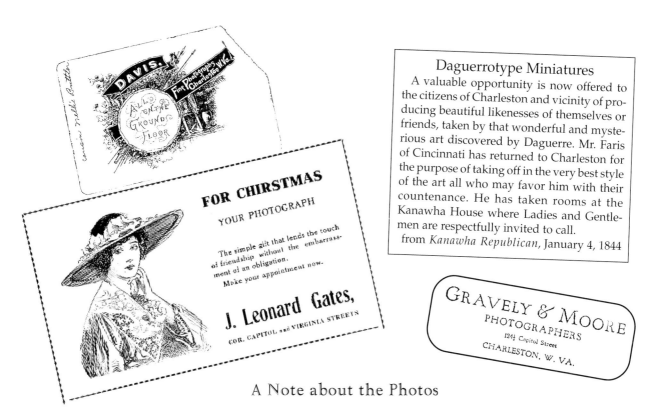

A Note about the Photos

The photos in this book range from over a hundred years old to less than 25.

They were taken by everything from primitive box cameras to the newspaper photographer's famous graflex.

Some of them are of the highest quality done by professionals while many others were taken by people from every walk of life.

Some of the photos in this book are very rare and may not be as clear as we would prefer, however, we believe our readers will agree that a dim picture of a rare scene is better than no picture at all.

Even in this age of computer enhancement there are still no miracles but we have done everything we know how to improve the faded old photos.

R.A.A. - S.B.C

Also note:

Occasionally the reader will note a circled number following a caption or a photograph. This means that the photograph relates to a page in Volume One of *Kanawha County Images*. This will enable the reader of the first volume to use it in conjunction with the second volume. For example: Volume Two has a section on motorcycling in the 1940s and '50s. As one comes to this section look for the circled number following a caption and it will direct the reader to page 190 in Volume One concerning motorcycling in the 1900-1930 period.

Photo Credits

SWV - West Virginia State Archives, Charleston
BK - Bob Kirk Collection, Belle
GA - Glenwood Archives, Charleston
C&OHS - C&O Historical Society Archives, Clifton Forge, Va.
RAA - Richard Andre Collection
BEA - B.E. Andre Collection
CET - C.E. Turley Collection, Milton
CN - Charleston Newspapers Archives
TH - Todd Hanson Collection, Given, WV
KCL-Kanawha County Public Library
DED-Daniel E. Davidson Collection
Other photos are credited to their source.

Kendall Vintroux - Artist

April 24, 1932

Born in Putnam County in 1896, Kendall Vintroux tickled the funny bone of Charleston readers for almost half a century.

His son John has devoted a labor of love to the task of assembling the thousands of his fathers' cartoons into an amazing chronicle- day-by-day- of the 46 years that Vintroux drew the passing scene.

Every morning it was almost a ritual to open the *Gazette* to see what "Vintroux" had to say about what was going on in the city, the state, the nation and the world.

When he passed away in 1973 after a long life, Columnist Don Marsh wrote the following, "Vinty was a nice guy. He was as polite and courteous toward the newest reporters as he was to the publisher. He lacked the meanness and maliciousness that seems to identify the political satirist. I thought as I looked through some of his drawings he made during his 46 years as editorial cartoonist for the *Gazette*, that making people laugh a little and think a little wasn't a bad way to spend a lifetime."

October 13, 1940

Kendall Vintroux.

KENDALL VINTROUX

Sunday on the Turnpike

November 16, 1954

Table of Contents

"A country with no regard for its past will have little worth remembering in the future."

- Abraham Lincoln

The price of freedom has always been high but Americans have willingly paid it.

As we go to press, the horrible images of the murderous attack on our country on September 11 are fresh in our thoughts.

Since 1776 we have met the worst the tyrants wrath could send against us and we have always prevailed.

As you read this history of our forebearers courage - take heart - The light of Freedom will not fail!

God Bless America.

R.A.A.

S.B.C.

As early as 1820, the failure of the first steamer that entered the Kanawha River to get up as high as Charleston, induced the state of Virginia to direct the James River & Kanawha Company to improve the navigation of the Kanawha River so as to give three feet of water from the mouth to Kanawha Falls all year.

The Way It Was
19th Century

This was one of a group of drawings that appeared in an 1891 issue of *Harper's Weekly*. The 1885 capitol is on the left with the beginning of an industrial complex on the south side of the Kanawha River where Camp White was located during the Civil War. (101)

Daniel

Boone

500 acres

Kenhawa

Exd & deld

to Robt W Keie

Feby 7, 1805

James Monroe, Governor of Virginia and later fourth President of the United States, signed this document in 1805 giving Daniel Boone, one of the original founders of Kanawha County, 500 acres of land in the county. Boone, however, left the County in 1799 and never returned, declaring Kanawha was becoming too crowded.⑬

James Monroe, Esquire, Governor of the Commonwealth of Virginia:

To All to Whom these Presents shall Come, Greeting:

Know Ye, That by virtue of a Land office Treasury warrant No 4,202 fmd the 21st day of March 1780. there is granted by the said Commonwealth unto Daniel Boone a certain tract or parcel of land containing 500 acres by survey bearing date the 8th day of September 1798 lying and being in the county of Kenhawa on or near the dividing ridge between the 16 and 18 mile creeks that runs into the ohio (the 16 mile creek runs into the Kenhawa) and bounded as followeth to wit. Beginning 100 poles north west of a large Deer lick on a small drain that runs nearly west and from the end of the said 100 poles at 2 black oaks 3 hickories and one white oak on the south side of a ridge E 200 poles to black oak and pine on a ridge S 400 poles to white oak black oak and hickory on a ridge near the head of a hollow W 200 poles to 2 small white oaks and 2 hickories in the head of a hollow thence N 400 poles to the beginning with its appurtenances

TO HAVE AND TO HOLD the said Tract or Parcel of Land, with its appurtenances, to the said *Daniel Boone* and *his* heirs forever.

IN WITNESS WHEREOF, The said *James Monroe*, Esquire, Governor of the Commonwealth of Virginia, hath hereunto set his hand and caused the Lesser Seal of the said Commonwealth to be affixed, at Richmond, on the 1st day of *April* in the year of our Lord one thousand & hundred and and of the Commonwealth the 24th

James Monroe

Seal.

Virginia, Kanawha County, to wit:

YOU ARE HEREBY COMMANDED, that of the goods and chattels of *Joseph Hunt* late in your district, you cause to be made the sum of *Twenty* ——— dollars ——— cents, for debt, with interest thereon, at the rate of six percentum per annum, from the 19— day of *June* 1839 until paid; for which *Wm T Stockton* has obtained a Judgment before me, a Justice of the Peace for said County; and also the further sum of 30 cents for costs about *his* said suit expended; and that you have the same before me, on the 19— day of *Decem* next, to render the said *Wm T Stockton* of *his* debt and costs aforesaid. Given under my hand, this 19 day of *Oct* 1839

David Ruffner

This summons is dated Oct. 19, 1839, and is signed by David Ruffner, Justice of the Peace for Kanawha County, and one of the pioneer salt producers of the area.

MEMORIAL

OF THE

MANUFACTURERS OF SALT

IN KANAWHA COUNTY, VIRGINIA

PRAYING FOR

A RESTORATION OF THE

DUTY ON IMPORTED SALT.

ADDRESSED TO THE SENATE AND HOUSE OF REPRESENTATIVES
OF THE UNITED STATES.

KANAWHA C. H. VIRGINIA,
PRINTED AT THE OFFICE OF THE KANAWHA BANNER.
1830

This is the earliest known booklet printed in Charleston. The area salt manufacturers prepared a petition to Congress in 1830 urging the restoration of the 20 cent duty on foreign salt. CET ㉟

The Salt Industry

This bill of lading, dated Nov. 19, 1851, was printed with William Dickinson's name on it. He and Joel Shrewsbury established a salt business in Kanawha Salines about 1810 and became the largest producers in the area. His name has been scratched out and Ruffner, Donnally written over it. This assocation had been formed in 1851 after the Kanawha Salt Association had been dissolved. The Ruffners and Donnallys were two large salt producing families in the area. Notice that the bill of lading was shipment by steamboat but his shipment was by wagon to Nicholas County Court House (now Summersville). CET

SHIPPED, in good order and well conditioned, by Ruffner Donnally by
WILLIAM DICKINSON, President of the Kanawha Salt Association.
On board the good Steam Boat Waggon
the following articles marked as below, which are to be delivered, without delay, in like good order and condition, at the
Port of Nicholas C. House (the unavoidable dangers of Navigation and Fire only excepted) unto I. H. Robinson or assigns, he or they paying Freight for said goods at the rate of (as agreed upon)

PRINTED ON THE STEAM PRESS OF E. SHEPARD, 41 SECOND ST. CIN.

In Witness Whereof, the owner, master, or clerk of said boat hath affirmed to 2 Bills of Lading, of this tenor and date, one of which being accomplished the others to stand void.
Dated at Kanawha Salines, this 19 day of Novm. 1851

MARKS.	ARTICLES.	WEIGHTS.
I. H. Robinson Nicholas C. House	9 Boxes Mdse 1 Cask Jonathan Dunbar	1547

-3-

Kanawha Court House Feb 10 1844

Dear Sir

Enclosed are the copies you wrote for. and below I give you the quantity of salt manufactured in the years stated - As to our approaching Spring Elections, althou we have two candidates (whigs) in the field. I have no fears but the matter will be compromised before election day - the Loco's however declare that they have no desire and do not intend running any candidate, but will leave a clear field for the whigs.

What think you of our Judge? what speaks of him as a kind hearted man and good lawyer though rather careless in manners and general appearance - the parties belligerent here for the office, have settled down here in quiet, and are preparing to receive him with a good grace - I have positively no news to write about except that Worths & English are making 45 barrels of salt per diem entirely without the use of coal and are rapidly extending their works so as in a short time to more than double the quantity. using now not to exceed one half of their water, - the gas brings up the water and then converts it into brine, then the steam from the pan makes the brine into salt. they have no need of horses or work cattle - and if they had a machine for hacking might almost do without human labor. Please present my best respects to Mrs. S.

respectfully yours

A.W. Quarrier.

G.W. Summers Esq

Salt manufactured inspected & weighed in the County of Kanawha State of Virginia, in the year named below. taken from the returns filed in my office - viz:

Year 1840 1.235.873 bushels - one return not made   say 1 80000 b.

" 1841 1.343.648   "   "   "   "   "
" 1842 1.819.394
" 1843 2.043.890

A.W. Quarrier Clerk
Kanawha County Court

Interesting voucher from the 1880s. Boone, one of the founders of Kanawha County had died years before. This store may have been located in the Snow Hill area on the north side of the Kanawha River.

Relics of a Vanished Industry ㊴

Bromine still at Dickinson Salt Works, circa 1970s.

Salt well at Malden, circa 1970s.

These three photos are of various tools
at Dickinson Salt Works, circa 1970s.

The salt producers along the Kanawha River formed the first industrial cartel in the United States in the 1840s a move that today would be in strict violation of the anti-trust laws. CET

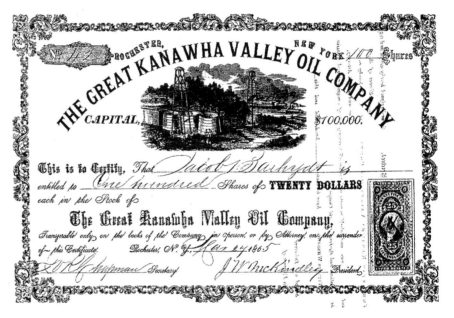

Cincinnati, 184

Received of

of

Barrels

Salt, which we promise and bind ourselves to sell strictly in accordance with the prices fixed from time to time by the *Kanawha Salt Association*, and to conform to all the regulations they have adopted or may adopt for the sale of Salt. Should it appear that we have intentionally violated by selling contrary to the prices and regulations aforesaid. we agree that the owners of the Salt or the Vigilance Committee of the Association shall take the Salt out of our possession without other charges on it than freight, inspection, labor, drayage and cooperage. The violation to be decided by said Committee upon reasonable notice given to us.

Nothing is known of this 1860s local oil company, but it was probably a company on paper only.

No. 42   ROCHESTER, NEW YORK   100 Shares

THE GREAT KANAWHA VALLEY OIL COMPANY

CAPITAL, $100,000.

This is to Certify, That Jacob Bashydt is entitled to One hundred Shares of **TWENTY DOLLARS** each in the Stock of

The Great Kanawha Valley Oil Company, Transferable only on the books of the Company, in person, or by Attorney, on the surrender of this Certificate. Rochester, N. Y. Mar 24 1865.

Chipman Secretary   J W McKindley President

This Internal Revenue form for excise tax on 35 tons of coal from Kanawha Salines is unusual as it is dated Oct. 2, 1863, when the Civil War was raging. CET

UNITED STATES INTERNAL REVENUE

No. _____   Collector's Office, 3d District, State of West Virginia

October 2nd, 1863.

Received of Walker & Schrewsbery of Kanawha Salines the sum of Twenty One 00/100 Dollars, in full for his Excise Tax on —

| 35 Tons Coal @ 6 | $ | 21.00 |
| Total | $ | 21.00 |

as per Monthly list of the Assessor of said District sent to me for collection for the Month ending August 31, 1863.

S. R. Dawson Collector

Charleston, May 25, 1827.

This day Mrs. Philena Whitteker appeared before the session, convened at her request, to give an explanation of her conduct in relation to a dancing party which occurred in her tavern, during the absence of her husband, William Whitteker; for which offence she had been informed she would be called to an account by the session.

The session having opened with prayer Mrs. Whitteker was heard. It appeared before the session that Mrs. Whitteker, in the absence of her husband, had not the control of the house, that her elder son, who was of age, had been employed to superintend the management of the house, in the absence of Mr. Whitteker, his step-father, and that he, in opposition to the wishes and advice of his Mother Mrs. Whitteker, did encourage the party at her house. Upon the evidence of this fact, in connection with Mrs. Whitteker's profession of regret and sorrow that the occurrence had taken place, and her promise in the future to guard against anything of the kind, the members of session expressed their satisfaction at the exhibition of a christian spirit on the part of Mrs. Whitteker, and affectionately admonished her to guard in future against anything which might have even the appearance on her part of giving countenance to a practice so injurious to the cause of piety as dancing.

At the same meeting of session Miss Jane Wolfington, formerly a member of the congregation of   presented a request to be received into connection with, and under the care of this church. Upon examination she was received as a member of this church.

Session closed with prayer.

N. W. Calhoun., Moderator.

From a history of the Presbyterian Church

This frame farmhouse at Quincy was built before 1820 by the Shrewsbury family. It was subsequently occupied by the Dickinson family for many years. The road in front is the old Midland Trail now U.S. Route 60. The house stood for almost 200 years. C.C. DICKINSON COLL.

Kanawha Salines July 1862

280   **Cabell & Donnally**   July 1st 1862

To 1 Cedar Faucet 13 (5c) 10th 4 D Nails 61 65 Casterbil 15   91

Order paid Wm Cundiff 300 P P Dean 700   1000

(4th) 1 Blind Bridle 125 1 Collar 100 (5th) P Albert $10.00   1225

9th Pm R W C 2 Cradles 200 16th Horse Shoe Irons 52 88   488

Paid Wm Cundiff 100 (9th) 2 Hay Forks 75 150 1 File 62   312

1 1/4 Auger 63 (14th) P P Dean 300 (21st) Linsed Oil 35   398

(22d) pd P P Dean 250 (23d) pd Wm Cundiff 450   700

(25th) pd Wm Cundiff 600 (31st) To A F D.   600

28 Yds Virginia Shirty 45 12.60 1 Gross H Buttons 25   1285

2 Hanks Blk Thread 20 (29th) 1 Mule Collar 100   120   6219

This ledger is interesting as it is dated July 1862, just two months before Confederate forces expelled Union troops from the Kanawha Valley and shipped salt from the Salines east for use by the Southern army. CET

Dr. Spicer Patrick

Dr. Spicer Patrick GA

One of the valley's most prominent early citizens was Dr. Spicer Patrick whose legacy lives on in Charleston. He was born in 1791 in New York and died at his home near Two-Mile Creek in 1884, thus living through the formative years of the United States and Kanawha County. He came to Charleston in 1816 to practice medicine and most of his patients at the time lived at Kanawha Salines (Malden). In the 1840s a great cholera plague hit the area, especially in the vicinity of the Salines, killing both whites and their slaves. Dr. Patrick worked day and night to care for the sick and was successful in controlling the disease. He became one of the largest landowners in the new development on the west side of the Elk River, thus Patrick Street and the bridge are named after him. He was a delegate to the Virginia Secession Convention in 1861 where he voted against succession and after the war became the first Speaker of the House of Delegates of the new state of West Virginia. His house "Beechwood" stood for many years on the hill at the end of Patrick Street. Dr. Patrick was truly a prominent individual in the shaping of Kanawha County history.

1850 MAP
of
KANAWHA SALT WORKS

REDRAWN BY

WILLIAM D. WINTZ

WITH PERMISSION OF THE CHESAPEAKE & OHIO HISTORICAL SOCIETY, CLIFTON FORGE, VIRGINIA

ORIGINAL MAP MADE BY C. B. SHAW, C.E., IN 1854 FOR THE COMMONWEALTH OF VIRGINIA IN CONNECTION WITH A SURVEY COMPLETED FOR THE COVINGTON & OHIO RAILROAD

LEGEND

SW	—	Salt Well
OSW	—	Old Salt Well
SF	—	Salt Furnace
OSF	—	Old Salt Furnace
CB	—	Coal Bank
	—	Residence
	—	Main Road
	—	Secondary Road
	—	Coal Bank Railroad

This wonderful look back at the Charleston of 1850 was discovered in the C&O Historical Society Archives in Clifton Forge, Va. It was done in preparation for the construction of the Covington & Ohio Railroad (later Chesapeake & Ohio). The Civil War interrupted the completion of the railroad and it did not reach Charleston until 1873. For years, Wheeling had the great advantage of the Baltimore & Ohio Railroad and that was often cited as a reason Wheeling, not Charleston, should be the capital. In 1873, that advantage vanished as the C&O gave Charleston main-line access to the rest of the nation. Note the 1850 surveyors plotted a line on *both* sides of the river, but chose the southside for actual construction. In 1884 another company utilized the northside route (now Norfolk-Southern).

TOM DIXON, C&O HISTORICAL SOCIETY ARCHIVES. CLIFTON FORGE, VA 206-224

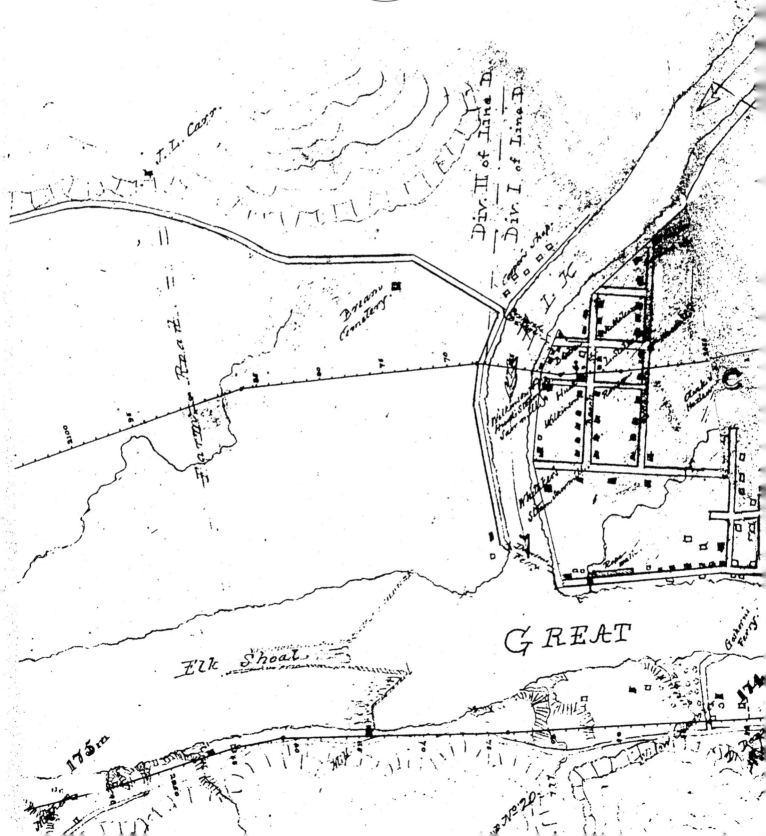

Note: Gallows

At the time of this interesting proclamation the Union Army was firmly in control of the Kanawha Valley. However, a month later the Confederate Army under General W.W. Loring drove the Federals from the valley and occupied it until October.

Head Quarters 4 Brigade
Charleston Aug 4, 1862

Col. Thos. Nutter

Col 153 Regt Va Militia
You will at once order the Captains of your Regiment to disarm all disloyal men belonging to their respective companies have the names of the owner placed upon the guns and have them sent to these head quarters, also to arrest and bring to these head quarters all person who they can prove are using treasonable and menacing lagnage (sic) against the U.S. Government or threatening uninion (sic) citizens. Hurrahing for Jeff Davis & C. any and all male persons violating as above stated upon testimony or affidavit will at once be arrested and brought to these head quarters.

By order of
J.A.J. Lightburn
Col Commg 4 Brigade
B Stanbury
Lieut

Above: an 1863 letter sent to Mr. E.A. Broun, Co. C, 26th Regiment O.V.I. at Charleston, Western Virginia.

At right: A soldier's letter from a J.R. McMullin, Capt. Independent Ohio Battery, stationed in Charleston, Nov. 1863.

A Civil War letter sent to Mrs. Almyra Brown in Ohio from Kanawha Court House, Virginia.

Headquarters 3d Division, Dep't W. Va.,

CHARLESTON, WEST VA., APRIL 29th, 1864.

GENERAL ORDERS.
No. 15.

I. Before a Military Commission, which convened at Charleston, West Va., on the 15th day of April, 1864, pursuant to Special Order No. 71, from these Headquarters, and of which Captain W. H. ZIMMERMAN, 23d Regt. Ohio Vol. Infantry, is President, were arraigned and tried:

1. Captain *Geo W. Cox*, of the steamer Victress:

CHARGE—"*Conduct highly prejudicial to the interest of the Government, endangering thereby the lives of its officers and soldiers, and rendering it's property liable to capture by the enemy.*"

Specification—In this, that Captain Geo. W. Cox, of the steamer Victress, a vessel then in service of the United States, did, on or about the night of the eighteenth of March, 1864, land and tie up the said steamer, some two miles and a half above Red House, a dangerous point on the Kanawha, and leaving the vessel at the mercy of the enemy, crossed over the river to Winfield, on a visit to his wife, and this was done in the face of the recent capture of Gen. Scammon and other officers, and the burning of the steamer B. C. Levi, and notwithstanding the best efforts of officers on board to prevent delay, and when ordered to put the boat, said steamer Victress, under way, the acting Captain refused to obey, saying that Captain Cox, on leaving the vessel, had ordered that she should not set out before four o'clock in the morning. The night was fine and clear, and the wind entirely lulled after ten o'clock.

To which charges and specifications the accused pleaded "Not Guilty."

FINDING—The Commission having maturely considered the evidence adduced, find the accused, Geo. W. Cox, Captain of the steamer Victress, as follows:

Of the Specification, (except in leaving the boat, and failing to run the schute after the wind lulled,) Not Guilty.
Of the Charge, Not Guilty.

SENTENCE.

And the Commission do therefore sentence him, the said Captain Geo. W. Cox, of the steamer Victress, "That he be not employed again in the Government service, and that he be not allowed to run a steamboat on the Kanawha river.

The evidence in this case does not warrant the finding. The whole proceedings are disapproved, and Captain Geo. W. Cox is released from his bonds.

The Charleston Bank

The legislature has authorized the Governor to make inquiry into the affairs of this institution, and we hope ere long to give our readers a full insight into what has been a costly mystery to some of them. Below we give the correspondence between the Governor and its late President:

STATE OF WEST VIRGINIA,
EXECUTIVE DEPARTMENT
WHEELING, July 18, 1864.

JAMES C. MCFARLAND, ESQ.:

Sir:-I am informed that the assets of the branch of the Bank of Virginia at Charleston are in your hands as its late President, and that in the absence of a Board of Directors you are disposing of such asssets to persons holding notes of the bank, and otherwise claiming to be creditors of the bank.

The Commonwealth of Virginia was a large stockholder in the Bank of Virginia; and whatever interest she had in the branch at Charleston was transferred by act of the General Assembly to the State of West Virginia.

Inasmuch, therefore, as in my opinion it is not proper for you in the absence of the legally constituted directory to be exchanging the assets of the bank for its notes, or otherwise transacting its business, except it might be to collect the debts due the bank, I feel it my duty on the part of the State, as I do hereby, to give you notice that if any detriment shall result to the interests of the State by your management of the affairs of the bank, the State will hold you personally responsible therefor.

Very Respectfully,
(Signed,)   A.I. BOREMAN.

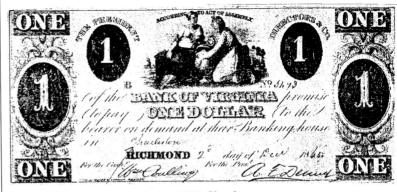

This interesting notice in an 1864 Charleston newspaper concerns the problems of the Bank of Virginia, Charleston Branch. McFarland's reply was that because of the present Civil War the former Board of Directors had scattered or left for parts unknown (some supposedly to the Southern Army) and he had no way to communicate with the mother bank in Richmond. In addition the bank building was burned in Lightburn's retreat from Charleston in September 1862. The bank was established in Charleston in 1831. ㉖

The Bank of the West was one of the oldest banks in the Kanawha Valley. Apparently its assets were taken over by First National Bank of Charleston in 1872. CET ㉛

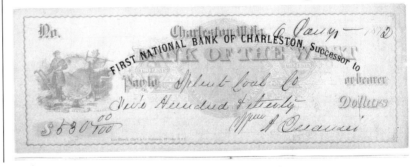

Rutland O., Dec. 10, 1908

Ed. Leader:-I recently made a visit up in Fayette county, W. Va., my old home county. I saw different places where I used to go to school when a small boy.

I could locate the ground where the old log building stood. I remembered one place distinctly where I went to school in an old log school house about 10x12 feet with no floor in it. There was another place where I went to school in an old store house, but it don't look like the same place now They now have fine school houses. A great many people who lived there before I left and who could not read or write have raised their children up under the free school system. Some are fine doctors, some lawyers and some ministers of the gospel. You can see what free schools have done for West Virginia.

Now one word to the old soldier boys. I saw several of our old camping grounds and several places where we had skirmishes and the place where Jenkins' cavalry was ambushed by the Union infantry right above Hawks Nest.

I came home by the way of Charleston and stayed two nights there with my sister. I would say to the soldier boys that they wouldn't know Charleston if they haven't been there since 1884. Where we formerly camped is built up with fine houses costing from $5000 to $50,000. Gov. McCorkle built his house across the river about half way up the mountain. It cost $72,000. He has a stone or a stick of timber from nearly every fort that was built in the time of the Civil War. I visited the cemetery back on the hill. It is about three-fourths of a mile long but I do not know whether our boys were removed from there or not. I know we buried several of our regiment up here. Boys, do you remember where Gen. Duffy's headquarters were? That is all covered with houses. I guess you've not forgotten how the old scamp used to tie the boys up by the thumbs. Fortunately he never got any of Co. A in his clutches. I for one was not sorry when old Mosby captured him. He would do to command foreign soldiers but we Americans had no use for him.

Well, I will close for this time. Would be glad to hear from any of the old boys of 1861 to 1865. Call and see me.

W.A. Hunt,
Late of Co. A 2nd W. Va. Cav.

President Grant's Visit to the Kanawha Valley, June 1874

————— :0: —————

THE PRESIDENT'S VISIT.-General Grant left Washington City on thursday, and going directly to the White Sulphur, will remain there until this morning, when he will come over the Road by day and arrive here about 3 o'clock this P.M. A special train went up yesterday, consisting of an engine and the new car of the Superintendent. He will be accompanied by Mrs. Grant and some other members of his family, all of whom will be the guests of Col T.B. Swann while here. During his visit to Kanawha he will spend sometime at his aunt's, Mrs. Tompkins, who lives about sixteen miles above the city. On tomorrow the President's party will attend Divine worship at State Street Church, where pews will be reserved for them. We are unable to say how long the Chief Magistrate of the nation will honor Kanawha with his presence, but bespeak for him that hospitality and courtesy which is due him as well as ourselves.

June 27, 1874
From a Charleston newspaper

President U.S. Grant
1869-1877

————— :0: —————

DEPARTURE OF THE PRESIDENT.-As he had announced would be the case, the President only remained with us a couple of days and left on the Eastern bound train yesterday for Washington, where he has no doubt already arrived. It had been his intention to go from here up to visit his aunt, Mrs. Rachel Tompkins, who lives above the city about eighteen miles. Finding her here at her son's in law, Col. Swann, upon his arrival, he gave out the idea and remained in the city all during his visit to Kanawha. On yesterday he received many of our citizens who called and it is rumored he expressed the hope and intention of revisiting the county sometime in the Fall. He frequently expressed his appreciation of the hospitality and courtesy shown him while here, and we are happy to say nothing occurred in any manner to mar the pleasure of his stay among us which was mutually enjoyable to him and our people.

June 28, 1874

For many years it was believed that President Grant came to Charleston by steamboat - this positively proves he came by railroad. -

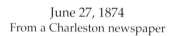

The State Street M.E. Church at the corner of State (Lee) and Court streets. This building later became a Jewish Synagogue. KCL

Glenwood

The historic house at Park Avenue and Orchard Street is known as Glenwood. It was built in 1852 for James M. Laidley, who sold the house and surrounding 366 acres to George W. Summers in 1857. Laidley had purchased the farm from Mrs. Betty Washington Lovell and her children in 1850 for $7,000. Mrs. Lovell was the daughter of Howell Lewis, son of George Washington's sister, Betty, who married Fielding Lewis of Fredericksburg, Virginia. Mrs. Lovell's husband, Joseph, was the son of Lord and Lady Lovell of England. After his death, Lady Lovell married Maj. James Bream who came to Charleston and bought up a considerable amount of the west side that had been owned by Thomas Bullitt. Glenwood is today a splendid museum house owned by the College of Graduate Studies of Marshall University. Many of the photos and documents in this book are from the Glenwood Archives.

Information about pioneer houses that were long ago lost is indeed rare and this 1939 article by George W. Summers describes what may have been the first house in Charleston that was not made of logs.

Summers wrote about the old Goshorn house in anticipation of its demolition to make way for the United Carbon Building on the northwest corner of Kanawha Blvd. and Broad St. The venerable old mansion fell- a victim of progress- in 1940.

Goshorn House Believed Oldest
Still Standing in Charleston

Perhaps the oldest house in Charleston, certainly one of the oldest now standing in the entire community, and known for much more than a century as one of the city's notable residences, this house has been the home of more than one of the most prominent families of old-time Charleston. And something of its history may prove interesting and instructive to those who have seen the old building, admired its style of architecture and have wondered about its origin and its past history.

No person living now can remember back to the time when it was built.

Traditions handed down in families which have occupied it indicate that the house was built in 1801, and therefore is 138 years old. The Daniel Ruffner house, known later as the Silas Ruffner house, now the Nash home, on Kanawha street a few doors below the capitol, was built in 1807 and often has been called the oldest house in Charleston. Perhaps it is. But, if the Goshorn house was built, as is believed by many, in 1801, then it is the oldest, without a doubt.

While the date when it was erected is somewhat vague, it is well established that it was erected by Andrew Donnally, a son of Col. Andrew Donnally of Donnally's Fort, near Lewisburg. Andrew Donnally was born at that fort.

Andrew Donnally had a large family and J.H. Fry married two of his daughters, the first dying in early life. Through these marriages J.H. Fry became a resident of the old house at Broad and Kanawha. He was the father of Joseph L. Fry, twice major of Charleston.

The Goshorn family originally came from Wales, settled in Pennsylvania and after living on both sides of the Ohio river about Wheeling, George came here in 1822. He settled at that time on the banks of the Kanawha river at the end of Goshorn street, which was given his name because of his high standing and the fact that he owned the property beside the street.

George Goshorn established the ferry which ran for many years across the Kanawha river from the end of Goshorn street.

Goshorn prospered and when members of his family wanted more privacy than they could get at the hotel, he bought the Andrew Donnally house, which by that time had become the J.H. Fry house and moved his family into it. And so it became known for years as the Goshorn house.

Birthplace of Mayor

It was in this house that the first mayor of Charleston was born, sometime before 1850, Jacob Goshorn, a son of George Goshorn, who ran the ferry and hotel, was Charleston's first mayor, elected in 1861.

Charleston had a city government many years before that date. But the early government was by a board of trustees, which had a president, a secretary and a treasurer. The president of the board of trustees corresponded then to the mayor of today and the trustees were something like the councilmen of today. But by 1861 the city established a more modern form of city government and Jacob Goshorn was its first elected mayor.

The Civil War was just starting when Jacob Goshorn came to take his seat as mayor of Charleston, he met conditions never faced before, or since, by any Charleston official. It seemed like being mayor of Charleston at that time was an almost impossible job. Goshorn also had kinsmen in one army and he vacated the office of mayor a short time after his election.

Back in the Civil War days, the yard around the Goshorn home was much larger than it is now, extending from Kanawha to Virginia street, and about half way from Broad to McFarland street. And in these grounds there was a garden, as was customary then, and, as was also customary, they kept a cow. When soldiers of the contending armies came into the valley, men in either army did not hesitate to forage for supplies and to take whatever they could find which might be useful to them, especially for food. And many a privately owned farm animal, hog or chicken was carried away by army men for food. And the owner had no recourse.

Cow Hidden in Attic

When sections of both armies were encamped here and harassing the owners of farms, gardens and livestock with their raids, the Goshorn house had an unusual experience. One of the prized possessions of the Goshorn family was a cow. It was stabled, fed and milked on the premises.

When news came one day that a raid on gardens, cow barns, hen houses and all such places was threatened, Mrs. Goshorn took novel steps to save her cow. The cow was led with a halter into the house. And then, with the aid of the servants, men, women and children, the cow was taken slowly up the steps-two flights of them-and tied securely in the attic.

Safe from the raids and raiders of either army, fed and watered in a barn she had never occupied before, the cow was kept in the attic of the house until all danger of further raids had passed. And all the time the cow was there the Goshorn family had its fresh milk every day, but the two armies had to get whatever meat supply they might have had from some other source.

The bricks used in the walls are all hand-made and doubtless were made just over the river bank. The wooden sills and joists in the house were all hand-sawed and all the nails in it were made by hand before nails were first made by machinery. But, despite all the evidence of its age, the old structure is in a better state of preservation now than many buildings half or a third as old.

— OFFICE OF —

James H. Sentz,

JOBBER IN THE PERFECTION COAL,

Charleston, Kanawha Co., W. Va., *April 30th 1884*

Mr J. G. W. Tompkins Prest
Of C. G. M. Co.

Dear Sir

Yours of this date rec. will make it a point to bring you a W.&S. Barge Thursday night as requested do not care to have W&S loaded in barge #25 but if I can posibly spare an other lump Barge will bring it up Thursday night we will Expect you to have the present W&S Boat ready Thursday night for Shippment

Yours Truly
J. H. Sentz

— OFFICE OF —

EDITH MARION MINES,
BLACKSB....

WM. SHARPE, PROP'R,

GAS, STEAM AND GRATE COAL.

Merchandise Department.

Hampton, Kanawha Co., W. Va., Oct. 1 1884

H. P. Tompkins Esq.

Letterheads of county natural resource companies in the 1870s and '80s.

Directors.
C. M. HOLLOWAY,
F. A. LAIDLEY,
J. B. SPEED,
G. Y. ROOTS,
LEWIS GLENN.

C. M. HOLLOWAY, Pres't.
LEWIS GLENN, Treas.

G. Y. ROOTS, Sec'y.
GEO. McQUIGG, Ass't Sec'y.

Cincinnati, _____ 187

M _____

BOUGHT OF Ohio River and Kanawha Salt Co.

MANUFACTURERS OF

OHIO RIVER AND WEST VIRGINIA SALT.

43¾ lbs. News   Paid   9 $3 96
                          S. S. Moore

-18-

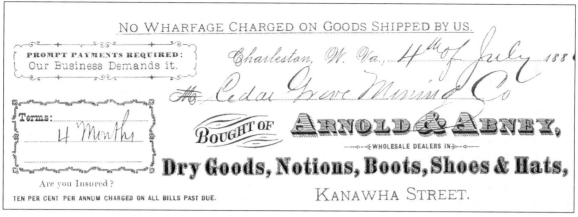

Late 19th century local businesses carried a wide variety of goods as we see here - from baby carriages to coffins.

At left: Ad from 1880s when their store was
on Front Street (now Kanawha Blvd.)
between Hale and Capitol streets.

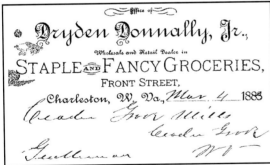
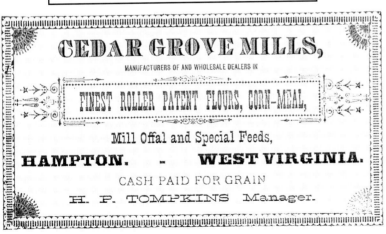

Charleston's First Bicycle 1878

George W. Summers grew up on Charleston's west side on his father's farm. In his adult years he went on to become a newspaper man and historian of considerable renown but long before, in 1878, he was an adventurous 10-year-old. Looking through a magazine one day he came upon a picture of a newfangled means of transportation called a bi-cycle. To the boy of 10, it was as fabulous and desirable as anything the modern generation might imagine. Young George wrote the maker-The Pope Manufacturing Co. and found out the price whereupon he set out to sell enough chickens and eggs to finance this wondrous device!

Before long he had the necessary sum and the grand day came when the gleaming bicycle arrived.

A bicycle was so new and strange that no one had ever seen one much less knew how to ride it. George had to learn the hard way-trial and error. Many bruises and skinned spots later he mastered his new-found delight and became a common sight on the dirt streets. For a while of course, horses bolted at the strange apparition. The contraption was of the high wheel type with a larger front wheel and a much smaller rear wheel. It could go to beat the devil but its design made for some nasty spills.

The particular bike Summers had was not even equipped with rubber tires-in fact it had iron rims. It was childs' size with a 36" diameter wheel to enable a youngster to handle it. In later years, Mr. Summers owned many different bikes and was very enthusiastic about the sport. At one time he was even a dealer for the famous Columbia Bicycle brand.

The Summers Family*

One of the most prominent pioneer families of the county was that of Col. George Summers[1]. He came to the county from Fairfax County, Virginia, in 1814 and died in Charleston in 1818. His oldest son, Lewis was a judge on the Kanawha County Circuit Court from 1819 to 1843. Col. Summers youngest son, George W. [2] was born in 1804 and died in 1868. He was a prominent local lawyer and served on the circuit bench from 1852 to 1858. He was also a member of Congress. He was a law partner of George S. Patton. George W. [2] had two sons, Lewis and George[3], who died during the Civil War. Lewis lived his entire life in the family home at Glenwood on Charleston's west side and had two sons named, Lewis and George W.[4] The last George W. (1868-1941) became a well-known newspaperman and historian and much of the early history of the county is taken from his writings.

*To reduce confusion, the names of the various George Summers' are numbered. George [2] was sent to the Virginia Succession Convention in Richmond where he gave a speech on Federal Relations. He returned to Charleston after voting against secession by Virginia from the United States. Summers County is named after him.

Speech written by George W. Summers[2].

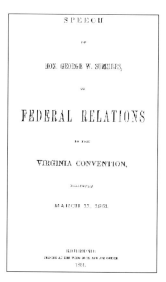

Newspaperman and historian George W. Summers in 1901 and the late 1930s.

This map of the Lens Creek area was published in a report in 1868 by S. Harris Daddow a "practical geologist." It shows present Marmet listed by its old name, Kanawha City and the present Chesapeake & Ohio Railway (now CSX) as the proposed Covington & Ohio Railroad, which merged with the Virginia Central in 1868 to form the C&O which came to the Kanawha Valley in 1873. A proposed but never built railroad and tunnel to Peytona are shown. The Federal Camp Piatt is also shown.

Lens Creek was named for the pioneer settler and Indian fighter of the 1770s, Leonard Morris, whose home was at the mouth of the creek.

Daddow reported that "The Kanawha region is still undeveloped, and the prize long sought by the dilatory Virginia slave master is still to be accomplished by the enterprise of free labor. In no other portion of our country, north or south, are there more inviting prospects to labor, enterprise and capital, than is now presented in the Great Kanawha Valley. Not only its unlimited mineral resources invite attention, but the best portion of the trade of the great Mississippi Valley may be diverted into the channel of the Kanawha by ordinary means."

Jedediah Hotchkiss

Jedediah Hotchkiss was a transplanted Northerner who sided with his adopted Virginia at the onset of the Civil War. He served as chief topographical engineer for Stonewall Jackson and subsequent commanders in the Army of Northern Virginia. After the war he became one of the principals trying to exploit the mineral resources of Virginia and the new state of West Virginia, especially the coal deposits of the New and Kanawha valleys. Hotchkiss, who worked out of Staunton, Virginia, had numerous coal properties in Kanawha County, especially in the Cabin Creek area. His detailed topo and geologic maps were the most accurate of the time. One of his most ambitious projects was the development of a new town to be called Kanawha City. He worked on this and other local projects with Dr. J.P. Hale, but many of these projects were never carried to fruition or ended up in long legal entanglements. Hotchkiss died in 1899 and his superb collection of Civil War and post-war maps of the Virginias is now housed at the Library of Congress in Washington, D.C.

Coal mining in the old days was extremely labor intensive. This 1890s employment agreement with the Cedar Grove Co. was very specific as to what they would pay a miner. CET

No._____ THIS CONTRACT, made this_____day of_____189__, between CEDAR GROVE MINING CO. of the first part, and _____ of the second part,

WITNESSETH, the said _____ agrees to mine coal for the said CEDAR GROVE MINING CO. in a skillful and workmanlike manner, to be paid for by weight, as hereinafter provided, and the weight of all such coal mined as aforesaid, shall be ascertained by weighing the same either in or out of the mine cars in which the same is loaded, and either before or after the same is screened, as the said CEDAR GROVE MINING CO. may elect. The said CEDAR GROVE MINING CO. shall have the right to pay for mining said coal as aforesaid either by run of mine or for screened coal only. The price of run of mine coal shall be _____ cents per bushel of eighty pounds, and for screened coal shall be _____cents per bushel of eighty pounds. This contract of employment shall cease and terminate at the will of either party thereto.

WITNESS

Stock certificate of The Coal River Boom and Driving Company, 1888. BK

The Charleston levee near Summers Street showing the waterfront and the south side, circa 1880. GA

The Charleston levee looking
downriver, late 1890s. GA

These two photos, taken by Miss Lucy Quarrier in 1896
from the old South Side bridge, show the Ruffner Hotel
on the left and, right, a steamboat leaving the levee with
the steepled Kanawha Valley Bank in the distance. GA

Mud streets and board sidewalks were the rule in these 1880 scenes of Charleston although brick paving was becoming common. GA

Little did this lady imagine that a century later automobiles would be whizzing by on the four-lane Kanawha Boulevard. GA

Looking west on old Kanawha Street near Capitol Street. The building on the right was the Kanawha Valley Bank. Before this was Kanawha Street it was simply called Front Street. GA ⓶⓵⓽

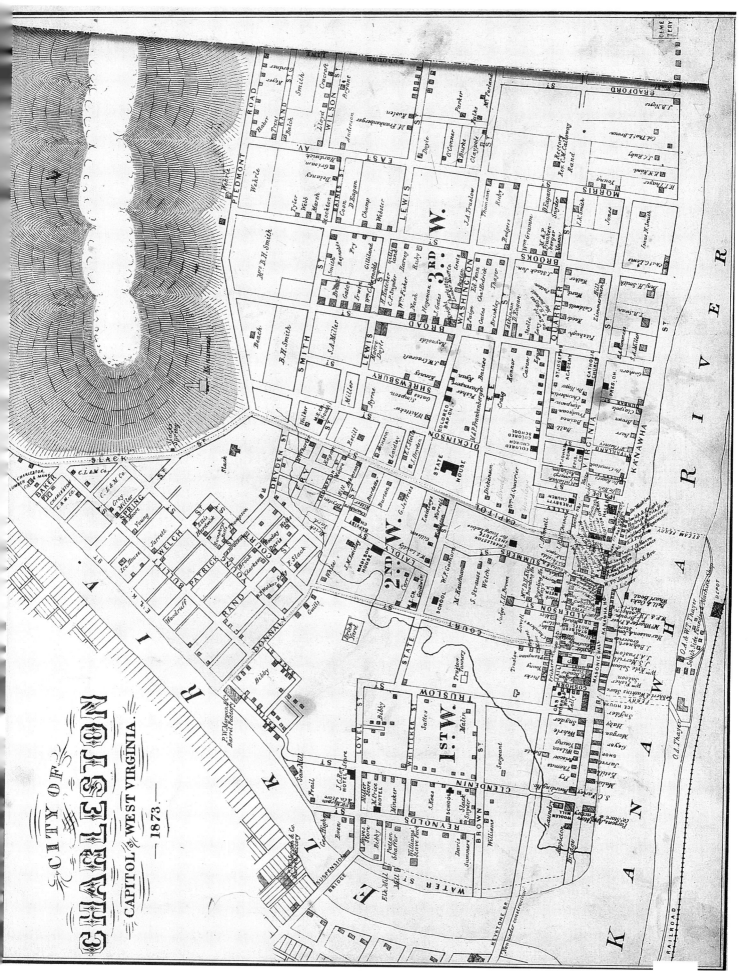

CITY OF CHARLESTON
CAPITOL OF WEST VIRGINIA.
— 1873 —

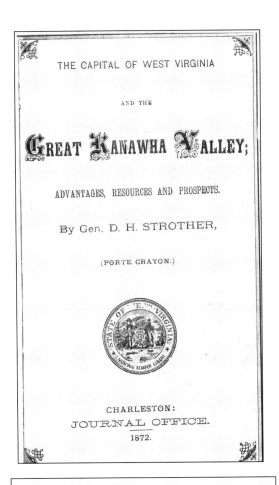

THE CAPITAL OF WEST VIRGINIA

AND THE

Great Kanawha Valley;

ADVANTAGES, RESOURCES AND PROSPECTS.

By Gen. D. H. STROTHER,

(PORTE CRAYON.)

CHARLESTON:
JOURNAL OFFICE.
1872.

32

FOR SALE.

IN THE CENTER OF THE

GREAT KANAWHA COAL FIELD,

COAL,

Cannel, Splint and Bituminous.

20,000 ACRES,

IN TRACTS SUITABLE FOR OPERATING.

Never Before in the Market.

EIGHT MILES OF RIVER FRONTAGE,

DEEP WATER FOR LOADING.

For companies seeking desirable coal lands for operating,
none better can be obtained.

TITLE PERFECT.

For particulars address

W. A. QUARRIER,
J. P. HALE,
Charleston, W. Va.

THE
WEST END EXTENSION.

Perfectly Level, Well Drained,

Broad Sixty-Feet Streets.

LARGE PUBLIC PARK.

Title Indisputable.

There are now Seven Factories in operation on the West End.

Two new Planing Mills; one Barrel Factory; one Tobacco Factory; one Machine Shop and Stove Factory; Mineral and Soda Water Factory. These establishments will employ in the neighborhood of 300 men during this year.

Thirty new buildings erected since last March. The Elk River railroad and the Parkersburg, Ripley and Charleston railroad will have their termini on the West End.

Every encouragement will be offered to mechanics and parties seeking a manufacturing location.

An alley gives access to the rear of each lot. Size of lots, 40x120.

PRICE--$300 AND $250.

Office REMOVED from Shields' Building to the corner of PENNSYLVANIA AVENUE and KANAWHA STREET—WEST END.

Office of the Kanawha  ills in, its sa Building.

Gen. David Hunter Strother, soldier, writer and artist from Martinsburg, West Virginia, was known by his pen-name, "Porte Crayon." His son-in-law, J. Brisben Walker, the developer of Charleston's west side asked him to write a pamphlet in 1872 extolling the virtues of the new development. Charleston at the time had an estimated 5,000 population and Porte Crayon made the following statement in his pamphlet: "Within a radius of 200 miles, there is no city of importance to stand as a rival in the business of the lumber, coal, salt and manufacturing interest of the Kanawha and its tributaries."

- The West Side -

By GEORGE W. SUMMERS

The present West Side of Charleston grew up in three separate and distinct sections.

Back in 1872 J. Brisben Walker, who later founded and for many years edited the Cosmopolitan magazine in New York bought all the land from Elk river west to a line which ran from the Kanawha river near the end of the present Delaware avenue to about the end of Fayette street at West Washington street, and extending from the Kanawha river to the present West Washington street. This he designated as the J.B. Walker addition to the City of Charleston, but it was commonly called the West End.

Walker laid off this section into a town site, with streets running in one direction and avenues in another. He named the streets for West Virginia counties, and the avenues for other states. His original plans, with a few changes in names, but little other variation, are still the plans of that part of the city. The story of the growth of this section, from the time P.M. Price helped his father and his brothers fence in 112 acres for a farm in the most thickly settled part of the city today, was told in a recent number of the Daily Mail.

Aided by Nicholas Bigley

Later Mr. Walker interested Nicholas J. Bigley, of Allegheny county, Pa., meaning either the city of Pittsburgh or one of its suburbs, and the two laid out and began the promotion of the Bigley and Walker addition, which later was known as Glen Elk. It comprised the territory in the Elk valley north of the present West Washington street.

The third section grew up in later years between the western end of the old West Charleston and Two Mile creek, and is now a flourishing and thickly settled portion of the city, with residences, stores, churches, school houses and manufacturing plants.

The section afterwards known as Glen Elk was laid out and promoted by Bigley and Walker. The present Bigley avenue was named for Mr. Bigley, but the name of J. Brisben Walker who was the real founder of the whole West Side of today, is not preserved in any way in any portion of the city.

Bigley and Walker based their hopes of a new city in the Elk valley, north of what was then Charleston street and now is West Washington street, on an industrial section they hoped to establish in that territory. And their first act in promoting the sale of home sites was to arrange for the building of a blast furnace. It was planned that it should utilize the iron ore which cropped out from the hills in the valley of Magazine creek and the surrounding territory.

There is still iron ore in these hills, but neither its quantity nor its quality would permit it to enter into successful competition with the rich ores from Minnesota.

Much of the land Bigley and Walker bought for their proposed city north of West Washington street in the valley of the Elk, belonged to Alethea Brigham, daughter of Major James Bream, who came to Charleston at the solicitation of Major Bream's stepson, Colonel Joseph Lovell and bought most of the land between Elk river and Two-Mile creek, from the hills to the Kanawha river and part of the Elk valley as well. Bigley and Walker also bought other smaller tracts in the same section and on them planned their industrial section.

On March 1, 1875 Nicholas J. Bigley, of Allegheny county, Pa., and Susannah L. Bigley, his wife; J. Brisben Walker and Emily Strother Walker his wife, sold to the Kanawha Iron company, a West Virginia corporation, the land on which the blast furnace was later constructed, perhaps an acre or two. The land was along the Elk river bank, just above the present Spring street bridge, and the furnace was located inside the present railroad yards.

Walker's Wife Author

Mr. Walker's wife was Emily, daughter of D.H. Strother, artist and writer of the early 1800's, who wrote under the name of "Porte Crayon." Her early volume on what was then a wilderness country along the western slope of the Allegheny mountains is fine in its descriptions and valuable for its illustrated accounts of the early country now in West Virginia.

While the blast furnace never was completed and consequently never gave employment to any one except the comparatively few who aided in its construction, the town planned by Bigley and Walker, to be based on the iron industry which it was thought would follow the iron furnace, grew from other reasons and based on other industry.

Glen Elk, as the Bigley and Walker addition came to be known, developed numerous saw and planing mills, a veneer factory and other wood working industries, and gradually grew into a town of considerable size.

The first post office on what is now the West Side was called Glen Elk. Later, Glen Elk and the "West End" were incorporated into a city known as "Elk City," which still later was merged into Charleston and is now part of the greater city.

Belsches First Postmaster

The "Glen Elk" post office was established under the administration of Grover Cleveland with George E. Belsches; father of W.H. Belsches, well known pharmacist of the West Side, as postmaster. His store, where the post office was located, was at 84 Washington street, west, where the Ratliff automobile tire store is now located. The Belsches store was a frame structure some feet above the street level. It was later lowered to the street level, and its walls were veneered with brick.

Later the Glen Elk post office was abolished and station A of the Charleston post office was substituted, with Mr. Belsches still in charge. This office was located on West Washington street, just east of the end of Bigley avenue.

When the J.B. Walker addition, between Washington street, west, and the Kanawha river, and the Bigley and Walker addition, north of Washington street, west, in the Elk valley, were in their infancy back in 1873, lots fronting on the present Washington street, west, in the heart of the present West Side business section, sold for about $10 a front foot, with a depth of 120 feet.

Choice Property Cheap

On October 8, 1873, Bigley and Walker sold to Starke Overstreet, a lot on "Charleston street, formerly the Parkersburg and Charleston turnpike." The boundary described started on Charleston street, "40 feet from Elk street, 120 feet deep and 40 feet wide at the rear. This is the property on which the Charleston Journal now has its publication office, and the Mount Vernon Meat company has its offices and sales room. The price for which this corner lot, 40 by 120 feet, sold in 1873 was $450.

In the same block, and about the same date, Bigley and Walker sold to Michael Quinlan 80 feet from on Charleston street and 120 feet deep, "with the improvements thereon," which included the house in which present members of the Quinlan family still reside, for $900, half cash. This property ran down old Charleston street to the present alley between Ratliff's store and the Bridge Cafe and included the lot where the Glen Elk post office was first located.

Down on the corner of Pennsylvania avenue and Washington street, west, where the first brick store on the West Side was built, which was the birthplace of Glen Elk lodge of Odd Fellows, and is now the business place of the Adkins plumbing supply store, the corner lot, 40 feet front, sold October 11, 1873, for $400

Old Blacksmith Shop

Next door to the present Charleston Journal office, when the West Side was just beginning to grow, was the blacksmith and horse-shoeing shop of Mose Leftwich, a Negro man who had belonged in the Leftwich family in slavery days and did much of the blacksmith work for farmers coming in from Two-Mile creek and the surrounding country.

About opposite the blacksmith shop, where Lane and Son's upholstery shop is now, was the store of Thomas Croghan, whose home faced the Kanawha river just south of Charleston street.

On the corner where the Mount Vernon Meat company and the Charleston Journal now are was Jack Holmes' saloon. It was a two-story front.

On the northeast corner of Charleston street and Pennsylvania avenue was for some years the old saloon of Cal. Summers, who came from up the Elk and catered largely to the up-Elk farmers and loggers when they came to town.

On the river bank, above Charleston street, was Morgan's barrel factory, where thousands of barrels used for packing and shipping salt from the Malden furnaces were made.

Once Tobacco Center

On Pennsylvania avenue, just above Charleston street was a tobacco warehouse, where tobacco from the surrounding farming country was pressed into hogsheads and shipped. But the big tobacco business was done by W.J. Lucado, who had a warehouse on Pennsylvania avenue, about opposite the end of Fayette street, from which in 1873 he shipped more than 240,000 pounds, or several hundred hogsheads of Kanawha county tobacco to English markets, shipping by the newly built C.&O. railroad to seaboard and thence by ocean vessel.

When construction work stopped on the blast furnace, just before its completion, so that it never was operated, and J.B. Walker's failure in business put a stop to his real estate operations, the Glen Elk section lay idle for a while. But sawmills and other wood working establishments sprang up in that section with the saw and planing mill run by J.C. Roy and H.W. Knight, the Dilcher veneer factory and others among them, and the Glen Elk company took over the old Bigley and Walker holdings and started the growth of that present populous portion of the community. E.B. Knight was president of the company, but George S. Couch was the most active official. J.C. Drouillard was one of the company's officers.

The development of the Glen Elk section was so rapid that more property was added and it was called Upper Glen Elk. Both upper and lower Glen Elk, and Walker's West End, south of Charleston street were combined some 30 or 40 years ago into the incorporated town of Elk City, which remained in existence until an extension of the city limits of Charleston took all the territory west of the Elk into its area and the West Side now is the most populous and one of the busiest sections of the capital city. (206)

To the Voters of Kanawha.

In 1861 you elected me, with General Lewis Ruffner, to the Convention, which framed our present Constitution. The Legislature and Convention sat at the same time; and as a member of both bodies, I found my hands full of labors and responsibilities in a time of more than ordinary perplexity and trial. I endeavored to do my duty in that behalf, nor ceased my efforts till the existence of the State was secured. Subsequently, while on the Bench, I abstained from participation in politics, content to exercise the right of the citizen-to vote as I thought right and best for the public good.

At the call of a convention of the people of the county who thought it unwise and inexpedient at this time to subject the people of the State to the unnecessary expense and burthen of a Constitutional Convention, to do what might have been done without such cost or hazard, I am again before you as a candidate for the Convention.

In 1861 the object was to form a Constitution for the proposed new State of "Kanawha;" (the name was afterwards changed to our present name,) now the object is to "consider, discuss, and propose a new Constitution" for the State of West Virginia.

A man's past history is the best evidence of a man's future conduct. And as promises on the part of candidates are so easily made and so easily broken, or soon forgotten, I prefer simply to rest on the record of my past acts, which have been done in your midst, and in public, and are open to your inspection. Nor am I a stranger among you, but "to the manor born," with every interest and relation common with your own:

I can only promise, if elected, to do in the future as in the past,-the best I can to secure the rights of the people, and promote the prosperity of the State. And this I propose to do by reserving, as far as possible, the great and fundamental principles of liberty so clearly enunciated and so carefully guarded in our present Constitution. In Other words, I propose, as far as possible, to preserve all that is good in the old, and keep out all that is bad from the new.

I believe in the principle of Democracy, which proposes the greatest good to the greatest number, enlarges the area of freedom, and secures the equal rights of all; and this is Republicanism. I am for the Union and the Constitution, with all the amendments, including the 15th; and conforming our own to harmony with it, in phraseology, as it is in spirit.

I am for preserving the reserved rights of the States and of the people, on the one hand; and the delegated powers of the Union on the other; each within the limits of their respective spheres.

I am in favor of universal amnesty and universal suffrage; and equally opposed to test oaths and proscriptive legislation.

All our Constitutions prohibit *ex post facto* laws, that is, laws of a criminal nature, acting retrospectively, but only one, and that of a New England State, so far as I remember, prohibits retrospective laws, relative to civil rights, affecting property.

And I am in favor of adopting that principle into our Constitution (save when the Legislation is purely remedial or curative,) as one both wise and just. Nor would the objection against Northern ideas and "Yankee notions" deter me from adopting what reason approved, whether it came from the North or the South, the East or the West.

General education among the people by means of the free school system is in the most danger from restrictions that may cripple its efficiency.

The name will doubtless be retained, but the vital power of the system may' be lost, for many of you will remember the hostility that was publicly proclaimed by distinguished gentlemen-leaders of the party calling this Convention-to the present free school system.

To change the system was one declared object of the call. The question, therefore, is not likely to be a dead issue when the election is over.

And next to that, is the danger of restrictions on the right of suffrage. This may be in the requirement of qualifications and conditions, such as payment of taxes, reading and writing, head of a family, or freeholder, &c., as of old; for it is useless to deny that there are widely different views on this subject, and not a few would return to the old order of things.

In the Convention of 1861, when the effort was made to carry these principles or restriction into the present Constitution, I opposed it; and still do so, believing that the citizen who perils his life in defense of his country shows as much devotion to his State as one who pays a few dollars taxes; and is, therefore, equally entitled to vote for its rulers. The rulers declare the war, and the people fight it through. They ought, therefore, to do the voting as well as the fighting. And since the non-payment of taxes or lack of education does not excuse from the draft, so neither should they exclude from the ballot.

The Legislative, Executive, and Judicial Departments, should be separate and distinct, and neither allowed to encroach upon the domain of the other. This is essential to liberty and durability. The province of the Legislature is to make the laws, of the Executive to enforce them, and of the Judiciary to interpret them.

The power of taxation is a necessary evil, and ought not to be used for other purposes than to raise revenue. It is an abuse of that power to make it the means of forfeiting the citizen's lands without his default; nor is it less so when the main object is to transfer the property of one man to another who has no right to it. I am in favor, therefore, of a Constitutional restraint on the Legislature, against such an abuse of the taxing power.

I was the first to propose, and shall be the last to abandon Charleston as the Capital of the State, which I helped to inaugurate, and of which I am proud.

And when I behold her advance in freedom, in progress, in population, in wealth, in education and power; I do not regret the part I have taken, nor repine at the past; but hopefully look forward to the future for still greater advance in all that can elevate and adorn a free people.

Mr. Truslow who is associated with me, is well known for his worth; and Messrs. Warth and Knight, who are our opponents, are gentlemen of whom I have nothing to say, except in their praise; however, they conflict on the main question of calling a Convention, for while Mr. W. voted for the call, Mr. K. voted against it. That they differ on many other, and important, points I have little doubt. What seems most strange in the matter is, that they should have been nominated on the same ticket. As they neutralized each other's vote at the election, will they not be likely to do so again, if elected? For instance: Mr. W. is opposed to the Township system and ballot, voting, while Mr. K. was raised in the State of New Hampshire, where; both were in operation, and has shown his approval of both here, by his vote against the Convention. Mr. W. would make the Constitution with a provision discriminating between citizens, and deprive one class of rights accorded to another, not withstanding the 14th amendment to the Constitution of the United States, which provides that "No State shall make any law which shall abridge the privileges or immunities of citizens; or deny to any person the equal protection of the laws."

Whether Mr. K. would go that far, I can hardly believe. It remains to be seen. At present the rights of all secure and equal, and each has a right to vote for whom he pleases.

And this is the liberty we would preserve, as including all the rest.

Then go to the polls on the 4th Thursday of this month-the 26th instant-and cast your votes for whom you please. If I should find favor in your eyes, I shall be grateful for your confidence, and endeavor to deserve it. But if another be chosen I shall not complain.

JAMES H. BROWN.

October 17, 1871.

Judge James H. Brown was born in Cabell County in 1818. After moving to Charleston, he was a member of the state supreme court and active in the formation of West Virginia. His son, James F. was a prominent Charleston lawyer and banker. He lived in the Brown estate on Alderson Street which was torn down in 1957 for the extension of Quarrier Street.

A Few Things Needed

In his pedal excursions around the city of the future, Carl observed that some things should be provided which are not. Among them that:

Virginia Street should be paved eastward to Broad and Capital Street paved north to the Ohio Central railway depot.

Fewer drains by small tiling across our streets, and at least a couple of large sewers through the city before water works undertaken.

Some method beyond, individual lanterns, to light our sidewalks and crossings at night and in muddy seasons. If not, there will be some heavy damage suits soon for broken ankles and dislocated shoulders;

A free wagon bridge over Elk into Charleston, so that the west portion of Kanawha can exchange merchandise and farm products without a trip tax;

A sloped wharf from Summers to Capitol along the river, a market house, an opera house in harmony with our capitol pretentions, our houses numbered systematically, and our streets lettered in one direction and numbered another;

Some one to push into being a building association. Every large town with enterprise has several. They inspire taste, a desire to acquire homes instead of paying rent;

A street railway from West End along Front street to the Ruffner ferry and out Capitol past the State House to the Ohio Central depot.

Carl Quiz.

This interesting piece appeared in a Charleston newspaper in the 1870s. No matter what time of history, there are always things to do in a community to improve the quality of life.

First Brick Pavement Laid in City

Charleston's early streets were mere mud holes. Regular thoroughfares were laid out, but they had no hard surface. After every rainfall vehicles which traveled on them cut deep into soft mud. No drainage was provided and surface water kept the roadways full of soft mud a great part of the time. Sometimes the summer sun would dry them up. But even then they were rough and travel over them was difficult at all times.

____ as far back as 1833 steps were taken to improve them. Feb. 19, 1833, the Virginia legislature passed an act authorizing the operation of a lottery in Charleston for the purpose of raising not more than $10,000 to be applied to the paving of streets.

There seems to be no record of any fund raised by the lottery. The probability is that the people of Charleston, which had a population of only about 800 at the time, failed to buy a sufficient number of the lottery tickets to justify its operation, and that the $10,000 authorized to be raised in that way never became available. The fact remains, however, that Charleston undertook to raise its first street paving fund through a lottery authorized by the legislature of Virginia.

Before the lottery plan of raising money for street improvements was devised, each of the male citizens was required to work on the streets as many days in each year as they might be called upon to do.

New Attempt Made

One of the first attempts to make a Charleston highway other than a mud street was about the close of the Civil War when armies hauling supplies had cut the streets down deep into the mud and left them in that way. Most of the traffic came into Charleston then from the Kanawha Two-Mile section, from the Elk valley and from down the Kanawha. All this traffic entered the city over the old "wire bridge" where the Washington street bridge now stands. The only route into town then was from the bridge up to Clendenin street, out that street to the Kanawha river bank and thence up Kanawha street.

Clendenin street became almost impassable from heavy usage and in its worst portion, about where it now crosses Brown street, the city built its "corduroy road." Saplings, or straight limbs of trees, two to four inches in diameter, were laid lengthwise across the street, close together and a wooden roadbed was made which kept vehicles and the animals which drew them from getting too deep into the mire to be pulled out.

In the 1870's what was known for years as "the plank road" was put down, also in Clendenin street. It reached from the end of the "wire bridge" to Clendenin and out that street to the Kanawha river bank. Girders were laid lengthwise, and boards were nailed to them, the length of the board being the width of the roadway. For a short distance at the west end of the bridge a similar "plank road" was built, reaching about as far west as Bigley avenue, where the road dropped into deep mud again and it was hard work to get a vehicle out of the mud up on the planks. But once out of the mud the plank road made traffic easy and teams could even trot along its course. But a team was not permitted to go faster than a walk on the old wire bridge.

Plank Road Noisy

The "plank road" made it easy to get into Charleston from the western end of town and brought business to the merchants. But when the planks seasoned with age the ends curled up, the nails rusted and came out and when vehicles passed over the boards they rattled so that school had to suspend in the little one-room schoolhouse between Whitteker and Brown streets, on the west side of Clendenin street, in which some of Charleston's older men of today received their earliest education.

A novel plan to get Charleston out of the mud was by means of the "cinder road." Which meant collecting cinders from the old salt furnaces near Malden for road building. Several barge loads of them were brought to Bibby's landing, where the east pier of the Lee-Fayette bridge has now been built, and the cinders were hauled across the bridge to start the cinder road at its western end and extend as far as the money available would permit. They were piled up a foot or more in depth and road ran about to where Virginia and Washington streets meet. It made a fine road, and kept traffic out of the mud. But when the cinders dried and were crushed by traffic, all the homes along the roadside were filled with black dust and housewives complained so that the system was abandoned.

The first attempt to build a hard-surfaced street in Charleston, after the plank road was found to be impractical, was when the block of Summers street between Kanawha and Virginia was paved with brick in the fall of 1873. And it was the first brick street paving laid in the history of the world.

Invented Method

The system of making a foundation and covering it with brick was devised by Mordecai Levi, close business associate of Dr. John P. Hale, who was then a man of means and financed the experimental block built by Levi.

Under the system used by Levi for laying brick streets which would carry traffic of the day, it was necessary to dig down to solid earth. This solid earth was arched between the curbs, high in the center and sloping toward the sides. The arched surface was covered with sand. Then oak boards covered with tar to keep out moisture were laid on the sand. They were covered with more sand and on it the bricks were laid.

The *Kanawha Chronicle*, printed in Charleston Oct. 15, 1873, said in that issue that "much work is now going on in the streets of the city. Summers street has been dug up for a new pavement." This was the local newspaper's announcement of the first brick street pavement in the world's history.

The Summers street paving was not by any means all the work of public improvement in which Dr. Hale and Mr. Levi were associated. When Charleston's first capitol was built, it was erected largely through public subscriptions accepted in payment by Dr. Hale, who erected it. Associated with him in its erection was Mr. Levi, who had charge of the construction work. When members of the legislature afterwards threatened to rescind their action in making Charleston the capitol unless some measures were provided for their housing and comfortable entertainment while attending legislative sessions. Dr. Hale arranged to build the Hale House, the state's largest and best equipped hotel. Contractors from the East wanted six months time in which to build the Hale House. But Mr. Levi told Dr. Hale he would build it in 90 days and lacked just one day of completing it in that time.

Building the Hale House in 91 days saved the capitol for Charleston. And in the erection of the Hale House and the Capitol building. Mr. Levi superintended the construction for Dr. Hale and made both buildings possible. To him, as builder, as well as to Dr. Hale, who financed these structures, Charleston owes much today. (257)

by George W. Summers

M.A. MILLER, ESQ.,

Dear Sir:-In answer to your inquiry in regard to brick street-paving, I will give you the history of an experiment I made here in 1871, the result of which has been very satisfactory.

The point selected was Summers street, between Kanawha and Virginia streets. Summers street is 30 ft. wide between the curb-stones, and the block is about 400 ft. long.

The street after being graded and rounded up to the proper convexity, was laid with common sheeting-plank boiled in gas tar; upon this was spread 2 ½ to 3 inches of sand, and upon this the brick were laid on edge and zig-zag, a coating of sand was then spread over the surface so as to thoroughly fill the spaces between the bricks, and the pavement was done.

Summers street is the third most used and traveled street in the city. Yet, after ten years use, there is not a hole, rut, or lump in the pavement. It is apparently as sound and as smooth as the day it was put down, and *in the ten years it has not cost one cent for repairs.* Having lasted ten years without apparent injury, it would be hard to fix a limit to its durability.

It is a delightfully smooth and even pavement to ride or drive over, just rough enough to give secure footing for horses, and does not get slippery with ice in winter.

I kept an accurate record of the cost of the pavement, but regret that I have mislaid it and cannot now find it; the data are free and simple, however, and an estimate can readily be made for any locality.

The success of this pavement I consider due, almost entirely, to the *character of the brick.* They were made by Mr. Levi, a brick maker and builder of large experience, of a very tenaceous clay, almost entirely free from sand, by machinery under heavy pressure, and were burned extra hard. Mr. Levi also superintended the laying of this pavement. I do not think that ordinary hand-made brick, from sandy clay and burned to the usual hardness of building brick would stand the test at all.

Very respectfully, yours &c.,

J.P. HALE.

Brick Paving for Streets.

GORDONSVILLE, VA., Aug. 3rd, 1881.

MAJOR JED. HOTCHKISS:-Some time ago I saw a statement in a newspaper to the effect that some of the streets in Charleston, Kanawha Co., W.Va., were paved with *brick*, and a rather sneering criticism on the material with which the people of that good city were satisfied to pave their streets. As I happened to have seen this brick paving put down, some ten years ago, I took occasion, on a recent visit to the place, to inquire about the durability and general service of it; also made a personal inspection. I find a universal expression of satisfaction with it, and my inspection showed it to be in apparently as perfect a condition as when first put down. I am informed that it has not had one dollar spent on it for repairs.

I take pleasure in enclosing a letter from Dr. J.P. Hale, giving the details of his experiment with this brick paving. You will see that the Dr. attributes the success of his experiment to four principal elements, the quality of the clay, machine pressure, the very had burning of the brick, which, however, are not vitrified, and the manner in which they were put down.

In localities like Richmond and elsewhere, where good granite Belgian blocks are to be had, they are probably to be preferred to the best of brick; but in very many localities whee excellent clay, free of sand, may be had, and where granite blocks are not to be had, good, hard-pressed, and hard-burned brick will certainly be found to make a paving of the very best character for streets, far superior to blocks of any kind of wood, sandstone or limestone, or any other kind of material that I know except the very best quality of granite.

Yours truly,   M.A. Miller

VOL. 1.   APRIL, 1901.   No. 2.

The West Virginia
Historical Magazine
Quarterly.

CHARLESTON, W. VA.

Published by the West Virginia Historical and Antiquarian Society.

J. P. HALE, Editor, President of the Society.

SUBSCRIPTIONS, per year, – – – – $1.00
SINGLE COPIES, – – – – – – – – .25
For Advertising, enquire of the Editor.

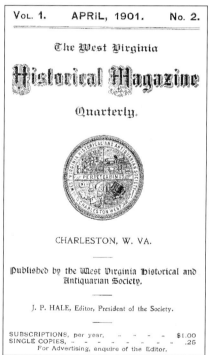

Grave of John P. Hale (1824-1902)
in Spring Hill Cemetery.

Head Quarters Democratic Congressional Executive Committee.

CHARLESTON, WEST VIRGINIA, April, 1880.

DEAR SIR:

I desire to call your attention to the fact that it is all important that there should be a thorough and complete organization of the Democratic party in every county in this district, and that said organization should be begun at once. I have written to several Democrats in your county, and in connection with them, I hope you will at once proceed to this business and manifest that interest in the success of Democratic principles which all good citizens so earnestly desire.

Let me call the attention of the Democrats of your county especially to the fact that various conventions have already been called: 1st, A Convention of the 3rd District at Huntington on June 2nd, for the purpose of appointing delegates to attend the National Convention to be held in Cincinnati, O.; 2nd, The Congressional Convention of this District at Hinton on August 14th, to nominate a candidate for Congress; 3rd, The State Convention to be held at Martinsburg on the 28th day of July. It is very important that these conventions should be well attended and all the counties be represented in each. Let me urge upon you to have a convention called to meet on the first day of the earliest court to which you can give ample and general notice, to appoint delegates for your county to these various conventions. And in order that you may not go unrepresented, appoint proxies of gentlemen from some of the counties who will likely attend.

The Congressional Committee would be pleased to hear from your county at all times during the approaching canvass as to the condition of things politically, and the probable result of the various elections to be held this Fall.

Respectfully yours,

CET

AN ORDINANCE!

Amending and Re-enacting an Ordinance entitled

AN ORDINANCE DEFINING THE CITY FIRE LIMITS.

Sec. 1. Be it Ordained by the Common Council of the City of Charleston,

That the Ordinance entitled "An Ordinance Defining the City Fire Limits" be and the same is hereby amended and re-enacted so as to read as follows:

From and after the adoption of this Ordinance, no new building, or extension of old ones, shall be erected within the limits hereafter described, except they be built of either brick, stone, iron or concrete, with fire proof roof.

The limits above referred to shall be known as the "Fire Limits," and the boundary of the same shall be as follows, to-wit:

Beginning at the low water mark on the Kanawha river at the foot of Broad street, on a line with the sidewalk on the Eastern side thereof, to a drain half way between Quarrier & Virginia streets, and from thence by a line parallel to and equally distant from Virginia street to Truslow branch, thence with said branch to Clendennin street, and thence with said Clendennin street along the Western sidewalk thereof to Kanawha river, and thence with the low water mark on the Kanawha river to the place of beginning.

SEC. 2. In all cases where the provisions of this Ordinance are being violated the Mayor shall have the power to stop the work of building or extending until the matter can be brought before the Common Council.

SEC. 3. Any person violating the provisions of this Ordinance, shall, upon conviction thereof, be fined in a sum not less than fifty dollars and not exceeding one hundred dollars.

Sec. 4. Such Ordinance or parts of Ordinance as conflict with this are hereby repealed.

A copy teste,
D. H. ESTILL, Recorder, R. R. DELANEY, Mayor.

For any violation of the above Ordinance the penalty will be rigidly enforced.
R. R. DELANEY, Mayor.
JULY 22, 1881

SUMMONS IN CHANCERY.

THE STATE OF WEST VIRGINIA,

To the SHERIFF OF KANAWHA COUNTY, Greeting:

We command you that you summon Martha A. Gibson widow, George Gibson John R. Gibson, Samuel Gibson George Gibson, James Gibson infant heirs of Wm H. Gibson decd if they be found within your bailiwick, to appear before the Judge of our Circuit Court for the County of Kanawha, at Rules to be held in the Clerk's Office of said Court, on the first Monday in November next, to answer a Bill in Chancery exhibited against them in our said Court, by Louisa W. Mais nee Gibson, & Nora Gibson

and have then there this writ.

WITNESS: THOMAS SWINBURN, Clerk of our said Court, at of said County, the 30th day of November, 1883, and in of the State.

Thomas Swinburn

Kanawha County Court, Oct. Term, 1879

Augustus Cohen is allowed $4.00 for his services at this Term as a Petit Juror, he having attended said Court 3 days at $1.50 per day,

to be paid by the County: which is ordered to be certified for payment.

Teste: Shurittan Morris Clerk.

CET

Mr. Snow Hill Salt Co in Malden District, 1878. To the Sheriff of Kanawha County,			Dr.
	Rate per $100	Capitation Tax	$
	20 cts. for	State Tax	1 50
	10 cts. for	State School Tax	75
Total Value of Personal Property $750	75 cts. for	County Tax	5 63
	50 cts. for	District School Tax	3 75
	25 cts. for	District Building Tax	1 87
		Total Tax $	13 50
Received Payment, R.A. Coleman			Deputy for J. H. ROSLER, S.K.C.

COMMITTIES,

COMITTEE OF ARRANGEMENTS.

E. A. Boone,   J. A. Rogers.

RECEPTION COMMITTEE,

Frank Woodman,   Mrs. W. B. Rooke,
A. W. Carpenter,   Mrs. J. W. M. Appl..
S. B. Miller,   Mrs. W. G. Norvel..
Capt. C. P. Snyder.

FLOOR MANAGERS.

Tom Reynolds, Geo. Byrne..

Estill & Trud...

Masquerade Ball,

HALE HOUSE,

TUESDAY EVENING, DEC. 20, 1881.

The Hale House was built by John P. Hale as an added incentive to move the capitol to Charleston in 1872. It was the second largest building in town, after the state capitol. It burned down in 1885. The Ruffner Hotel was later built on this site.

Monday Morning's Fire

Caused by a Boiler Explosion in Ruffner Bros.' Basement.

Hale House Destroyed.

+‡+ NOTICE +‡+

Having taken Capt. D. P. Woodward into partnership with me and the Hale House now being run by Fitz & Woodward, it is desirable that all the old business be closed up.   I wish, therefore, that all those to whom I am indebted, as well as those who owe me, would call and settle.

HALE HOUSE.   Respectfully,
    Charleston, W.Va.)
    June 19, 1883.   )   J. M. Fitz.

Monday morning at 7:45 people on Front and Virginia streets and at the Hale House were startled by a loud explosion, and rushing in the direction of the noise found that the building occupied by Ruffner Bros' wholesale grocery house had fallen. The fire department was notified and finally responded, but owing to some misunderstanding went to the Skees-Oney block, the basement of which is filled with water. It was seen at a glance that they were out of position and the engine was then taken to the river. The windows in the Hale House toward the ruined building were all blown in by the explosion, and in a few minutes all that side of the building was on fire. Every effort was made by the guests and servants of the house to check the flames but it was impossible to do so, and it was seen by all that the building could not be saved. Then everybody's attention was turned to removing the goods. Almost every thing of value was removed from the first and second floors. The upper, or fourth story, was a mansard roof, built mostly of wood, and burned so rapidly that nothing in it was saved. The fire burned rapidly, and by 10 o'clock the building was a complete ruin.

It was a quarter of an hour before the cause of the explosion was known. Buildings in the vicinity were shaken from the top to the bottom, and the shock was felt out Capitol street as far as the Custom House. The cause of the accident was the bursting of the boiler in the basement used for warming the building. George Welcher, a colored man who has long been employed by the firm went into the basement to fire up, at which time Joel Ruffner and an employee named Kannis were the only persons on the first floor. Mr. Ruffner was in the office over the boiler while Kannis was nearer the door. In about fifteen minutes after Welcher went below the crash came, and Mr. Ruffner was thrown from his chair to the back wall as it fell in around him. It is a mystery to all how he escaped instant death. He was taken from the ruins a few minutes afterwards bruised and bleeding, and strange to relate was not fatally injured, his principal injuries were a broken jaw and a few cuts about the head not considered dangerous. Kannis escaped from the building but how he himself can not explain. Wilcher was undoubtedly killed instantly. His body was taken from the ruins Tuesday morning.

Mr. Ruffner thinks that the water in the boiler was low and the explosion was caused by turning in cold water.

Ruffner Bros.' loss is estimated at $38,000, the house being valued at $18,000 and the stock at about $20,000. Insurance $20,000. The loss of Fitz & Woodward, including building and furniture, is in the neighborhood of $75,000. Insurance $24,000 on the building and $4,000 on the furniture.

Messrs Fitz & Woodward after years of work had succeeded in making the Hale one of the best hotels in the State, and their loss is sincerely regretted by the people of the city. A new hotel will be put up, no doubt, as soon as possible, as the St. Albert, which is now crowded, cannot possibly accommodate the traveling public.

The above article appeared in the *Star Tribune*, March 28, 1885.

COURSE OF STUDY AND BOOKS

USED AT THE

Kanawha Military Institute.

FIRST CLASS—FOURTH YEAR.

SUBJECTS.	TEXT BOOKS.
Mathematics.	Peck's Mechanics, Ray's Astronomy. Integral Calculus; (Buckingham,)
Natural Science.	Dana's Mineralogy and Geology.
Logic. Psychology.	Jevon's Logic. Munsel's Psycology.
Military Engineering. Ordinance and Gunnery.	Mahan's Engineering. Benton's Ordnance and Gunnery.
German.	Hans Anderson's Märchen. Goethe or Schiller, Lessing. Otto's Grammar. Exercises.
Military Law.	Halleck's International Law. Benet's Military Law and the Practice of Courts-Martial.

13

SECOND CLASS—THIRD YEAR.

SUBJECTS.	TEXT BOOKS.
Mathematics.	Analytical Geometry.(Robinson's) Differential Calculus. (Buckingham.)
Latin.	Gildersleeve's Grammar and Original Exercises. Horace. Tacitus and Livy.
Natural Science.	Youman's and Roscoe's Chemistries. Physiology.
English Literature. Rhetoric.	Brooke's Primer, Shakespeare's Works, Bain's Rhetoric.
German.	Stern's Studien und Plaudereien. Otto's Grammar; Conversation. Exercises.
Tactics.	Practical instruction in the Schools of the Soldier, Company and Battalion.

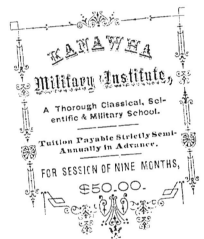

Bottom: The Kanawha Military Institute was founded by Maj. Thomas Fife Snyder in 1879. He was a graduate of the Virginia Military Institute and modeled his school after it. The school's first location was on Laidley Street in Charleston, but later it was moved to a site bounded by Summers, State (Lee) and Capitol streets. Major Snyder's health however prevented the school from becoming a major military school in the south. The students were prepared for entrance to some of the most prominent universities in the country. Many well-known business and professional men of the county were graduates of the institute. This rare and only known photo of the cadets was probably taken at their new school site in Charleston. GA
Right: Cadet George W. Summers (1868-1941). GA

THE KANAWHA MILITARY INSTITUTE.

In the demand of the Kanawha Valley for a good school, where her young men could obtain a fair education the Kanawha Military Institute originated.

Its founders wished, in the Institute, a happy combination of the high Military and Mathematical training of the Virginia Military Institute and the English and Classical Culture of Randolph Macon College.

The Kanawha Military Institute aims to give her Cadets a good practical education, that, when they leave here, not only will they be able to take a high stand at the University of Virginia or at any first-rate college, but they will be fitted for real life at once, and for honorable positions amongst their fellowmen. Thus her function is two-fold.

To those wishing for their sons a University education, the importance of having such a school near their homes cannot be over estimated. Upon the strength of the ground work rests the value of the superstructure. To send a boy off to college before he can take a good stand among his class-mates is tempting Providence. Ten to one, becoming discouraged, he will join the band of loafers that curses every college and his manhood will be of the animal type. Let parents, therefore, and guardians, take care how they send the sensitive beings entrusted to their care among college students before their moral courage and manliness are sufficiently developed to work for duty's sake. First, let the ground-work be laid at a High School near home, and then let the College or University build upon that a noble and enduring structure.

19

While, however, we are tenderly nursing the mind we should not neglect the body. A leaking ship, with never so good a crew, can accomplish but little. The military training will assist nature to strengthen the body and make it a fit home for the real man. Besides gaining by the drill a manly bearing and a good physique, the Cadet learns the lessons, that in our country are of special importance, of submission to proper authority and of strict performance of duty. These will weave themselves into a habit that a lifetime will hardly unravel.

LOCATION.

Charleston, situated in the valley of the Great Kanawha River and on the line of the Chesapeake and Ohio Railway, presents many advantages for the location of a school. It is *central, accessible and healthful.* The city has a population of 6,000, and is the political and commercial centre of a large district. It contains the State Capitol, an elegant Music Hall, nine Churches and one Synagogue, splendid Hotels, a large number and variety of manufacturing establishments and handsome stores, both in wholesale and retail branches of trade. Charleston has been selected as the permanent Capital of the State, and the present Capitol itself a fine one, is rapidly giving place to a new structure, which when completed will be probably the most magnificent State House in the South. For beauty of situation our pretty little city is almost without a rival in this country. Indeed the romantic loveliness of the Kanawha Valley is becoming world famous, so much so, that many travelers take the Chesapeake and Ohio Railway simply on account of the scenic

attractions of the route. The Ohio Central Railway is now complete to Charleston, thus rendering our city doubly accessible. Charleston is also connected daily with Gallipolis, and weekly with Cincinnati, Wheeling, and Pittsburgh, by lines of elegant steamers.

HEALTHFULNESS.

The annual reports of the health officer show that few cities of this size are so healthy. In the suburbs are two Chalybeate and Alum Springs. The late Dr. McChesney, an eminent physician of this city, pronounced these Alum Springs to be superior to the celebrated Rockbridge Alum of Virginia.

THE SYSTEM OF INSTRUCTION AND GOVERNMENT.

The system of instruction and government in the Kanawha Military Institute, is *distinctive*, and is founded as near as will be practicable upon that of the Virginia Military Institute. The Cadets are lodged and boarded in the Institute, their clothing, books and other supplies being furnished at cost by the authorities of the Institute; the sick will be placed under the special care of the Surgeon.

MILITARY.

The *energy, system, subordination* and *self reliance* which the *Military Government* of the Institute cultivates will give a *practical* character to the education which it will supply. The high reputation which the graduates of the United States Military Academy and the Alumni of the Virginia Military Institute have established for themselves as citizens and soldiers is sufficient evidence of the value of such education.

21

ARMS.

The arms, accoutrements and equipments supplied the Cadets are new and of the latest improved pattern.

ENCAMPMENT.

The Institute is supplied with Tents and Camping Equipage, and during a portion of the summer months the Cadets are placed in camp and instructed in the practical duties of a soldier in camp and on the march. These summer encampments have proved of signal value in improving the physique of the corps. During the encampments the Cadets are accompanied by the Professors, and the health of the command is under the especial care of the Surgeon of the Institute, who is a distinguished physican and has been an able and successful practitioner for nearly forty years.

UNIFORMS AND OTHER CLOTHING.

As cadets are required to wear a prescribed uniform at all times, it is only necessary to bring a full supply of *under-clothing.* The cost of the uniform with cap is $16.50.

EXAMINATIONS AND REPORTS.

During the year there are two examinations, chiefly written, one at the close of each term. A Cadet failing to pass an approved examination loses his title to advance from a lower to a higher class.

At the close of each term a report, combining the results of the examination and the average class-standing during the term will be sent to each parent or guardian. Monthly reports showing the class-standing and deportment will also be issued.

ADMISSION.

No person who is under thirteen years of age or who is physically unable to perform military duty can be admitted as a Cadet.

EXPENSES.

Tuition payable semi-annually *in advance,* for
 session of nine months, - - - $ 50 00
Estimated expenses for board at $3.50 per week, 133 00
 When a Cadet enlists, he pledges himself to comply with our terms, *which are strictly in advance, as noted above.*
 Except in case of protracted illness, no deduction will be made for absence; nor will money be refunded, should a Cadet be withdrawn or dismissed during the term, unless at the direction of the Faculty.

CALENDAR.

The session is divided into two terms. The first term begins on the first Wednesday in September. The second term begins on the third Wednesday in January, and closes on the first Wednesday in June.

ROLL OF CADETS OF THE KANAWHA MILITARY INSTITUTE.

As we think it may interest our readers we publish in this issue the following roll:

1. Barr.....................Charleston, W. Va.
2. Brabbin.....................Coalburg, "
3. Botkin.....................Charleston, "
4. Brooks.....................Kan. Salines, "
5. Broun, E. F.....................Charleston, "
6. Broun, H. L.....................Virginia.
7. Campbell.....................Charleston, "
8. Clarkson..................... " "
9. Caruthers.....................Buffalo, "
10. Dickinson.....................Malden, "
11. Dryden.....................Charleston, "
12. Du Bois..................... " "
13. Farrar..................... " "
14. Fife.....................Buffalo, "
15. Fisher.....................Charleston, "
16. Flagg..................... " "
17. Frey..................... " "
18. Goshorn..................... " "
19. Hoge.....................Winfield, "
20. Hubbard.....................Charleston, "
21. Kaufmann..................... " "
22. Knight, E. W..................... " "
23. Knight, H. W..................... " "
24. Kyle..................... " "
25. Laidley..................... " "
26. Lewis, C. C..................... " "
27. Lewis, J. D..................... " "
28. Lovell..................... " "
29. Loyd..................... " "
30. McChesney, H..................... " "
31. McChesney, R..................... " "
32. Morris..................... " "
33. Norman.....................Kan. Salines, "
34. Patrick.....................Charleston, "
35. Peyton..................... " "
36. Putney..................... " "
37. Quarrier, A. W..................... " "
38. Quarrier, J. S..................... " "
39. Quarrier, R. G..................... " "
40. Ruffner, A..................... " "
41. Ruffner, D. L..................... " "
42. Smith..................... " "
43. Summers..................... " "
44. Tompkins.....................Malden, "
45. Thayer, G. T.....................Charleston, "
46. Thayer, J. J..................... " "
47. Thayer, J. R..................... " "
48. Thayer, W. T..................... " "
49. Ward..................... " "
50. Whitehurst..................... " "
51. Winkler..................... " "

Total number cadets.................51.

THE MONTHLY CADET.

Published by the CADET LITERARY SOCIETY.	*Multum in Parvo.*	Terms: 30 Cents For Term of Nine Months.

VOL. I.   CHARLESTON, W. VA., OCTOBER 20, 1881.   NO. 2.

1883

This rare photo shows downtown Charleston in the 1870s. The Hale House, the city's social center, is the large building on the left. The large building in the upper right is the 1870 capitol building. The population at this time was approximately 2,000. JULIUS JONES COLL.

Downtown Charleston in 1896 at the corner of Capitol and Kanawha streets. GA

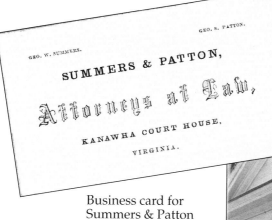

Business card for Summers & Patton prior to the Civil War.

Mayor Elmer Dodson, left, and architect Clarence Moran and two members of the Colonial Dames of America view the Craik-Patton house at its second location at 1316 Lee Street in 1971. It was built in 1834 by James Craik, grandson of George Washington's personal physician and the son of President Washington's secretary. Located on Virginia Street, the house, known as Elm Grove, was moved to Lee Street in 1907 and to its present site adjacent to Daniel Boone Park in 1971. The house has been restored by the Colonial Dames of America and is open to the public.⟨452⟩

Early Kanawha County Justice

STORIES COURTESY GERALD RATLIFF

Charleston, W.Va., March 7, 1890

Felix Kampf was visited this morning by several of his old friends together with his counsel. He passed the night as usual, and bade all an affectionate goodbye. The death warrant was not read by his request. He said he was greatly provoked when the murder was done and expressed perfect willlingness to die, saying he hoped the execution would take place as early as possible. He asked the sheriff not to tie him and at 10:57 o'clock he left the jail, accompanied by Father Stenger, of the Catholic Church, the county officials and attending physicians led by the city police who kept back the crowd.

Kampf took the arm of sheriff Pickens and mounted the scaffold with a firm step. Pickens adjusted the rope around the prisoner's neck, and the trap was sprung exactly at 11 o'clock. Kampf falling with a prayer on his lips. All occurred so quietly that a crowd of about 2,000 people scarcely realized what was going on. The execution took place at the Courthouse yard, about 150 feet from the jail.

Kampf died without a struggle, and life was pronounced extinct twelve minutes after the fall. The remains were placed in a handsome coffin bearing the inscription, "At Rest." Funeral ceremonies were held in the Catholic Church and the remains were laid to rest this afternoon in the Catholic Cemetery.

The floor of the scaffold broke through shortly after the drop fell to the ground, but no one was hurt.

The crime for which Kampf suffered death was the murder of his daughter Mary aged twenty years and his son William aged nineteen. Their mother had been dead several years, and owing to their father's disagreeable disposition they left his home several months previous to the murder, and were keeping house for themselves about a quarter of a mile from their father's home.

Upon going home on the night of October 4, 1889, Kampf found that a window had been raised and some flat irons were missing. He made up his mind that Mary had taken them, and went over to her house at once, taking with him a large dirk knife which he had carried for years. He accused her of having taken the irons, and according to Kampf's story, she called him a liar and picked up a hatchet as though to strike him, when he drew his knife and cut terrible gashes in the girl's abdomen. Her brother, who was lying in bed, sprung up to defend his sister and was also cut about the abdomen by his inhuman father who then coolly went home and went to bed where he was arrested about an hour later. Both his victims died within twenty-four hours. Journal.

June 26, 1891

It is estimated that not less than 6,000 people witnessed the execution of "Sim" Johnson in the jail yard at Charleston last Friday morning. People had come for hundreds of miles from all parts of the country for several days and the ropes stretched around the scaffold failed to keep back the crowd. Women were jammed in among the men close to the scaffold, it being utterly impossible to keep back the crowd. The work of execution was quickly done. At 10:57 Johnson appeared on the scaffold with Sheriff Pickens, Rev. Father Stenger and the others who had been permitted to enter the jail. At 11 o'clock the trap was sprung aand in a few minutes "Sim" Johnson was dead from strangulation. He was executed on the same scaffold that Felix Kampf, the murderer of his two children was hung in March 1890. Though the crowd was large it was orderly and not trouble of any kind occurred.

The crime for which Johnson was hanged was committed on the seventh of April 1891. He was at once arrested and narrowly escaped being lynched while crossing the new bridge into Charleston. On the next day he was indicted by the Criminal Court grand jury. On the 10th his trial was begun and on the 11th he was convicted. On the 20th of April he was sentenced and on Friday last, scarcely two months from the commission of his awful crime, he paid the death penalty. Nothing that has ever occurred in Kanawha County aroused so much public feeling. Had it not been for the speed with which he was tried and convicted, justice would long ere this have been meted out to him. The crime was one of the most revolting ever known in that county and it's details are too horrible to be printed. On at least three previous occasions, Johnson, had followed and seized young girls, evidently with the same purpose as on this occasion but they had all escaped his clutches, and he had escaped the law. Johnson was a young fellow probably twenty-one or twenty-two. The guesses at his age vary. All through the trial and for some time after he was sentenced, he maintained an air of dogged indifference, but a short time before the date of the hanging he began to realize his fate, and to Rev. Father Stenger his spiritual adviser, he professed religion and was baptized. The girl is a comely creature of about fifteen years who has lived back in the country all her life until recently. Her stepmother was unkind in her treatment of the girl and when her sister, she was living in Charleston, sent word that she had a place for her, she came to town. It was while returning for her clothes that she was assaulted. The poor creature has never recovered from the shock, and today is as timid as a hare. She is now living in Charleston but is afraid to step outdoors after dark. She is an honest, modest girl, who never says a word to a man unless spoken to and not a word has ever been breathed derogatory to her character although an effort was made in the defense to show that she had consented to the crime.

Through the years Charleston and the county had dozens of newspapers published with a wide range of political views.

MacCorkle late in life.

Belle F. (Goshorn) MacCorkle. The MacCorkles married in 1881, and she died in 1926.

W.A. MacCorkle in 1893.

William A. MacCorkle (1857-1930) was a statesman, lawyer, author and the youngest governor of West Virginia until Cecil Underwood was elected. He served as the Democratic governor from 1893 to 1897. For many years he was one of the most prominent men of the state and his mansion "Sunrise" overlooking Charleston, was one of the most well-known homes in the state. For many years his mansion was owned by John A. Kennedy, a local broadcasting executive. He donated his home to the Salvation Army who sold it to the Sunrise Foundation in 1961. At the time of this publication, it is not known what will happen with the property.

Vice-President Marshall was my guest several times at Sunrise. He was a peculiar man, at times genial beyond expression, and at other times absolutely silent. He loved to go out on the porches, away from the people, with one or two men, and talk to them about every-day matters. He also delighted in getting away in some quiet corner, with the great valley before him, and the two rivers, and to sit there for an hour alone in silence.

Sunrise, my home, is named for my ancestral home in Rockbridge County, Virginia, and is full of interesting things, interesting to West Virginians and Virginians, and to the people of this Valley. I have made it a rule to entertain everybody who comes, because I like people. Many of the religious gatherings, many of the political, social and scientific assemblages in Charleston, for 30 years have been guests in my house, and anybody who comes to Charleston, if he desires, may come to Sunrise.

Mr. Marshall was seated one morning at Sunrise on the river porch. It was in his second term of office as Vice-President. He was looking over the sweep of the two rivers, with their embowering hills. The beautiful valley of the Elk with its blue hills and misty vistas, and the Kanawha flowing just below, and the crescent of the city, were spread out before him. After awhile, he awoke from his reverie and abruptly said to me, "Governor, you are an ambitious man," and without any explanation lapsed into silence. I replied: "I am not generally ambitious, but only in certain directions." He said, "This place of Sunrise is wonderfully beautiful." Again he paused, and looking out over the Elk Valley said, "You would like to be Vice-President of the United States, wouldn't you?" I said, "Yes, I believe I would. I do not care anything about going to the Senate or the House, but I would like to be Vice-President." "Well," he said, "if by any sort of necromancy I could turn over to you the Vice-Presidency, with all the honors that go with it, and if I could have this place in exchange, I would be very glad to make the trade." That was his point of view. W.A. MacCorkle

From *Recollections of Fifty Years*

Governor MacCorkle was an avid horseman as we can see from this 1908 photo in front of his mansion, Sunrise..
KCL

Notice the number of prominent names on this letterhead, including Governor MacCorkle. All important businessmen, lawyers and politicians were enlisted to promote the virtues of Charleston.

Governor MacCorkle on the steps of Sunrise with his feed pail for the birds.

The following eight pages provide a panoramic photo of the city riverfront, circa 1915. (200)

C&O Railway
Main Line

Thayer
Foundry

Ward Boiler and
Shipbuilding Works

Railway
Express Co.

RIVERS

Mouth
of Elk

Virginia St.
Bridge

Washington
St. Bridge

Kanawha Cou
Courthouse

Sternwheel regatta, 2001.

St. Albert
Hotel

City Hall

Union School

Union Building

Old Kanawha
Valley Bank

1885 Capitol

Ruffner
Hotel

Hale St.

Capitol Annex
(later Kan..Co. Library)

Toll Booth on
1891 South Side Bridge

Kanawha
Presbyterian
Church

Sacred Heart
Catholic Church

Mercer
School

The New Steamboat

KANAWHA PACKET, designed as a regular weekly packet between Cincinnati and this place will be finished, & is expected here, on the 15th April. She will have comfortable accommodations for Cabin and Deck Passengers. Persons travelling on horseback, or in carriages, and movers, will be taken on board at Samuel Shrewsbury's, Col. D Ruffner's, and at Charleston; and will be landed at Cincinnati, or at any intermediate port.—Charges will be moderate. *Apply to*

ROGERS & SHREWSBURYS,

Charleston, Va.

April 2.   [37

DAILY STAGES

ARE NOW RUNNING BETWEEN

Charleston and Guyandotte;

CONNECTING AT GUYANDOTTE WITH

THE FOLLOWING LINE OF FIRST CLASS

STEAM PACKETS:

FORMING A DAILY LINE TO CINCINNATI.

Sunday	Little Ben	Capt.	Thacker	Up
	Majestic		Bennett	Down
Monday	Brunette	"	Irwin	Up
"	Cutter	"	Collins	Down
Tuesday	Clipper	"	Crooks	Up
"	Monongahela	"	Stone	Down
Wedn'day	Majestic	"	Bennett	Up
"	Hibernia	"	Klinefelter	Down
Thursday	Cutter	"	Collins	Up
"	Little Ben	"	Thacker	Down
Friday	Monongahela	"	Stone	Up
"	Brunette	"	Irwin	Down
Saturday	Hibernia	"	Klinefelter	Up
"	Clipper	"	Crooks	Down

Passengers leave Cincinnati on the above boats every morning, arrive at Guyandotte next morning, and Charleston next evening, or in 35 hours.

Passengers leave Charleston every morning in superior four horse Post Coaches, arrive at Guyandotte same evening, and Cincinnati next morning, or in 24 hours.

☞ Passengers by this line have precedence in the Eastern Stage over all others. WM. PETTES.

June 25, 1844—tf

1844

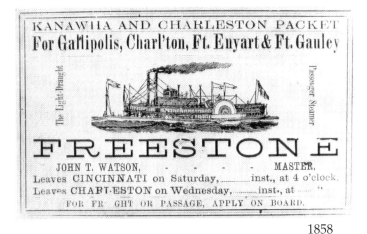

KANAWHA AND CHARLESTON PACKET

For Gallipolis, Charl'ton, Ft. Enyart & Ft. Gauley

The Light-Draught   Passenger Steamer

FREESTONE

JOHN T. WATSON, - - - MASTER,

Leaves CINCINNATI on Saturday,_____inst., at 4 o'clock.

Leaves CHARLESTON on Wednesday,_____inst., at ''

FOR FREIGHT OR PASSAGE, APPLY ON BOARD.

1858

KANAWHA ND CINCINNATI PACKET

The new, light-draught, and substantial steamer PLANET, RICHARD ROBERTSON Master, having been purchased expressly for the above trade, will commence her regular trips in due season; leaving Kanawha every Wednesday morning at 9 o'clock, A.M. and Cincinnati every Saturday at 12 o'clock, M.

The Planet's accommodations, for speed and comfort, will not be surpassed (if equalled) by any boat in the trade. Shippers and passengers may rely on her punctuality, and all business entrusted to my care will meet with every necessary attention—in return for which I only ask of my friends, and the public generally, a *deserving share* of their patronage.

October 22, 1845

1845

The *City of Charleston* operated briefly as an excursion boat on the Kanawha River in 1919-20. It then moved to Pittsburgh to operate on the Monogahela River. It burned at Gallipolis, Ohio, on May 5, 1921. (58)

Fast Side-Wheel Electric Light

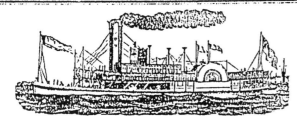

STR. LIBERTY

Gallipolis, Pt. Pleasant and Charleston Packet

Will Enter the Trade about May First.

Leaves Gallipolis at 6 A. M., Central Standard Time.
Leaves Pt. Pleasant at 7:30 A. M., Eastern Standard Time.
Making the following Landings on Hail
Lock Eleven, Beach Hill, Leon, Lock Ten, Buffalo,
Fraziers, Oak Forest, Red House, Winfield, Plymouth,
Raymond, Poca, Lock Seven, St. Albans, Lock Six.
Arriving at Charleston 2 P. M. Returning leaves Charleston 4 P. M.,
East. Stan. Time; Arriving at Gallipolis about 9 P. M. Con. Stan. Time.

Special Attention and Rates to Excursion Parties.

SUNDAY, MAY 3, 1903.

Steamer LIBERTY will Make an Excursion

Leaving Gallipolis 6 A. M. Central Standard Time and Pt. Pleasant 7:30
A. M. Eastern Standard Time to

$1   Charleston $1 Round Trip $1

From Gallipolis, Pt. Pleasant and Leon. 75 cents Round Trip from Buffalo,
Fraziers and Oak Forest. 50 cents Round Trip from Red House and
Winfield. Returning leaves Charleston 4 P. M. East. Stan. Time.

Don't Miss this Chance, Delightful Day-Light Trip.

See the Six Locks and Large Coal Mines. The Great Kanawha River is
one of the most beautiful streams in America and increasing in picturesque interest with each advancing hour. Good Music, Good
Order. Don't forget   st Excursion Sunday

For further information, excursion rates and dates apply to Capt. S. A.
Dunbar on board, or to Harry Maddy, Manager Gallipolis, Ohio.
GALLIPOLIS TRIBUNE PRINT.

1903

COMING!

Excursion Steamer

HOMER SMITH

Saturday, May 8th
Sunday, May 9th

First special excursion leaves wharf May 8th at 3 P.M.
returning at 9 P. M., personally conducted by J. R.
Shanklin, S. M. Snyder and Col. R. S. Carr, for the
Ladies First Division M. E. Church South. Drop your
business and take a delightful outing for six hours up
the beautiful Kanawha. The boat is steam heated and
will run regardless of the weather. Six o'clock dinner
will be served on the boat. The boat is equipped with
lunch counter, soda founta n, ice cream parlor, pop
corn roaster, orchestra and choir. Mr. Edward
Lauhon, Baritone, from Cincinnati, Ohio will render
several selections for the occasion.

Bring your lunches and have party picnics, tables and
chairs will be furnished free. Mrs. B. called up yesterday and said "I want 20 tickets, I am going to give
a party on the boat for Mrs. C.".

Everything sold on the boat at reasonable prices and
no comfort neglected. The boat is nothing short of a
floating hotel and summer resort, capacity 3000 people.

Tickets sold for this special excursion will be honored
for any one of four excursions advertised. Prices 75
and 25 cents.

On sale at Coffey's and Moore's book stores, Ladies
Committee and at the ticket booth on the levee. Get
tickets before going on the boat as the Ladies First
Division only get commission on tickets sold off the boat.

1915

-53-

Kanawha Packet Company
Pittsburg, Pa.

Bell Phone 1604 and 2358 Court.   P. & A. 2915 Main.

Str. KANAWHA.

W. E. Roe, Master.
J. H. Wolfe, Purser.

Independent Wharfboat at the foot of Wood Street.

¶ The only boat giving two days in Pittsburg. Leaves Pittsburg for Charleston Tuesdays at 4 p. m. Leaves Charleston for Pittsburg Thursdays at 10 p. m.

¶ Connects at Gallipolis with the Greene Line Steamers for all points in the South and West.

The *Kanawha* was built at Ironton, Ohio in 1896, for the Pittsburgh-Charleston trade. The boat spent almost 20 years on this route until tragically sinking in the Ohio River on Jan. 5, 1916, with the loss of 16 lives.

TIME AND DISTANCE CARD
EASTERN TIME

Read Up	Ohio River	M	Read Down
Sunday, 10:00 p. m.	Pittsburg	0	Tuesday, 4:00 p m.
8:30 p. m.	Sewickley	13	5:00 p. m.
6:00 p. m.	Rochester	26	6:00 p. m.
5:00 p. m.	Shippingport	35	7:00 p m.
4:00 p. m.	Georgetown	40	7:30 p m.
3:00 p. m.	East Liverpool	44	8:00 p. m.
2:30 p. m.	Wellsville	48	9:00 p m.
1:30 p m.	New Cumberland	56	10:00 p. m.
1:00 p. m.	Toronto	58	10:30 p. m.
11:00 a. m.	Steubenville	67	11:00 p. m.
9:30 a. m.	Wellsburg	74	Wed'd'y, 1:00 a. m.
7:00 a. m.	Martin's Ferry	88	2:00 a. m.
6:00 a. m.	Wheeling	90	4:00 a. m.
5:00 a. m.	Bellaire	94	4:30 a. m.
4:00 a. m.	Moundsville	102	5:00 a m.
2:30 a. m.	Powhatan	109	5:30 a. m.
1:30 a. m.	Clarington	117	6:00 a. m.
Saturd'y,12:00 nig't	Proctor	122	6:30 a. m.
11:30 p. m.	Hannibal	126	7:00 a. m.
11:00 p. m.	New Martinsville	128	7:30 a. m.
10:30 p. m.	Sardis	131	8:00 a. m.
9:30 p. m.	Sistersville	137	8:30 a. m.
8:30 p. m.	New Matamoras	142	9:00 a. m.
6:00 p. m.	St. Marys	154	9:45 a. m.
5:30 p. m.	Newport	155	10:00 a. m.
4:30 p. m.	Waverley	164	11:00 a. m.
3:00 p. m.	Marietta	171	12:0 noon
12:00 noon	Parkersburg	183	2:00 p. m.
10:00 a. m.	Little Hocking	191	4:00 p. m.
8:30 a. m.	Hockingport	197	4:30 p. m.
7:00 a. m.	Belleville	201	5:00 p. m.
6:00 a. m.	Long Bottom	208	5:30 p. m.
4:00 a. m.	Portland	215	6:00 p. m.
Friday, 9:30 p. m.	Ravenswood	219	7:00 p. m.
8:00 p. m.	Millwood	231	8:30 p. m.
7:00 p. m.	Letart	234	9:00 p. m.
6:00 p. m.	Racine	240	9:30 p. m.
5:30 p. m.	Syracuse	244	10:00 p. m.
5:00 p. m.	Hartford	245	10:30 p. m.
4:30 p. m.	Pomeroy	248	11:00 p. m.
3:30 p. m.	Middleport	250	11:30 p. m.
2:00 p. m.	Cheshire	256	12:00 nig't
1:30 p. m.	Addison	260	Thur'd'y,12:30 a. m.
1:00 p. m.	Point Pleasant	264	1:00 a. m.
12:00 noon	Gallipolis	268	1:30 a. m.

Read Up	Kanawha River		Read Down
Friday, 10:30 a. m.	Pt. Pleasant	0	Thur'd'y, 3:00 a. m.
10:15 a. m.	Lock 11	1	3:30 a. m.
10:00 a. m.	Brighton	6	3:45 a. m.
9:30 a. m.	Leon	13	4:30 a. m.
9:00 a. m.	Arbuckles	16	5:00 a. m.
8:00 a. m.	Lock 10	19	6:00 a. m.
7:30 a. m.	Buffalo	22	7:00 a. m.
7:00 a. m.	Lock 9	25	7:30 a. m.
6:45 a. m.	Midway	26	8:00 a. m.
6:30 a. m.	Winfield	31	9:00 a. m.
6:00 a. m.	Red House	31	9:00 a. m.
1:30 a. m.	Lock 8	36	10:00 a. m.
1:15 a. m.	Raymond City	38	11:00 a. m.
1:00 a. m.	Poca	39	11:30 a. m.
Thurs'y 11:30 p. m.	Lock 7	44	12:30 p. m.
11:00 p. m.	St. Albans	46	1:30 p. m.
10:30 p. m.	Lock 6	54	2:30 p. m.
10:00 p. m.	Charleston	58	4:00 p m.

The *Valley Belle* is handling a wharfboat at the city levee during the 1915 Kanawha River flood. The *Belle* was built in 1883 and ran 34 years as a packet.

Daily packet *J.Q. Dickinson* making a landing somewhere along her Charleston-Montgomery route. Built on the hull of the side-wheel steamer *Zanetta* with the engines from the *Kanawha Belle* in 1906, the *Dickinson* was owned and operated by the Calvert Brothers of Charleston. This photo circa 1915. GA

The *Tacoma* possibly holds the record for a continuously operating packet for not having a name change or alteration in appearance for her entire 39-year career. Built in 1883 for the Ohio River Packet Co., the *Tacoma* was sold in 1904 to run in the Cincinnati-Pomeroy-Charleston trade. She burned in 1922 while still in this trade. Photo circa 1915 in Lock #8. GA

The *Greenland* was designed and built for the Pittsburgh-Charleston trade in 1902 and ran most of her career in the Cincinnati-Pomeroy-Charleston trade. Photo taken in Lock #8. GA

Locks and Dams

ON THE GREAT KANAWHA RIVER.

What the Government Has Done to Improve Navigation.

The United States Government has appropriated three million eight hundred and eighty-five thousand and two hundred dollars, ($3,885,-200) for creating slack water navigation on the Great Kanawha river from the Ohio river at Pt. Pleasant to a point near the Kanawha Falls, in Fayette county, W. Va., distance ninety miles.

With this money the following locks and dams have been constructed towit:

Lock and Dam No 2, near Cannelton. Finished in 1887.

Lock and Dam No. 3, near Paint Creek. Finished in 1882.

Lock and Dam No. 4, near Coalburg. Finished in 1880.

Lock and Dam No. 5, near Brownstown. Finished in 1880.

Lock and Dam No. 6, below Charleston. Finished in 1886.

Lock and Dam No. 7, below St. Albans. Finished in 1893.

Lock and Dam No. 8, below Raymond City. Finished in 1893.

Locks and Dams Nos. 9, 10 and 11, now under construction, and nearly finished, are located as follows:

Lock and Dam No. 9, above Buffalo.

Lock and Dam No. 10, below Buffalo.

Lock and Dam No. 11, near Pt. Pleasant, at the mouth of the river.

This entire slack water navigation will be completed for the 90 miles when Locks and Dams Nos. 9, 10 and 11 are finished, which will be in the year 1897.

This important government work is now in charge of Col. Peter C. Hains, of Baltimore. The U. S. Resident Engineer is Addison M. Scott, whose office is in this city.

COAL SHIPMENTS.

The shipment of coal in bushels from the colleries on the Great Kanawha river, below the Kanawha Falls, for fiscal years (ending June 30th) by river, and for several years by railroad, is given in the following table, which has been furnished us by the Resident Engineer:

Year.	River.	Rail.	Total.
1875	4,048,300		
1876	6,024,000		
1877	5,183,600		
1878	no report		
1879	"		
18-0	"		
1881	9,628,695	6,631,660	16,260,356
1882	no report		
1883	15,370,418	13,290,255	28,660,713
1884	18,421,084	12,059,172	30,480,256
1885	17,812,323	12,972,217	30,784,540
1886	17,861,613	13,953,745	31,815,358
1887	23,233,374	19,160,896	42,394,270
1888	20,100,525	20,962,686	41,063,611
1889	26,921,788	22,031,121	48,842,909
1890	24,161,554	27,433,925	51,591,979
1891	25,761,316	28,668,025	54,429,371
1892	26,787,888	30,814,100	57,631,888
1893	22,983,000	no report	
1894	25,821,000	" "	
1895	21,882,600	" "	
1896	23,050,000	" "	

The first two locks and dams of the system, as noted above, were completed in 1880.

If such has been the increase of the coal traffic from the locks and dams already constructed and in operation, how much greater will that increase be when locks and dams No. 9, 10 and 11 are completed, and thereby six feet of water for 90 miles on the Great Kanawha will be furnished during the entire year?

We will here add that the shipments during the last four years have been materially cut down by unusually low water in the Great Kanawha below the locks and dams already constructed—that is, below lock and dam No. 8, situated below Raymond City. This will, however, no longer be the case after locks and dams 9, 10 and 11, now under contract, are completed. It may be added that the coal shipments by river particularly during the last two years, have also been materially affected by the prevailing "hard times"—the depression in manufacturing, and in business generally.

FREE NAVIGATION.

By an act of Congress passed in 1882, the navigation of the Great Kanawha was made free and no tolls are charged thereon.

On the Monongahela river tolls are charged thereon by the Monongahela Navigation Company which was chartered by the Legislature of Pennsylvania many years ago, with authority to lock and dam the Monongahela river and charge tolls thereon. The Kanawha river being free of tolls gives the Kanawha coal operators a very great advantage over the Monongahela coal operators.

Furthermore this free slackwater navigation is a permanent guarantee that the coal operators on the Great Kanawha river and its tributaries, Elk and Coal rivers, cannot be controlled in their shipment of coal westward by freight rates of either Chesapeake & Ohio R. R., or the Kanawha & Michigan R. R. which roads are constructed on and along the banks of the Great Kanawha river. This slackwater navigation will always furnish the Kanawha collieries with free transportation to Point Pleasant on the Ohio River.

ADVANTAGES ON THE OHIO.

Pittsburg is 262 miles by the Ohio river above Point Pleasant, and the coal boating stages are therefore more frequent at Point Pleasant than at Pittsburg.

From gauge records kept at Pittsburg and Point Pleasant for a number of years, as shown by U. S. Engineer reports, it appears there are, on an average, 155 days in a year when coal boats and barges drawing six feet of water can be taken down the Ohio from Pittsburg, whilst there are, on an average, 251 days in the year when coal boats and barges drawing the same depth of water can be taken down the Ohio river from Point Pleasant at the mouth of the Great Kanawha river.

FREEDOM FROM ICE.

The Great Kanawha, owing mainly no doubt to its source being so far south (New river, the principal tributary, rises in North Carolina), is but little obstructed by ice. Records kept at the U. S. Engineers office here show that during the last twenty-three years (beginning with 1873) navigation on the Great Kanawha has been suspended wholly or in part, an aggregate of only 195 days, or on an average less than 8½ days per year. The longest suspension was 30 days in the winter of 1892-3. During eight of the twenty three winters there was no suspension on the Great Kanawha by ice.

COMMERCIAL ADVANTAGES.

The great commercial advantages yet to be given to the coal and timber lands of the Great Kanawha and its tributaries, Elk river, Coal river, &c., will be seen when locks and dams 9, 10 and 11 are completed. That is, when ninety miles of slackwater navigation of the Great Kanawha are completed, collieries on the Great Kanawha, Elk & Coal rivers will have very great advantages over those on the Monongahela and Youghiogheny rivers in the shipments of coal down the Ohio to the western and southwestern markets.—*From Kanawha Gazette, West Va., April 21, 1897.*

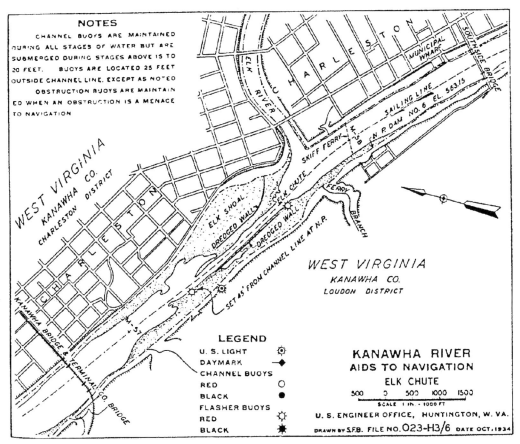

LEGEND
U. S. LIGHT
DAYMARK
CHANNEL BUOYS
RED
BLACK
FLASHER BUOYS
RED
BLACK

KANAWHA RIVER
AIDS TO NAVIGATION
ELK CHUTE
500   0   500   1000   1500
SCALE 1 IN. - 1000 FT
U. S. ENGINEER OFFICE, HUNTINGTON, W. VA.
DRAWN BY S.F.B. FILE NO. O23-H3/6 DATE OCT. 1934

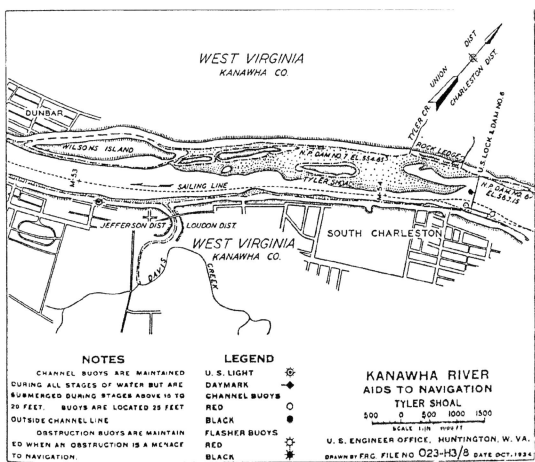

LEGEND
U. S. LIGHT
DAYMARK
CHANNEL BUOYS
RED
BLACK
FLASHER BUOYS
RED
BLACK

KANAWHA RIVER
AIDS TO NAVIGATION
TYLER SHOAL
500   0   500   1000   1500
SCALE 1 IN - 1000 FT
U. S. ENGINEER OFFICE, HUNTINGTON, W. VA.
DRAWN BY F.R.G. FILE NO. O23-H3/8 DATE OCT. 1934

1934

Marmet Locks and Dam #2, March 29, 1936. The Dupont Works can be seen in the extreme right across the river. U.S. ARMY CORPS OF ENGINEERS COLL.

The Marmet Lock Disaster

At 9:50 p.m. on Saturday, April 23, 1932, a landslide collapsed the river bank on the Belle side of new construction of the Marmet locks. It came without warning and 100 tons of earth crashed down on workers at the site. At least 10 were killed and nine injured. Rescue crews from throughout the valley, totalling over 150, toiled for hours with heavy equipment and hand tools digging out the dead and injured. Over 5,000 spectators came to the scene causing the authorities to declare semi-martial law. A broken gas line in one of the buildings owned by the construction company filled the air with gas. State police rigidly enforced a "no smoking" ban fearing a deadly explosion. Two spectators were injured by subsequent small landslides in the same area.

The crews of workman caught under the slide were doing excavating work for a foundation for the landward wall of the second of the twin locks at Marmet. Heavy rains and recent flood waters of the Kanawha River hammered the site and a layer of sand beneath the river bank was thought to have given way contributing to the disaster.

Opposite page, bottom: The *Wild Goose* had an internal combusion engine and was unique in having a two-part paddlewheel that could operate separately - that is one could go faster, slower or even in reverse. The goal was better handling, but the screw propeller made it obsolete. (176)

Lock #6 just east of Dunbar, looking toward South Charleston, 1921. This was one of the locks completed in the 1880s by the U.S. government to make the Kanawha River navigable from its mouth to above Charleston. A boat would be locked through; that is, enter a chamber where the flowing water would raise or lower it to the next level. The 1880s dams and the later much-improved roller design of the 1930s created a series of pools, thereby taming the old natural river for commerce. Of course, in times of flood nothing could be done except lower the dam and stand clear. Before these series of locks and dams were built, there were places where in the dry season a person could walk across the river. Old-time steamboats had to wait for the times when there was enough depth to get through, sometimes scooting across sandbars. It was not unusual to have to tie up for weeks. This lock and dam system was demolished in 1936. GA ⑥⑦

This second *Wild Goose* was given its trial run on Sept. 25, 1926.

Launching the river towboat *Destrehan* at Ward Engineering in 1922. Two seagoing ships, built for the U.S. Army, are nearing completion. GA ⑰⑥

The Ward Engineering Company

A shoemaker's son, Charles Ward grew up in Leamington, England, where he was apprenticed to a pipe fitter at age 16. After working for gas and iron companies in Leamington and Liverpool, he emigrated to America during the early 1870s. Settling in Charleston, he received employment supervising a new gas works and also opened a store that sold gas fittings and provided plumbing services.

Ward soon left the gas company to concentrate his efforts upon designing and manufacturing steam boilers for transportational use. Rather than relying on traditional boiler design in which coils of hot air were used to bring drums of water to a boil, Ward developed a method in thich coils were water were heated in a chamber

of hot air. The result represented a dramatic increase in heat production per unit of water. Ward tested his new design on a steam packet called the *Wild Goose* with mixed success during the late 1870s. When he finally patented the Ward Water Tube Boiler in 1879, his new invention was met with skepticism by most riverboatmen who were accustomed to the old "Scotch Boiler" design. Yet, gradually over the next two decades, water tube boilers built by Ward and his competitors came to dominate the industry.

Ward faced similar skepticism when he advocated the elimination of the bulky, if picturesque, paddle wheel as a means of propulsion in favor of the screw propeller during the 1890s. After testing screw propulsion on small family yachts, Ward offered to build a towboat for the U.S. Engineering Service that he claimed would be the equal of any boat then in government service. When the boat was launched in 1902, the U.S. Government had every intention of holding him at his word. In response to ridicule by veteran rivermen, an inspector from the Engineering Service's Pittsburgh Office was brought in to pass judgment on the slender craft, which Ward had named the *James Rumsey* after the Shepherdstown steamboat pioneer. When the inspector pronounced it inferior to a sternwheeler, a duel was arranged between the *Rumsey* and the sternwheeler *D.T. Lane*, one of the most powerful boats on the Kanawha.

Thousands of spectators lined the banks of the Kanawha as the

Rumsey and the *Lane* were lashed together on Saturday, March 7, 1902, on the Charleston riverfront. To many it appeared to be a battle between David and Goliath, as indeed it proved to be. Despite a poor start, the *Rumsey* was soon pushing the *Lane* about at will as the throng looked on in amazement. In the words of a *Pittsburgh Gazette* correspondent who was in attendance, the sight of the powerful "Little Giant" manhandling the majestic *D.T. Lane* was one that "broke old hearts and changed a river axiom" forever.

Though the advantages of screw propulsion were convincingly demonstrated in this and subsequent trials, acceptance came slowly, compelling Ward Engineering to continue manufacturing sternwheel vessels while simultaneously developing and building propeller-powered craft.

With the failing of Ward's health, Charles Ward's son, Edwin, assumed stewardship of the company in 1909. When Charles Ward died on Jan. 7, 1915, he left an admirable legacy - from humble beginnings his company had achieved a position of leadership in marine engineering recognized around the world.

Continuing in his father's footsteps, in the ensuing decades Edwin Ward developed Ward Engineering into a major supplier of "shallow draught" boats capable of functioning in as little as two feet of water. The times were ripe for such a craft as this was truly the heyday of the barge age. From 1920 to 1930 Ward Engineering produced about 80 hulls and many more boilers for vessels such as barges, ferries, lighthouse tenders, packet boats, and towboats for service throughout the United States and beyond.

Among the most impressive boats built by the company during this period was the immense ferryboat *Sainte Genevieve.* Constructed to transport railroad cars across the Mississippi River, the craft was 360 feet in length and could carry as many as 21 freight cars in a single trip. The *Vicksburg* (1921) and the *Indiana* (1930) were the most powerful boats ever built by Ward, each with 2,500 horsepower. The U.S. Lighthouse Tender *Greenbrier* was reportedly "the most beautiful steamboat ever built" in the Kanawha Valley. President and Mrs. Hoover rode the *Greenbrier* during a regatta celebrating the completion of the canalization of the Ohio River by the Ohio Valley Improvement Association in 1929.

With the onset of the Great Depression, declining health, resistance to unionization, and increasing government regulation combined to induce Edwin Ward to close the Ward Engineering plant in December 1931. Thus ended a notable chapter in the history of maritime technology and Charleston's history as well.

The launching of the *Indiana* on June 16, 1930. It was the first river towboat to have a steam tube-electric drive and, along with other boats being built, were the largest and the last Ward-built boats.

Most of Charleston must have turned out at the levee to see the launching of Ward boats.

NATCHEZ -1920

MASCOT - 1893

JAMES RUMSEY -1903

J. B. BATTLE -1923

GEO. T. PRICE - 1925

DWIGHT F. DAVIS -1929

W. A. SHEPARD -1927

ESTABLISHED in 1872, The Charles Ward Engineering Works have always been pioneers in improving the design and construction of River Craft of all types. Here are 13 illustrations of Ward products, each an outstanding achievement of its period.

MASCOT—Built in 1893—the first tunnel boat on the Western Rivers.

JAMES RUMSEY—Built in 1903—the first twin screw tunnel towboat built in America.

J. B. BATTLE—Built in 1923—the first Diesel electric stern wheel towboat built in America.

C. B. HARRIS—Built in 1924—the first Suction Dredge, with direct Diesel engine driven pump. built for River service.

DUNCAN BRUCE—Built in 1929—the largest and most powerful stern wheel towboat with direct Diesel drive.

THE CHARLES WARD

DESIGNERS AND BUILDERS OF RIVER CRAFT OF ALL TYPES

Leadership

GEORGE T. HARRIS (1925): W. A. SHEPARD, (1927); INCOR, (1928). The first three twin screw tunnel towboats of 720 h.p., each equipped with Diesel engines.

DWIGHT F. DAVIS—Built in 1929—the first vessel actually designed and built to use pulverized coal under its boilers.

TWO TOWBOATS—Twin screw tunnel towboats with Turbo-Electric drive—the first of their type—building for the Standard Unit Navigation Company.

WHITE SWAN—The largest modern passenger vessel designed and proposed for Western River service.

GEN. FRANK M. COXE and GEN. JOHN McE. HYDE—Built in 1922—the first twin screw passenger vessels built on the rivers for ocean-going service.

NATCHEZ—Built in 1920—the first of a fleet of 2000 h.p., twin screw tunnel towboats.

INCOR - 1928

GEN. FRANK M. COXE -1922

WHITE SWAN

SUNCO

DUNCAN BRUCE -1927

C. B. HARRIS - 1924

ENGINEERING WORKS
CHARLESTON, WEST VIRGINIA

The *Ada V* docked opposite the Campbells Creek area in the early 1900s. KCL

Ferryboat owned by Edward U. Beene and used on the Kanawha River at St. Albans from the 1920s to 1934. PHOTO BY DON GREENE, J.W. WILLIAMS COLL.

NEW BATHING BEACH TO BE OPENED TODAY

Spot Lies Just Before Plant of Standard Oil Company and Can Be Reached by Clendenin Street Ferry

Today Charleston's new city bathing beach, sanctioned by Mayor W. W. Wertz and other city officials, will be thrown open to the public on the south side of the Kanawha river, opposite the mouth of Elk river. The privileges of the beach and picnic and recreation grounds will be free to the public, all donated by one of Charleston's public spirited citizens who refuses to allow his name to be mentioned.

The spot lies just before the Standard Oil company plant and the mouth of Ferry branch and is reached by the ferry at the foot of Clendenin street or by automobile through the Ferry branch undergrade crossing and a new roadway just south of the culvert where signs show the way.

The beach is rapidly being transformed into one of the beauty spots of the section. The plot of ground contains more than five acres and the beach is 1,000 feet long. Nearly 700 feet of floats have been anchored at the place for divers and those who desire to take sun baths and the ground beneath the large willow grove has been cleared and placed in presentable condition with the trees nicely whitewashed.

Chief of Police John Britton, who has been exerting every precaution to prevent deaths by drowning in the rivers about the city, officially inspected the beach last Friday and placed his stamp of approval on it. Mayor Wertz looked it over yesterday and stated that the city would place a life guard at the place to make it doubly safe for bathers.

The beach is a sandy one and the slope is gradual for at least 200 feet from the shore before the water becomes too deep for wading. There is little current at the place but the guard will patrol the outlying section in a boat at all hours of the day and evening. Some distance below the beach are the "chutes" where strong and experienced swimmers may swim at great speed for nearly half a mile, returning by boat inside the wing wall.

There is automobile space sufficient to accommodate 700 cars in an open flat tract adjoining the grove and there is ample room for automobile tourists who desire to avail themselves of the camp site and the privilege of the beach. Large signs along the Midland trail will direct them to the spot.

Preparations are being made for a large attendance at the beach on July 4, next Saturday. The entire city administration has been invited to call on that day and inspect the grounds. The Dokkies will also go to the beach July 4 for an all-day outing and picnic, given as a benefit to their drum corps.

There will be no bathing suits furnished at the beach at this time but a large house has been renovated and placed in condition where clothing may be changed. The privileges of the beach will be available for night bathing parties, the grounds having been well lighted by a large number of electric lights. This is the first free bathing beach that Charleston has had, a privilege afforded citizens of nearly every city in the country that is situated on a body of water.

Swimming at Lick Branch, 1920s.

There were four recognized swimming places in the Kanawha River in the old days. Lick Branch, at the mouth of the creek of the same name, Splash Beach, across from the mouth of Elk River, "the Rock," at the mouth of Hale's Branch, across from Broad Street, and a beach near the old C&O Railroad transfer site at the upper end of South Ruffner.

Lower Falls Beach on Coal River. Bathers would park their vehicles on one side of the river, buy a ticket and board a barge. The barge was connected to a cable that was pulled to propel the barge across the river. Eventually a suspension bridge was built across the river. The river is still popular with bathers. PHIL GOLDSTEIN COLL.

LOWER FALLS BEACH
Now Open At Lower Falls on Coal River
Picknicing, Swimming, Diving and Camping
The Largest and Best All Sand Beach in Southern West Virginia. Free Parking.
Under Management of
Jas. F. Sattes, Jr.

Trying to escape the summer heat, bathers would swarm to the Lick Branch swimming beach on the Kanawha River, circa 1920s.

In one year of the 1920s, 18 deaths by drowning were recorded in Charleston. But the summer heat was relentless and the river worth the risk.

Lick Branch swimming in 1910. (372)

Originally built at Virginia Street across the Elk River about 1873, this suspension bridge was dismantled in 1907 and rebuilt upriver at the Spring Street location. This circa 1910 photo was taken at Spring Street. The swimmer on the left is Raymond "Buzz" Andre. BEA ⑤⑦

Lick Branch swimming, 1910.

OLD DIVING PIER PASSES AWAY IN A BLAZE OF GLORY

Placid as fabled mirror lake lay the stretch of the waters of the Kanawha near Lick Branch last evening. The cooling down-river breeze fanned from the fast departing day the sweltering heat, yet so gently that no riple showed upon its silver undulations in the new moon's light.

Lazily in canoe and motorboat, devotees of summer glided silently in the deepening dusk about Lick Branch pier to the heart of swimmer and pleasure seeker.

Almost it was "The Perfect Day" when apparently from the waters surface rose a tiny tongue of flame. In an instant, it had grown to a pillar climbing to the sky, across the silence came the crackle and roar of burning timber, a million golden sparks danced and swirled in clouds of purpling smoke.

Like awed creatures of its depths the river craft stood still, while many hearts were saddened by what they perceived was a golden glorious transition of the Lick Branch Pier diving tower, into memory.

Contractors had poured kerosene over the logs of the old river pier, condemned as dangerous to navigation, and were using fire to eliminate the long loved landmark.

Newspaper story - May 31, 1914

Swimming in the Kanawha River, 1915.

- Candid shots of a steamboat ride -

On the Kanawha River with the Charleston High School Senior Class Excursion - 1915
The steamer is the "Valley Belle." GA

Class members. Lucy Quarrier is on the right.

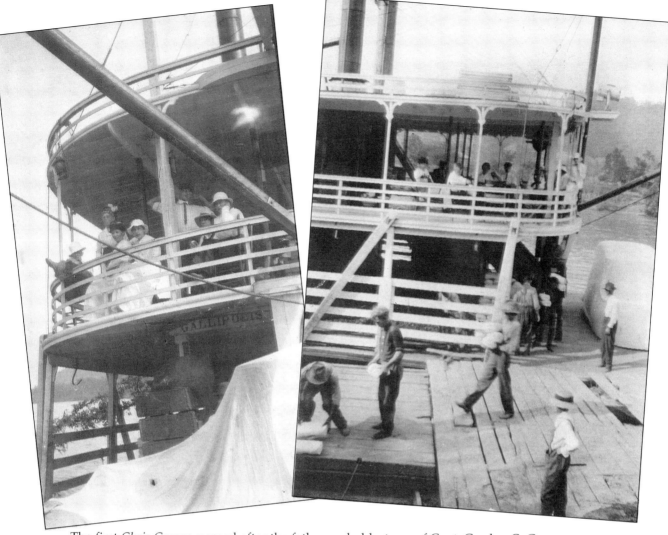

The first *Chris Greene*, named after the father and oldest son of Capt. Gordon C. Greene ran the Gallipolis-Charleston route from 1915 to 1918. Notice the covered car on the deck. Automobiles were often transported from town to town since roads were so bad. GA

Friends gather to swim on the Kanawha River, circa 1915. What would these girls have thought of today's bikini swimwear? We can guess what the fellows would think. GA

Shanty boats on the Elk River behind the present Civic Center. This was typical housing for many people during the Depression years, circa 1935. The Virginia Street bridge is in the background.

The *Taric* was originally named *H.St.L. Coppee* when built for the U.S. Army Corps of Engineers in 1904. Bought by the Raymond City Coal & Transportation Co. in 1935 and renamed, it towed coal to Louisville until dismantled in 1947. Note the Elk River Boulevard Bridge in the background, circa 1943.

The *E.D. Kenna* was built in Charleston in 1925 for the Ohio River Company. It worked on the Mississippi, Ohio, Kanawha and Illinois rivers until 1952 and was dismantled in 1953. This is believed to be her trial run steaming under the South Side bridge in 1925.

Two of the 12 houses which were moved by barge across the Kanawha River in 1923 to make room for the new state capitol on the tract comprising the 1900 and 2000 blocks of Kanawha Street. They were moved to the south bank below 20th Street. The house on the left was occupied by the de Gruyter family, the other by the C.B. Couch family. Total cost to move all 12 houses was $42,000. Over the years with a growing Charleston - more than a few houses have been moved by barge including a few from the Morris Harvey College site and Southside Expressway construction. ③00

Built in 1927 for the Federal Barge Line at Dubuque, Iowa, and named *C.C. Webber*, the *Ellen Hatfield* was bought by the Ohio & Kanawha Transportation Company in 1947. The name was changed in May 1948 to honor the wife of James T. Hatfield, Sr., by the Hatfield-Campbell Creek Coal Co. Transferred to the Amherst Barge Company in 1953, she was dismantled in 1956. The *General Ashburn* was raised and renamed *J.T. Hatfield* when the Ohio & Kanawha Transportation Co. was absorbed by the Hatfield-Campbell Creek Coal Co. in April 1945. Six years later, the *J.T. Hatfield* (2nd) became a part of the Amherst Barge Co. fleet until sold in 1957 to Armco Steel Corp. who renamed her *Charles R. Hook*.

The "Queen of the Kanawha," the *P.A. Denny* sternwheeler has had a long, hard and colorful history. It was originally built in the late 1920s at Ward Engineering and named *Scott* for Addison Scott, the engineer who constructed the original Kanawha River locks. The U.S. Army Corps of Engineers used her to push barges and dredge silt until 1954 when she was sold and taken to Alabama. Long-time riverman Peter A. Denny bought her, brought her back to the Kanawha and started to rebuild her. He rechristened her *Robin D Too* after the first sternwheeler he owned, the *Robin D*. Denny died in 1975 before the boat was finished, but well-known valley businessman, Lawson Hamilton bought her, finished the rebuilding, even after a fire caused extensive damage, and renamed her the *P.A. Denny*. Hamilton put her into excursion service on the river in 1976 and entered her in Charleston's annual Sternwheel Regatta. In January 1981 bad luck hit when frozen pipes caused her to sink. Hamilton raised her, refitted her and again put her into service plying the river as a charter and excursion boat. After 25 years of service, the *P.A. Denny* is truly the "Queen of the Kanawha."

The Kanawha River reached almost record heights in 1915.

Two views of the Kanawha River levee at Charleston in 1915. The famous excursion boat the *Delta Queen* is docked at the present levee in the modern photo at left. The courthouse and new Federal Building are in the background. The 13-story Union Building is still the most prominent building on the boulevard. The *Delta Queen* was too large to venture up the Kanawha to Charleston until the new Winfield Locks was opened in 1999. HAROLD FIELD COLL.

SUNSET SPECIAL
TO
ST. ALBANS
AND
MOONLIGHT
ON
LARGE STEAMER
G. W HILL

SUNDAY, SEPT. 17
TO ST. ALBANS
Lv. Charleston 2:30 P. M. Returns
6:30 P. M.
Arrive St. Albans 4:00 P. M Leaves
4:30 P. M.
Famous New York 20th Century
Orchestra
A Treat to Hear Them.
5—ROOMY DECKS—5
MOONLIGHT
Leave Charleston 8:15 P. M. Returns
11:30 P. M.
The Event of the Season. Don't Miss
It. Best of Order Maintained. No
Rowdyism Permitted.
Fare on Either Trip 75c

Returning to the Kanawha River to run excursions in 1914, the *Ohio* had originally run on this river as the steamer *Avalon* in 1907. In 1908, she was given the name *Ohio* and operated about a year on the Kanawha before being placed in the Cincinnati-Pittsburgh trade. She burned on Feb. 2, 1916, at Parkersburg.

1922

Big Excursion
STEAMER "OHIO"
Will Run a Moonlight Excursion
THURSDAY SEPT. 10, 1914
Will leave Charleston Wharf at 7:30 p. m. and return at 11:30 p. m. same evening. The boat carries their own orchestra. Dancing will be free.
Tickets 50 Cents---Pays All

This will give the people of Charleston an opportunity to make a trip on the finest Excursion Boat on the waters of the Mississippi River. All Fraternal Organizations and the public invited.

The boat reserves the right to reject all objectionable parties.

Just below Charleston's city levee showboat, *Majestic* with its towboat, the *Attaboy* of Pittsburgh, 1950.

The *Gordon C. Greene*, seen here at the Capitol levee in 1947, was one of the best-known steamers on the Kanawha River. Originally named *Cape Girardeau* when built in 1923, her name was changed in 1935 when acquired by the Greene Line Steamers for the company founder. She made many excursions on the Kanawha River until she was retired in 1952 and became a floating restaurant at a number of locations on the Ohio and Mississippi rivers. The boat sank at St. Louis in 1967. (59)

The highlight of *F.M. Staunton*'s career was towing *Edward's Moonlight* excursion barge with Vice President of the United States Charles Curtis on board at the dedication of the Marmet Locks in September 1932. Originally built as the *Winifred* in 1903, this towboat had been named *C.F. Colbert* and *Governor Harding* before becoming the *Staunton* in 1930 for the W.Va. Sand & Gravel Co. (68)

Still running today as the very successful *Belle of Louisville* stationed at Louisville, Ky., the *Avalon* is one of the most widely traveled steamboats ever. Originally named *Idlewild* when built in 1915, this boat is remembered by many along the Kanawha for enjoyable summer afternoon and moonlight excursions in the 1940s and '50s. This view circa 1959. CN (58)

STEAMER
AVALON

MOONLITE
EXCURSION
NITELY 9 PM

ONLY BOAT THIS YEAR!
CHARLESTON — 4 DAYS
THUR. **19** thru SUN. **22**
MAY **19** MAY **22**
Moonlite Nitely 9 p.m. Foot Capitol

Bring the Kiddies Sightseeing
Sat.-Sun. Aft. LVS. 2:30 PM
RTS. 5:30 PM
FARES: Child 50¢ Adult $1.00

RHYTHM MASTERS ORCH., All Trips
MOONLITE DANCING
STARTS 8 PM
LVS. 9 P.M. FARE: At Boat $1 50 ADV. $1.25

EXTRA **SAT. MIDNITE**
TRIP Lvs. 12:30 AM - Rts. 2:30 AM

Advance Tickets WHELAN'S DRUGS,
Capitol and Quarrier Sts.

1955

The towboat *Omar* was built in 1936, decommissioned in 1961 and rebuilt in 1962 as a museum/ showboat theater by the State of West Virginia as part of the state's 1963 centennial celebration. It was renamed the *Rhodo-dendron* and was towed along the state's waterways. She was sold to the city of Clinton, Iowa, in 1966 and renamed *Showboat* for use on the Mississippi River. This photo was taken Feb. 10, 1966. CN

Built at Point Pleasant, W.Va. in 1940 by the Marietta Manufacturing Co., the Union Barge Line named the boat *Jason* when they bought it in 1941. The name was changed to *Herbert E. Jones* in 1951 after being bought by the Hatfield-Campbell Creek Coal Co. The *Jones* was the last large sternwheel steam towboat to operate on the Kanawha. The last owner of the *Jones* was the Amherst Industries, Inc., of Port Amherst (Charleston) which is owned by the Jones family. Decommissioned in 1961, the 25-foot diameter sternwheel from the *Jones* is now a permanent display at Station Square in Pittsburgh.

Another house move on the river in the 1950s when houses were barged to new locations to make way for the South Side Expressway. Note that one of these is a brick structure.

Above and far right, top: These giant stone pillars could easily be some artifact of ancient Egypt but actually they were a part of early Charleston which stood from 1852 until 1904.

Pictured here are the westerly suspension towers of the old Washington Street bridge.

The first link across the Elk River, this cable suspension bridge had quite an eventful life in its 52-year history.

In September 1862 during the Federal Army's retreat from Charleston the Yankees burned the bridge to try to slow down the on-rushing Confederate troops. It was soon rebuilt and served until a fateful morning in December 1904.

On that cold winter day several heavy freight wagons were crossing the bridge and their weight was just too much for the old cables. One broke and dumped horses, wagons, and unfortunately, a few people into the frozen Elk.

Eleven horses were drowned along with two children who were on their way to school.

The bridge we cross today is the third to span the Elk at Washington Street and many of us can recall the iron truss bridge that existed from 1907 until the 1970s.

These stone masons built the piers for the 1905 Washington Street Bridge that replaced the fallen suspension bridge.

Steamboats on the Elk River help to rescue people and horses from the icy water after the collapse of the Lovell (Washington) Street bridge on December 15, 1904. BEA ⑦⑤

Above: Pouring the deck on the Charleston and South Charleston (Patrick Street) bridge on March 7, 1930. GRAVELY & MOORE PHOTO Below: Dedication ceremony for the new bridge in 1932, scene looking north. GA ⑦⑨

Charleston Mayor DeVan is the bald-headed man in the middle of the platform.
K-Mart of today would be visible to the distant left.

Erection of Bridge, Below Present Structure, Proposed to Relieve Existing Traffic Congestion

Two Ramps on South Side of River Would Aid Much in Directing Traffic in Either Direction

A new bridge over the Kanawha river, extending from the city levee to a point about the old stone building below the Chesapeake and Ohio passenger station, is proposed today by a prominent Charleston business man who has made a sketch of the plan and who goes into a detailed explanation of it. The sketch, though easily understood, is, of course, not drawn to scale.

The location of the bridge would throw the north end about midway between Capitol and Summers streets, west of the Union building. It would be a drawbridge, gaining its maximum height about 30 feet above the street level on an easy grade reached at about the river's edge. The north-end approach would be fan-shaped with a small park in the center of the fan where, it is suggested, a piece of statuary, such as the Stonewall Jackson statue that still stands on the old capitol site, could be placed.

The bridge would be sufficiently wide to take care of all needs for many years to come, this to be estimated by experts. There would be ample sidewalks on each side. Southbound traffic would approach from Summers and lower Kanawha streets and northbound traffic would flow east with Kanawha street or into Capitol street. It is seen that this would necessitate the changing of the direction of the one-way arteries of the city but, it is pointed out, this would prove more convenient, the only reason for routing traffic east on Virginia street having been because of the location of the approach to the old South Side bridge.

On the south side of the river there would be two ramps directing traffic up and down the river on easy grades. Another ramp, or really an extension of the bridge, would go straight ahead over the Chesapeake and Ohio railroad tracks to connect with the present road below the MacCorkle drive. Thus all railroad crossings at the point would be eliminated.

Could Enter Station

It is suggested that under this plan there would be plenty of space for station extensions. The present building could be extended on over the tracks to the road along the hillside and there is plenty of room for an additional building below the proposed bridge approach. Room for additional trackage could be provided by eliminating the grade floor rooms of the present station.

Another advantage would be the providing of plenty of room for the parking of automobiles and taxicabs under the east and west ramps.

Span Would be of Drawbridge Type, but Rivermen Agree that Opening of It Would be Small

there would be considerable parking space left under the north side approach.

The bridge would be of the draw type. While at first this appears to be somewhat of a disadvantage, it is shown that the necessity for opening the draw would occur only at long intervals. At the proposed height, all steamboats could pass under the bridge during normal or usual stages of the river. During high water, few, if any, boats run.

While the Kanawha county court owns the old bridge and its rights-of-day, it is suggested that the county would probably co-operate with the city in the matter and make available the revenue that would come from the sale of the old bridge approaches in the event that the old bridge is abandoned. This would make available for sale two large business frontages on Kanawha street and one on Virginia street.

The suggestions are nothing more than merely that, it is pointed out. They are made by a practical business man who has given the matter considerable study but does not want free discussion hampered by giving his name at this time, he says. Full criticism of the plan is invited by The Gazette, and any drawbacks that seem apparent to anyone will be given full consideration by this newspaper if communications are properly addressed and signed. Any one who has additional suggestions to make or can work out any improvements in the plan is urged to do so and inform The Gazette fully in regard to his ideas.

Proposed new bridge over the Kanawha river at the city levee. Proportions and distances are not drawn to scale.

Diagram labels: OLD BRIDGE SITE; BRIDGE AVE.; MacCORKLE'S DRIVE; PRESENT C. & O. BRICK STATION WITH POSSIBLE EXTENSION; TO KANAWHA CITY; RIVER BANK; RAMP; TO SOUTH CHARLESTON; POSSIBLE NEW ADDITION TO STATION ON WEST; KANAWHA; RIVER; PROPOSED NEW BRIDGE; LEVEE; LEVEE; LAND BANK BLDG.; UNION TRUST BLDG.; CAPITOL STREET; KANAWHA VALLEY BANK; KANAWHA STREET; FRANKENBERGER BUILDING; SUMMERS ST.; PEOPLES STORE

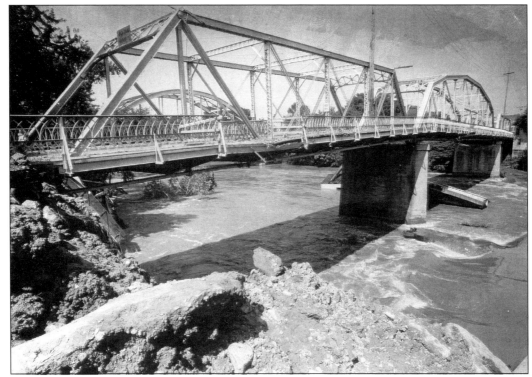

On Sept. 16, 1971, several barges owned by Burdette Asphalt & Paving Co. broke from their moorings, striking other barges, including one housing a giant derrick. In all 10 vessels slid downstream bumping several bridges over the Elk River. The Washington Street bridge was the only one damaged as seen in this photo. Surrounding earth on the eastern abutment was washed away and it started to settle. The bridge was replaced by a modern multi-lane arch.

The infamous crooked bridge on U.S. Route 60 at Belle crossed over the railroad and was the scene of many accidents in its history. Photo circa 1955.

The Kanawha City Bridge was originally built for streetcars in 1915 and it served well until 1975 when it was demolished by explosives. The new arch bridge was built first to take care of the traffic and we see it standing as the old bridge goes crashing to its grave. ⑦⑧

The old Chelyan bridge over the Kanawha River was finally replaced in 1999. As bridges go, one might say it was rather odd but it served for many years. ⑦⑨

This interesting photo of the Elk River at Spring Street circa 1920 shows clearly the suspension bridge that was originally built at Virginia Street. When the 1907 vintage iron bridge was built to cross the Elk at Virginia Street, the city fathers decided the old 1873 suspension bridge was still serviceable and it was disassembled and moved up to Spring Street when it was finally replaced in about 1923. The city water works reservoir is seen under construction, and near the K&M (now NS) Railroad bridges we see the smoke stack of the streetcar power generating plant. ⑭

The old
Montgomery
bridge over the
Kanawha
River in 1915.

WON'T USE BRIDGE

After Hearing Report of Engineer

WAIT FOR THE NEW

Unless the city compels the Kanawha Valley Traction Company to run their cars over the present Keystone bridge the company will continue to transfer its passengers at Virginia street crossing to the West Side. This was decided yesterday after the report of the bridge expert, William Farris of the Penn Bridge company, of Pittsburgh, had been seen.

Mr. Farris informed the street car company that the small cars which had been in use before the large cars were purchased, would be safe in carrying passengers across the bridge, but the street car officials when seen today say they cannot abide by this decision and therefore will not use the bridge for street car traffic unless compelled by the city and it is safe to say that the city will not ask the company to undertake anything that would look like endangering the lives of any citizens.

"We have not enough of the small cars," said Mr. W.E. Chilton, "to accommodate the people and it would cost a large sum to repair the ones we have on hand now in order to use them; so there is nothing to do but to wait for the new bridge, which will be pushed as rapidly as possible now."

Mr. Farris is preparing the plans for the new bridge and will submit his work to the bridge committee and the traction company in a few weeks in order that they may make any needed changes before the election on the bond question on the 19 of November, calling for $250,000 to be issued in bonds with which to build the bridge and complete the sewerage system.

The report of Mr. Farris which was submitted to the council Thursday night was as follows:

Charleston, Oct. 18, 1906.
The Hon. Mayor and City Council,
Charleston, W. Va.

Gentlemen: In response to the request of your bridge committee, we examined the suspension bridge over Elk river, on Virginia street, and respectfully report as follows:

We did not find any breaks nor apparent defects in the main factors of the bridge, to-wit: The main cables, towers, floor beams, anchorages nor piers.

We found eight breaks in the auxilliary cables, and two in the stiffening trusses; these were repaired in a substantial manner. We also found the auxilliary cables, several of the vertical suspenders and truss rods out of adjustment and carrying unequal shares of the load. We brought these all into proper adjustment.

The bridge is now safe for the small cars, one at a time and running not over (5) miles per hour. EXCERPTED FROM A 1906 CHARLESTON NEWSPAPER.

Yourself and Lady are respectfully invited to attend a ball and banquet to be given in honor of the completion of the Capitol building, Charleston, W. Va., January 5, 1887.

Construction view apparently taken in late 1886. Probably one of the earliest views of the capitol building. The clock has not yet been installed in the tower. View looking to the northeast showing the corner of Lee and Capitol streets. swv

The Capitol

This is the only known photograph of the first Charleston capitol building, built in 1870, by the State House Company for the sum of $79,000. Dr. John P. Hale was the prime motivator for moving the capitol site to Charleston and ended up financing most of the construction. In 1875, the capital was moved back to Wheeling. This view is from a stereograph card owned by Julius Jones of Richwood, West Virginia. (228)

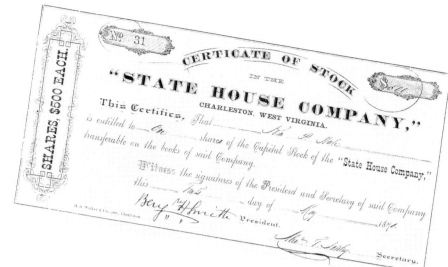

No. 31

CERTIFICATE OF STOCK

IN THE

"STATE HOUSE COMPANY,"

CHARLESTON, WEST VIRGINIA.

SHARES, $500 EACH.

This Certifies, That _____ Mrs. P. Hale _____ is entitled to _____ One _____ shares of the Capital Stock of the "State House Company," transferable on the books of said Company.

Witness the signatures of the President and Secretary of said Company this _____ day of _____ May _____ 187_.

Benj H Smith President.

Alex T Laidley Secretary.

Stock in the first Charleston capitol building. The 1870 building was built by this company and leased to the state. This, along with building of the Hale House, was the enticement to lure the capitol to Charleston. Two prominent local citizens, Benjamin H. Smith and Alexander Laidley were also officers.

The 1870 capitol was built on the same site as the later 1885 capitol. The block bounded by Washington - Lee - Dickinson and Capitol streets was in later years the site of the Diamond Dept. Store as well as Stone & Thomas, the Telephone Building and the 20-story Kanawha Valley Bank Building.

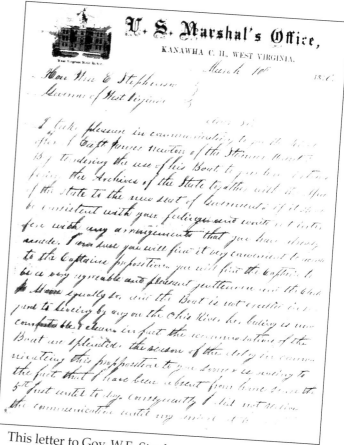

This letter to Gov. W.E. Stephenson, March 10, 1870 offers the use of Capt. James Newton's steamer *Mountain Boy* to transport the state government archives and papers from Wheeling to Charleston.

Telegraph above:
To S. Brady   1880
        Secy of Capitol building
Sir, after I arrived home last night I made a careful examination of my estimate for building the capitol at Charleston and I found that I had make a large mistake so that I will look to raise my bid so you will please add the sum of twelve thousand dollars to my bid which is now in the hands of the board of public works.

        G A Cochran

This letter dated May 14, 1875, concerns an injunction to stop the transfer of public property to the new capitol in Wheeling. The government was moved to Wheeling for 10 years until permanently locating in Charleston in 1885.

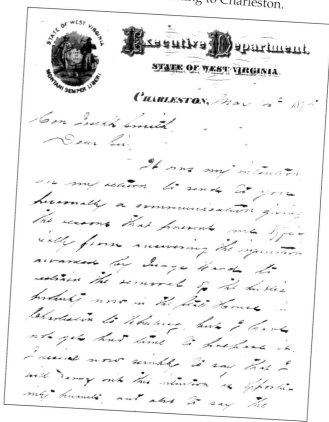

This is the only known view of the 1885 capitol in wintertime. This view is from the corner of Lee and Capitol streets. What we now call the Lee Street Triangle was the southwest corner of the capitol lawn as seen here.

The 1885 capitol building was destroyed by fire of unknown origin on Jan. 3, 1921. This fire photo shows the steeple and clock still intact. When the clock finally fell, the chimes rang prompting tears to fill the eyes of many spectators.

A very early view of the capitol fire from the Lee Street side. Note the fire engine on the lawn. Spectators and firemen are seen dashing about. The ammunition stored in the attic started going off about this time. A volunteer fireman, Charles Walker, was killed by a falling chimney. (235)

These two Charleston fire engines are at the corner of Lee and Dickinson streets. The old steam pumper, now on display in the Civic Center lobby, is going full-blast while next to it is a more modern hook and ladder truck. This fire would mark the end of steam fire engine use in town. Some accounts have suggested the pumper was actually brought to the fire by a motor truck.

The awesome destruction of the January 3 fire.

HUNDREDS COME FROM DISTANCE TO VIEW STATE CAPITOL RUINS

Souvenirs Taken From
  State House Lawn By
  Visitors; Firemen On Job
  All Monday Night.

STATE POLICEMEN
  GUARDING PROPERTY

Debris Is Removed From
Rear of Burned Building But
No Trace of Other Casualties
Is Found.

January 4

"A New Capitol is Born"

Setting the cornerstone for the capitol's west wing on May 1, 1924, the first part of the building to start. Construction was well along in this June 16, 1924 photo. The wing opened in 1927. CN

The ornate carvings above the doors were carved in place by skillful Italian stonecutters.

The carved mythological figures, Hera (Juno), Prometheus and Perses, stand guard over the entrance to the east end of the main building. SWV

Construction view of main building on Jan. 2, 1931. Structured steel is going up for the massive dome. SWV

Capitols Have Big Domes

West Virginia's Building Compares Very Favorably With Other Government Structures Erected by the 48 States in Union

A MAJORITY of the capitols of the 48 state and the national capitol at Washington have domes.

West Virginia's capitol dome seems to outrank all others, including the famed one in Washington, in several details. An instance of this is shown in height. The dome here reaches a height of 292 feet, measuring from the ground to the eagle that tops the bell over the dome.

The dome at Washington measures 287 feet, 5 1/2 inches up from the east base line to the statue of freedom on top of it.

Nowhere else in the country, excepting a few instances, where the chief capitol adornments seem to be a belfry or a tower, do the dome structures reach such heights as they do in Charleston and Washington.

The dome at Washington is more compact in appearance than the West Virginia dome. Its diameter is greater by several feet.

The rotunda at Washington has a greater diameter than the rotunda in West Virginia's capitol. Its diameter is 88 feet, and the one here is 75 feet.

The length of the national capitol is 751 feet, 4 inches. The length across the main unit building here is about 560 feet.

The area of the capitol grounds at Washington is 58.8 acres. The area of the capitol grounds here is approximately 16 acres.

The cost of the capitol building at Washington has been placed at $14,-000,000. West Virginia's capitol, including the ground, cost less than $10,000,000.

Since the capitol at Washington was completed in 1818, many millions have been spent on improving it and in adding new features. West Virginia's capitol was built also with an eye on the future, when, in time, many millions may be spent in improving it, and adding interior decorations, including mural paintings, statuary and by increasing the size of its ground.

There is a strong resemblance between the West Virginia capitol and the national capitol, but primarily in the style of architecture. An examination of details will demonstrate that they are entirely dissimilar in construction and in general arrangement of the units. The two wings of the national capitol connect with the main unit at their centers. The West Virginia capitol units are connected at their ends.

Alabama's capitol, at Montgomery, rests on a hill in a park and is surrounded by small trees. Its front entrance is approached by terraced steps, leading from outside the grounds. The building has a small dome.

The capitol of Arizona at Phoenix, has the appearance of a public library, and is topped by a low dome. The lawn around it, is well kept, and there are a variety of tropical plants and trees growing around it.

Arkansas' capitol is at Little Rock and California's is at Sacramento. Each of these buildings which are somewhat similar in general appearance, has a dome.

Colorado's capitol at Denver and Connecticut's at Hartford, also are somewhat similar, with small domes over their centers. These two buildings resemble somewhat West Virginia's old capitol.

Delaware's capitol at Dover, and Florida's, at Tallahassee, in general design, have the appearance of a church. Each has a small tower over its main section.

Georgia's capitol at Atlanta, Idaho's at Boise, Illinois' at Springfield, Iowa's at Des Moines, Indiana's at Indianapolis, Kansas' at Topeka, Kentucky's at Frankfort, and Maine's at Augusta, are somewhat similar in design, each being adorned by one, or several small domes.

Louisiana's capitol, which is at Baton Rouge, resembles a skyscraper office building and in this respect is much like Nebraska's new capitol at Lincoln.

The capitol of Maryland, which is at Annapolis, in general appearance is like a court house. Its central portion is topped by a tower.

The capitols of Massachusetts, at Boston; Michigan at Lansing; Mississippi at Jackson; Minnesota at St. Paul; Missouri at Jefferson City, and Montana at Helena, are largely alike in general appearance, each having a conspicuous adornment outside.

Small domes are on top of Nevada's capitol at Carson City and New Hampshire's at Concord. The main buildings are very much like those that are used as court houses.

New Jersey's capitol at Trenton, has no dome feature and it appears much like a building that might be used as a university of an art museum.

New Mexico's capitol at Santa Fe, has the churchy appearance and the same might be said of North Carolina's capitol at Raleigh.

In contrast with the size of the state, New York's capitol is small. It appears to be no larger than West Virginia's old capitol. There are other buildings in Albany, however, which house the empire state's governmental departments. North Dakota's capitol at Bismarck, also has the college appearance and is entirely lacking in any dome effect.

Ohio's capitol at Columbus, except for its peculiar kind of dome-which looks like a huge drum, because of its flat top, is like West Virginia's capitol in one respect. There are tall columns at its main entrance and broad terraced steps.

The main entrance to Oklahoma's capitol at Oklahoma City, is modeled after the Parthenon, but the structure has no dome.

Oregon's capitol at Salem, is topped by a small dome as also are the capitols of Pennsylvania at Harrisburg; Rhode Island at Providence; South Carolina at Columbia; South Dakota at Pierre; Texas at Austin; Utah at Salt Lake City; Vermont at Montpelier; Washington at Olympia; Wisconsin at Madison and Wyoming at Cheyenne.

The front of Tennessee's capitol at Nashville, has the Parthenon effect. Its center has over it a tower.

Virginia's capitol at Richmond, also is a replica of the Parthenon. There is no dome.

"Gold Dome Cheaper" Architect Asserts

West Virginia's "gold dome" towering above the new capitol building is not a lavish expenditure of money, but in reality will save the taxpayers thousands of dollars in years to come, according to Cass Gilbert, the architect.

If we had built the dome of stone, as in the Arkansas state capitol, or of marble as in the Minnesota state capitol or the Rhode Island state capitol, it would have cost five or ten times as much money and probably would not have excited any comment whatever." Gilbert said.

"In other words the bell of the dome of this dimension, in marble, might easily have cost $500,000, whereas the comparatively modest expense for covering it with newly developed material of lead coated with copper and using gilding has reduced the cost to a minimum."

The use of gilding is not at all unusual, Gilbert said, citing the fact that the dome of the capitol at Trenton, N.J., is gilded as well as the dome of the state house in Boston and the dome of the library of congress in Washington.

"I would like to point out," Gilbert continued, "that if the bell of the dome were of limestone it would be, in that climate, susceptible to expansion and contraction and the joints would have to be constantly repaired in order to preserve it."

If metal was used without gilding and was painted it would be an additional yearly expense, the architect said.

· D E V E L O P M E N T · F O R · T H E · S T A T E · C A P I T O L · G R O U N D S ·

· CHARLESTON · WEST · VIRGINIA ·   · CASS · GILBERT · ARCHITECT ·

· JUNE 20 1932 ·

This architect's rendering dated June 20, 1932, the day the Capitol was dedicated, shows Gilbert's vision of the grounds extending beyond Piedmont Road into the hillside. His apparent four-lane roadway along the Kanawha River was a reality by 1940. The landscaping, reflecting pool and some type of small structure behind the Capitol, which today is the site of several state office buildings and a parking lot, was of course not yet built. The Capitol Complex has changed considerably since the 1932 dedication and is today considered one of the most beautiful of the 50 state capitols. WVSA

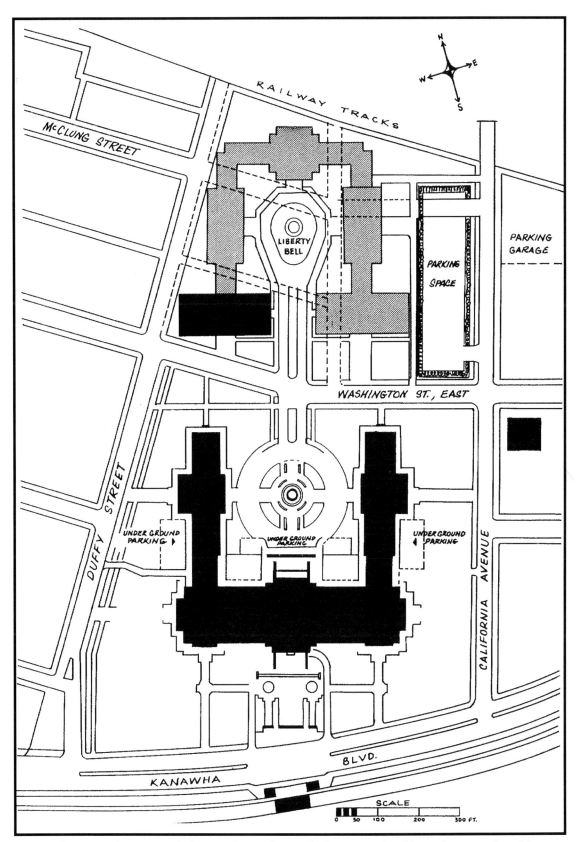

A 1962 drawing of an expanded capitol complex, including considerable underground parking. The existing Department of Motor Vehicles building was to be duplicated along with the gray outline buildings.

THE CAPITOL?

"Yes, I Helped Put It Up There On That Beautiful Location"

... and the Street Car can say in all truth that it did help put the new Capitol on its beautiful location, for so busy a place as the State's business headquarters must be served by quick, safe, dependable and economical transportation. Both state employees and visitors must be able to get to and from the Capitol quickly and easily, comfortably and economically. . . The Capitol's completion and dedication is but further evidence of that for which your Street Car Company has labored from its beginning—progress. . . We join with West Virginia in welcoming her proud sons and honored guests to this memorable event. ... But ever concerned about our guest's comfort and convenience while with us, we suggest the Street Car as the quickest, safest and most comfortable mode to travel to and from the Capitol Dedication!

Charleston Interurban
RR Co

Quick, Safe, Dependable and Economical Transportation

All three items 1932.

Judgment of This Work in Hands Of People, Says Gilbert, Architect

Editors Note: Below, The Gazette presents to you exclusively, the personal message of Cass Gilbert, noted architect who designed the new capitol building.

By Cass Gilbert

I have endeavored to the best of my ability to respond to the confidence which my appointment as architect of the capitol implied, and I trust that the result will be approved by the people of West Virginia.

I must leave it to others to judge of the results of our work, but I can say with confidence that my associates and I have most earnestly and conscientiously endeavored to honorably fulfill our obligations, whether actual or implied; that in this we have had the helpful cooperation of Governor Morgan, Governor Gore and Governor Conley, and the members of the State Capitol Building Commission under whom this work has been carried on. We have had the cooperation of able and experienced contractors.

The buildings are well built and the cost is well within the amount appropriated by the legislature and very much less than was originally proposed by the state.

I have endeavored to make this group of buildings useful, and also to give it dignified and beautiful character without elaboration or extravagance. I hope tht we my now complete the work with suitable sculpture and mural decoration, that the grounds may be properly developed and that these buildings will be preserved as among the many evidences of the dignity, importance and civilization in the state of West Virginia.

An aerial view of the capitol complex in 1955. At the time, there were only two nonattached buildings. Duffy Street is at the bottom which was removed to make way for the Cultural Center and Washington Street is shown cutting through the complex on the left. Parking was allowed around the oval at this time.

Old Capitol Bell Is On State House Lawn

The huge bell resting on the capitol lawn is a grim reminder of the disastrous fire of 1921 that destroyed the statehouse building in 1885. The bell for years tolled the time for hundreds of townspeople and there was more than a passing touch of sorrow in its fall to the ground, causing a crack extending almost around its surface.

The figure "3" of the clock tower that housed the bell was salvaged from the ruins and presented to the department of archives and is now on display in the museum.

Weighing several tons, the bell was cast by the Clinton H. Meneely company of Troy, NY. in 1887. The state board of public works accepted the bell July 7, 1888.

The old bell went to a World War Two scrap drive.

NEWSPAPER ARTICLE OF 1932

These two views of the state museum in the basement of the Capitol in 1957 should bring back many memories for people of the county. One of the most popular exhibits were the dressed fleas which one could see plainly through a magnifying glass. How many of these priceless artifacts can one see today in the present museum? CN

CALL FOR PROPOSALS.

Sealed proposals for the erection and completion of the Capitol Annex for the State of West Virginia, at Charleston, in accordance with drawings and specifications prepared by Harrison Albright, Architect, will be received until 2 P. M., Eastern Standard time, Thursday, Sept. 14th, 1899, at which time all proposals will be opened.

Drawings and specifications may be seen at the Senate Chamber in the Capitol, between the hours of 9 and 11:30 A. M. and 2 and 5:00 P. M. Monday, Aug. 14th and every day thereafter, except Sundays, until Sept. 14th. Each proposal must be accompanied by a certified check for 2 per cent. of the proposal tendered, as a guarantee that the bidder will furnish bond for fifty per cent. of amount of proposal and enter into a contract with The Board of Public Works for the construction of the building. Upon failure of successful bidder to furnish bond and enter into contract, the check submitted with his proposal will be forfeited to the State. All checks will be retained until successful bidder furnishes bond and enters into contract; after which the checks of all bidders will be returned to them.

Address all communications regarding drawings and specifications to Harrison Albright, Architect, Charleston, W. Va. Make certified checks payable to the order of the State Treasurer. Address all proposals to the undersigned marked on the outside "*Proposals for Capitol Annex.*"

The right is reserved to reject any and all proposals.

WM. M. O. DAWSON,
Secretary of State.

Charleston, W. Va., August 7th, 1899.

The Capitol Annex was designed by local architect Harrison Albright and opened in 1903. Albright gained national acclaim when he was hired by Mr. Lee Sinclair to design a hotel in West Baden Springs, Indiana, which would be called the "Eighth Wonder of the World." When the Hotel opened in 1903 it was the largest domed structure in the world and would remain so until the Houston Astrodome was built many years later. Albright was from Pennsylvania but moved his office to Charleston in 1891. He apparently had little formal training in architecture, gaining most of his knowledge "on the job." Soon however he gained the prestigious position as West Virginia State Architect. One of Albright's signature elements was the use of reinforced concrete which he used extensively in earthquake prone Los Angeles where he and his family moved about 1903. Gaining in prominence, he became a popular architect for homes of wealthy patrons as well as continuing to design public buildings. The old building that housed part of the state government, the library and Morris Harvey College finally succumbed to the wrecking ball in 1966.

The old capitol annex, the public library in this 1928 photo, is decked out for the Memorial Day holiday. (233)

Skyscraper Capitol
Once Was Proposed

A skyscraper capitol building for the state was one of many suggestions made in the crisis of the homeless state house employes. While individuals offered choice sites for the capitol, J. S. Darst, state auditor, came forward with the skyscraper proposal

Mr. Darst stated that the annex foundation was substantial enough to support eight or ten extra floors. In part he said, "I think the board of public works should be given power to add eight to ten stories to the capitol annex at once. The building is one of the best constructed in the state and is practically fireproof

Incidentally the state of Louisiana has since erected a skyscraper capitol which is considered one of the finest examples of the modernistic school of architecture.

This interesting newspaper article appeared in 1932 in regards to the 1921 Capitol fire.

Scene on the steps of the new capitol during the inauguration of Herman Guy Kump in 1933, the state's 19th governor. Both he and his predecessor, William G. Conley, served only one term.

1966

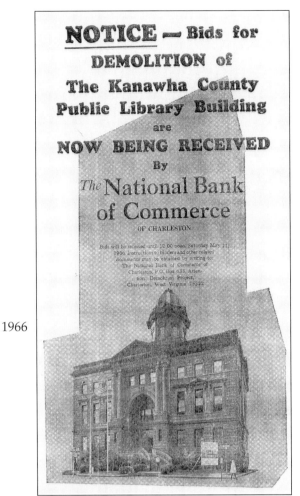

NOTICE — Bids for DEMOLITION of The Kanawha County Public Library Building are NOW BEING RECEIVED By The National Bank of Commerce OF CHARLESTON

Bids will be received until 12:00 noon, Saturday May 21, 1966. Instructions to bidders and other related documents may be obtained by writing to: The National Bank of Commerce of Charleston, P.O. Box 633, Attention: Demolition Project, Charleston, West Virginia 25322

A bill for the inauguration of
Howard M. Gore, the state's
17th governor.

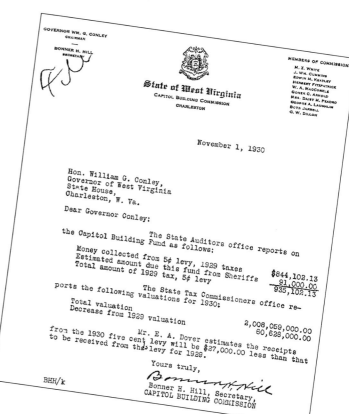

STORE
TELEPHONE CONNECTION 1875

GREENHOUSES
TELEPHONE CONNECTION 1169-W

Winter FLORAL CO.

Florists and Decorators

Kearse Theatre Bldg.
Summers St.

CHARLESTON-KANAWHA, W. VA.   March 4, 1925 192

Original

The Inaugural Committee,
M   c/o Mr. Walter Hallanan,
Vice Chairman,
Charleston, West Virginia

DATE	ARTICLES	CHARGE		CREDIT	BALANCE
	To 3 cases of Southern Smilax @ $12.50	37	50		
	3½ dozen Palms @ $6.00 per dozen	21	00		
	24 dozen cut Jonquils @ $1.50 per doz	36	00		
	6 doz Pink Carnations 2.00 per doz	12	00		
	5 doz Snapdragons @ $4.00 per doz	20	00		
	2 doz Roses pernet(Yellow) $5	10	00		
	10 doz Pink Roses @ $3.00 per doz	30	00		
	12 bunches of Asparagus @ 1.00 each	12	00		
	1 Basket of Calendulas	3	50		
	Ferns and foliage	1	00		
	3 Pans of Jonquils @ 1.50 each	4	50		
	4 doz Pussy Willows long stems $4.00	16	00		
	Table smilax	3	00		
	2 doz lilium rubrum @ $3.00 per doz	6	00		
	Baskets, vases and service	10	00		
		221	50		
	For state Armory				
	To 4 cases of Southern Smilax 12.50	50	00		
	18 palms @ $6.00 per dozen	9	00		
	1 Large vase of Carnations 6 doz	16	00		
	with asparagus etc				
		75	00		

Quality and Service Our Motto

MANUFACTURED BY AMERICAN SALES BOOK CO., LIMITED, NIAGARA FALLS, N. Y.

GOVERNOR WM. G. CONLEY
CHAIRMAN

BONNER H. HILL
SECRETARY

State of West Virginia
CAPITOL BUILDING COMMISSION
CHARLESTON

MEMBERS OF COMMISSION

M. Z. WHITE
J. WM. CUMMINS
EDWIN M. KEATLEY
HERBERT FITZPATRICK
W. A. MACCORKLE
GOHEN C. ARNOLD
MRS. DAISY M. PEADRO
GEORGE A. LAUGHLIN
BOYD JARRELL
C. W. DILLON

November 1, 1930

Hon. William G. Conley,
Governor of West Virginia
State House,
Charleston, W. Va.

Dear Governor Conley:

The State Auditors office reports on
the Capitol Building Fund as follows:

Money collected from 5¢ levy, 1929 taxes	$844,102.13
Estimated amount due this fund from Sheriffs	91,000.00
Total amount of 1929 tax, 5¢ levy	935,102.13

The State Tax Commissioners office reports the following valuations for 1930:

Total valuation	2,008,059,000.00
Decrease from 1929 valuation	60,628,000.00

Mr. E. A. Dover estimates the receipts
from the 1930 five cent levy will be $27,000.00 less than that
to be received from the levy for 1929.

Yours truly,

Bonner H. Hill, Secretary,
CAPITOL BUILDING COMMISSION

BHH/k

ESTABLISHED 1865   INCORPORATED 1913

SECTIONAL
BOOK CASES
IRON and STEEL
SAFES
DESKS, CHAIRS
and FILING
EQUIPMENT

THE S. SPENCER MOORE CO.
OFFICE OUTFITTERS
STATIONERS ✦ PRINTERS
BOOKSELLERS

115 Capitol Street, CHARLESTON, W. VA.,

BOOKS
KODAKS
FOUNTAIN PENS
STATIONERY
SPORTING GOODS
PICTURE FRAMES
WALL PAPER

July 5, 1929

Mr. Geo. W. Sharp
Charleston, W. Va.

Dear Mr. Sharp:

Herewith you will find enclosed complete bill for
moving the Archives & History Dept. and the Museum to its new
location in the Capitol. This is complete and included everything. Since speaking to you this morning I have added three
metal book ladders. These are absolutely necessary for the
librarians to reach the top shelves and I am sure this meets
with your approval.

Yours very truly,

THE S. SPENCER MOORE CO.

GJH/LB

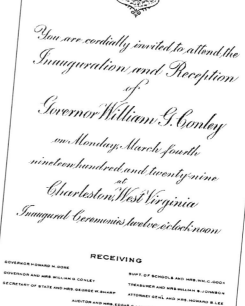

You are cordially invited to attend the

Inauguration and Reception

of

Governor William G. Conley

on Monday, March fourth

nineteen hundred and twenty-nine

at

Charleston, West Virginia

Inaugural Ceremonies twelve o'clock noon

RECEIVING

GOVERNOR HOWARD M. GORE

GOVERNOR AND MRS. WILLIAM G. CONLEY

SECRETARY OF STATE AND MRS. GEORGE W. SHARP

AUDITOR AND MRS. EDGAR C. LAWSON

COMMISSIONER OF AGRICULTURE AND MRS. JOHN W. SMITH

SUPT. OF SCHOOLS AND MRS. WM. C. COOK

TREASURER AND MRS. WILLIAM S. JOHNSON

ATTORNEY GENL. AND MRS. HOWARD B. LEE

RECEPTION EIGHT-THIRTY TO TEN-THIRTY P. M.

EXECUTIVE MANSION

HISTORY OF OUR WEST VIRGINIA CAPITOL

EST VIRGINIA moved its seat of government so many times during the first twenty-two years of its existence that popularly it was said to have a "Capitol on Wheels." In brief the capitol was located heretofore as follows:

At Wheeling from June 20, 1863 to April 1, 1870. (6 years, 7 months, 11 days.)

At Charleston from April 1, 1870 to May 21, 1875. (5 years, 1 month, 20 days.)

At Wheeling from May 21, 1875 to May 1885. (9 years, 11 months, 11 days.)

At Charleston from May 1, 1885 to the present time.

When the state was created the temporary seat of government was at Wheeling, and the meetings at which our independence was determined were held in Washington Hall, popularly known as "The Birthplace of West Virginia." This building of brick construction had been erected in 1851 by the Washington Hall Association at a cost of $46,000. It was destroyed by fire on November 30, 1876.

The first capitol was the Linsly Institute building of brick construction, erected in 1858, by the trustees of that school, and was used as the capitol from June 20, 1863 to April 1, 1870, and again from May 23, 1875 to December 4, 1876.

In 1869 the legislature passed an act, effective April 1, 1870, making Charleston the permanent seat of government. When the "moving day" came, the steamer Mountain Boy literally became the capitol for on it all the officials with the state's records and other property moved at midnight on March 28th down the Ohio and up the Great Kanawha to Charleston where it docked at eleven o'clock on the morning of the 30th.

The first Charleston capitol was erected in 1869-1870 by the State House Company, a corporation, at a total cost of $71,000.00. It was of brick construction and was used as the capitol from December 20, 1870, to May 21, 1875, when the seat of government was moved to Wheeling. The state officials made the journey (May 21-May 23) on the steamer Emma Graham to Parkersburg and from there to Wheeling on the steamer Chesapeake. An injunction to prevent the removal of the state archives and records by citizens of Charleston failed to halt the transfer to Wheeling, and all state property was taken there by the steamer Iron Valley and two barges, September 22-25.

While awaiting the erection of a new capitol building at Wheeling, the Linsly Institute building was occupied a second time. The second Wheeling capitol was erected by the City of Wheeling in 1875-76, at a cost of $82,940. It was of stone construction and housed the state government from December 4, 1876 to May 1, 1885. At the present time it is being used as a city and county building.

As the result of an election held on August 7, 1877, Governor Jacob issued a proclamation declaring that after the expiration of eight years Charleston, having received a majority of the votes, was to be the permanent seat of government. When the time for removal from Wheeling came, May 1, 1885, all state officials and state property embarked on two steamers,

the "Chesapeake" and the "Bell Prince" with the barge "Nick Crawley" in tow, and made a historic "home run" to Charleston.

The second Charleston capitol, and the fourth building used as the official home of the state government, was erected on the site of the first at a total cost of $389,923.58, including the cost of the building and grounds of the first which had been transferred to the state by the State House Company. This was of brick and stone and was occupied by the state from May 1, 1885, to January 3, 1921, when it was destroyed by fire.

A temporary office building popularly known as "The Pasteboard Capitol" was speedily erected in forty-two working days after January 14th, 1921, at a cost with equipment of $225,000. This building was of wood and wall board construction and contained 166 rooms. It was destroyed by fire March 2, 1927.

In 1921 a State Capitol Commission was created to supervise the erection of a modern home for the state government. The old site was sold and a new one in the east end between Duffy and California streets secured. The services of Cass Gilbert, a noted architect, were secured and plans were drawn for a fine new capitol. By the summer of 1925 the first unit was completed and occupied by offices that had been in the temporary structure. By January, 1928, the second unit was completed and occupied shortly thereafter. Each of these units cost approximately $1,250,000. Work on the construction of the main or central unit which will cost approximately $5,000,000 was begun in March 1930 and was completed and occupied on the 15th of February, 1932.

Marble figures extensively in the interior finish the state's new capitol unit.

The walls are of Imperial Danby, a white marble from Danby, Vt., while floods are of travertine, a buff-colored stone. Some idea of the amount of marble used can be had from the fact that more than 200 railway freight cars were required to transport it from the Vermont quarries to Charleston.

Directly inside the main entrance of the ground floor there is a marble rotunda from which one may look up 180 feet to the sky-blue interior of the dome. Around the circumference are huge monolithic columns supporting the rotunda balcony of the first flood, the floor of the legislative halls.

The main central corridors of the ground floor and the corridor at either end of the central building, connecting with the office building units, are lined with marble to the ceilings. Marble walls decorate the two foyers which lead to the chambers of the senate and house of delegates. These foyers, measuring 80 by 20 feet, with marble benches for visitors and crystal chandeliers, will serve as reception halls for the legislative bodies.

Imperial Danby marble on a base of Verde Antique, a dark green marble from Roxbury, Vt., gives beauty to the senate and house chambers. The stone reaches up to the arches over the three balconies and the presiding officer's rostrum in each chamber while between the arches are dark maroon panels.

—*W. S. Johnson*

Program

JUNE TWENTIETH

One O'Clock P. M.

PARADE Forms at corner of Broad and Kanawha Streets, marches down Kanawha Street to Capitol Street, out Capitol Street to Lee Street, east on Lee Street to Morris Street, south on Morris Street to Quarrier Street, east on Quarrier Street to Capitol Grounds.

Chief Marshal_____General C. C. Pierce

Adjutant _____E. T. Williams

Program

JUNE TWENTIETH

Two O'Clock, P. M.

DEDICATION WEST VIRGINIA CAPITOL BUILDING

Speaker's stand will be located on north portico, facing Washington Street.

Presiding:
  Honorable Wm. E. Chilton

"America"—
  201st Regiment Band

Prayer:
  Dr. Wilbur V. Mallalieu

Address:
  Miss Anna Jarvis
    Founder of Mothers Day

Dedication Address:
  Colonel Guy D. Goff

Address:
  Accepting the Capitol Building on behalf of the people of the State—
    Governor Wm. G. Conley

"West Virginia Hills"
  201st Regiment Band

Eight-Thirty O'Clock P. M.

PUBLIC RECEPTION

By the Board of Public Works and the Capitol Building Commission, Governor's Reception Room, Capitol Building

Members of Capitol Building Commission

Gov. E. F. Morgan
Gov. Howard M. Gore
Gov. William G. Conley
Hon. Gohen C. Arnold
Hon. Edwin M. Keatley
Hon. Herbert Fitzpatrick
Hon. George A. Laughlin
Hon. Mont Z. White
Hon. J. William Cummins
Mrs. Daisy M. Peadro

Hon. Charles W. Dillon
Hon. Charles K. Payne
‡ Hon. William McKell
*Hon. Frederick M. Staunton
*Hon. Harry P. Camden
*Hon. N. Price Whittaker
*Hon. Virgil L. Highland
*Hon. W. A. MacCorkle
*Hon. Boyd Jarrell

‡Houston G. Young, Secretary
Bonner H. Hill, Secretary

Board of Public Works

William G. Conley_____Governor
George W. Sharp_____Secretary of State
W. C. Cook_____Superintendent of Schools
Edgar C. Lawson_____Auditor
W. S. Johnson_____Treasurer
Howard B. Lee_____Attorney General
Howard M. Gore_____Commissioner of Agriculture

*Deceased.

‡Resigned

Cost of New Capitol

The net cost to the taxpayers in property taxes for the completed Capitol was $6,412,373.60.

The following is a condensed statement of all receipts and disbursements incident to its construction:

EXPENDITURES

Purchase of new site (Including expense of grading, and sundry expenses in preparing for construction)	$2,111,825.43
Office Building, Unit No. 1 (Total cost of construction)	1,216,967.66
Office Building, Unit No. 2 (Total cost of construction)	1,354,525.94
Capitol Building, Main Unit, and interest (Total cost of construction)	4,807,861.00
Total cost of New Capitol	$9,491,180.03

RECEIPTS FROM SALE OF OLD CAPITOL SITE, INSURANCE, ETC.

Received from sale of old site, etc.	$1,551,000.00
Received from sale of old Annex	501,256.59
Received from sale of site of old temporary Capitol and Mansion	352,223.84
Insurance on old buildings and contents	533,455.23
Received from sale of houses on new site	104,586.52
Interest received on deferred payments	36,284.25
	$3,078,806.43
Total Cost of New Capitol	$9,491,180.03
Less Total Salvage from old Capitol	3,078,806.43
New Cost to Taxpayers	$6,412,373.60

The amount authorized by the Legislature to be expended in erecting the Main Capitol Unit was $5,000,000.00. The amount actually expended was $4,627,278.00, or $372,722.00 less than the amount authorized.

June 20, 1932

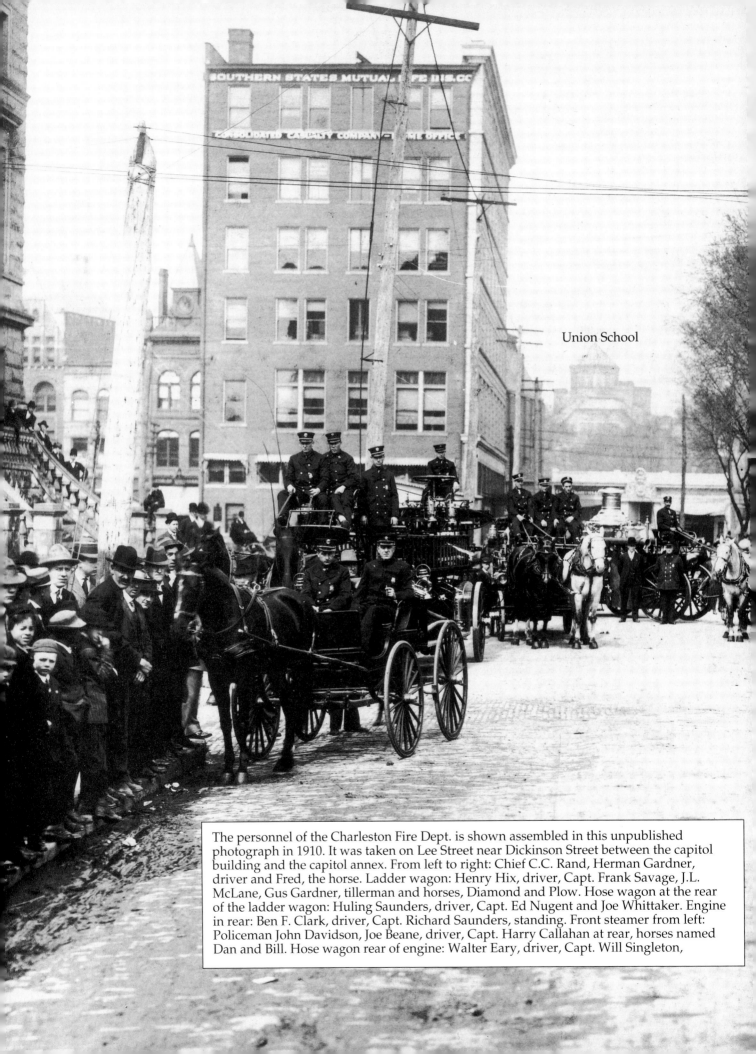

Union School

The personnel of the Charleston Fire Dept. is shown assembled in this unpublished photograph in 1910. It was taken on Lee Street near Dickinson Street between the capitol building and the capitol annex. From left to right: Chief C.C. Rand, Herman Gardner, driver and Fred, the horse. Ladder wagon: Henry Hix, driver, Capt. Frank Savage, J.L. McLane, Gus Gardner, tillerman and horses, Diamond and Plow. Hose wagon at the rear of the ladder wagon: Huling Saunders, driver, Capt. Ed Nugent and Joe Whittaker. Engine in rear: Ben F. Clark, driver, Capt. Richard Saunders, standing. Front steamer from left: Policeman John Davidson, Joe Beane, driver, Capt. Harry Callahan at rear, horses named Dan and Bill. Hose wagon rear of engine: Walter Eary, driver, Capt. Will Singleton,

Fire, Flood, Public Safety

Leo Price. W.M. Whatley, Robert Given, Howard High, Arnold Dame, horses named Barney and Bailey. Second hose wagon: Howard Dawson, driver, Capt. Charley Stalnaker, Lt. Ira Ellis, Tom Timlin. Third team from engine: Capt. Jack Adams. In the distant background the Union School can be seen. Note the policeman on the right wearing a London-style "Bobbie" hat.

J. LEONARD GATES PHOTO

The same scene today.

One of the oldest Charleston Fire Department photos showing a steam pumper, circa 1880s.

Long-time chief, D.L. McLane related a story years ago about his hottest fire: "Some blazes get so hot that the thickest stream of water evaporates into steam a few feet within the burning building. Such a blaze was the fire which destroyed the temporary 'pasteboard' capitol in 1921 with a loss of $50,000. The flames, fanned by the draft through the large corridor that ran the length of the building on the first floor, swept through the flimsy building, located where the Daniel Boone Hotel now stands, and it was a total loss in 25 minutes."

"It was so hot," McLane remembered, "that it broke 18 windows in the YMCA building, separated from it by the distance of two sidewalks, a street and a parking lot. People a block away turned from the heat. Firemen couldn't even get close to the walls; the fire burned up their hose. There was nothing to do but watch it burn and try to keep it from spreading." (237)

Charleston Fire Department at the Court Street Station, circa 1918. This is a light vehicle intended to get to the scene first in hope of controlling a fire when slower heavy equipment followed.

Early aerial tiller wagon, Charleston Fire Department, Court Street, circa 1920. The tiller ladder wagon had steerable rear wheels. City hall is in background. Note seated fireman above rear wheels.

C.F.D. wagon on Court Street circa 1920 near the end of the romantic era of horse draw equipment.

Fire engine manufactured by the Kanawha Chemical Fire Engine Company on Virginia Street, circa 1910 in front of the Central fire station in the old city hall.

Charleston Fire Department Station #4 on Washington Street near Elizabeth Street, circa 1930s. Left to right: Daddy Coleman, policeman, Capt. Dickie Barrett, Happy Shaffer, driver, E.E. Withrow, fireman and Harley Sheets, fireman. The building still stands and houses a restaurant. DED

An article by Geroge W. Summers in the May 8, 1938 issue of *The Charleston Gazette*.

Within the memory of many persons here to tell of it, before the days of motor vehicles, a fire alarm would bring out the old fire engine, gleaming with all its burnished, polished metal; smoke rolling in black clouds through the flues and out its smoke stack; as it was drawn by powerful galloping horses toward the burning property. It would pump from the river's edge, or the nearest cistern, the water used in fighting fire, and force it through the hose which was taken as close behind the pumping engine as possible to every fire. The hose was wound up on the hose reel, like thread upon a spool, and was unrolled in such lengths as were needed.

Charleston had its old fire engine of this kind. Fires were kept burning in it constantly, so there would be steam always ready to start the pump as soon as a supply of water could be reached, as close as possible to the fire, and the hose could be connected.

But back before the days of the horse-drawn steam fire engine Charleston had its old-time volunteer fire department, which hauled its hose and its old hand-pump to every fire. These volunteer firemen, with their primitive apparatus, did efficient work at a time when buildings were small, never more than two stories high and were built too far apart for flames to spread, except when heavy winds would carry burning sparks and embers and deposit them on distant shingle roofs, thus starting new blazes to be fought.

Before the present street was opened up, and only a pathway toward the east from Capitol Street, where Quarrier Street is now, a small brick building, something like 20 feet square, with a low-roofed second story, stood where the entrance to the Rialto theater is now. It was erected for the use of Mercer academy, where a higher education was given to those of Charleston's young men who wished it, many years ago. It was also used for public meetings and religious services and was one of the early landmarks of the town.

But after it had served its purpose and had been used as a place for the education of many eminent Charleston men of generations now all gone, this building became headquarters for Charleston's volunteer firemen. They were all young, vigorous and earnest, efficient in the performance of their duties and worked arduously when called upon to fight a fire. These volunteer firemen came from the professional, commercial and other walks in life, and it was considered an honor to be made a member of the volunteer fire department. Their organization to some extent included social activities and their firemen's balls, musical or literary gatherings attracted many from what were regarded as the town's best people.

Outside the building which faced the present Quarrier Street, a steel triangle hung, each side of it about a yard in length, and beside it hung a heavy hammer. Together they constituted the town's fire alarm system. Whoever discovered a building to be on fire would rush to the headquarters of the volunteer firemen and hammer on the steel triangle as hard and as fast as he could. The alarm, which could be heard

This is the last team of horses that would pull Charleston's fire department horse drawn equipment. The horses were named Ben and Morgan respectively. The driver is J.H. Homes, seated beside him is Captain J.A. Hamilton and standing in the rear are Roe Miller and Sanford Walker. On May 5, 1923 this team of horses made their last run on an emergency call to the 1500 block of Quarrier Street to put out a minor grass fire. All the other motor fire engines were out on other calls.

all through the town, brought the volunteers as fast as they could get there, perhaps but partly clad, and fastening buttons as they ran, if it were a night alarm, to do whatever might be done to save the burning building.

That they feared no hardship and spared no pains to do their work well may be shown by the plight of one of these volunteer firemen who became afterwards one of the leading members of the Kanawha bar, who got back home one midwinter night after working as a fireman, with his clothing so stiffly frozen on him, that he could not sit down till they were thawed enough for him to get them off. All this was before the time of the steam fire engine with its pump and spool-like hose reel.

When the triangle brought these young men to the fire house, they grabbed hold of a long rope which was attached to the light wagon frame on which the pump was fastened. Running as fast as they could they dragged the pump to the river, well or other water supply as close to the fire as they could get and then a score or more of them would climb upon the wagon and work the old hand pump to force the water on the flames.

But as the town grew and buildings spread over wider areas it was often difficult to find water near enough to pump into a fire. And then the old fire cisterns, some of which are still in existence, came into use. They were dug in the earth at strategic points and were kept filled with water hauled in the water-carts of the time from the river. Each cistern might hold about 100 barrels—not much water for fighting a modern fire, but enough for the kind of service then required.

One of Charleston's old horse-drawn steamers was donated to the city's scrap drive during World War Two. Like so many historical artifacts that were hastily sent to scrap, this fire engine would be very valuable today.

Scrapping of Metallic War Relics Is Urged

Gov. Neely has again called upon West Virginia counties and cities to co-operate in the drive to turn relics and memorial pieces into war needs.

Neely said he urged all mayors, county court members and others having old cannons, cannon balls or other metallic relics to deliver them at once to local salvage committees or the War Production board's general salvage office in Charleston.

Sept. 4, 1942

Fortunately, the last remaining steamer from the horse-drawn days has been saved and is now on display at the Charleston Civic Center. This machine is reported to have been used to fight the 1921 Capitol fire.

Morgan Lumber Co. fire, early 1920s. A number of railroad cars were destroyed in the conflagration.

A little known or remembered fire occurred on Capitol Street on July 20 1936. The Fleetwood Hotel was destroyed along with considerable damage to two women's apparel stores, La Mode and Mangels, Silver's 5-10, Dan Cohen's shoe store, the Darling Shop and the dental office of Dr. Jim Davidson. Five people were injured.

Looking east on Virginia Street at Capitol Street.

The following four pages show dramatic scenes of the devastating fire that destroyed several large buildings adjacent to the South Side bridge in January 1946. Near-zero temperatures caused the water to freeze to everything it touched. (276)

Four Injured; Property Toll Hits 2 Million

Cause Still Mystery As Firemen Labor in Near-Zero Reading

By Vint M. Jennings

Weary after 34 hours of constant duty, most of Charleston's firemen were still playing six streams of water onto the smoldering ruins of 10 office and warehouse buildings in downtown Charleston which were destroyed by fire early Sunday at a total loss estimated to run as high as $2,000,000.

A virtual inferno in the 800 block of Virginia Street.

Near South Side Bridge, looking west on Virginia Street.

Looking south on Hale Street toward Virginia Street. Masonic Building is on the right. Note smashed Packard automobile in distance. Wind blown ashes were seen as far away as Kanawha City.

View from across the river—the Ruffner Hotel was scorched but did not burn.

Hale Street at Virginia Street.

800 block of Virginia Street.

South Side bridge ramp showing debris from adjoining building.

Ruffner Hotel

Two Turn in Alarm

There seems to be some doubt as to who turned in the first alarm on the Virginia Street blaze. Kenneth Beleher, a taxicab driver said he first discovered the blaze at 3:25 a.m. in the Rose City building. He said he used his pocket knife to break the glass on a call box at Virginia and Hale streets to pull the alarm signal.

Destroyed Buildings Listed

Buildings destroyed in the fire included:

Two five-story structures occupied by the Rose City Press at 819-821 Virginia St., East.

The five-story Kanawha Valley Leather Co. building at 817 Virginia St.

The five-story Cobb Wholesale Clothing Co. building, 813 Virginia St.

A smaller structure housing the Rose City office machine repair service, 811 Virginia St., Watch Repair Service, 811 Virginia St., and the Friden Calculating Machine Agency Sales and Service, 811 ½ Virginia St.

The five-story building occupied by the Save Supply Co. and the National Cash Register Co. at 17-19 Hale St.

The four-story warehouse of the Cohen Drug Co. at 905 Virginia St.

Severe damage was done to the five-story building owned by Guthrie-Morris-Campbell Co. and occupied by the Copley-Mullen automobile agency at 901-903 Virginia St. but a sprinkler system prevented its destruction.

Southwest view at the corner of Hale and Virginia streets. The Rose City Press building was destroyed. Site is now a drive-in bank. NORMAN FITZHUGH PHOTO

Looking north on Hale Street from Kanawha Boulevard. McMillion Motors, the Chevrolet dealer is on the right, Ruffner Hotel on left. NORMAN FITZHUGH PHOTO

Aerial view of the tragic March 4, 1949 Woolworth fire in downtown Charleston. Capitol Street at the bottom, Summers Street at the top. Prominent building in center was old Charleston National Bank—next door to Woolworths.

Two members of the Skating Vanities of 1949 appearing in the municipal auditorium earned off-stage praise of many people Friday for their assistance in battling the Woolworth building fire.

Billy Lee of New York City, one of the show's comedians, manned a fire hose during late morning and early afternoon hours, then made a quick change to appear in Friday night's performance. Mick Frazier of Denver, Colo. aided radio broadcasting stations in providing on-the-spot recordings of the holocaust.

Damage to the rear of the Woolworth Building after the fire was put out. Kearse Theatre in the middle distance. CN ⟨277⟩

-118-

On March 4, 1949, the greatest loss of life in any fire in West Virginia occurred when the Woolworth Store on Capitol Street caught on fire. Seven firemen died when the wooden floor collapsed into the basement. Fifteen people were injured and the loss amounted to over $1 million. ㉗

15 Men Injured; Damage Placed At Million Mark

Kresge Store, Stock Is Severely Damaged; Flames Out of Control Eight Hours; Two Victims Critically Hurt

By Neil P. Boggs

The most tragic fire in Charleston's history took the lives of seven firemen yesterday as it raged out of control in the downtown shopping district for eight hours.

Fifteen other persons were injured, at least two critically fighting the blaze, the origin of which was not immediately determined.

Smoke Concealed Deadly Trap During Early Fire-Fight Stages

By James A. Hill

Survivors Relate Fight to Escape Store's Inferno

By William E. Garrett

Firemen's Loss Heaviest In West Virginia History

By William H. Maginnis

IN MEMORIAM

THIS TABLET ERECTED BY
THE CITIZENS OF CHARLESTON
IN MEMORY
THOSE VALIANT FIREMEN
WHO GAVE THEIR ALL IN THE
DISASTROUS "WOOLWORTH" FIRE
OF MARCH 4, 1949

IN SORROW AND RESPECT THE
NAMES SO INSCRIBED ARE HONORED
FOR THEIR HEROIC DEEDS

G. A. COATES, JR.
J. P. LITTLE
R. E. McCORMICK
F. N. MILLER
E. C. PAULEY
T. F. SHARP
F. C. SUMMERS

AND TO THOSE OF
THE CHARLESTON FIRE DEPARTMENT
WHO SURVIVED, AND WHO CONTINUE
TO GUARD WITH VIGILANCE AND
VALOR THE LIVES AND PROPERTY OF
THE COMMUNITY, TRIBUTE IS PAID.

Recovering bodies from the Woolworth fire scene in the alley to the rear. CN

The St. Albert Hotel fire on Kanawha Blvd. on March 10, 1932 completely destroyed the old hotel.

Old Lyric Theater on Summers Street going up in flames in the mid-1970s. Note marquee film title: "Teenage Sex Kitten" rated X. CN

Kings Cafeteria fire across from the Virginian Theater at the northeast corner of Lee and Summers streets 1956. Note Christmas decorations. CN

The major part of Christ Church United Methodist at the corner of Quarrier and Morris streets was totally destroyed by fire in 1969 but the bell tower was saved and the church rebuilt.

The Charleston fire chief's 1954 DeSoto automobile shown behind old station on Lee Street at Tennessee Avenue, west side.

The St. Albans Volunteer Fire Department equipment in 1949. Smaller towns often received former Charleston equipment such as these.. CN

Showing their pride, Charleston Fire Department personnel in 1955. Left to right: Lawrence Kitts, Richard Blackshire, driver, Ted Leekis, Habard Jones. Engine is a Seagrave V-12. Note open cockpit and racy design. Modern fire engines tend to be just square boxes—very efficient but not very attractive. CN

In 1901 the Kanawha River again left its banks and flooded parts of the city. The top view is at the corner of Clendenin and Virginia streets. The view at right is at the lower end of Virginia Street looking towards the Elk River.

A 1913 flood covered the west end of the city at the Elk River boundary. This view is now the site of the Charleston Civic Center.

Flood damaage to the highway and interurban railroad bridges at the mouth of Cabin Creek in 1916. The AEP power plant is in the background.

The Aug. 9, 1916 flood on Cabin Creek was one of the most disastrous in this part of the county. This view is of the coal mining community of Eskdale.

The Hansford-Pratt area was flooded in 1916. The hills in the background are across the Kanawha River. JERRY SMITH COLL.

On August 14, 1958, a flash flood hit the Piedmont Road area. This view is at Wertz Avenue. CN

The following three photos show some of the damage from the great cloudburst of July 19, 1961 in the Charleston area that killed 21 people. This view is toward Garrison Avenue with the Midwestern Little League ballfield in the background. CN (283)

The National Guard was called out to patrol and maintain order. View on Garrison Avenue. CN

The heartbreaking task of recovering the dead. CN

LAW AND ORDER

The Charleston Police Department stands assembled in full regalia on the steps of city hall, circa 1934. The police cars are all 1934 Fords, as their V-8 engines made them a favorite of departments all across the country for their jack rabbit agility. These policemen are very serious about their work. Every one has a white shirt and necktie along with what was called a Sam Brown belt. The belt was designed to take the weight of a heavy revolver off the waist and place it on a shoulder. When World War Two began, U.S. Army officers preferred Sam Brown belts as a spiffy accessory, but they were forbidden because of the similarity to the Nazi uniform.

A few officers' belts are white, no doubt indicating traffic assignment. Charleston's finest of 67 years ago are not lightweights because to be a policeman meant lots of rough stuff handling rowdy drunks. In 1934, each patrolman carried a hickory nightstick that was sort of a small baseball bat. Anyone resisting arrest was likely to wake up in jail with a big headache. The streetcar tracks in the middle of Virginia Street are apparent as is the ornate streetlight. Otherwise, take away the people and the cars and this scene hasn't changed much in a lifetime. CHARLESTON POLICE DEPT. COLL.

Charleston motorcycle patrolmen pose at City Hall in 1934. A continuation of the previous photo.

Rev. Billy Sunday poses with Charleston's Finest in 1925. Sunday is in the middle, with Chief of Police, John Britton on his right and Gov. E. F. Morgan of West Virginia on his left. Mayor Grant Hall is next to Morgan.

The motorcyclist on the right is T. Carey Taylor of Staunton, Virginia, who was killed in an auto race in Clarksburg in 1931.

Strong Men Shed Bitter Tears As John Barleycorn Is Buried

$3,150 Worth of Confiscated Liquor Poured Into Sewer With Appropriate Ceremony—Was Result of Two Months' War on Illicit Trafficking in Booze.

Strong men shed bitter tears. Mayor Grant P. Hall stood with bowed head and members of the Charleston police department stood at attention with night sticks held in salute position and caps were held over hearts. It was a sad and solemn occasion as the beloved comrade was laid in his last resting place.

No. Don't be misled. No one is dead around the city hall for office holders never die. Nevertheless, it was the occasion of a burial and the center of interest in the ceremony was our long lost but ever present acquaintance of other days known familiarly as "Old John Barleycorn."

Chief of Police John Britton has it all figured out. There was just $3,150 worth of liquor withdrawn from circulation and poured into the sewer. There were 26 quarts of Black and White Scotch which smelled like the "real stuff" and which was valued at the retail price of $25 or $650. Six quarts of "good old red licker," Melwood brand, was worth to the trade $150; 30 quarts of real Gordon gin, manufactured in England and which experts with watering mouths declared was genuine, would have brought $750 if handled by a seasoned bootlegger, and 200 gallons of moonshine, of doubtful age, vigor and wholesomeness, was quoted at the opening of the local curb market yes-

terday morning at $8 per quart or a total of $1,600.

The supply has accumulated since the police headquarters moved to the new city hall about two months ago. The Scotch whisky was found in an unoccupied private garage in the upper part of the city several weeks ago. The owner of the property reported the find to the police but the owner of the whisky was never caught.

The gin was captured in a leading hotel in the city, concealed in specially constructed trunks and its alleged owner is now serving a sentence of 90 days in jail and will have to pay a fine of $100. The other stuff was taken in small quantities at various times.

The "pouring out" was accomplished by the colored janitor, whose solemn mien bespoke the depths of his feeling. Some wag poured a quantity of flour on the janitor's head without his knowledge and he was then informed that the shock had turned him gray. A glance in a mirror convinced him that this was true and he departed with trepidation in search of medical attention.

"Kanawha river catfish will indulge in that popular custom of long ago known as the Saturday night jag," remarked Chief Britton as the ceremonies were concluded.

1922

This interesting antedote was published in the *Charleston Gazette* in 1922. Kanawha County was certainly not immune to the war against alcohol. There were probably hundreds of illicit stills hidden in the county's hills and even bathtubs in the city proper. Nationwide prohibition lasted from 1919 to 1933.

Note policeman weights.

Long-time city policeman Dan Prowse, left, and Robert McIntosh pose in 1930.

1925

Smith was a constable at the time of McKinley's assassination in 1901 by Kanawha City resident Leon Czolgosz. See page 210 for details.

—1942—

Basement Gym

In 1942, 12,622 arrests were made, an average of 36 per day. There were 1,107 arrests for vagrancy, most of whom were suspected prostitutes; 284 arrests for breaking and entering, and 138 for driving while drunk. There were 73 arrests for gambling, 165 for grand larceny, 117 for petty larceny. Sixteen persons were arrested for murder, five for manslaughter, 18 for operating houses of prostitution, 201 for reckless driving, with only 15 dismissals. There were 82 arrests for violation of the city code, three for window peeping. Other arrest classifications include those made on charges of drunkenness, disordery conduct, investigation, forgery, turning in false alarms and for other violations of the law.

These are views of the Charleston Police Department in 1942. Basement gym, City Hall radio room, target range in the basement of the Municipal Auditorium.

Charleston had a police department personnel of 79 people, which include a Chief, three Captains, three Lieutenants, five Sergeants, four Dectectives, three Patrol Drivers, fifty-three Patrolmen, one Humane Officer, a Police Woman, two stenographers, a mechanic, a painter and a Detective Sergeant assigned to the Health Department.

The annual budget for the department totaled $154,804 which included $13,500 for traffic lights, materials and supplies, gasoline and oil. The highest salary was $250 per month, the lowest $60. In addition to its task of law enforcement, the Police Department assigned part of its force to traffic regulation in the business district, at schools and special events.

City Hall Radio Room

Target Range

Target Range

One of Charleston's most controversial police chiefs died of an apparent heart attack at age 55 on June 6, 1971. Dallas W. Bias was found dead on his boat which crashed into the rocks on the bank of the Kanawha River near the junction of Elk River. He was appointed by Mayor John Copenhaver in 1956 and was asked to resign in 1970 by Mayor Elmer Dodson after Bias filed for the mayor's race himself as a Republican candidate.

Bias, a recovered alcoholic who helped out many alcoholic prisoners, drove his men hard but when one of the department's members came up with personal problems he was quick to offer his help. He worked well with the black community and prevented several potential race riots. He got along well with the old conservative members of Charleston's society, but not as well with the younger set. He also got along well with his controversial boss, Mayor Copenhaver. In 1970 the Fraternal Order of Police booted him from the lodge after he sought an ordinance giving him a stronger hand in dealing with malingering and sick leave.

Chief Dallas Bias demonstrates a spray can of mace (tear gas).

Charleston police department's first K-9 dog meets Mayor John Shanklin on Aug. 2, 1962.

A World War Two vintage article in the *Saturday Evening Post* first coined the phrase "Magic Valley" to describe the awesome concentration of industry in the Kanawha Valley. This circa 1950 aerial view shows the Kelly Axe Factory in the foreground–Union Carbide in the middle and the Naval Ordnance Plant in the distance.

Industry and Commerce/
The Magic Valley

This business, near Morris and Smith streets, was destroyed in a 1920s fire, photo circa 1907.

Plant of the Tanners & Dyers Extract Company. Established in 1891 it manufactured refined chestnut oak bark extract for tanning high-grade oak and union leathers. Located on the south side.

This building still stands, just east of the state capitol on the railroad right-of-way, circa 1907.

This rare 1885 photo is a rear view of the Kanawha Woolen Mills, one of Charleston's major industries for years. It was located near Virginia and Clendenin streets and was owned by well-known businessman, Frank Woodman. ④52

Part of the Ward Engineering works on the south side. ①76

The Kanawha Chemical Fire Engine Mfg. Company was located on Charleston's south side. It built horse-drawn fire fighting equipment.

The Ohio Valley Furniture Company was located near the K&M Railway on Bream Street and was in business in the early 1900s.

M. T. Davis Jr. started the Kanawha Mine Car Co. in 1902 on Charleston's south side. In 1915 the name was changed to Kanawha Manufacturing Company and the business diversified into manufacturing mining machinery and equipment for the newly established chemical industry. This is a 1911 view when the company was still housed in wooden buildings.

A turn of the century industry believed to be a lumber mill between Broad and Morris streets. On the hilltop in the distance the victorian Savage mansion is seen.

A sawmill somewhere in the county, circa 1900.

Buff Lick logging camp near Ward, 1901.

Inside Bowman's Sawmill in St. Albans. (174)

Chain dogs were used to fasten logs together. The ring dog was used when tying logs with a rope. BILL WILLIAMS PHOTO (70)

Interior views of Gravely Tractor Company, 1964. CN

The first experimental Gravely Tractor was powered by an Indian motorcycle motor provided by B.E. Andre. Ben Gravely was also a prominent Charleston photographer. (177)

History tells us that it was the invention of the crude wooden plow that began the rushing tide of human development. A regular and methodical supply of food through agriculture is the basic foundation of modern society—without that we can count on nothing except the prospect of starvation.

The tilling of the soil was one of man's first technological problems. It is a job that requires considerable energy and it soon became apparent that man's old ally the beasts of burden—oxen, donkeys and horses were necessary to supply the power to turn the soil.

Now the horse is a noble creature that has walked alongside mankind in the long path of human development but as we all know they are creatures of flesh and blood and as such must be subject to all the natural shortcomings of living things.

B.F. Gravely had observed the many problems associated with the attempt to maintain a small farm or garden. A horse had to be fed and guarded against disease. A horse could only work so long without rest and of course finally it required a good deal of plain old sweat to convince a horse to do the job.

The gasoline age had recently dawned upon the face of America and men were absolutely obsessed with applying the new found source of power to anything and everything that needed power.

B.F. Gravely was a dreamer and America was built by dreamers.

The initials B.F. stood for Benjamin Franklin and it was no coincidence that Gravely emulated his inventor namesake. His plant was established in Dunbar in 1922 and moved out of state in 1968.

Early oil wells at Dawes, Cabin Creek. The Dawes brothers of Marietta, Ohio opened up the Cabin Creek oil field, forming the Pure Oil Company in 1914.

Oil wells in the Blue Creek, Pinch area, circa 1918. Four companies initially opened up the field. United Fuel & Gas Company, Hope Natural Gas Company, South Penn Oil Company, and Elk Refining Company. (163)

West Virginia was the nation's leading oil and gas producing area for a period of time after the Civil War. A major production area was south of the Little Kanawha River in the central part of the state. But production declined between 1901-1908 and in 1911-1912 the Blue Creek field in Kanawha County was developed. This field extended up to Clendenin and embraced 10 to 20 square miles around the mouth of Blue Creek and on both sides of the Elk River. Capacity began to drop between 1913-1916, and new wells drilled in that period brought in many small quantities of oil and gas. Producing wells were brought in on Cabin Creek in 1914. The Ohio Cities Gas Company opened the field drilling 268 oil wells and six gas wells with only six dry holes. The outgrowth of this discovery was the launching of what would become a major national oil company called The Pure Oil Company. In 1918 a refinery was built on Cabin Creek to handle the flow from that field.

Oxen hauling a boiler in the oil fields at Tad on Campbells Creek. Five thousand year old technology meets the 20th century!

A small Heisler type locomotive that was more often found in the logging industry but shown here in the oil field at Dawes.

The true meaning of "man power." Oil field workers at Dawes.

Elk Refinery at Falling Rock, 1950s. One of the largest refineries in the state, it was built by the Weir family at the previous location of one of the early cannel coal oil refineries from the 1850s. (166)

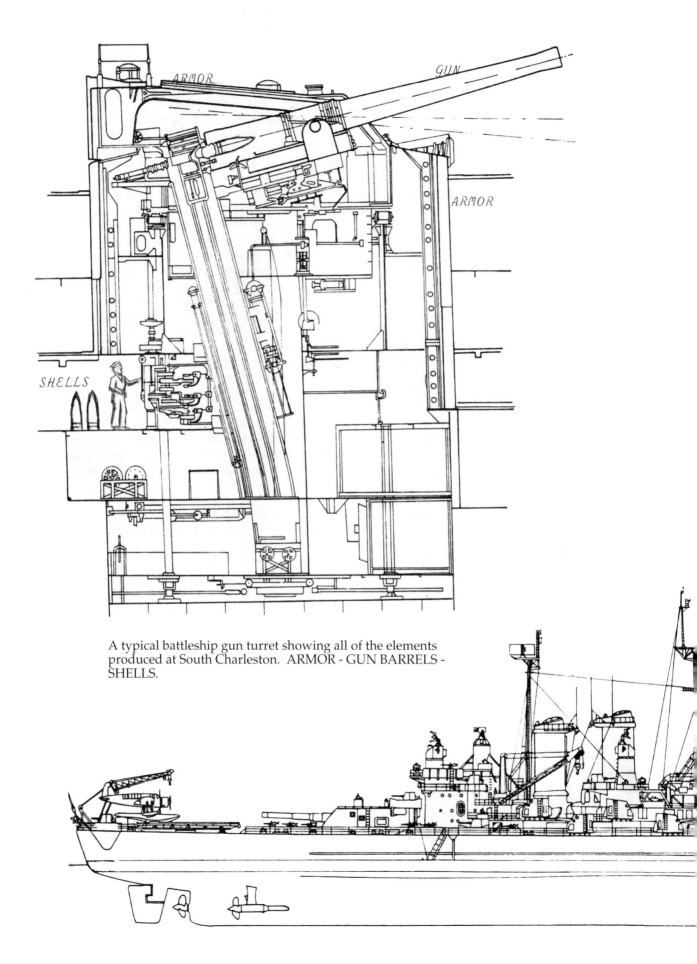

A typical battleship gun turret showing all of the elements produced at South Charleston. ARMOR - GUN BARRELS - SHELLS.

Big Guns and Hard Steel

The South Charleston Naval Ordnance Plant and the Battleship Navy

In 1916, the U.S. Congress passed a naval armaments bill providing for the construction of the world's greatest war fleet, brought on by the looming American involvement in World War One. The nation's leaders wisely concluded that if America were to protect herself and remain free it would be necessary to equal or better the great battleship fleets of the other world powers—notably Germany, France, Japan, and even traditional ally, Great Britain.

The 1916 act called for a superb fleet of battleships and battlecruisers without peer in the world.

The immense plan was thrown into question however by the Allied victory in November 1918 in which the German fleet was vanquished. Some then saw little need for such a powerful American fleet. Others still believed that a strong defense was crucial regardless of the world situation.

Thus the Navy Department pushed ahead with construction of the South Charleston Naval Ordnance Plant even though World War One had ended in victory for the Allies.

It is most interesting to note that in 1920 - a year of great activity in the building of the South Charleston plant - the powerful British Navy was considered a potential adversary. This sounds strange today, however the naval planners of 1920 were well aware that America had fought Great Britain twice before in our history and a friendly Britain could conceivably change into a bellicose foe. And, foremost in the formulation of American Naval strategy was the expansion of Japanese power in the Pacific.

It may be said, of course, that the South Charleston plant was born of World War One. In 1914, when the war began in Europe it was a good bet that the U.S. would become involved eventually and prudence dictated that the American military forces be brought to a state of readiness.

West Virginia Sen. William E. Chilton was an influential Democrat and a friend of the Wilson administration. It was Senator Chilton and former Gov. William A. MacCorkle's pleadings that had the most influence in the locating of the plant ordnance works in West Virginia — rather distant from the seashore and shipbuilding yards. One strong argument, however fantastic, was that South Charleston was remote from the Atlantic Coast and therefore immune from attack by enemy forces. Aside from Chilton and MacCorkle's influence, there were several distinct advantages to a location in Kanawha County. Abundant water, energy, land and transportation, not the least of the inducements was the donation of the 265 acre site to the government by means of a $300,000 public subscription on the part of local citizens.

On Aug. 30, 1917, Secretary of the Navy Josephus Daniels turned the first spade of soil to begin construction.

Nearly everything about the new plant was, in a word, remarkable. The biggest and best in the world. It is astonishing to note that the projectile facility was set up to produce up to 20" shells although the largest naval guns ever mounted on a battleship were 18" on the huge World War Two Japanese battleships *Yamato* and *Mushashi*. In actual practice the South Charleston plant turned out 16" shells like those used on American battleships *Missouri* and *Iowa* in World War Two.

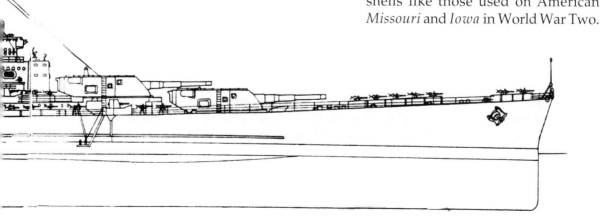

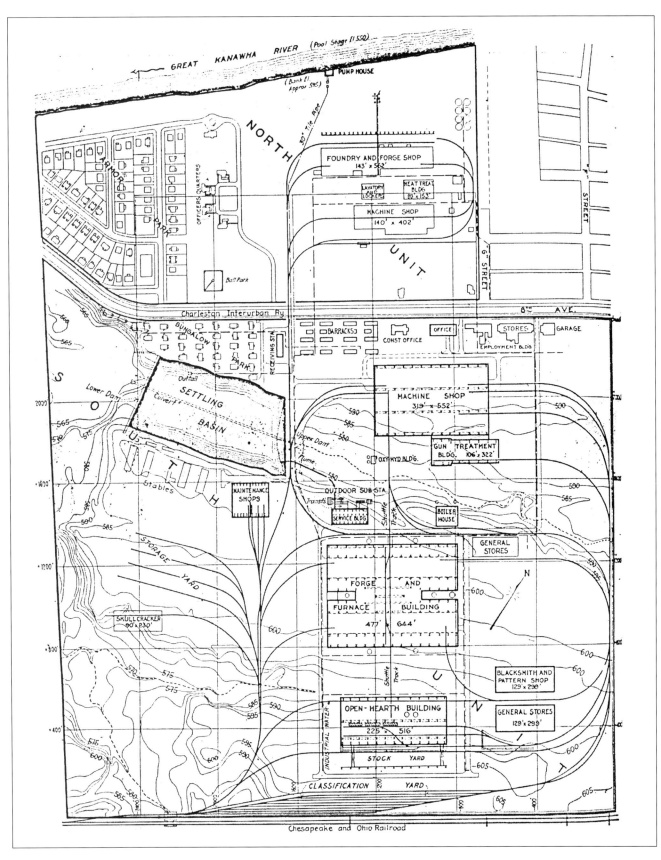

This 1920 map shows the original World War One facility. Considerable new construction occurred during World War Two. The flow of production went from raw metal in the railroad yard through the various processes toward the river.

There is the question of why the U.S. Government decided to build and operate an armament plant when general practice throughout the world was to contract out to private industry. The answer lies in the fact that the U.S. Navy had become the victim of price gouging by the giant steel companies who possessed a virtual monopoly on the manufacture of armor plating.

Another factor for the Navy was the distastrous experience of "cost-plus" system allowed companies to collect a set percentage profit on the gross cost of a plant - thus it was to their advantage to run costs up as high as possible. The powder plant at Nitro was one example. The Navy was determined not to let such a situation arise at South Charleston.

The Feb. 3, 1921, issues of the Charleston newspapers carried the headlines: "First Ingot of Steel is Finished at Naval Plant." This ingot, weighing over 70 tons marked the climax of over three years of work by thousands of laborers and the expenditure of a virtual fortune out of taxpayer's pockets.

Incredibly a few months later in November 1921 the world powers met in Washington and signed the "Washington Naval Treaty" which drastically limited the size of naval forces and rendered the splendid South Charleston plant unnecessary.

Oddly enough, this was not an uncommon story in America following World War One. To a great extent the nation had geared up for a long war which actually ended less than two years after U.S. entry into the conflict.

It is interesting to note that the Japanese signed the "Washington Treaty" with every intention of violating it. The rules allowed heavy cruisers to mount only eight-inch guns. The Japanese built their cruisers with the allowable eight-inch guns but cleverly designed the turrets to accommodate 12-inch guns. Thus when Pearl Harbor was attacked the Japanese cruisers were quickly fitted out with the vastly more powerful 12-inch guns. The bitter lesson learned here was the unreliability of a treaty with those determined to cheat.

The giant works were closed in 1922 and put on reserve status to await another war.

On April 26, 1939, after 17 years of inactivity, the ordnance plant was leased by the Carnegie-Illinois Steel Co. to facilitate the heat treatment of steel armor plate.

The actual plate was produced at the Great Homestead Works in Pittsburgh and then sent to South Charleston for the heat treatment which resulted in a hardening of the armor.

Thus began the rebirth of the South Charleston Ordnance Plant which led to a vast and diverse contribution to the nation's World War Two victory. To detail all of the elements of work done during World War Two at the plant would require a book of its own—here are a few of the high points:

A total of 131,000 gun barrels were produced from 6-inch to 8-inch—more than all other U.S. factories combined.

The number of employees reached 7,400 in 1944—about half of them women.

The first production of air to ground rockets with monthly count reaching 8,600 in May 1945.

Thousands of torpedo flasks manufactured for the Navy, 12-feet long by 21-3/4" in diameter.

The plant boasted one of the largest machine shops in the world.

On July 22, 1942, the coveted "E" award was given for "High achievement in the production of war equipment."

DEPARTMENT OF THE NAVY
OFFICE OF THE UNDER SECRETARY
WASHINGTON

July 22, 1942

Mr. Alfred Weiland, Vice President
General Machinery Ordnance Corporation
U. S. Navy Ordnance Plant
South Charleston, West Virginia

Dear Mr. Weiland:

This is to inform you that the Army and Navy are conferring upon your organization the Army-Navy Production Award for high achievement in the production of war equipment.

The patriotism which you and your employees have shown by your remarkable production record is helping our country along the road to victory. The Army and Navy are proud of the achievement of the men and women of the U. S. Navy Ordnance Plant of the General Machinery Ordnance Corporation.

In conferring this award, the Army and Navy will give you a flag to fly above your plant, and will present to every individual within your organization a lapel pin, symbol of leadership on the production front.

May I extend to the U. S. Navy Ordnance Plant of the General Machinery Ordnance Corporation my congratulations for accomplishing more than seemed reasonable or possible a year ago.

Sincerely yours,

James Forrestal

The ordnance plant received the Army-Navy Production Award in 1942.

Ordnance plant workers sit on a box that reads - bottom forging die 14,000 ton press. Everything that had to do with the plant, i.e. buildings, equipment and products were all oversized.

In 1939 the South Charleston ordnance plant was leased to the National Youth Administration (NYA) for an "experiment in occupational guidance." Five hundred youths, half from West Virginia, gained an exploratory work experience set up for the purpose of giving needy young men an opportunity to explore the fields of the metal and mechanical trades so that they could discover whether or not they had aptitudes in these trades.

Again in 1946 the plant was closed due to victory and lay idle until the 1950 Korean War. Utilization of the plant was minor and only a few hundred were employed.

On April 13, 1961, the government sold the ordnance plant to the F.M.C. Corporation for over $4.3 million. F.M.C. remodeled the plant to build M-113 armored personnel carriers for the Vietnam War and employed 1,800 people.

The South Charleston Ordnance Plant played a very important role in American history. It helped to give birth to the great Pacific fleet that took the Japanese surrender in Tokyo Bay in 1945. Many of the guns of the battleship *Missouri* were produced in South Charleston. Indeed if Hitler or Tojo might have had a wish fulfilled—it could have been for the destruction of the South Charleston Ordnance Plant.

Charleston-1900-1950

Middle Westerners Boom Charleston

Navy Secretary Josephus Daniels and former Governor MacCorkle participated in the dedication of the Ordnance plant on Aug. 30, 1917.

The election of R.P. Devan Jr. as president of the Charleston Chamber of Commerce in 1957 calls to mind the events of 1911 when two hustling young men from Oklahoma came to Charleston and aided in changing the entire history of the Kanawha Valley. They were S.P. Puffer and the late R.P. Devan Sr. They came in an Oklahoma booster car that was sidetracked at Charleston and they sold Oklahoma real estate.

After a brief stay in Charleston, they decided that West Virginia presented more opportunity than Oklahoma and remained in Charleston. Puffer became secretary of the Charleston Chamber of Commerce, Devan was his assistant but later went into the insurance business and eventually became president of the Rotary Club, president of the Automobile Club, president of the Chamber of Commerce and mayor of Charleston.

As far back as 1876, a book, *Mineral Resources of West Virginia* by Messrs. Fontaine and Maury pronounced the Kanawha River as having "more manufacturing advantages combined than at any other point in the country."

The description continued: "with cheap salt, cheap coal, cheap sulphurets, cheap manganese, cheap limestone, cheap timber, cheap labor, and cheap transportation, there is nothing lacking but capital to make the Kanawha the Tyne of America."

However, Charleston was torn in factions following the Civil War and nothing was done, until

Puffer did it. Charleston had one major industry in 1911, the Kelly Axe Manufacturing Company. But there soon followed two chemical companies, at South Charleston, the Rollin Chemical Company with English affiliation and the Warner Klipstein Chemical Company with German affiliation.

Puffer had been a reporter on the *Chicago Tribune* and often did a pinch hit for this writer when there was a difficult story. He was a high-powered publicity man.

The big test came for Charleston in 1917, when with national publicity the federal government sought the best location for making armor plate for the navy. Charleston won this contest amid much fanfare and followed by a wild real estate promotion of the Kanawha Valley in which old-timers were shocked by the prices paid, but no one lost any investment.

Cumberland, Maryland was adjudged the next best location. Huntington was in the running, and when it lost, Boyd Jarrell, the brilliant editor of the Huntington *Herald-Dispatch* wrote a scathing editorial accusing the late U. S. Senator, William E. Chilton of having used his influence in favor of the selection of Charleston, the senator being a staunch supporter of the Wilson Administration.

Col. Herbert Pfahler, the editor of the senator's newspaper, the *Charleston Gazette,* admitted privately that this may have been true with respect to Charleston and Huntington, since there was but little difference between costs of steel manufacture between the two cities.

But most persons gave Puffer the top credit, he was the spark plug, and the advertising that the Kanawha Valley got from this victory boomed the Kanawha Valley with such industries following as the powder plant at Nitro, the Libby-Owens sheet glass and Owens-Illinois bottling plants, Carbide, Dupont, Westvaco and Barium Reduction. Also came a host of smaller industries.

One wonders just how much the arrival of the Oklahoma Booster car and the breezy, hustling of Messrs. Puffer and Devan changed the history of the Kanawha Valley. For until they came to town, little or nothing had been done although for 45 years industrial engineers had pronounced the Kanawha Valley as the foremost spot in the nation for manufacturing.

These two photos show the immense size of the interior of the U.S. Naval Ordnance plant at South Charleston, circa 1940s. Top 500 ton press in Forge Shop #1. Bottom: Machine shop view from east end. Note gun barrels.

In 1961 the F.M.C. Corporation bought the ordnance plant from the U.S. Government and utilized it for the production of the M-113 armored personnel carrier.

Motors for the M-113 vehicle. CN

Demonstration of a heavy howitzer mounted on an M-113 chassis at the F.M.C. Ordnance plant, 1963. CN

Testing the M-113 vehicle in Davis Creek. CN

Assembly line for the Army M-113 armored personnel carrier at the F.M.C. Ordnance plant, 1963. Many of these vehicles were used in the Vietnam War. CN

Walter Clark contractor is hauling a special pontoon barge made by West Virginia Steel Corp. for use in building the Kanawha Boulevard, circa 1939. Ward Engineering Works is across the river.

Carbon Fuel Company's coal tipple at Cabin Creek, 1951.

Fletcher Enamel Company in Dunbar produced a large percentage of the enameled ware used in North America. It produced more than 268 items and during World War Two 650 people put out over 20,000 pieces of product per day. The company was started in 1908 by the Fletcher brothers in Anderson, Indiana and moved to Dunbar in 1914. The company also produced aluminum ware between 1914 and 1934. Enameled ware is composed of glass on steel and requires a chemical process and a high degree firing in an oven. The business closed in the 1960s.

The pressing of Steel utensils before the enamel coating is applied and baked and after the enamel has been applied, 1946.

The Stonewall Jackson Station, Hope Natural Gas Company in Chelyan, 1953.

The Cobb Compressor Station near Clendenin, 1953.

Hubert Jones trucking company, 1940s.

Wartime cartoon by Vintroux.

West Virginia's Great KANAWHA VALLEY

The narrow 97–mile-long valley of the Kanawha River is unique because of its unlimited supply of coal, its oil, the availability of gas in large quantity and its brine, coupled with its strategic location, low cost electricity, excellent transportation and abundance of native born labor.

Fortune Magazine has called the Valley the "Ruhr of the United States Chemical Industry." Saturday Evening Post has named it "Magic Valley" because of the manner in which research, engineering and management utilize its advantages to produce modern miracles of chemistry. The same resources, in some plants, serve both as fuel for steam and electric power and as basic raw material.

This brochure indicates that many of the nation's industrial giants are now profiting from the Valley's riches. Plant and warehouse sites are available. For information concerning them, communicate with:

CHARLESTON CHAMBER OF COMMERCE   Chamber of Commerce Building   CHARLESTON, WEST VIRGINIA

The Dunbar Glass Company in 1955. It was founded in 1912 as the Dunbar Flint Glass Company making flint glass lamp chimneys. Through the years it expanded to include hundreds of glass products ranging from gift items to home and industrial products.

The Libby-Owens-Ford plate glass factory under enlargement in Kanawha City, April 1920. The part of the plant on the east end was built prior to 1920. KENNY SHOCK PHOTO

Glass Cutting
by Paul Marshall

July 19, 1946, was a red-letter day for me! It was my 16th birthay and the first day I could become an apprentice glasscutter to my father. I was excited.

We went to the Libby-Owens-Ford Plant No. 1 on 57th Street in Kanawha City and were greeted by the Boss Cutter. I was issued a leather apron, wrist cuffs, rubber-coated cotton gloves and a table brush, then taken to Dad's cutting stall.

The cutting stall was a rectangular work space about 15 feet wide and 20 feet deep with a high ceiling. Just in front of the windows was the cutting table which was 8'-6" long, 4'-6" wide, covered with thick felt and edged by a steel square numbered in inches. The left edge was adjustable so that the cut glass would be perfectly sized. To the left of the table was the cullet (waste glass) box which led into a chute that was emptied in the basement. Cullet was used in making new glass. It was melted along with chemical ingredients.

The right side of the stall was where sheets of glass were stacked. The left side of the stall was made up of heavy shelving where the cutter would place small sizes of cut glass, such as 10"x12", 8"X10", etc. In the center of the stall was a "buck," a free-standing unit with sloping sides where larger sizes of glass were leaned as they were taken from the table. In later years the center bucks were removed and replaced with movable bucks which could be handled by electric trucks.

There were 12 cutting rooms on the production level (2nd floor) of the plant, corresponding with the number of lehrs which carried the annealing process of glass production. There were 12 furnaces each having two lehrs (A and B). The ribbon (or sheet) of molten glass was drawn out of the furnace and flowed over a large smooth steel roll, then proceeded along a 200 foot long lehr slowly cooling in the annealing process until it reached the end where a man controlled a cutting wheel device called "the rabbit" which cut the ribbon into sheets. The sheets were placed on wheeled "trucks" for delivery to the cutting rooms.

The thickness of glass was determined by the speed of cold water traveling through pipes on both sides of the ribbon as it came over the big roll - the faster the water, the thinner the glass. Most glass was either single or double strength, but there was thick glass (7/32" to 3/16") and very thin glass (like used in picture frames or microscope slides). During my 18-1/2 year tenure at the plant, I cut all thicknesses at one time or another.

Not all cutting rooms were in production. Actually cutters worked in rooms 6 through 12 and rooms 11C and 12C in the basement, where the very thin glass was cut. It was referred to as picture glass. Room 6 was where oversized sheets were handled by two men. Those stalls were referred to as the "Big Place" and it took seniority to work there. Rooms 7, 9 and 10 were for single strength. Room 11 had double strength and Room 8 was for "heavy" (3/16" to 7/32"). At the time I left (spring of 1965) to spend full time in Architecture, I was the chief inspector in Room 8.

Due to Dad's handicap (he was missing four fingers on his right hand) he usually could handle glass sheets only 24" wide x 96" long. After I joined him and began to learn the way to grade glass to

remove unwanted defects, wider sheets of glass were brought into Dad's stall because I was handling most of the heavy work. If I do say so myself, I learned quickly and was able to increase the family take-home pay significantly. When I started I made 30 cents per hour. I also made extra money counting-off for other cutters.

Counting-off was the term given to setting the day's production out in front of each stall beginning with the largest size and progressing, in line, to the smallest size. Two cutters, Joe Hilton and Quentin Joslin, paid me 1 cent per box to count off for them.

Before the introduction of electric trucks which moved "bucks" from the stall to a basement packing area, packing was done in the cutting rooms.

First the "paper boys" would slip a sheet of paper between each lite of glass. Then the "packers" would slip a cardboard-backed box (which had boxwood ends) over each box and the "nailer" would nail the lid in place. When the packing of a cutter's count off was completed, an electric truck would be loaded by a "trucker" for delivery to the basement warehouse, ready for shipping by rail or truck.

A glass cutter was paid by the piece (piece rate). Each box of cut glass was worth so many cents per box. Each box contained about 4,800 sq. inches. A very good day's work would be about 100 boxes of production (single-strength glass). In the 1950s that production would earn over $25 per day. The glass cutter was one of the highest paid journeyman in the Kanawha Valley.

The basic work of a cutter was to cut sizes of glass from sheets, based on orders submitted to him each week or day depending upon the size of the order (number of boxes). The orders were matched by width of sheets. For instance, 24x24 sizes could be cut from 24 or 48 inch-wide sheets; 24x36 would be cut from 36 inch-wide sheets, and so on. There were also fractional sizes. The orders for fractions, were coveted by the cutters because there was a premium per piece for fractions.

The cutter was expected to remove defects such as blisters, carbon, dirt, etc., and produce a finished product which would pass inspection for the quality designated on the order. Grades were AA, A, B, windshield, and greenhouse. Grade AA had to be almost perfect because the pieces were to be used in mirrors. Of course the finest mirrors were of plate glass, which we did not handle in Charleston. The usual grade for window glass was B. Grade A was used in fine cabinet-work and other special applications.

Grade AA and A were always inspected - every lite of glass. As much B grade was inspected as possible depending upon the overall work load for inspectors. To be an inspector was an honorable position and was filled by cutters of tenure. Chief inspectors were in charge of quality and production of an entire room of about 24 cutters and a staff of about three inspectors.

The Libby-Owens-Ford plant in Charleston was, in its prime, the largest window glass plant in the world. When I started there in 1946, there were over 350 hand glass cutters employed. When I left in the spring of 1965, there were less than 100.

Glass cutting was good, well-paying work but it could be dangerous. Several men had injuries which cost them work days but, in the L.O.F. period of glass cutting history the work place was much safer than when window glass was produced by a glass blower. Those shops ended, for the most part, early in the 20th century. Today, as far as I know, there is not one production glass cutter in the country. Window glass is today produced by floating the glass sheet over molten tin, resulting in a much flatter product which has even replaced plate glass. All cutting is by machine.

When the continuous sheet of flat drawn glass emerged from the long lehr or annealing oven, it was cut into large sheets which were then washed, inspected and turned over to crews of cutters who cut it into smaller sizes for shipment. LOF was the largest window glass plant in the world, circa 1946. BOB DEAHL PHOTO

South Side Foundry and Machine Works workers, circa 1905. This business would eventually become the present Trojan Steel Company. BRENDA THAYER COLL.

A mining machine invented by O. A. Thayer and Joseph L. Beury, circa 1900. Built at the South Side Foundry. G.T. Thayer Jr. is pictured. BRENDA THAYER COLL.

The petrochemical industry got its start in a small natural gas/gasoline plant at Clendenin in 1920 operated by Union Carbide. In 1925 the operation was moved to South Charleston.

This is the Rossler & Haslacher Chemical Company plant, located at "Chemical City" on the west side of St. Albans, west of the Coal River. It was one of the first chemical plants in the valley, built in 1916. It is believed to have made "Torpedo Fuel" during World War One. During the Civil War it was the site of the Valcoulon Mansion and Confederate Camp Tompkins. The Valley Drive-In Theater was also on this site. The plant shut down in the 1920s. DR. WILLIAM DEAN PHOTO ⑧⑨

The first office building for Union Carbide was constructed on MacCorkle Avenue in South Charleston in 1930. ⑮⑤

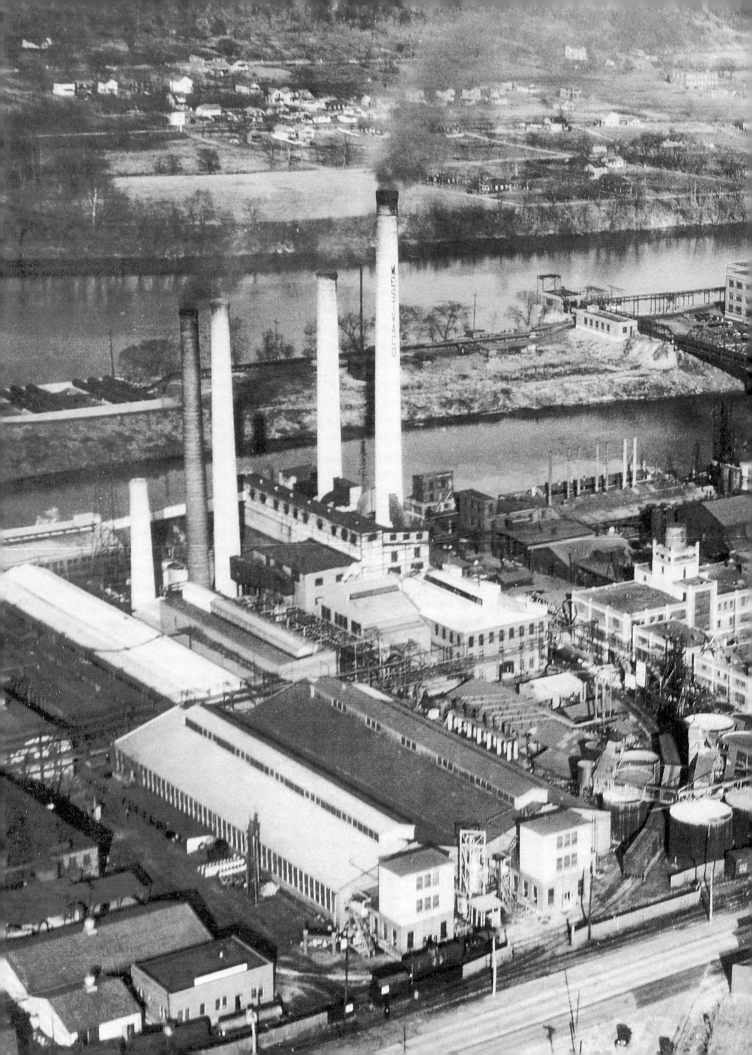

The huge complex of the Carbide and Carbon Chemical Company and Westvaco at South Charleston, 1930s.

An old joke stated that one evening a drunk was going across the Patrick Street Bridge and looking at Blaine Island declared. "Good Gosh— what a battleship!"

Blaine Island in the Kanawha River at South Charleston, part of the large Carbide and Carbon Chemical (now Dow) Company complex.

Teeth of Skeleton Cleaned, Put Back

Maybe you've heard this story, and maybe you haven't.

Blaine's island, on which the Carbide and Carbon Chemical corporation has built, at one time was an old burying ground. Bodies had been buried there, according to record, for 115 years or more.

Carbide began extending its island plants, last year, and caskets were dug up and reburied.

N. A. Barth, mortician, was called in. He got the job of moving and reburying 12 caskets.

All that remained of those pioneers of course, were the skeletons. In one casket, which was believed to contain the remains of an ancestor of a local doctor, Mr. Barth found a solid gold upper plate, with the teeth and plate perfectly preserved. The teeth were of ivory. Each was drilled and attached to the gold plate with little gold pins.

The plate was taken out and cleaned, and the doctor wanted to present it to the dental society, but for one reason and another the plate was returned to its resting place, and the remains of the old pioneer were transferred to another cemetery.

1928

-164-

Union Carbide Corporation

In 1920 the petrochemical industry started in a small building in Clendenin producing products from chlorine. In 1925 the Carbide and Carbon Chemical Company moved to a larger facility in South Charleston, taking over the Rollin Chemical Company which was next door to the Warner-Klipstein plant. Antifreeze was produced along with other products using local raw materials.

· A large flat island in the Kanawha River, Blaine Island, was purchased in 1928 and a huge chemical complex was constructed. The company name was changed to Union Carbide and a research and development center was started. With the advent of World War Two, the company became the largest employer in the county and a major supplier of vital war materials including supplying chemicals for the adjacent synthetic rubber plant.

After the war a large technical center was established in South Charleston (1949) and enlarged in 1959 and 1962.

The Linde division was formed in the 1920s making air products including acetylene for metal working.

In the latter years of the 20th century, Union Carbide along with other valley chemical plants, began to down size and in 2000 the company was sold to the Dow Chemical Company.

The Westvaco plant in South Charleston was formed from the Warner-Klipstein interests in 1928 to furnish chlorine to the Carbide plant next door. The plant produced a variety of chemicals including a highly secret catalyst used in the manufacture of most of the synthetic rubber and the new insecticide DDT. In 1948 Westvaco became the Chloride Alkali Division of FMC. PHOTO FROM 1957

The Synthetic Rubber
Manufacturing Complex at Institute

In August 1940, Carbide and Carbon Chemicals Corporation was asked to aggressively pursue investigations to produce butadiene and styrene in anticipation of the possibility that large-scale production of both chemicals might someday become a pressing necessity.

Carbide proceeded immediately with its research and engineering work on a round-the-clock basis to find out how to produce large quantities of butadiene and styrene as primary products. Within six months, Carbide had perfected a practical process, as well as advanced designs for equipment, to convert ethyl alcohol into butadiene.

On June 3, 1941 Carbide was asked to submit estimates for possible styrene and butadiene production. The need for conserving construction materials, the necessity for using a raw material that was readily available, and the extensive research that had started early in 1940, all culminated in the decision to meet the national emergency—to make the needed tonnage of butadiene from grain alcohol.

Charleston mayor, D. Boone Dawson holds a Treasury Department flag before hoisting it at the rubber factory during World War Two. Plant officials and workers look on.

BFGoodrich

RUBBER *and* SYNTHETIC *products*

Two months later, in August 1941, the government specifically authorized Carbide and Carbon Chemicals Corporation to design and build a

Goodrich-Gulf

A riverfront view of the rubber manufacturing facility in early 1945. Note old Wertz Airfield in top right corner.

plant for the Defense Plant Corporation at Institute, for making 10,000 short tons of butadiene a year. Immediately after the declaration of war in December 1941, this capacity was increased to 20,000 tons. This in turn was increased shortly to 40,000 tons and then finally to 80,000 tons of butadiene a year. It was also decided to add a plant for producing 25,000 tons of styrene a year. Carbide was also asked to design, build, and operate all the utilities for the butadiene and styrene plants and for the adjacent rubber polymerization plant.

U.S. Rubber, one of the leading American rubber companies, was asked to design, build, and operate for the government an adjacent plant for consuming this 80,000 short tons of butadiene and 25,000 short tons of styrene and combining them to make 90,000 long tons of Buna S synthetic rubber a year. There would thus be in operation at Institute the only government synthetic rubber plant that was totally integrated. It was also the largest of the synthetic rubber plants.

Construction work on the first two alcohol-to-butadiene units at Institute was started in April 1942 by Ford, Bacon & Davis, Inc. the first of four butadiene units started producing on January 29, 1943, less than 10 months after ground had been broken and more than two months ahead of the originally scheduled date. All utilities for the plant were ready for operation. Raw materials were available. The first tank car of butadiene was shipped three weeks later. The construction of the two styrene units began in July 1942, and the first operation began seven months later in March 1943. The first shipment of synthetic rubber Buna S left the plant on March 31, 1943, as the Institute Plant went to war. By May 31, 1943, one million pounds of Buna S synthetic rubber were produced at the Institute Plant.

The plant continued in operation until 1969 partly as a large-scale development unit where new polymers were made. In 1970 Union Carbide bought the now obsolete plant and most of the original facilities were demolished to make way for new installations.

FIRST SYNTHETIC RUBBER SHIPMENT

On March 31, 1943 there were no ovations, no speeches, no bands played as freight car 28012 rolled slowly down the tracks and out the gate with the first shipment of synthetic rubber. *Institute had gone to war.* Car 28012 and many others like it will arrive at their destination with their loads of synthetic rubber to be made into tires, tubes and many products so vital to our armed forces.

Our plant, the largest of its kind in operation today, will eventually have a capacity of 90,000 tons of Buna-S synthetic rubber.

Synthetic Times - April 1943

The Institute Plant in 1952.

The Belle Works of E.I. Dupont de Nemours & Company in the 1930s.

The DuPont Belle Works

A landmark in the history of the American chemical industry the Dupont Belle Works has been a mainstay in the prosperity of Charleston and the great Kanawha Valley for the better part of the 20th century.

Located 11 miles east of the capital city on U.S. Rt. 60 and the old Midland Trail in the little town of Belle—this pioneer plant of the E.I. DuPont de Nemours Company at its zenith employed over 5,000 people in the early 1950s.

The wonderful story of the Belle plant began in the mid-1920s when DuPont decided to commence the manufacture of ammonia using new technology developed during World War One. During the war the United States imported all of its nitrates from mines in South America. Nitrates were essential for the production of explosives and ironically also of agricultural fertilizer.

Cut off from access to imported nitrates, Germany developed a process to compress coal gas or coke gas in which pressures of up to 15,000 lbs. per sq. inch were attained by the use of giant mechanical compressors.

The original German invention was improved upon in France and the French "Claude" system was the basis for the Belle plant.

On April 1, 1926 the first ammonia was produced at Belle thus providing the raw material to manufacture a myriad of chemical products including methanol.

Since coal was the primary ingredient of the process it was natural for the plant to be built in the heart of coal country and on the abundant waters of the Great Kanawha River.

The Belle Works played a crucial part in the victory of World War Two as all of the nylon used by the U.S. Armed Forces during the war came from the Belle Works.

The basic nylon raw material was produced at Belle and shipped to other plants where it was woven and turned into the parachutes and instruments of war.

During World War Two very many Belle Works employees served in the armed forces and 31 lost their lives.

Nitrates were also used to make fertilizer that led to the amazing ability of farmers to feed millions who would have otherwise starved.

In 1998 the last of the giant hyper compressors were cut up into scrap and today in the first year of the 21st century the Belle Works still manufactures considerable product but with automation and new technology the work force is under 500 and ammonia is no longer produced.

Oil is now the key raw material of chemical production and the work is carried out in areas where oil is readily available.

The Belle plant today produces specialty chemicals but the smoking coke ovens with their gleaming fires showing through the night are gone forever.

These historic compressors nicknamed "hypers," were installed in the 1920s and removed in 1998. Photo circa 1946.

In 1929 when Monsanto purchased the Rubber Service Laboratories in Nitro, four local men formed a company called Kavalco Products, Inc. to manufacture some of the same products as Monsanto was producing. In the early 1930s the name was changed to Apex and then to Ohio-Apex Chemical Company. Bernard H. Jacobson and Kenneth H. Klipstein took over the company in 1936 and manufactured plasticizers. In the early 1950s F.M.C. purchased the company and added several new products. The plant was located in Nitro. Photo circa 1961.

One of the pioneer chemical plants in the Kanawha Valley was Belle Alkali Company at Belle, established in 1919. Coal from a nearby mine was used to generate process steam and power for electrolysis of local brines. First products were chlorine, caustic soda and liquid bleach. In 1953 the plant was purchased by Diamond Alkali Company which later became the Diamond Shamrock Corporation. Note West Virginia Turnpike under construction across the river. Photo circa 1954.

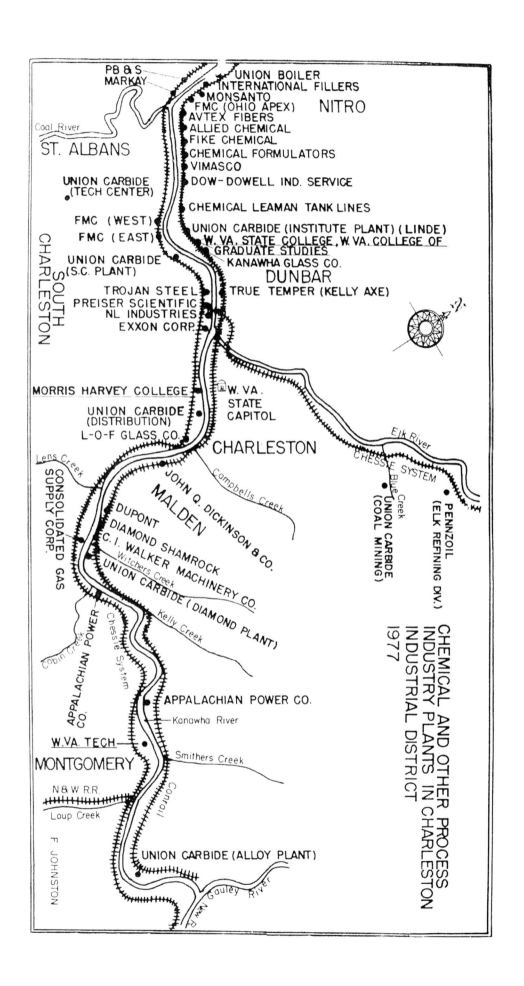

CHEMICAL AND OTHER PROCESS INDUSTRY PLANTS IN CHARLESTON INDUSTRIAL DISTRICT 1977

Three coal miners pose with their mules at the boat landing at Crown Hill in eastern Kanawha County. The year was about 1910. Note the buckets used for carrying food and the horse whips around the men's necks. The mules are Shad, Bird and Old Dave. The men are (from left) Ben Hudnal, Emory Massey and Julius Clark.. WILLIAM KELLY COLL.

Kelly's Creek Coalburg Block, No. 2 mine, 1920s.

Miners on an electric tram about to enter a mine in the Kayford area, 1916.
C&OHS #6341

Strikers Tent Colony To Be Set up in City This Week, by Miners

The West Virginia Mine Workers union will begin Wednesday establishing a tent colony at the Splash beach property on the south bank of the Kanawha River, opposite the mouth of Elk, President Frank Keeney reported yesterday. Shower baths and other sanitary facilities now being installed will be completed by then, Keeney said. The union has 47 tents, purchased with funds donated by Mrs. Ethel Clyde of New York, and will purchase 53 more shelters.

The colony, which will house the families of miners evicted at Ward by the Kelly's Creek Colliery company, will be lighted with flood lights.

"We're going to erect signs so that all of Charleston, Charleston's visitors and passengers on railway trains may see and know why the miners are camping there," Keeney said.

The Charleston Gazette, Oct. 25, 1931

Underground scene in the Ward area. TH

Deep in the earth where its dark and
*   damp*
a miner labors by a carbide lamp
and the cities light up and factories
*   roll*
all because a miners loading coal!
   Lyric from an old song

Hazel Hamrick and "Jay Bird" Knapp with the Valley Camp Coal Company on Kelly's Creek, 1944. TH

Jay Dean and Bud Leftwich on an electric tram car at Campbells Creek, early 1940s. TH

-173-

The Diamond's size was doubled in 1949.

1949

New Diamond Invites Public

Open Houses Mark

Expansion Program

West Virginia's largest retail merchandising establishment, the Diamond department store at Capitol and Washington streets, Friday begins a series of open houses to acquaint its thousands of customers with the extent of its now nearly completed $1,250,000 expansion modernization program.

The program is the culmination of planning that was begun two years ago by Wehrle B. Geary,

● ● ● ● ● ● ● ● ● ● ● ● ● ●

Tribute to Workers

Employee loyalty has been a principal contribution factor in the growth and success of the Diamond department store, President Wehrle Geary said Thursday.

"Many of my department heads have been with the store for 30 years," he said. "Their loyalty to the store and their personal friendship has been one of the most valuable assets which the Diamond possessed and an always significant factor in the growth of this establishment."

● ● ● ● ● ● ● ● ● ● ● ● ● ●

president of the store, and A.W. Cox, vice president.

Actual construction of a four-story addition to the northern wing of the store began 15 months ago and is now in the final stages of completion.

The installation of escalators leading to all of the five merchandising floors of the big establishment began 11 months ago and was completed and placed in operation Nov. 15. Since that time they have carried more than 350,000 persons to the various levels during their shopping and inspection trips. The average has been around 3,000 daily.

In addition to the escalators, the store has also installed two new elevators, making a bank of five and assuring a rapid movement of traffic between all shopping levels regardless of the size of store crowds.

During the Christmas shopping season, the store in one day had more than 80,000 persons enter and leave the building and was able to handle the huge crowd without undue congestion.

Diamond officials said Thursday that visiting store officials from several department stores in larger eastern and midwestern cities are expected here for the opening and to inspect the design, installation and equipment that has been called the most modern and functional to be found in any but a relatively few stores in the nation - all of them in cities of much larger population.

Present work completed at the store includes completely new treatment and rearrangement of fixtures, displays and lighting, together with the major enlargement of virtually all departments on the first, third, fourth and fifth sales floors.

Work on the modernization of the second floor has not been started, but is scheduled for the immediate future. When completed, the store management asserts that it will be an ultra-modern fashion salon comparable only to those found in the nation's largest cities.

The sixth and seventh floors will not be for merchandising. The sixth will be a marking and stock floor and all offices will be on the seventh floor, along with a personnel training section, rest rooms and a first aid department.

Mr. Geary, head of the Diamond, born on a Roane County farm, came to Charleston as a young man in 1906 and after doing odd jobs for a time, opened a small shoe store on Capitol Street a few months later.

Holding to the belief that "the recollection of quality remains long after price is forgotten," Mr. Geary's business prospered and he moved to larger quarters at 209-211 Capitol Street. There he later installed a ready-to-wear department and a men's store that had grown to the city's leading shopping center by 1920.

During the boom period of 1926, he purchased the site where the old Capitol building had stood until destroyed by fire and erected what was the first unit - a five-story brick structure - of the present Diamond building.

Through the depression years that followed the boom, the Diamond survived in staunch financial condition, and in 1940, Mr. Geary made the first major enlargement, virtually doubling the floor space by erecting three stories on a lot between the first unit and the corner of Capitol and Washington. The second unit to be added is the four-story addition to that section.

1949

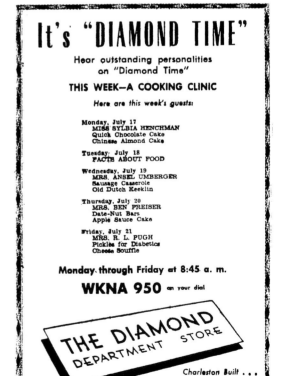

The above photo shows a picture of the Frankenberger clothing store taken in 1898 at a location on the corner of Kanawha and Summers streets.

Philip and Moses Frankenberger came to Charleston from Columbia, PA, in 1860 to open a men's clothing store. Unfortunately, the Civil War soon interrupted their business and Confederate troops confiscated their stock and sent the brothers to prison in Virginia. They soon escaped and returned to Charleston and reopened their store. Philip took over the business after the war and about 1882 moved the store from its original location in the 500 block of Kanawha Street to the corner of Kanawha and Alderson streets. The same year Henry Kleeman, who would be associated with the store over 50 years, was employed. In 1895 the store was moved to the corner of Kanawha and Summers streets and in 1915 to its last location in the Security Building on Capitol Street. Philip died in 1908 and his son Max took over. The store became the premier men's clothing store in the state but because of changing buying habits finally closed in the early 1980s. The store and the Frankenberger and Kleeman families were very involved in community activities for over 100 years. Many boys will remember the Franco Club organized in 1932 which eventually had over 5,000 members. (258)

Maintenance work on
the big neon sign, 1940s.

Frankenberger's front window, 1949. Lavishly
expensive curved glass in an era before vandals.

Coyle & Richardson preceded the Diamond as Charleston's premier department store from the 1880s up until the 1930s. It was the choice of the well-to-do and survived on into the 1970s. Always dignified Coyle's, in its last years, was almost like stepping back in time. This building at the corner of Lee and Dickinson streets survived as state offices. Photo circa 1975.

Interior of the Coyle and Richardson Department Store on Lee Street in the 1940s.

Ruffner Hotel

A description of the venerable Ruffner Hotel would not be complete without first recalling its predecessor the "Hale House" which occupied the same site as the Ruffner on the northwest corner of Hale and Kanawha (Blvd.) streets from 1871 to 1885.

When Charleston became the capital of West Virginia in 1870, Dr. John P. Hale with a group of local boosters built the capitol building which was then leased for a nominal amount to the state. Dr. Hale was clearly the leader of the group responsible for having the capitol located in Charleston.

Realizing that to accommodate the legislature the small town would need a fine hotel, Dr. Hale built the Hale House which was a handsome four story building with a French roof complete with dormers. One hundred foot square, it contained 100 bedrooms and was billed as the finest in the state.

It is interesting to note that Dr. Hales residence was right across the street on the northeast corner.

The coming and going of the capitol from Charleston to Wheeling and back again in 1885 wrote the destiny of both the Hale House and the later Ruffner Hotel.

The Hale House burned in 1885 making way for a new and finer hotel—The Ruffner—which was owned and operated until about 1900 by A.L. and Meredith Ruffner and the Charleston Hotel Company.

The Ruffner was grand in every way and it was quite an addition to Charleston along with the splendid new Victorian statehouse (1885-1921).

Containing 180 bedrooms, the Ruffner as originally built featuring a spire on one corner of the roof and an elegant portico facing Kanawha Street.

Aside from the capitol, the red brick Ruffner was by far the biggest building in Charleston in the late 19th century and its elegant profile was familiar to generations.

Whether by coincidence or careful scheming, the first bridge across the Kanawha River was built almost at the Ruffner's doorstep in 1891 allowing easy access to the south side and the C&O Railroad depot directly across the river.

At the turn of the century, the Ruffner stood as the city's prestige hotel but naturally as Charleston grew other fine hotels were built—The Kanawha—The Holley, and finally, in 1929, The

Daniel Boone.

Up until its demolition for a parking lot in 1970, the Ruffner never fell into ill repute, and even into the 1950s, its restaurant was noted for fine cuisine.

In January 1946 an historic fire destroyed nearby buildings and almost reached the eight-story Ruffner.

After 1900 the Lilly family owned the hotel and from 1941 until 1963, A.A. Lilly resided in the elegant penthouse which was added circa 1907, when the spire was removed and a floor added. The ground level was the site of the restaurant in later years.

One of the Lilly family recalled that her father raised flowers and even corn in the penthouse garden hothouse.

The list of famous guests is far too long for enumeration but suffice it to say the historic old Ruffner in its 84 years saw Charleston rise from a sleepy little river town to a robust, modern capital city.

1925

Notice the scrip spelled Ruffner with a "B."

-180-

Gen. Jubal A. Early had lived for a short time in the Charleston area prior to the Civil War. He led a famous raid in 1864 with his Confederate troops, threatening for a time the nation's capital. He visited the hotel on Feb. 8, 1890.

BK

The stately old historic Ruffner Hotel met its end by a wrecking ball in 1970 and the site has been a parking lot ever since. Not a fitting end to a grand old building. ㉘

In 1933 the major hotels in Charleston with number of room and rates were: Daniel Boone (200) $2.50; Holly (225) $.75 to $1.50; Kanawha (200) $2.00; Worthy (80) $1.25; and Elk (70) $.75.

1903

WHEN IN CHARLESTON, W. VA., VISIT THE

ST. ALBERT HOTEL

ON EUROPEAN PLAN. ONLY EUROPEAN HOTEL IN THE STATE

Refurnished, Remodeled and Up-to-Date in every respect.

Rooms 75c and up, Cafe open from 6 A. M. to 9 P. M.

Cuisine of Superior Excellence.

FREE BUS TO AND FROM ALL TRAINS

YOURS TRULY,

HARRY E. ROBINSON,

514 TO 520 KANAWHA ST.

HARRY E. ROBINSON, Proprietor
ST. ALBERT HOTEL AND HOTEL ROBINSON.

ST. ALBERT HOTEL.

The old St. Albert hotel on Kanawha Street circa 1917. The hotel was destroyed by fire on March 10, 1932. The site is now occupied by the municipal parking garage next to City Hall.

The Hotel Kanawha opened for business in 1903 as the largest hotel in the state. A fire in 1906 changed its appearance on its upper floor. It was taken over by the Job Corps in the 1960s and is now scheduled to be turned into a first-class luxury hotel. During its heyday it was especially known for its fine food. (289)

Charleston's premier hotel, The Daniel Boone was opened on Feb. 1, 1929 on the site of the 1920s pasteboard capitol. Wehrle B. Geary who developed the Diamond Department Store was the organizer of a community corporation to build the hotel. Its original 251 rooms were increased to 340 in 1936 and 465 in 1949. The hotel, managed for many years by Roger Creel was the social and political center for Charleston and much of West Virginia. Many famous people were guests at the hotel through its four decade history but due to changing lodging trends it was forced to close in the 1980s. The building is now known as 405 Capitol Street. The photo was taken about 1949. JAMES BARTH COLL. (237)

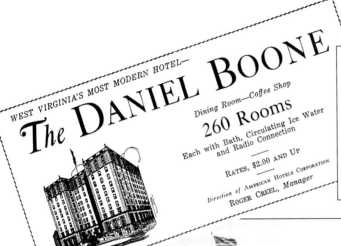

WEST VIRGINIA'S MOST MODERN HOTEL—

The DANIEL BOONE

Dining Room—Coffee Shop

260 Rooms

Each with Bath, Circulating Ice Water and Radio Connection

RATES, $2.00 AND UP

Direction of AMERICAN HOTELS CORPORATION
ROGER CREEL, Manager

SOME OF THE DANIEL BOONE'S FAMOUS GUESTS:

Evangeline Booth	Robert Cummings	President and Mrs.
James Farley	Tyrone Power	John F. Kennedy
Lord Halifax	Bob Hope	Dwight D. Eisenhower
Rear Admiral Felix Stump	Lloyd Nolan	Bette Davis
Herbert Hoover	Jeannette McDonald	Charles Laughton
Harry S. Truman	Sigmund Romberg	Lily Pons
Fay Emerson	Wendell Wilkie	Debbie Reynolds
Victor Borge	Jack Dempsey	Bess Myerson
Walter Brennan	Earl Warren	Nelson Eddy
		Eddie Fisher

and many business and professional people of national prominence.

-184-

1895 photo of employees of Beller's Place, 808 Kanawha Street between Capitol and Hale streets. George Beller is sitting in the middle.

Charleston's favorite watering hole, frequented by doctors, lawyers and workingmen, was Beller's Place. It was owned by Malden native George Beller, who opened his first saloon in the St. Albert Hotel in 1890. The next year he moved to the Kanawha Street location. With the state adopting prohibition in 1914 the saloon business was over until 1933.

Exterior view of Beller's Place, 808 Kanawha Street, circa 1895.

Interior views of Beller's Place when it was in the St. Albert Hotel, circa 1890.

BK

This was the site of the Kanawha Valley Bank from 1892 to 1929 at the corner of Capitol and Kanawha streets. The six-story, 77 office room building was called the Pioneer Building. It was demolished in the 1962 urban renewal project. ㉒⑲

John L Dickinson, president of the Kanawha Valley Bank, turns the first shovelful of dirt for their new building in 1928. Many bank directors were in attendance. The site was occupied by the 1885 state capitol which was destroyed by fire in 1921. Judge Andrew Alexander, representing a Philadelphia buyer, bought the site from the state and resold it to the bank. In 1929 West Virginia's tallest building and major bank opened for business.

The Kanawha Valley Bank building construction on Dec. 12, 1928. Note Christmas trim on the Diamond Depart–ment Store next door. For years it was the tallest building in West Virginia and people came to Charleston just to see it. ⟨220⟩

The Kanawha National Bank on the northeast corner of Capitol and Virginia streets opened in February 1892.

Interior view of the Kanawha Banking & Trust Co. building, 1951.

The Kanawha Banking & Trust Company was incorporated in August 1901. It's first site was at 13 Capitol Street with a staff of five. C.C. Lewis of the Lewis-Hubbard & Co. was elected the first president followed by F.M. Staunton, I.N. Smith, Sr., Harrison B. Smith, N.B. Lewis, I. Noyes Smith, Sr. and I. Noyes Smith, Jr. In June 1903 the bank moved to the old Coyle & Richardson building at the corner of Capitol and Quarrier streets. With the bank's continual expansion it built their new building on Capitol street in September 1918. The bank continued in operation until moving to its new site at the corner of Virginia and Laidley streets in 1984 and merged with United Bank in 1986. The old building has been converted into office and residential space by McCabe-Henley-Durbin LP. (221)

The Bank of Cabin Creek located adjacent to the AEP plant at the mouth of Cabin Creek, 1920s.

Charles Powell Mead founded the Charleston National Bank in 1884 at 614 Front Street (Kanawha Boulevard). George S. Couch was chosen president and after six months a larger building was needed and the bank moved to the Wagner Block, at the southeast corner of Virginia and Capitol streets. It was a national bank, meaning it could issue its own bank notes. Larger quarters were again needed by 1889 and a new building was built on the south side of the old custom house (the old KB&T building). In 1906 this building was opened at seven stories and served the bank until it was demolished in 1969. Through the years the bank merged with the National City Bank, the Merchants and Mechanics Bank and the Citizens National Bank, making Charleston National Bank the largest national bank in the state in 1929. A year later it merged with the Kanawha National Bank. With urban renewal beginning in the 1960s the bank built its present 17-story building in the first block of Capitol Street in 1969, and the former bank building was torn down.

Photo circa 1967.

EVENING DINNERS — ● — EXCELLENT FOUNTAIN

MEET·ME·AT

The Ritz

CLUB
BREAKFAST

"SMART PEOPLE"

SPECIAL
LUNCHES

Just Off Capitol On Quarrier Street

(1939)

The Dog Wagon was not the only little diner in Charleston! Here we see the White House somewhere in downtown. Photo circa 1915. GA

The Strand has been a downtown Charleston institution for many decades on Hale Street. A shiny new Cadillac sits outside. Photo circa 1941.

The Idle Hour Billiards Parlor on Summers Street near Virginia Street. A drive-in bank is now on the site.

Dog Wagon

Charleston's most famous little restaurant the Dog Wagon, was actually built on wheels and opened in 1910 by Clint and Levi Litton. By the time it shut down in 1971, it had moved from Summers Street to Post Office Square on Capitol Street to the corner of Summers and Quarrier streets and finally in 1950 to the Arcade. It became famous for its hamburgers and baked beans. Businessmen and governors frequented the eatery throughout its history and *Gazette* cartoonist Vintroux made it a regular feature with imaginary characters such as a wise-cracking country jake named "Fishook."

John Burdette, center front, remained with the Wagon until closing in 1971. Photo 1920s.

Dedication of the statue at the United Carbon Building in 1941. From left: Rev. Herman Mees Meyer of St. Paul Lutheran Church; Oscar Nelson with daughter, Anna Marie Nelson; architect Walter Martens. Note WCHS radio microphone.

We've "COOKED UP" SOMETHING SPECIAL For YOU Today!

King's Terrace

Special Sunday DINNER

King's Terrace
UNITED CARBON BLDG.

RECOMMENDED BY DUNCAN HINES

We Also Feature A Complete SEAFOOD MENU

PHONE 6-2841

ON BEAUTIFUL KANAWHA RIVER . . . where you can enjoy King's Traditional GOOD FOOD in the air-conditioned Dining Room or on the Patio

1950

At the northwest corner of Broad Street (now Louis Sullivan Way) and Kanawha Boulevard stands the 12-story United Carbon Building. It was built in 1940 by a partnership of T.A. Whelan and T.F. Koblegard of Weston and Oscar Nelson of Charleston. United Carbon was formed in 1916 and in 1925 the properties were combined with 15 other corporations. The company was the largest producer of carbon black in the world and one of the county's largest natural gas producers. Noted Charleston architect, Walter F. Martens designed the building and it stands today as one of the most distinctive and beautiful buildings on Charleston's waterfront.

Valley Bell Dairy was started in the early 1900s by the Lewis family. At first the dairy was located where Memorial Division, CAMC now stands, then it moved to the present site of George Washington High School and in 1918 to Court Street and formed the Lewis Brothers Dairy. In 1922 they took over Tip Top Dairy on Roane Street, and incorporated as the Valley Bell Dairy Co. By 1942 the dairy was a statewide company and had 13 restaurant-type dairy stores. The last of the large family dairies in the state was sold in the 1980s to Borden's Inc.

The VALLEY BELL STORES
INVITE YOU
TO EAT FOR HEALTH'S SAKE

Ice Cream Sodas   Dairy Drinks   Sundaes
                    Sandwiches   Malted Milk

Eat The Dairy Products Way For Better Health

NINE CONVENIENT RETAIL STORES   *Valley Bell* DAIRY CO. INC.   GOOD THINGS TO EAT FOR OLD AND YOUNG

"The Aristocrat of Dairy Products"

One of the fondest, some might say the sweetest, memories of Charleston were the art-deco Valley Bell soda fountains.

Bonham Dairy on Sissonville Road was in business for many years in the county, photo circa 1931.

Now, I've never stood on ceremony when it came to food and drink, I've always made my meals of things that keep me fit and in the "pink." That's why I've a Milk-fed complexion . . . oh, I'm just as wholesome as they come, so everybody drink a toast to Mount Vernon Milk . . . cause it helped me get my man, by gum!

MOUNT *Vernon* DAIRY

800 Pennsylvania Ave.   Phone 2-3108

1950s

Headquarters of the Mt. Vernon Dairy was on Pennsylvania Avenue on Charleston's west side, circa 1964. The site was taken by the Interstate highway. The building was of course designed to resemble George Washington's home, Mount Vernon.

Navy and City
Restaurant.

Is serving the best meals in the city for 25c. Everything new, neat and clean. Ladies and gentlemen cordially invited to try our

25c Dinner

1906

Once you try us you will come again. Short orders served both day and night. Chop-Suey from 8 p. m. to 4 a. m. We serve to white people only.

A. Boan, Prop, 801 Kanawha St

Steward in U. S. Navy for past 20 years

1953

1940

TONY'S GOLD DOME BARBECUE
Open 24 hrs. Daily—Curb & Tray Service

OUR ALL TIME SPECIAL—HOT DOGS	.15
FOOT LONG HOT DOGS	.30
All Orders to Go are 10¢ Extra for Boxes.	

DINNERS

STEAK DINNER	2.00
SEAFOOD DINNER	2.00
OYSTER & SHRIMP DINNER—LARGE	2.00
SMALL	1.50
★ SPECIAL—21 SHRIMP WITH TOASTED BUN	1.20
BAR-B-QUE CHICKEN DINNER	2.00
BAR-B-QUE RIB DINNER	2.00
FRIED CHICKEN LIVER DINNER, WITH FRENCH FRIES & SALAD	2.50
9 INCH PIZZA PIE—PLAIN	1.20
EXTRAS	1.40

SANDWICHES

FRENCH FRIES	.30
★ BIG TONY—3 Slices, Salami Dipped in Our Own Special Sauce, 2 Slices Cheese, Slice of Onion & Pickle all served on a Jumbo Seeded Bun	
CHEESEBURGER	.75
STEAK SANDWICH	.45
BAR-B-QUE—PORK OR BEEF	.75
CHICKEN SANDWICH	.45
HAMBURGER	.75
RIB SANDWICH	.35
BACON, LETTUCE, & TOMATO ON TOAST	.75
HOME MADE, FRESH, ITALIAN HOT SAUSAGE ON ITALIAN BREAD	.45
KING SIZE ROAST BEEF ON ITALIAN BREAD	.60
★ GOLD BOY—DOUBLE DECKER—HAMBURGER & CHEESEBURGER	.75
FISH WITH TARTER SAUCE, LETTUCE & LEMON	.65
MYSTERY SANDWICH—SHAVED HAM, LETTUCE, TOMATO & MAYONNAISE ON LARGE SEEDED BUN	.45
PLAIN SHAVED HAM WITH LETTUCE & MAYONNAISE ON LARGE SEEDED BUN	.65
WESTERN SANDWICH	.55
★ TONY'S SPECIAL—MADE FROM PERSUTTI HAM, MOZZARELLA CHEESE & PEPPERONI WITH LETTUCE & MUSTARD ON ITALIAN BREAD	.65
HOT BOLOGNA	.85
LARGE HOT FRANK—DIPPED IN HOT SAUCE	.50
	.35

DRINKS

Small Fountain Drinks (9 oz.)	.15	
Large Fountain Drinks (16 oz.)	.30	ICE COLD BEER
Thick Milk Shakes, Lg.	.30	Standard & Premium
Vanilla, Choc. & Strawberry, Sm.	.20	

ICE CREAM AND SUNDAES
We Serve Breakfast on Trays

1950s

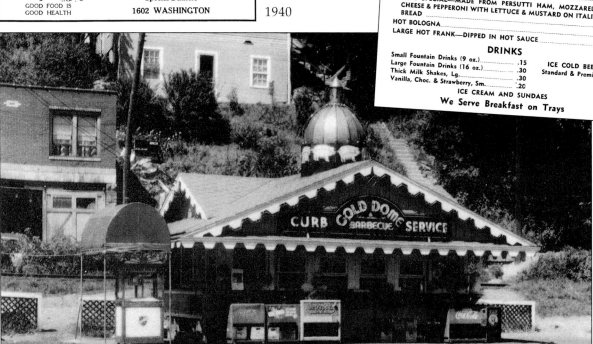

The Gold Dome Drive-Inn at the west end of Kanawha City. ㉙④

A cafe in the segregated Charleston Triangle District, circa 1960.

1947

DINE & DANCE
AT
John Pauley's
Featuring
- SIZZLING STEAKS
- SOUTHERN STYLE FRIED CHICKEN
- SPAGHETTI
  - SALADS
- SANDWICHES

CHICKEN BOXES

- MICHELOB ON TAP

SOUTH RUFFNER
COFFEE SHOPPE
1810 MacCORKLE AVE.

"WHERE REAL FOLK RENDEZVOUS"
HEAR ARLENE and HER SOLOVOX with soothing song and melodies of Today and Yesterday, in our dining rooms 11:00 to 11:30 P. M. and OVER WKNA at 11:15.

EAT IT HERE—OR TAKE IT WITH YOU
Sterling CHICKEN IN THE ROUGH
Is something to "Write Home" about!

½ Fryer
Shoestring Potatoes
Pot o' Honey-Buttered Rolls
$1.25

STERLING
RESTAURANT
NEXT TO DIAMOND ON WASH. ST.
PHONE 3-2243 or 3-6244
WE DELIVER

1953

The Empire Diner was located on Summers Street next to the Virginian Theater. Photo circa 1975.

GOLDEN BROWN, SKILLET FRIED
CHICKEN DINNERS
WE SERVE THE FINEST
SPECIAL LUNCHEON OR DINNER!
FRIED A CRISP, DELICIOUS GOLDEN BROWN—SERVED PIPING HOT WITH COMPLETE MEAL
EMPIRE DINER
194 SUMMERS ST.

1940

Thumms store on
Bigley Avenue,
circa 1910.

Thumms store,
circa 1925.

National Store chain McCrory's was located at
218-20 Capitol Street. This type of store was
popular until the advent of discount stores.
PAUL MARSHALL & ASSOC. COLL.

Lewis Hubbard & Co. was organized in
1896 succeeding Noyes, Hubbard & Co.
and P.H. Noyes & Co. The original building was destroyed by fire on Dec. 27, 1896
and a new one was built in 1898. The
company was the largest wholesaler of
groceries in the area with a side business
selling grain and feed. This photo, circa
1938 shows the main warehouse at the
northwest corner of Morris and Lewis
streets.

State Street (Lee Street) lunch, circa 1920s.
JERRY WATERS COLL.

In the 1920s, stone from the 1885 capitol was used to build the Crystal Laundry Company on Florida Avenue. Photo circa 1950.

Company store of the Red Warrior Coal Company on Cabin Creek, circa early 1900s. Note the coal tipple behind the store.

This 1940s vintage photo shows a typical neighborhood Kroger Store believed to be on Charleston's west side. They were smaller and more numerous since most people had to walk to get groceries.

Lee Street between Capitol and Summers streets, 1958. Charleston had two famous dairies–the Blossom Dairy and the Valley Bell Dairy. They competed vigorously and this Blossom Dairy store was on Lee Street near the Virginian Theatre. It was demolished but fortunately the other Blossom art-deco store still exists on Quarrier Street near Hale Street.

The first mill in the area was a little floating tub mill, built below the mouth of the Elk River at Elk Shoals in 1802. About 1842 a Burr type mill was built on the Kanawha River east of the mouth of the Elk River. About 1894 the mill was converted into a roller mill, one of the first in the state. In 1902 the Charleston Milling and Produce Company was formed with Peter Silman as president. The mill burned in 1913 but was rebuilt the same year at the corner of Morris and Baines streets. This view is from 1911.

1939

1929

One of Charleston's most popular markets was Reeves Food Market, owned by George W. Reeves Sr. on Quarrier Street near Dickinson Street, 1932.

People's Grocery Store at 1513 Washington Street East near Ruffner Avenue served the east end neighborhood from 1929 to 1937. Owner E.B. Hardin is in the doorway, his wife, Ruth is inside with clerk, Armond Ancion. The building later became Peerless Auto Supply.

This photo of J. Sodaro fruit store, located in the 1200 block of Washington Street East was taken in 1908.
VINCE SODARO COLL.

There was a produce stand of some type for decades on the Virginia Street side of the Arcade. The most recent was Corey Brothers. This view is from 1905. Notice the window poster for Buffalo Bill's "Wild West" show.
VINCE SODARO COLL.

1903

SIMPSON & STEELE,
UNDERTAKERS AND EMBALMERS

FINE
FUNERAL
FURNISHINGS.

Both Phones No. 71.

CALLS
Answered Promptly
Day and Night.

BRANCH OFFICE:
Furniture and Undertaking,
Montgomery, West Virginia.

BEST LINE OF CARRIAGES IN THE CITY.

CHARLESTON, W. VA.

VIRGINIA STREET,

George T. Barlow opened his undertaking parlor in the Eagen Building on lower Front Street opposite the Court House in 1875. Shown here is "Uncle" Billy Clarkson apparently a hearse driver for John Barlow.

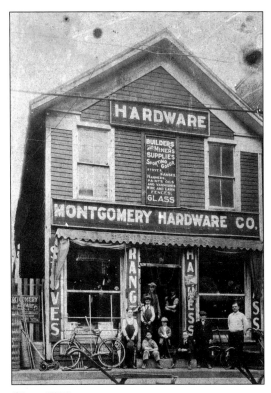

Circa 1920.

A familiar sight to all older Charlestonians was Joe Popp's plaster horse that stood in front of his shop. It is believed to still exist out of state. The store was located at 613-15 Kanawha Street. ㉑③

1928

Offices and salesroom of Butler Chevrolet Co. at 1016 Lee Street, 1928. This building later became the Midelburg Auditorium, and later housed WCHS radio. In 1958 Chuck Berry of rock and roll fame did his signature shuffle across the stage. Post office complex is now on the site.

Employees of Butler Chevrolet, 1932.

Patrick Street
Farmers Market,
1958. Washington
Street is in
distance.

Corner of Truslow and
Washington streets, 1910.

An early 1900s view of the
Cabin Creek Land Co. store.
A soft drink factory was
connected to the main
building. Barrels and crates
can be seen on the porch.

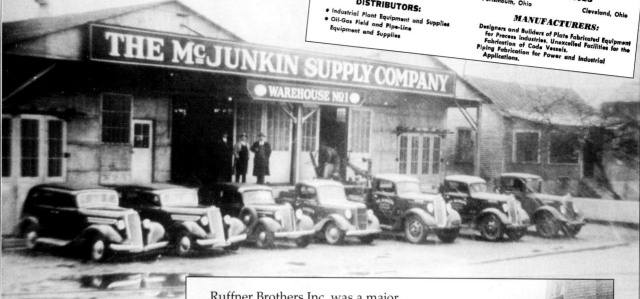

A 1935 photo of the McJunkin Supply Co. warehouse No. 1 on Hansford Street. The company has been a major supplier to the oil and gas industry for many years.

Corner of Quarrier and Dickinson streets, 1912. This was the site for the first Kroger store in Charleston.

Ruffner Brothers Inc. was a major wholesaler of grocery items in the area for many years in the 20th century. This early 1900s view was taken at the Kanawha & Michigan freight depot. SWV #1634.12

1904

Interior of the Frasier Motor Company on Hale Street, 1921. The company handled Hupmobile autos.
R.P.BARE COLL.

1914

Packard

TRADE-INS

Come to you direct from the original owners and represent the best obtainable on the Used Car market today.

39 PACKARD 120 TOURING SE-DAN. This car comes to you direct from original owner. We sold it new and know every service mile. Has very low mileage, cost over $1,600. Beautiful Black finish. White side-wall tires like new. Packard heater and radio. Seat covers put on when car was bought. Many trouble free miles to you. Price ... **$795**

38 PACKARD 130 SEDAN. This car has original Robin Egg Blue in wonderful condition, low mileage. Heater, Radio. Just traded in on 41 model. Priced to sell **$545**

38 PONTIAC SILVER STREAK COUPE. Heater. Radio. All good tires. Upholstery like new. Motor perfect. Has J. B. Ruby's famous guarantee. Reduced from $495 to **$425**

37 LINCOLN ZEPHYR 4-DOOR SE-DAN. This is a local owned car from an owner who has two cars Chauffeur driven. Priced **$395**

39 STUDEBAKER COMMANDER SEDAN. Black finish has original tires. Locally owned by a lady. Has had perfect care and will give new car service **$575**

38 PACKARD SIX SEDAN. Beauti-ful Black finish like new. Heat-er, Radio. All new tires. Local owner. One of the finest Packard trade-ins on our lot. Price **$545**

37 HUDSON-TERRAPLANE COUPE. This is a Packard trade-in that has gone through our shop. Has fa-mous Hudson motor. Built for speed and low mileage gasoline consump-tion. We trade and price to sell **$345**

37 CHEVROLET 4-DOOR DELUXE SEDAN. Heater. Radio **$425**

36 CHEVROLET MASTER DELUXE TUDOR **$275**

36 FORD TUDOR All new tires **$265**

35 OLDSMOBILE TUDOR **$285**

This is a few of the many PACKARD TRADE-INS we have for your approval.

Buy your PACKARD from your PACKARD DEALER and save the difference.

J. B. RUBY MOTOR CO.

Cor. Virginia at Tennessee Ave.   Phone 21-741

Cheapest Transpor-tation on Earth---

HENRY FORD'S AUTOMOBILE

Touring Car $360
Roadster - $345

THE WHOLE FAMILY CAN RIDE!
BUY A FORD NOW.

TRIPLE-STATE ELECTRIC CO.
16 McFarland St.   Phone 717.

1940

Southeast corner of Washington and Laidley streets.

The garage later
became the
Midelburg
Auditorium.

1948

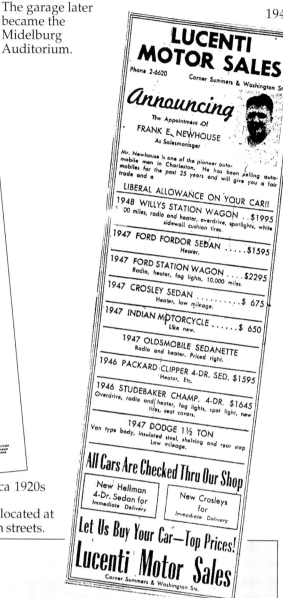
Lucenti Motor Sales and tire shop was located at
the corner of Summers and Washington streets.

The Way It Was
20th Century

We can only wonder what became of these youngsters playing nearly a century ago next to the old federal building where Quarrier Street now connects Capitol and Summers streets. Perhaps one of them became a millionaire or a famous doctor and some may not have come home from World War One - but we do know they were happy and full of life in this circa 1907 photo.

264

THE ASSASSINATION OF PRESIDENT WILLIAM MCKINLEY

The pistol, bullets and handkerchief that Leon Czolgosz used to shoot President McKinley at the Pan American Exposition in Buffalo, New York on Sept. 6, 1901. McKinley died on Sept. 14. BUFFALO & ERIE COUNTY HISTORIAL SOCIETY (420)

ASSASSIN CZOLGOSZ

Said to Have Been Married in Charleston

CHARLESTON, W.Va., Sept. 11. - It seems that Czolgosz, the anarchist who attempted the life of the President, was at one time a resident of Kanawha City, where he was employed in a nail mill as a wire drawer.

It is learned that such was the fact, and upon some inquiry at the mill it was learned that something more than a year ago a man giving his name as Czolgosz, and his home as Cleveland, with the same street address as the anarchist, was employed there as a wire drawer; that upon one occasion Chief of Police Starks and Constable Smith went up there and arrested him and brought him down here in connection with some trouble with a woman.

Although the man gave his name as Czolgosz when he first went there he afterwards became known as Neiman, and when asked about it said his stepmother's name had been Neiman, and that he was very small when his father married her he was known both as Neiman and Czolgosz.

When the matter was mentioned to other members of the staff it was remembered that a quick-shot marriage had been performed by Father Stenger about the time spoken of, in which the high contracting parties were from Ohio.

Constable Howard Smith was out of the city today and could not be interviewed about the case, but ex-Chief Starks, who is now an officer on the present force, was found on his beat. He said:

"Early in the spring, about a year and a half ago, a few months before the death of Mayor Smith, I was coming up from the poor farm one afternoon on the K and M., when a lady passenger on the train noticing my uniform, came to me and told me her troubles. She said she was from Cleveland and was coming here after her lover, who worked in a nail mill near. She gave a good reason why the young man should marry her and do it right away. I took charge of the girl and placed her in a boarding house on State Street. Then Constable Howard Smith and I went up to the man. We brought him down and he readily consented to a marriage and a license was issued by Deputy County Clerk Pres Smith along about dark. We had to send for Smith, as the office had been closed. The couple wanted to be married by a Catholic priest, but the late Rev. Father Stenger refused to perform the ceremony without communicating with the girl's parish priest in Cleveland. Accordingly, Father Stenger wired to Cleveland, and receiving a favorable response, he married the couple at the parish house. Some time after that I saw the woman in the jewelry store of the late Mayor Smith. She was buying a clock, said she was keeping house and was happy. I don't think I ever saw either of them again."

At the County Clerk's office, Deputy Pres Smith remembered the peculiar circumstances of the wedding, and that the girl was locked up for safe keeping while the parley was going on with the priest. Of course, he remembered nothing of the names, except that they were foreign. Looking through the marriage records of the spring referred to, the name Czolgosz could not be found, but a record of what seems to be the identical couple referred to was readily found. On the date of January 14, 1900, a license was issued to Frank Nauman and Emma Wisiemki. Rev. Father Joseph Stenger was given as the officiating minister, and Constable Howard Smith as the witness to the license. This notation seems to make it certain that this is the couple referred to, whether Nauman is the same man as the assassin or not. He gave his birthplace as Buffalo, and his residence at that time as Kanawha county; she gave her birthplace as Germany and her home as Cleveland. He gave his age as 23 and she hers as 17.

The name understood by the Clerk was Nauman, but that given at the mill was Neiman, and that and other circumstances point to the unwilling benedict as being identical with the man who attempted the President's life.

FROM A PARKERSBURG NEWSPAPER, SEPT. 12, 1901

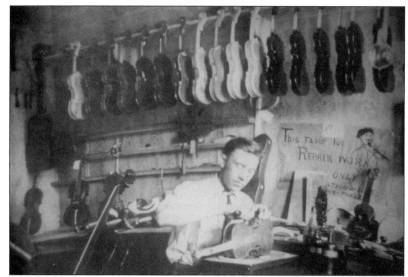

In the early 1900s a man named Mr. Perkins got the idea that with all the wood in the state, it would be a good place to make violins on an assembly-line basis. He hired a violin maker from Cincinnati and by the time the factory closed about 1914, hundreds of violins had been produced at about $150 each. It is thought that the factory was located on the West Side on West Washington Street. SWV HARRY BRAWLEY COLL.

Frozen Paint Creek, circa 1910. These ladies are standing on the ice near the C&O Railroad bridge. One is believed to be Eleanor Bailey. The Bailey family lived for many years in the historic brick Hansford house nearby. In the summertime this place was a favorite swimming hole for local youngsters.

Below: Some dapper Charleston gents pose in front of the I.O.O.F. building at the corner of State (Lee) and Capitol streets, circa 1910. The building is still standing. SAM FLOURNOY COLL.

Below right: A group of young men standing on a rock outcropping overlooking the C&O depot. Future Charleston mayor John Shanklin is the second man from the right. GA

One of Charleston's most prominent business-men of the late 1800s and early 1900s was Frank Woodman, whose beautiful Victorian home, pictured here, still remains at 1210 Kanawha Boulevard. Woodman, who was born in Wisconsin in 1846, studied and worked in civil engineering in the United States and Europe and moved to Charleston in 1875. He immediately invested in many area businesses including the Burlew Opera House, Vulcan Iron Works, Kanawha Woolen Mills and the Kanawha Brick Company. In 1884 he married Nannie Cotton, the daughter of well-known Charleston physician, Dr. John Cotton. They had two children, Ashton Fitzhugh and Charlotte. Woodman would be involved in politics and many civic endeavors until his death in 1918. His home was built in 1891 and sold to the United Mine Workers in 1950. In 1976 the house was purchased by the Old Colony Co. (Better Homes & Gardens Realty) and remains their headquarters today. Some remodelling has been done to the front porch. The carriage house on the northeast corner of the property has been renovated to be used as a rental home. The children in the front are Van and Dorothy Donnally. The grave of Charles Clendenin is in front of the house next to the boulevard. Photo circa 1900. NORMAN FITZHUGH COLL.

Old Colony Company 2001.

This World War One tank was brought to Charleston for a war bond parade in 1918.

At 4 P.M. attended a meeting of the finance Committee of the Law & Order League. They made me
chairman & directed me to prepare a circular to be
sent to persons from whom financial assistance is
hoped for, asking for subscriptions. We hope to find
10 people who will give $100. each.

SATURDAY 5

Temp 40° – 50°

Mr. EA Barnes & I, for the Law & Order
League went around to get subscriptions to
defray the Expenses of the League – We got the
following   Dr Prichard $100. Houghton Robson 100.
Ruffner Bros. 100.   Geo Price 100.   F. Woodman 100
EA Barnes 100.   F.W.Abney 50   J.E.Dana 50.   John Q
Dickinson 50.   Chas Sterrett 50.   J.D.Barnes 50.   Jas M.
Payne 50.   Mr. Jas F Brown did not subscribe.
and he is the only other one we saw.
      Law & Order League met at 4 P.M. and voted to offer
rewards for information leading to conviction of any
one for buying or selling votes or abetting same.

54° – 52   THURSDAY, APRIL 3, 1902

Notice rec'd this morning of my appointment as a member
of a secret sub-committee of the Law & Order League,
composed of
      E.A. Barnes, J. M. Payne, Geo. E. Price, Willis
Landon, & F. Woodman.
      Committee met at Mr. Payne's office at 8 P.M. Decided to
to prosecute some people for illegal voting, and to seek
the assistance of John B. Floyd at not over $50. as a kind of
general manager.
      —

Mr. Geo S Price & I have today received into our
custody $1000. contributed by various people
incl. ourselves, for the purpose of stopping the
usual corrupt practices, at the coming
Election. All the banks were successively
asked to hold the money & all declined.

Entries from Frank Woodman's diary in April 1902 discussing the Law and Order League formed to combat the corrupt practice of vote buying in local elections.

A rare Charleston newspaper that did not last long. The official armistice was signed on Nov. 11, 1918, in France.

THE CHARLESTON LEADER

HUNS QUIT!

ARMISTICE SIGNED, FIGHTING STOPS
GERMANY COMES OVER UNDER WHITE FLAG

Dr. Timothy L. Barber (in uniform under sign) formed an ambulance corps of volunteers from Charleston and other parts of West Virginia. The group was known as the 313th Ambulance Corps attached to the 79th Division in France, photo circa 1917 in front of Barber Sanitorium and Hospital at 364 Virginia Street. This site eventually became the Kanawha Valley Hospital. Dr. Barber died on Oct. 10, 1918, as a result of an explosion in a bomb crater that had been mined by the Germans. (222)

This Red Cross building on the right was constructed during World War One at the city levee to house relief workers. The building was a long frame structure, shingled on the outside, built by volunteer tradesmen. It was used as a recreation center for servicemen and later as a hospital during the flu epidemic, a library, headquarters of the Girl Scouts, an army recruiting station and as the John Brawley Post of the American Legion. Mike Kelleher is standing next to an unknown lady believed to be a Salvation Army volunteer.

K.K.K.

Memorial Services, Spring Hill Cemetery, Friday Night, May 27th, 8:00 P. M.

Music by Klan Band.
Singing by Klan Quartette.
Memorial Address by a Prominent Minister of the State.

All Klansmen, Klanswomen, Krusaders, Junior Klansmen and Tri-K's are urged to take part in this ceremony. Report at headquarters, 7:30 P. M. with robes. **PUBLIC INVITED**

Kanawha County was not immune to the popularity of the Ku Klux Klan in the 1920s. This service took place at Spring Hill Cemetery in 1927.

Rock crusher at Pinch, circa 1918. ED O'DELL COLL.

Judaism has a rich history in Charleston and a good deal of the area's prosperity can be attributed to Jewish families such as the Frankenbergers, Midelburgs and others. This Jewish family proudly poses on the front porch of their home in Charleston in their best finery, circa 1910.

A huge crowd on Hale Street at the *Charleston Gazette* office awaits the outcome of the second Jack Dempsey - Gene Tunney prize fight on Sept. 22, 1927. The fight was climaxed by the famous long count. Dempsey knocked Tunney down in the seventh round, but he did not go to a neutral corner immediately, so the referee delayed starting the count over Tunney. Tunney rose at the count of 9, but it was estimated that this was equivalent to a count of 14. Tunney went on to win the fight.

THE DEMPSEY—TUNNEY FIGHT, SEPTEMBER 27, 1527

The present West Virginia State College opened in 1892 as the West Virginia Colored Institute. By the 1920s when these photos were taken at the Institute depot, the name had been changed to the West Virginia Collegiate Institute (changed in 1915). In 1929 the name was changed to West Virginia State College.

The first city delivery of mail in St. Albans occurred on Sept. 11, 1928, apparently the date of this photo. The post office was located on C Street and 6th Avenue at the time. ST. ALBANS HISTORICAL SOCIETY

Nina Hamrick of St. Albans with her collection of carnival kewpie dolls in the late 1920s. She died young of tuberculosis and is buried in Teays Hill Cemetery in St. Albans.

Making molasses on the Simm's property in 1920 at the location of the Central Elementary School on Kanawha Terrace. J.W. WILLIAMS COLL.

A roving photographer traveled from town to town taking pictures of children in this miniature wagon in 1927. We can only wonder how much he charged, but a proud mother would be happy to have this memory on film. TH

Needless to say this little fellows' mom and dad were pretty well off to afford this pony cart for junior - complete with a groom to lead the way. This photo circa 1900 somewhere in the then prestigious East End of Charleston. GA

Not every little boy had a toy horse complete with wheels to bring him dreams of riding the purple sage chasing the bad men. This timeless photo, circa 1902, of Alexander Quarrier, 1901-1950, (Lucy's brother) wipes away a century and we can almost hear him shouting - Giddyup Boy, Giddyup! Little knowing what life had in store or that he would die at the tender age of 49. GA

Jimmie Lucenti and his son in Kanawha City just after World War Two. The bridge ramp is in the distance. JOHNNIE LUCENTI COLL.

The Richardsons (he just retired from the New York Central Railroad) are leaving on a train trip to California in 1939. The NYC was the former Kanawha & Michigan Railroad. Taken at the old depot at the north end of Broad Street.

A group of West Virginia State College students in their party attire for the 1937 prom. WEST VIRGINIA STATE COLLEGE COLL.

Some type of promotion for an automobile testing device which was broadcast on WCHS radio, circa 1930s.

In a local World War Two scrap drive, German relics from World War One were donated to be "sent back to Hitler." Yes, that's a real machine gun the boy's holding.

East End city limits of Charleston in January 1939. This photo was taken by famous Depression-era photographer, Arthur Rothstein. One of thousands of photos taken around the country for the Farm Security Administration. LIBRARY OF CONGRESS #26789-D

Nothing like a new car. Elizabeth Quarrier poses with her 1924 Jordan. GA

Chevrolet dealers from West Virginia, Ohio and Kentucky converged on Kanawha County Club in the 1930s for a regional meeting. They all had numbered arm bands, white shirts and ties. One wonders how many cars they were selling in the height of the Depression?

Some of the luckiest kids in the world in 1945. The war was over and they never were in any danger like children in Europe and Asia. Like most boys of the time however, they liked to play army. Johnnie Andre holds the Kerry Drake comic, Dickie Andre has the helmet and rifle and Larry Field sits in the middle front, at the Andre home, 311 Duffy Street. RAA

Eagle Scout ceremony for Sam C. Hill III, Troop 5, First Presbyterian Church. (1) Gene Stump, (2) Echols Hansbarger, (3) John Hover, Scoutmaster, (4) Sam Hill, (5) Mrs. Sam Hill, (6) Sam Hill III and (7) William Woodroe, Buckskin Council President in 1947. FIRST PRESBYTERIAN CHURCH COLL.

Third annual banquet of the Ohio Valley Zionist Region at the Daniel Boone Hotel, June 15, 1941. How many of these men would eventually be on the front lines fighting Hitler's troops?

Much is said about recycling these days but it is nothing new. A familiar sight 50 years ago was the roving junkmen who patrolled the alleys of downtown Charleston picking up anything they could sell at Silverstein's scrap yard at the railroad end of Summers Street. They gathered mostly cardboard. Incredibly they pulled their small homemade wagons by hand, usually fitted with old auto tires. There was very little welfare in those days and this was a means to get by. Hard to believe that men were almost reduced to "beasts of burden." DED

President Harry Truman is seen here helping celebrate the 100th anniversary of the state of West Virginia in 1963. He spoke on the riverside capitol steps and is also shown getting out of his limosine. President Truman was no stranger to Charleston having attended the inauguration of Gov. Matthew M. Neely in 1940 and on Oct. 1, 1948, while running for president.

The Jean Sirk Dancers performed at the "March of Dimes Revue" in 1955 at the Municipal Auditorium. Also performing were area vocalists Floyd Ellis, Clyde Hager, Louis Husson and Louis Haddad. From left to right: Reva White, Patty McMains, Barbara Ramsey, Martha Robinson, Barbara Ziegler, Bonnie Johnson, Carolyn Wilson and Joan Wheeler. CN

Children at the Kiwanis Club Boys' Farm in 1955 watching a turtle race. Area kids could spend two weeks there in the summer, paid for by area Kiwanis clubs. CN

Camp Galahad was opened in 1956 near Pinch as the new outdoor center for the county's handicapped children. CN

The Beni Kedem Shrine Circus brought sick children to view the show at the Municipal Auditorium in 1961. Note the Capitol Bus Lines. DED

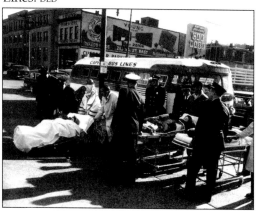

Election night, 1956 at WCHS radio studios. Well-known broad-caster and historian Harry Brawley is on the left, Ross Edwards on the right. His brother was Cliff Edwards, the voice of Walt Disney Studios' cartoon character, Jiminy Cricket. WILLIAM KELLEY COLL.

Dick Reid, one of the area's early TV personalities on WCHS-TV, 1956. The Lucky 8 Ranch ran from 1954-56, sponsored by Valley Bell dairy.

Neil Boggs, well-known Charleston TV news reporter in the 1950s.

August 26, 1955

Hollywood actress, Jayne Mansfield in front of Charleston's city hall. She was brought to town by Fred Haddad to help open a new Heck's Store on MacCorkle Avenue between South Charleston and St. Albans.

Photographer Bill Kelley gets an autograph from Pat Boone who's plane landed at Kanawha Airport with mechanical trouble, 1960s.

Gov. W.W. Barron, Congressman John Slack and Sec. of Defense Cyrus Vance (from Clarksburg) visiting the F.M.C. plant in South Charleston, early 1960s.

On June 20, 1963, West Virginia's centennial year, President John F. Kennedy spoke from the State Capitol steps during a downpour. Many dignitaries were in attendance including from left: ex-Governors Okey L. Patterson and Homer Holt. Native son Col. Charles "Chuck" Yeager, in uniform, was also in attendance. CN

How many state residents can remember the long wait for automobile license plates at the Department of Motor Vehicles? This line stretched clear around the building, circa 1961. Top photo on Duffy Street. CN

KANAWHA SCHOOLS MAKE IT WORK
County Integration Quiet

Marchers protested the urban renewal and interstate projects that were forcing them from their homes in this July 11, 1969 photo. Rev. Moses Newsome (left center in suit) led the march through downtown Charleston. CN

More than 57,000 boys and girls marched into classrooms today and, seemingly unaware of their parts, wrote an epochal chapter in Kanawha County school history.

The county has about 3,200 Negro students and 700 or 800 of them today were integrated into what previously had been white schools.

Reactions from administrators, teachers and children on mingling of students were the same.

Kanawha County's first day of integration went without trouble. First, second and seventh grade students attended mixed classes today. Next year all grades are expected to be integrated.

A small group of Negro seventh grade students failed to enroll in their new junior high school, but their absence was attributed to timidity and shyness.

One principal said he thought he might find one or two sets of parents objecting to a dance class.

Some Negroes are teaching in what previously were all-white schools and principals at the schools reported everything was going without a hitch.

From a Charleston newspaper Sept. 7, 1955

The old Kanawha County jail in 1960. It was demolished in the 1990s when the new justice building was opened on Virginia Street.

Charleston, like many other cities in the nation, experienced protests against the Vietnam War. This march in downtown Charleston in front of the library took place on Oct. 15, 1969.

The Charleston High School Band and Majorettes performed at the dedication of the new West Virginia Turnpike at the Kanawha City entrance, Nov. 8, 1954. The glass plant stacks are in the background. The new toll road reduced the time to travel between Charleston, Beckley and Bluefield.

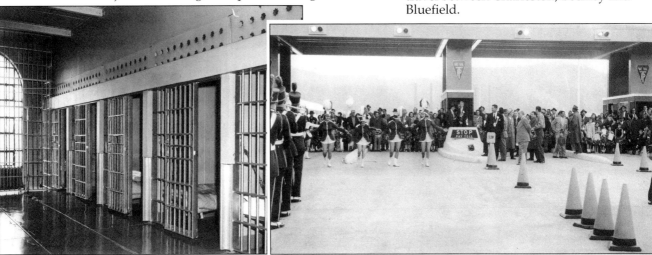

The YMCA was established in Charleston in 1904. Many prominent valley businessmen funded the organization. Henry Gassaway Davis donated a parcel of land at the corner of Lee and Capitol streets, known as the Fontaine property in 1906. The long-standing YMCA building was opened in 1908 and torn down in 1981. Davis' statue remains today in Davis Square. The YWCA was organized in 1912 by five local women. The present facility on Quarrier Street was opened in 1923.

Modern 2001 view of Davis Square with the statue of Henry Gassaway Davis.

The intersection of Capitol and Quarrier streets in 1972 waiting for the start of the annual Christmas parade.
CN

The next four pages are Bollinger photos taken in 1936 for a presentation of the blight in Charleston. This led to the building of "Washington Manor," a WPA project.

Washington Street near Elk River.

702 Court Street.

104 Slack Street.

This old building was on the riverbank side of Kanawha Street at Truslow Street and was later removed for boulevard construction.

A once fine house in the Triangle District.

This ramshackle tenement on Clendenin Street is an example of what the W.P.A./ Washington Manor project replaced.

These mischievous kids followed the photographer through several photos. They have waited over 60 years to be immortalized in history but their precociousness finally succeeded, 107 Clendenin Street.

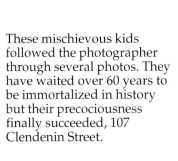

An old woolen mill at the corner of Virginia and Clendenin streets.

An outdoor beer garden in the Triangle District.

Present site of the Charleston Civic Center.

Houses and store on
Court Street next to
the railroad.

This site is now occu-
pied by the Sears
Monument Co. store at
the corner of Virginia
and Clendenin streets.

Gilbert Avenue
from Estill Street,
Triangle District.

Photos on these two pages from Emil Varney Collection All these buildings were demolished in 1963.

Urban renewal in downtown Charleston, 1962, looking west on Virginia Street at Capitol Street.

Looking south on Summers Street from the Kanawha Hotel.

STORES EVERYWHERE   FIT GUARANTEED

LET

A. S. WOOLEN US MILLS COMPANY

TAILOR YOUR CLOTHES

An Opportunity Like This   Extra Pair of $6.00   FREE   WITH SUIT TO $15.
Seldom Comes Your Way   Pants to Order   YOUR ORDER
                                   TO ORDER

31 Capitol Street Corner Va. Street, CHARLESTON, W. VA.

Looking south on Capitol Street toward the boulevard. The Union Building is in the background - this entire block is now occupied by Bank One. This scene is familiar to author Stan Cohen as his father owned a store in this block, 1943-1960.

This block of businesses bounded by Kanawha Boulevard, Virginia, Laidley and Court streets date from the 1870s. Looking south on Summers Street at Virginia Street.

Looking east on Kanawha Boulevard at Laidley Street. Levin Brothers Department is on the extreme left.

Looking east on Kanawha Boulevard at Summers Street intersection, (far left).

These two views show the house known as Henry Bradley's "Noah's Ark." He was an itinerant Black man known for his high "plug hat" and bony horse hitched to an old-style, high buck board buggy. His "ark" full of a variety of supposedly salable junk was located on East Virginia Street. The city condemned the property in about 1905 and it took considerable doing to get Henry out of the house, after which the city burned it.

This area of coal miner's houses at Ronda on Cabin Creek was taken out for construction of the West Virginia Turnpike in 1953.

Phillips Drive-Inn was a popular "hangout" for high schoolers in the 1950s. Shown here is the 1957 Stonewall Jackson High School majorette corps sitting on a Cadillac convertible at the Kanawha City location. One of Phillips' specialities was a variety of hot dog called a "French Frank."

Heavy snow and harsh winter conditions are unusual for this part of West Virginia but on Jan. 19, 1978, snow began to fall and by the 21st there were 24 inches on the ground and a broken record for the most accumulation in a 24-hour period. The airport, schools and most businesses were closed for several days. This scene was taken on Lee Street. The deepest snowfall in Charleston however was the great Thanksgiving storm of 1950 when 25 inches accumulated over a five-day period. It was called the worst snowstorm in the state's history. CN

Charleston's first federal building was constructed in 1884 on the present site of the Kanawha County Library. At the time, the city had about 5,000 residents. Prior to 1884 the post office was first housed in the Hale House and later moved to a storeroom in a building at the corner of Summers and Kanawha streets. This new building served for 26 years. The second building (now the library) was opened in 1911. From about 1806 until Sept. 13, 1879, the post office's official name was Kanawha Court House, Virginia and then West Virginia.

The old post office/custom house, constructed in 1884 was demolished in 1910 to make way for the new federal building. The Kanawha County Public Library now occupies the building. The Kanawha Hotel can be seen behind the mostly demolished building with the Charleston National Bank building on the extreme right. At this time Quarrier Street ended at Capitol Street. At right, same scene today. GA (344)

A 1938 view of the classic revival style Federal Building on Capitol Street. The Kanawha County Library moved here in 1966. Through the years this building has provided a platform for many political rallys and patriotic celebrations. At left is the front of the old federal building today. ③45

Hatted ladies viewing the laying of the new federal building cornerstone on April 3, 1911.

President Herbert Hoover giving a speech in 1932 at Laidley Field during his bid for re-election. He was beaten in the election by Franklin D. Roosevelt. (298)

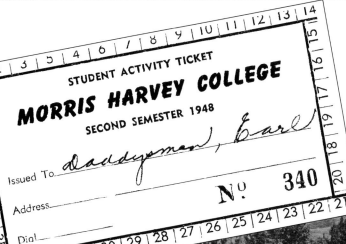

Morris Harvey College

Morris Harvey College showing the temporary buildings put up after the war for classrooms and dorms.

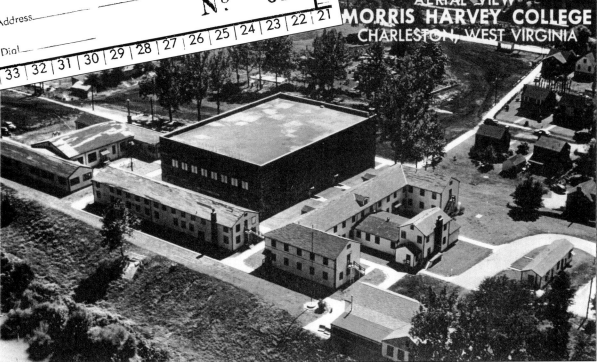

Morris Harvey College was founded in 1888 as Barboursville Seminary. Maintaining a school without regular funds was a hard task, so the citizens of Barboursville convinced the West Virginia Conference of the Methodist Episcopal Church, South, in making it a denominational college. In 1889 it became a Methodist school known as Barboursville College. In 1901, the name was changed to Morris Harvey College in honor of Morris Harvey of Fayetteville. In 1919 it became a junior college and achieved senior college status in 1921. The school was moved in 1935 to the old capitol annex buiding but after World War Two, the building was inadequate and a site was purchased in South Ruffner for a permanent campus. Former army barracks were brought by river barge to the South Ruffner location in 1947 for use as temporary structures until permanent buildings were constructed. The campus has expanded through the years and is now known as the University of Charleston. CN

Commencement day at Morris Harvey College, which in 1946 was housed in the old capitol annex (public library).

1925

Only known photo of the back of the first Mercer School from Lee Street. This later became the site of the last Charleston High School building opened in 1926. GA ⟨308⟩

Mercer Student.

VOLUME I. NUMBER 5.   CHARLESTON, W. VA., MARCH, 1896.   30 CTS. PER YEAR. 5 CTS. PER COPY.

Poe at College.

It is with no little tinge of pride—pardonable pride—that the University of Virginia reckons, among her numerous renowned offsprings, the illustrious Poe. However he may be regarded by others, erring, or reckless or profligate, he is dear beyond measure to her. As do all mothers, she loves her wayward son none the less because he was wayward. Fondly, however, as the memory of Poe is cherished by his proud parent, few traditions concerning him linger any more about the University. Nevertheless, enough of the facts relative to his habits and deportment during his college days are preserved to throw much light upon his inclinations and character during that early portion of his career.

Poe attended the University of Virginia during the session that began February 1, 1826, and terminated December 15, of the same year. The University had been opened to students the previous year, so that this was the second session in its history. He matriculated February 14, being at the time a little over seventeen years of age. The original of his entry upon the matriculation book is not preserved, the records having been later recopied. He entered the school of Ancient and Modern Languages, attending lectures in Greek, Latin. Spanish, French and Italian.

The majority of Poe's biographers, ill-informed as to the facts of his college life, assert that, even in those days, he continually indulged in the most shameful debaucheries; that already he was a drunkard, a libertine, and a profligate; that he was reckless and careless in his studies, and that it was only his natural ability which enabled him to maintain a fair scholarship in his classes; and that but for his numerous vices, which at length caused his expulsion from the University, he would have graduated with high honors. These statements, with few exceptions, are glaringly false. As a matter of fact, Poe was never expelled from the University. He remained as a student in good standing throughout the entire session. His passion for gambling, it is true, had already displayed itself. But as to the other accusations, we will endeavor, in the

1896

Swamp College Times.

VOL. 1. ST. ALBANS, W. VA., FRIDAY, NOVEMBER 3, 1899. No. 2

Price 20c per year.

Price of this paper is 20c per year.

Mr. Harry Kerns is back to school again.

Miss Abbie Meadows has started to school.

Prof. G. W. Leonard was here Saturday.

The goal poles were raised on Sat. Oct. 14, 1899.

Thomas Davison was in Charleston, Saturday.

The German class is now divided into three parts.

We need some blackboard erasers for the 4th room.

Mr. Harry Crawford has quit school and gone to work.

We would like to have items from all the schools in Kanawha Co.

Miss Willie Sams, of Prof. Mitchell's room, is very low with fever.

The Swamp College football team played a practice game Saturday.

The colored school is flourishing under the management of Mr. Wm. Preston.

Prof. F. A. Mitchell, of Swamp College was in Charleston, Saturday.

Master Lovell Meadows is improving slowly from typhoid fever.

We would like to have a correspondent at the Warth school house.

Hon. W. T. Barbe was well pleased with his visit here so report says,

Miss Eva Samms is home on account of the serious illness of her sister, Willie.

Prof. B. H. White, of Fairview Academy, was at Pt. Creek, Thursday and Friday.

The new history chart is quite an improvement on 'the old way of teaching history.

We are glad to see the lumber hauled to the new school house yard as it is a good sign.

The new green blinds in the school room are quite an improvement, both inside and out.

The Morgantown University has an attendance of 850 scholars now and is expecting over 1000 of which 26 are from Kanawha county.

The Swamp College was a humorous nickname for a St. Albans school that was located on wetland where mud was not unusual, 1899. BK

This school is thought to have been located near Corridor G. There were 53 students and three graduates. Graduation was in March so the students could do their spring farming chores. Phil Conley, long-time editor of *West Virginia Review* magazine, was the teacher. BK

All the Charleston public school teachers on the steps of the old Union School on State Street (Lee Street) in 1906. Superintendent George Laidley is marked with the white X. (302)

George S. Laidley (1855-1938) was superintendent of city schools for 42 years from 1878 to 1922, except for the years 1881-1883. Laidley Field is named for him. His contributions to the Kanawha County school system were so profound that he remains without peer 63 years after his death. Photo circa 1910. (304)

PROMOTION CARD
Charleston Public Schools.

This is to Certify,

That *Marcelline Potterfield*

Has passed a satisfactory examination, receiving *94* per cent. and is promoted to *3rd* Grade; 80 per cent. being requisite for promotion.

Geo. S. Laidley Supt.

CHARLESTON, W. VA. *May 27,* 189_

Tiskelwah Grade School children who were members of the Rainbow Club in 1915. The school was located on Charleston's West Side and is soon to be converted into a community center.

Charleston Business College moved to the Morrison Building on Capitol Street in 1925. This building eventually became the home of the Rialto Theatre.

Charleston Business College

Visit us in our new home

For comfort, convenience and attractiveness our new college home will be a revelation to you.

At home to friends, patrons and former students after August 24.

COURSES: Bookkeeping, Shorthand, Typewriting, Secretarial, Office Training, Higher Accountancy.

Fall Term September 1–8

E. C. STOTTS and A. H. DANGERFIELD
Owners and Managers

Morrison Bldg., Quarrier Street.   Phone 4833

1926.

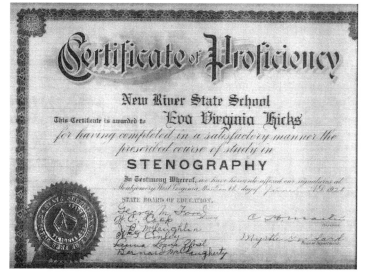

Certificate of Proficiency

New River State School

This Certificate is awarded to *Eva Virginia Hicks*

for having completed in a satisfactory manner the prescribed course of study in

STENOGRAPHY

Mr. & Mrs. Leo Chatfield

You are cordially invited to attend

An Informal Dance

Sponsored by Koppers Stores, Inc., Powellton District

Thursday, December 28, 1933

9:00 p. m. to 2:00 a. m.

New River State Gym   Montgomery, W. Va.

Music by Harry Bowman and his Generals

Committee:—F. E. Holman, R. C. Walker, P. A. Martin

Please Present Invitation At Door

CHARLESTON SCHOOLS

All school photos not credited individually
are from Jim Barth collection.

The old Cabin Creek
District High School was
built in 1912 and later
became East Bank High
School. This view was
taken before additions
were added. BK

Roosevelt Junior High School,
in 1958, was built in 1922 and
closed recently. The building
has been proposed to house
the city's police department or
a community center.

Fruth School between Court and Summers
streets on Lee Street in 1958. It was built in the
early 1930s on this site of the old Union School.

Fernbank Grade School on Bridge Road in 1958. It was
demolished in the 1980s.

Bigley Elementary School was demolished for interstate construction in the 1970s. Photo circa 1958.

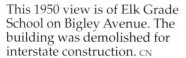

Mercer School on Quarrier Street in 1960. This building, constructed in 1903, was Charleston's first free-standing high school. It was demolished in 1973 and is now a parking lot next to the YWCA. (309)

The oldest part of Lincoln School on the west side was built in 1890. In 1918 it became a junior high school. The building was demolished in 1990 to make way for a Kroger Supermarket at 502 Delaware Avenue. Photo circa 1957.

This 1950 view is of Elk Grade School on Bigley Avenue. The building was demolished for interstate construction. CN

Dunbar High School in 1951. The building was demolished in the 1990s.

Kanawha City High School at Owens, 1929. The school served primarily the children of glass plant employees. This building is now Chamberlain Elementary School.

Junior High School at Ward.

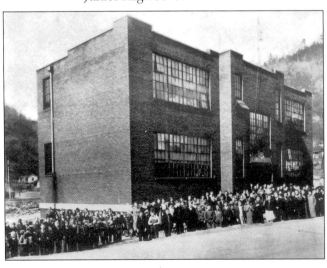

Woodrow Wilson Junior High School on West Washington Street in 1960. The building was built in 1925 and demolished in the 1990s.

Students at the Quarrier
Street high school, 1912.

Students in 1915 line up to walk
the two blocks to their new high
school building at the corner of
Quarrier and Morris streets. This
building then became Central
Junior High School and then
Mercer Grade School.

In 1956 the 50 year reunion of
the first Charleston High
School graduating class was
held. B.E. Andre is the first on
the left in the second row. BEA

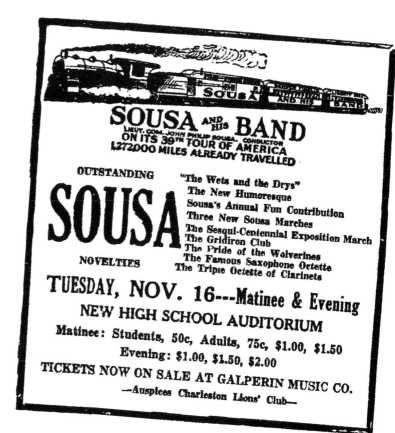

C. H. S. Mountain Lions' BASKETBALL SCHEDULE [1934-35] VARSITY			
Jan. 5	Nitro	Here	51-26
Jan. 8	So. Charleston	There	47-25
Jan. 11	St. Albans	There	51-24
Jan. 12	Clendenin	Here	49-25
Jan. 15	Montgomery	There	44-31
Jan. 19	Parkersburg	Here	
Jan. 23	Huntington	There	
Jan. 26	East Bank	Here	
Jan. 29	Beckley	There	
Feb. 2	Montgomery	Here	
Feb. 5	Clendenin	There	
Feb. 8	Bluefield	There	
Feb. 9	Princeton	There	
Feb. 14	Parkersburg	There	
Feb. 16	So. Charleston	Here	
Feb. 19	East Bank	There	
Feb. 23	Huntington	Here	
Feb. 27	St. Albans	Here	

Head Coach:
CLYDE "PUD" HUTSON

Managers:
William Shook - Richard Nichols

Captain: Cramon Stanton

C. H. S. "Little" Mountain Lions' BASKETBALL SCHEDULE [1934-35] "B" TEAM			
Jan. 5	Huntington	There	13-20
Jan. 12	Beckley	There	19-25
Jan. 15	Oak Hill	Here	
Jan. 16	East Bank	There	
Jan. 23	Wash. Dist.	Here	
Jan. 25	Parkersburg	There	
Jan. 29	Beckley	Here	
Jan. 31	Clendenin	There	
Feb. 1	Elkview	Here	
Feb. 5	Parkersburg	Here	
Feb. 8	Oak Hill	There	
Feb. 9	Huntington	There	
Feb. 12	Elkview	There	
Feb. 14	East Bank	Here	
Feb. 15	Clendenin	Here	
Feb. 20	So. Charleston	Here	
Feb. 26	So. Charleston	Here	

Head Coach:
RUSSELL "RAT" THOM

Managers:
Vernard Faigley - Bob Washington

Captain: Mitchell Haddad

1934-35

John Philip Sousa was one of America's most famous band leaders. Known as the "March King," Sousa composed 136 marches, 12 operettas (one included the hit *El Capitan)*, 11 band suites, and 70 songs. He even invented an instrument, the sousaphone. He performed in Charleston in November 1926.

Laidley Field circa 1930s. (389)

Charleston High School on Washington Street was opened in 1926 and closed in 1989. The site now houses a unit of CAMC's Charleston General Division.

Heartbreaking view of the classic 1926 Charleston High School in 1989.

Through the financial backing of members of the CHS Class of 1940, the Lee Street arched doorways of the 1926 school were disassembled and rebuilt on the grounds of the new Capital High School at Meadowbrook. Richard Andre (CHS 1958), who conceived the idea and guided the project, is seen speaking at the 1989 dedication of the archlike monument. Phil Goldstein, a great CHS booster of the class of 1940, stands inside the arch. CHS reunion gatherings are often held at the site and alumni have a deep sentimental feeling for this last surviving piece of their old school.

The 1905 Baptist Temple at the corner of Washington and Capitol streets was put up for sale in 1924 and some of the stone was used to construct a residence on Woodward Drive in West Charleston. The stone has a unique red hue. ③③③

The Christ Church Methodist seen here in a 1950 photo was partially destroyed by fire (see page 122) but was rebuilt with the distinctive bell tower remaining.

The Free Will Baptist Church in East Bank, 1900.

Members of St. Marks Methodist Church at Dickinson and Washington streets, 1930. DED

The Union Mission
Memorial Auditorium
on Washington Street
near Clendenin Street
in 1962. ③③②

The end was near in 1969 when
this photo was taken of Schwamb
Memorial Presbyterian Church on
Bigley Avenue. It was in the path
of I-77.

Metropolitan Baptist Church on Court Street in 1951.

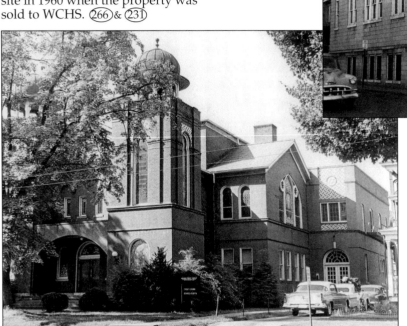

The Virginia Street Temple on Virginia Street in October 1959. This building was built in 1894 and the congregation moved to its present site in 1960 when the property was sold to WCHS. (266) & (231)

Bream Memorial Presbyterian Church on West Washington Street, circa 1940s.

The First Baptist Church (Black) on Washington Street near Dickinson in 1951. It was demolished in the 1960s to make way for the expanded post office.

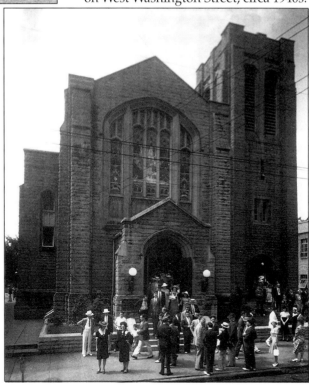

The Kanawha Baptist Church at Pratt.

Community Church at Ward.

Baptisms at Kelly's Creek, circa 1920s.

Billy Sunday came to Charleston and preached his "fire and brimstone" in a wooden tabernacle (not a tent) located on the southeast corner of Lee and Dickinson streets where Coyle and Richardson was. Pat Withrow was instrumental in bringing him to Charleston. Homer Rodehaver was with him as his choir leader. Boy, how he could sing "The Old Rugged Cross." Sunday, the acrobatic evangelist and former professional baseball player was the most popular fire and brimstone preacher of his time. BILL GUTHRIE COLL.

REV. W. A. SUNDAY

The American Legion was formed at the end of World War One. The "Kanawha Post" No. 20 of the Legion was formed in August 1919. In the summer of 1923 another post was formed in Charleston, "John Brawley Post No. 61," named in honor of Brawley who was killed in action. The post met in the chapel of the Owen and Barth Funeral Home. Nick Barth was elected first commander followed by L.O. Gastineau and B.E. Andre. In 1925 the two posts consolidated as John Brawley Post No. 20. Through the years the post has been involved in many civic and patriotic endeavors including purchasing Legion Field, erecting several monuments to World War Two dead, sponsoring baseball teams, disaster relief, oratorical contests, Civilian defense work and many other projects. In 1955, the post home was the former C.K. Payne residence on the northwest corner of Brooks Street and Kanawha Boulevard. The present post headquarters is at 415 Dickinson Street. (356)

JOHN BRAWLEY POST No. 20

Grand Opening of New Post Home

SATURDAY, MARCH 12, 1955

CELEBRATING THE

Thirty-Sixth Birthday of the American Legion

VISITING HOURS 10:00 TO 5:30 P. M.

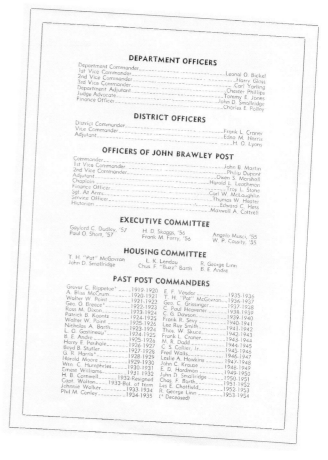

An early 1900s view of South Hills looking southeast out Oakmont Road. Oakmont Road was formerly Neale Avenue. DOUG NEALE COLL.

The Davis Child Shelter on Washington Street between Broad and Brooks streets has been extensively remodeled in this 1920s view from its original 1896 look. It was the primary care facility for children in the area for over 50 years.
(351)

Mountain State Memorial Hospital at the corner of Virginia and Morris streets in 1958. It later became the Capital City Nursing Home and is now vacant and awaiting its fate. D.E.D.

The Littlepage Mansion at North Charleston in the 1930s. View taken during the construction of the Littlepage Terrace Apartments. The mansion was built in 1845 by Adam Littlepage. ⑧

Wartime photo of Confederate Lieutenant General Jubal A. Early.

This is a 1910 photo of the home, constructed in the 1840s, five miles from the mouth of the Elk River on the north side. Confederate General Jubal A. Early lived here for a short period of time. Ruth Hill Wilson stands in the front yard. See *Bullets and Steel*, page 7 for the full story.

This old house on Kanawha Street just east of Hale Street appears on the 1890 riverfront photo on page 269 of *KCI #1*. By 1900 when this photo was taken the 1891 South Side bridge had been built to the west. BETTY & SAM MCCORKLE PHOTOS

The interior of the house gives us a good view of a late 1800s Charleston home probably owned by someone of middle-income status by today's standards.

Lee Street looking west toward Dickinson Street, circa 1930. The old Coyle and Richardson Department Store is now a state office building. BOLLINGER PHOTO ㉓㉓

Present-day scene of Lee Street looking west. The Huntington Bank building is on the site of the old Capitol Annex.

World War One had ended only three years before the 1885 Capitol burned in 1921 and a group of American Legionnaires conceived the idea to turn the Triangle into a memorial site. The World War One monument was soon dedicated and thereafter the Triangle was a gathering place where people of the area assembled to remember their fallen heroes. The ceremonies are now rarely held and only a shadow of those depicted in these scenes from the 1950s. CN

Lee Street looking west with Hale Street on the left, circa 1930. The Triangle in the background occupies part of the site of the 1885 capitol. BOLLINGER PHOTO 220

Inset below: the Triangle today.

A 1914 view of Quarrier Street looking east from Capitol Street. All these buildings still exist. Note hoop style street lights over intersection. B.E. Andre's cycle shop at 913 Quarrier Street is about next to the Florist sign on right. (264)

The same scene in 1999 before the Capital State Bank was built. As you can see, most of the buildings have survived 70 years. The old Kanawha Hotel awaits restoration.

Looking east on Virginia Street near the corner of Summers Street, 1930. The corner building across from the hotel is now occupied by the new Capital State Bank.

A rare view looking north on Capitol Street, circa 1910. The ornate roof of the old Burlew Opera House is visible on the left. Later the site of O.J. Morrison Department Store. RAA

Capitol Street looking south, 1914. Most of the buildings on the east side of the street are still in existence.

A recent view of Capitol Street looking north from the boulevard.

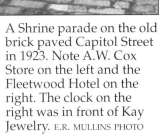

A Shrine parade on the old brick paved Capitol Street in 1923. Note A.W. Cox Store on the left and the Fleetwood Hotel on the right. The clock on the right was in front of Kay Jewelry. E.R. MULLINS PHOTO

A busy day on Capitol Street looking north, 1925. Now part of the historic district.

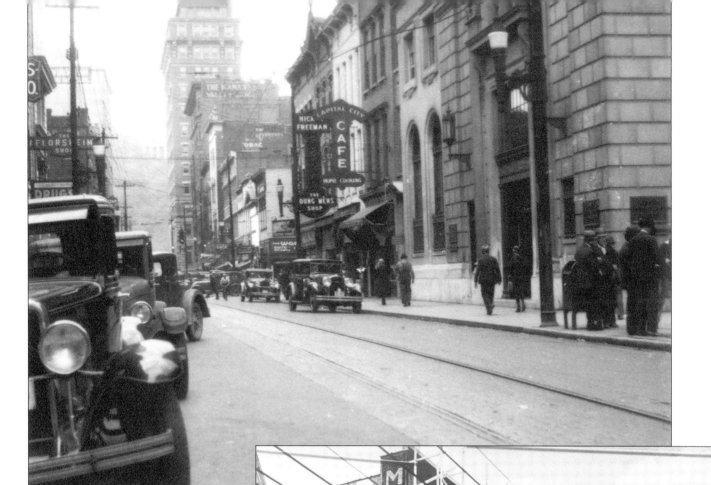

The 100 block of Capitol Street in the early 1930s. The big building on the right is the Kanawha Banking and Trust Co. KCL GRAVELY & MOORE PHOTO

O.J. Morrison's store on Capitol Street gets a face lift in the 1930s. The building was built on the site of the old Burlew Opera House in 1920. Morrison was one of the leading department store chains for more than four decades. Scott Brothers Drug Store is to the far left. KCL (291)

Capitol Street just past Lee Street, 1941. Taken from a window of The Diamond Department Store.

This is what life was before the mall in downtown Charleston. It was wall-to-wall people on the sidewalks during the Christmas holidays, circa 1930s.

Recent view of Capitol Street looking south near Brawley Walkway (old Fife Street).

The Shriners bringing their usual brand of laughable excitement on Capitol Street, circa 1970s. CN

Building the
Kanawha Boulevard
1939-1940

View toward Patrick Street bridge.

These photos were taken by Cramer Bollinger in February 1939 of the area along the Kanawha River which would be cleared for construction of the new WPA financed Kanawha Boulevard.

Kanawha Boulevard was originally named Front Street, then later Kanawha Street. There was a strong interest to name it Kanawha Parkway rather than Kanawha Boulevard.

Typical riverbank scene looking west toward Patrick Street.

Building the Boulevard

Part of old Kanawha Street was Charleston's backyard just a little more than a year ago. It is all front yard now. Serving to relieve the crowded traffic condition of West Virginia's capital city, and with a view toward preventing soil erosion on the banks of the Kanawha, diminishing flood hazards and improving facilities for water-borne commerce, the boulevard, to the casual observer, belies its utilitarian purposes. Riprapping - a method of surfacing with stone to prevent bank erosion of rivers and streams - necessary because the banks of the Kanawha are subject to rapid shifts and changes due to erosion, lends a certain symmetry to the boulevard as one views it on the river side.

The riprapping of Charleston's river front with heavy stone is, according to engineers, comparable to the building of the Pyramid of Cheops. Nine hundred thirty-eight thousand cubic yards of material were used to fill in the bank, all of it being handled, twice, first, in dredging, and second, in placing. Waste materials disposed of totaled 20,000 cubic yards. The "toe wall" required 106,000 cubic yards of rock fill, and 28,500 cubic yards of gravel were used for the foundation of the riprapping. Fifty-seven thousand cubic yards of stone were required for the riprapping, and steps placed at intervals in the riprapping took 656 cubic yards more. Eighty-three thousand five hundred square yards of grass sod were laid and 12,700 square yards of surface were seeded.

Sand and gravel filling for the bank was taken directly from the riverbed by huge dredges. It was then loaded into barges and towed by tugs to where it was needed. Stone for the "toe wall" was quarried a short distance up the Elk river, which empties into the Kanawha in the city. Pavements, curbs, and sidewalks - 47,600 square yards of material - were removed to make way for the new thoroughfare. Preparation for the new pavement called for 41,600 cubic yards of sub-grading and fine grading, and 25,800 cubic yards of concrete were poured to lay new pavement.

Connecting the east and west sections of the boulevard, the bridge which spans the Elk river is considered by engineers as a remarkable piece of construction. Designed and built so that the flow of traffic on the floor of the bridge is not an added strain to the part of the structure intended to support its own weight, it tends to relieve that strain and convert it into a tension or another part of the fabrication.

Sodium vapor lamps, like those used on San Francisco's Golden Gate Bridge, light the boulevard from end to end. These lights do not glare in the motorist's eyes. Their rays penetrate mist and fog, adding to travel safety on the new thoroughfare.

Charleston's Kanawha boulevard was completed at an approximate cost of $3,500,000. Nine hundred and eight thousand dollars was paid by the city for rights-of-way; ground made usable, however, through construction of the boulevard is estimated to be worth more than the amount paid.

Excerpted from Alice Partlow Curtis' article in the July 1940 issue of *West Virginia Review*

It was boasted that enough fill was dumped in the construction of the boulevard to equal the cubic volume of the Great Pyramid of Egypt.

Beginning of construction of the boulevard at the Elk River junction, 1939. Some building and debris to the left has not yet been cleared. The Elk River bridge construction has not yet begun. The Virginia Street bridge is at the top of the photo.

Aerial view of construction progress on the boulevard on the West Side at Ohio Avenue, 1939. Notice that a few houses still remain on the riverbank A magnifying glass will reveal a streetcar on Virginia Street about the middle of photo. 1939 saw the last of the trolleys. The Superior Laundry, started in 1921 by the Young Brothers, was located at Kanawha Boulevard and Truslow Street, circa 1940s.

The boulevard looking west, circa 1940s.

The boulevard looking west, 1946. Glenn Clark's seaplane base at the city levee is on the left. Inset is recent view of Haddad Park. The Ideal Furniture Co. was founded in 1906 by Harry Bloomberg. It moved to the Summers Street corner in 1927.

Photo from the South Side bridge looking east at the almost completed Kanawha Boulevard, circa 1940s.

The boulevard looking east, 1950. All the buildings on the left from Capitol Street west were demolished during urban renewal in the 1960s.

West Virginia's Centennial parade on Kanawha Boulevard, June 20, 1963. President Kennedy came to Charleston for the ceremonies.

Looking east on Lee Street toward the pride of Charleston in 1930, the new 20-story Kanawha Valley Bank Building. At left, the same view today.

In the years before the interstates were built - traffic in Charleston was often bumper to bumper and moved at a snails pace. This 1958 scene taken from the steps of the old library on Lee Street at Hale illustrates the frustration of those days. This picture reminds us of the bustling downtown where we grew up. If we could talk to these folks they might tell us they had just had lunch at the Diamond Cafeteria or seen a matinee at the Rialto Theatre.

An early 1900s view of Charleston Street (West Washington Street), looking west near the Elk River.

Inset: West Washington at Bigley Avenue.

View on Washington Street East at Morris Street, looking west, with Charleston High School on the left in background, 1957.

Washington Street at Summers Street, 1962. This scene is very familiar to author Andre since his dad's bicycle shop was in the basement of the Capitol View Apartment building in the 1950s.

Can it be 36 years since you could buy a "Burger Boy" hamburger for 15 cents on the northwest corner of Washington and Laidley streets? The photo is dated January 1965 and the site is now occupied by the city parking building and the cinema.

At right: This scene is not recognizable today as virtually everything in this view of Washington Street near Summers Street fell prey to the wreckers' ball, photo circa 1965.

In 1958, Dickinson Street had just been extended through from Quarrier Street to Virginia Street.

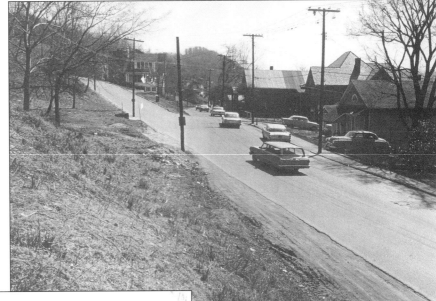

Piedmont Road at Farnsworth Drive (entrance to Spring Hill Cemetery), 1962. The road all but vanished with construction of the interstate highway. CN

Now directly beneath the interstate highway, this view of Greenbrier Street at Piedmont Road in 1962 reminds us of once familiar scenes - gone forever. CN

The C&O Railway underpass at Montrose Drive in South Charleston about 1953 will be recalled by many. A diesel locomotive roars past secure in its recent victory over steam. The interstate construction of course, completely changed the Montrose Drive area.

Piedmont Road at Wertz Avenue, 1960. The old "Gold Dome" Drive-In was just behind the photographer. Today, thousands of vehicles a day roar across this area high above on the interstate fill. CN

Co-author Richard Andre had the good fortune to grow up on Duffy Street in the third house from the right. This once happy neighborhood is all gone now - lost to the state parking lot in 1969. The McClung Street intersection shows in this 1966 photo. Children could walk to school and the State Theatre provided Saturday thrills. Playing outside until dark - hide and seek - cowboys and Indians - listening for mothers' call to come home! RAA

In 1908 the capital city of West Virginia was bursting at the seams with a population that doubled about every 10 years. This view of Capitol Street as it crossed the K&M Railroad yards (later New York Central - now Norfolk Southern) clearly shows the grand 1885 capitol building and its 1902 companion, the annex in the upper left. Near the center at the corner of Capitol and Christopher streets we see the roof the the house where well-known historian, William Wintz was born. Almost all of the buildings in this photo are gone but a few endure. Go up on Capitol Hill to the overlook and try to pick them out.

This recently discovered 1910 Haines Photo Co. photo of the Broad to Brooks Street area of east Charleston was found in the Library of Congress collection. For the first time in nearly a century we see long vanished elements of the old capital city from a very rare perspective. Beginning at the far left, we see the steam and smoke of an ever-present switcher locomotive working near Brooks Street in the Kanawha and Michigan yards. In the distant skyline, the towers of Mercer School stand out (demolished in 1925 for construction of the last Charleston High building). Note that the lower third of the photo shows fields and standing water as that area north of the train tracks was notoriously wet. As we can see much of the photo shows the warehouse district which existed hand-in-hand with the railroad. Near the center we observe the Victorian roof of the K&M depot which was a hub of activity competing with the C&O depot across the river.

CHARLESTON, W. Va. K. & M. Depot.

The Elk Hotel appears just to the right of the station and above and further right the dome of the Capitol Annex (built in 1902) and of course, the unmistakable steeple of the 1885 Capitol. Middle right: the yards and freight depot of the K&M Railroad (now the Capitol Market) are seen. The interstate highway now covers most of the lower part of this scene where old Piedmont Road ran along the foot of the hill. Recently the name of Broad Street was changed to "Leon Sullivan Way" to honor the world-renowned economist and civil rights activist who was born in Charleston in the very area this photo covers.

The Elk Hotel.

This 1918 view from the roof of Woodrums Furniture Store shows a truly vanished part of Charleston, lost in the 1963 urban renewal project. Note that the motor age did not yet have its grip on Charleston as the only thing in view on Virginia Street are horse-drawn wagons. The creases are from folding the photograph.

Pepsi-Cola has been around a long time as the 1918 sign indicates on a Summers Street building. Across the river is the huge Ward Boiler and Shipbuilding Works. The narrow building near the middle is the St. Albert Hotel which burned in 1932 (see page 122). On the right the Kanawha County Courthouse, with its 1918 Kanawha Street addition, has just been roofed. Atop the steeple is the eight-foot bronze Goddess of Justice that was lost to a scrap drive during World War Two. On the far right is a very rare glimpse of the roof and steeple of the old city hall that was replaced in 1922.

SOUTH SIDE HIGHLANDS
PROPERTY SAMUEL STEPHENSON

STANDARD OIL CO

COURT HOUSE

SOUTH SIDE

The Harris Photo Co.
Conneaut. O.

Recent view looking toward the north end of Capitol Street and up Elk River shows the changes wrought by over 70 years. Taken from the top of the 20-story Kanawha Valley Bank building - just as in the lower 1929 photo.

This 1920 view to the south show the busy yards of the Baltimore & Ohio Railroad. The steeple of the 1885 capitol can barely be seen in the upper left. Capitol Hill is on the lower left.
RAA

This unique view toward Elk River and the north end of Capitol Street shows the K&M Locomotive Round House in the center. Steam locomotives needed a turntable to be turned around since, unlike the modern diesels, they could not be run backwards for much distance. On the lower right the building which now houses West Virginia Public Radio is seen. The unmistakable smell of coal smoke hung over the old time railroad yards. The human nose - as well as the eyes - can bring back memories!

This 1948 East End view of Charleston was a century after the Ruffner Family farm. About 1900 Charleston was growing by leaps and bounds and the historic East End residential neighborhood that we know today was building up steadily. When the state capitol burned in 1921, a search was begun for a new, permanent site. Over half a dozen locations were considered including the area at the confluence of the Elk and Kanawha rivers. Even the hilltop above Piedmont Road was considered as well as a Kanawha City site. Finally the site in the East End was chosen and the area was changed forever. The Kanawha Grade School and Annex, where author Richard Andre went to grade school is in the bottom left. The large California Apartment complex is seen just to the left of the east wing of the capitol. The old saying is: "Nothing is forever" and so it is that the old neighborhood has changed but that is the nature of life. Centuries ago the Shawnee and the Cherokee lived there, then the pioneer Ruffners and one cannot help but wonder how it will be when the 21st century has passed? Will the capitol still stand in golden splendor? Will someone read these words and wonder about us?

This circa 1951 photo of the West End of Kanawha City holds many memories. The new Charleston Memorial Hospital was built on the site of the old nine hole "Capitol View" golf course. On the bottom right is the Watt Powell baseball stadium and next to it the old riding stable. Many will recall the "Casa Loma" nite club, which was a favorite of area residents in the 1940s. It can be seen just to the lower middle and near the railroad tracks. The club featured an open air dance floor and most of the famous big bands of the era played there, such as Miller, Goodman and Dorsey. In the 1920s the commission charged with finding a site for the new capitol building almost chose the golf course location but that would have required another bridge across the Kanawha River so the plan was dropped. 1951 was a great year to live in Charleston - prosperity abounded and only the Korean War disturbed America's happiness. (377)

This aerial photo of the heart of downtown Charleston dates from about 1952 and gives a pre-urban renewal view of the old town. Near the center left the remarkable 19th century Brown family home is visible amid the trees. Quarrier Street had not been extended beyond Capitol Street as yet and the home sat nestled in its leafy glade looking like a scene from "Gone With The Wind." The 1958 Federal building was later built on the Brown property. At the lower left can be seen the many homes that use to be on the present site of the Town Center Mall. Tag Galyean's Chrysler dealership is at the lower right. The huge roof of the Kearse Theater appears just above the Brown mansion and next to it is the Greyhound Bus Depot. The Woodrum Furniture building appears at the middle left (see page 282).

This aerial view freezes Charleston in a moment of its history circa 1959. The East End borders the downtown and Laidley Field is in the right bottom. The field in the 1940s and '50s used to attract huge crowds for Friday night high school football games and the annual Charleston High - Stonewall Jackson High game. The field has been greatly remodeled but the large crowds are seldom there anymore. The most striking change in this photo is the wide swath cut by the interstate highway. Considerable industry and warehousing had occupied this section until the interstate highway was constructed in the 1970s. Old East End residents will be able to locate Kanawha Grade School, Asbury Church, Roosevelt Junior High, Charleston High, the C&O Railroad yards, McJunkin Corporation and even the Daniel Boone Hotel. The historic Spring Hill Cemetery near the top right overlooks the city. At the very top left, the new Civic Center can be seen thus dating this photo.

If your memory dims as to how much of Charleston was lost to the interstate highway, these two photos will help. The top photo illustrates the Elk River-Washington Street area of the West Side in the mid-1960s.

The lower photo clearly shows the Washington Street bridge across the Elk, circa 1965. The center of this photo shows homes and buildings later crushed under the bulldozers tred. Old Bigley School is visible near the center. (See page 247).

MacCorkle Avenue at Jefferson Road in South Charleston with Davis Creek emptying into the Kanawha River, photo circa 1952.

This view was taken to show the proposed site of the new Civic Center, circa 1957. It also shows most of the residential area taken by the second urban renewal project in the 1960s which resulted in the construction of the Town Center Mall. The Virginia Street bridge across the Elk River is seen at the lower right. It was built in 1907 and was designed to hold four big streetcars. It was replaced in the late 1990s.

This circa 1950s view shows the South Side west of the train depot showing the ESSO (Exxon) gasoline storage facility near Ferry Branch. Much of this scene has changed first by construction of the Southside Expressway and in later years by the four-lane Corridor "G" Highway that obliterated the old Ferry Branch Road.

Big and Little Tyler Mountain roads come together in this aerial view of the Cross Lanes area, circa 1970.

The scenic Elk River defines the east and west sides of Charleston and this pre-interstate view shows the many buildings and residences that belong only to history. The Civic Center is a landmark and in the top midsection Stonewall Jackson High School (now Junior High) stands out. Undeveloped Magic Island is visible on the left, circa 1960.

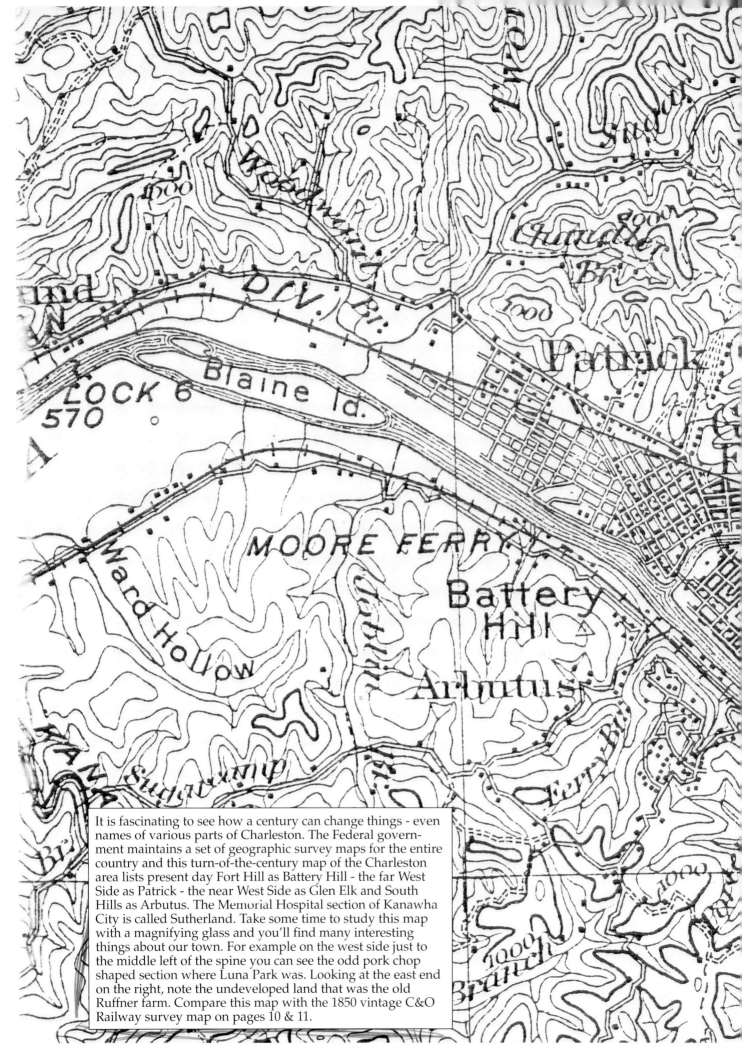

It is fascinating to see how a century can change things - even names of various parts of Charleston. The Federal government maintains a set of geographic survey maps for the entire country and this turn-of-the-century map of the Charleston area lists present day Fort Hill as Battery Hill - the far West Side as Patrick - the near West Side as Glen Elk and South Hills as Arbutus. The Memorial Hospital section of Kanawha City is called Sutherland. Take some time to study this map with a magnifying glass and you'll find many interesting things about our town. For example on the west side just to the middle left of the spine you can see the odd pork chop shaped section where Luna Park was. Looking at the east end on the right, note the undeveloped land that was the old Ruffner farm. Compare this map with the 1850 vintage C&O Railway survey map on pages 10 & 11.

Sports

Old Wehrle Park in Charleston East End was generally in the block bounded by Quarrier, Virginia, Elizabeth and Greenbrier streets. High School games were played here until Laidley Field was opened.

Rare photos of a 1909 football game at Wehrle Park. The hollow in the background is present-day Greenbrier Street leading to Yeager Airport. MRS. J. KENNEDY RIPPETOE COLL.

The 1908 Charleston High School football team pictured behind the school on Quarrier Street. (1) Burdette, (2) Dilcher, (3) F.L. Rippetoe, (4) Stein, (5) Bill Patrick, (6) Nib Donnally, (7) Ford, (8) Donald Cork, (9) George Burns, (10) John Ray, (11) Bill Lively and (12) Sam Chilton.

Lane Anderson, Charleston High School class of 1916, was the first West Virginia trackster to run the 100-yard dash in 10 seconds. Anderson is shown here at Wehrle Park.

The oldest V.F.W. post in the state, founded as the Elk-Kanawha post in Charleston on Jan. 5, 1920, was moved to South Charleston and renamed Lane S. Anderson Post No. 297 in honor of the sports star. Lieutenant Anderson is pictured at left and was killed in action in the Argonne Forest campaign in 1918.

Paul "Monk" Hager shown in his Marine Corps uniform in 1918.

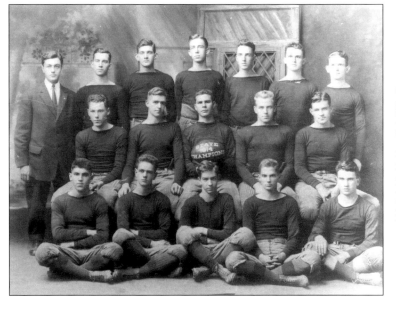

Charleston High School state football champions in 1914. Renowned coach Rocco Gorman is at top left, Lane Anderson, bottom left, and Paul "Monk" Hager holds the ball. Hager was the oldest living CHS and WVU football player, until he passed away a few years ago. ③⑧⑦

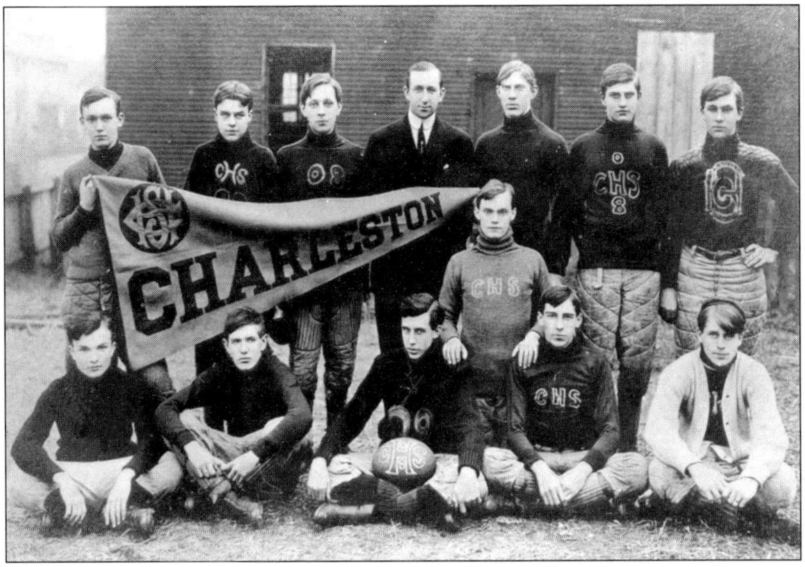

The 1908 Charleston High School football team wore a variety of uniforms and lettering on their jerseys. MRS. J. KENNEDY RIPPETOE COLL.

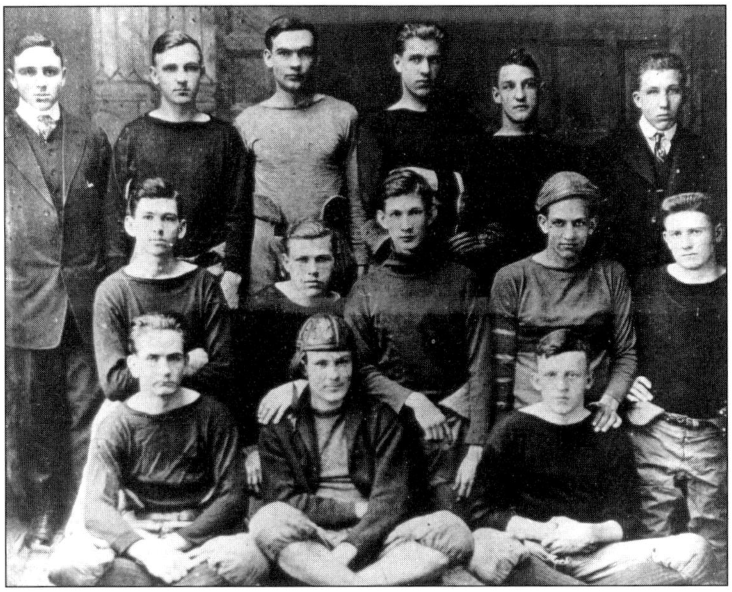

First St. Albans High School football team, 1914. Front row: Burke Rich, Ruel Hanks, Roy White. Second row: Capt. Hobart Shrewsberry, Murray Chandler, Francis Turner, Park Tudor, Marvin "Red" Bartlett. Third row: Coach Brownie Fulton, Hudson Chandler, Claude Holstein, Garrett Fogle, Lovell "Sheenie" Meadows and Dana "Cobby" Webb. BILL BURDETTE COLL.

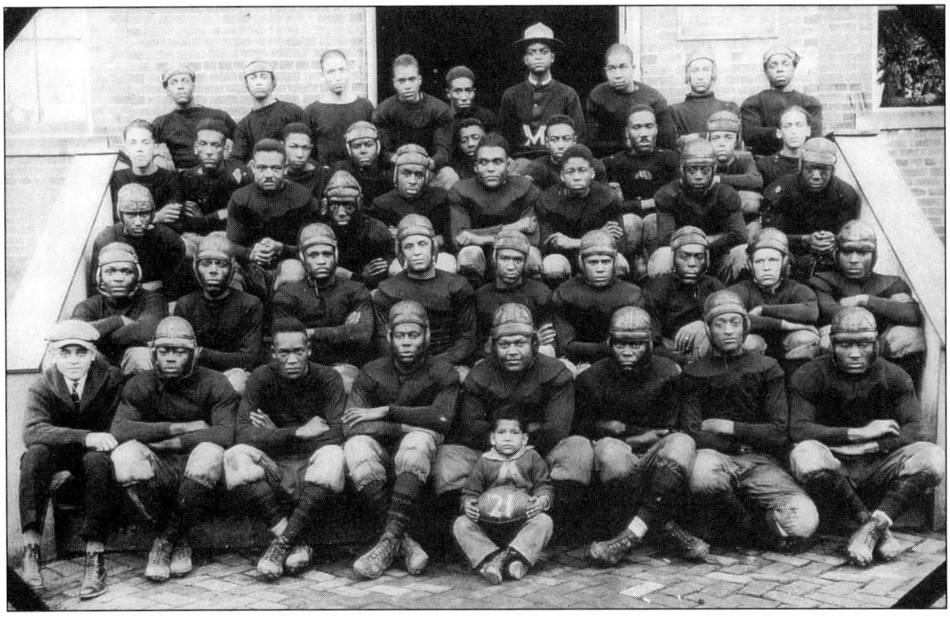

The 1921 West Virginia Collegiate Institute football team. (314)

The first football team of Cabin Creek District High School, the forefunner to East Bank High School, takes its stance on the front lawn of the school. The year was 1914, when teachers and coaches could play on the team with students. East Bank won one game and lost three, including an 80-0 pounding by Charleston High School, the state football champs that year. K.E. Chenoweth was coach of East Bank and Rocco Gorman was in his second year as coach and science teacher at Charleston High. Gorman had three undefeated CHS teams: 1914, 1920 and 1924. His 1920 team shut out opponents while scoring 379 points. ROBERT CRAIGO COLL. (389)

From left: Coach Lyle Rich, team captain Jimmy Marie (Miragliotta), Denver "Red" Hill and Billy "Stonewall" Thomas after the CHS-SJHS football game. Hill, a former CHS football and basketball player, originated the "Old Elk Bucket" trophy which CHS won in 1941. Marie later played center at the University of Virginia at 140 pounds and was a star intercollegiate boxer as well. Red Hill was tragically murdered by two robbers shortly after World War Two. DICK HUDSON COLL.

A 1920s basketball team representing the *Charleston Daily Mail.*

The Kanawha City High School basketball team in 1928. Danny Davidson's father is on the bottom left. DED (315)

Members of the Charleston and Huntington High baseball teams, circa 1906. B.E. Andre is pictured second from left in second row. RAA

The 1940 Handley
baseball team.

Charleston baseball 1907. B.E. Andre is second from left, top row.

The 1922 West Virginia Collegiate Institute (West Virginia State College) baseball team.

In 1923 the bleachers at Laidley Field collapsed at a football game between West Virginia University and Washington and Lee University. Sixty people were hospitalized. New stands were built the next year. ⓷⑧⑨

In June 1952 Mayor John Copenhaver welcomed the new Class AAA American Association Charleston Senators to the city at the C&O Station. The team moved from Toledo and stayed in the league until 1960.

Kanawha Park on the site of present Watt Powell Park in Kanawha City opened in 1916 with a seating capacity of 3,500. The park played host to professional and amateur baseball through the 1942 season despite a 1939 fire that destroyed much of the grandstand.

1957. BK

BK

Watt Powell Park in 1959. The stadium was opened in April 1949 and named for prominent baseball player, coach and promoter Watt Powell, who was State Parks Chief at the time of his death in 1948. The first team to use the park was the Charleston Senators of the Class A Central League. It was the renewance of professional baseball in the city that was curtailed in 1942. ⟨382⟩

1954.

A large crowd watched the
Charleston Marlins on
May 18, 1961. CN ③82

BK

Photo circa 1949.

Club house 1949.

The Meadowbrook golf course was the first public golf course in Charleston opened for daily fee play. The course was built on the old Cabell farm by H.B. and T.L. Embleton in 1930. It consisted of nine holes with sand greens. Because of increased demand, an additional nine holes were added in 1932 making Meadowbrook the only 18-hole public course in Charleston. In 1936, the sand greens were converted to grass and a clubhouse was constructed. In the mid-1950s the Dupont Company bought the property and operated it as an employee club but left it open to the public as well. In the mid 1980s the property was bought by the county school board and the new Capital High School was constructed there.

In the late 1940s and early 1950s, the annual fall boat races on the Kanawha River provided thrills and spills for free. Thousands of spectators in a picnic mood lined the boulevard riverbank. In 1948, Col. Chuck Yeager flew his P-80 jet fighter under the South Side bridge in a surprise bit of aviation showmanship. This view is from 1957. 61

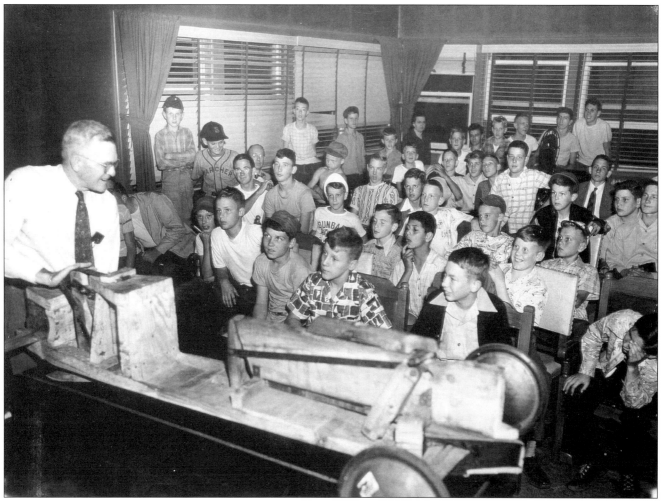

A driving force behind the derby in the 1930s, '40s and '50s was B.M. Higginbotham. He served as Derby Director and was responsible for many technical innovations that revolutionized racer designs nationally. When World War Two ended and the derby resumed, the race was moved to Cross Lanes to a long gradual sloping hill. The track was closer in appearance to the All-American track in Akron. It was felt that this would allow the Charleston derby to select the best representative to compete in the All-American Derby. In 1949, the derby was moved from Cross Lanes to the hill leading east from the Union Carbide Technical Center in South Charleston. Higginbotham gives a Soap Box Derby construction demonstration at the North Charleston Recreation Center in 1948. The boy in front with the pattern shirt is Harold Williamson.

Bottom photo, previous page: Fourteen-year-old Kenny Holmboe of Charleston won the 1947 All-American and International Soap Box Derby champion at Akron, Ohio. He was sponsored by the *Charleston Gazette* and Ken and his family were invited to appear on NBC's national program "The Firestone Hour" in Cleveland, and later went to New York where he received national attention. Ken won the derby before a crowd of 100,000, a full length ahead of the second place finisher. For his win he received a four-year college scholarship which he used to attend Morris Harvey College. In 1940-41 Charleston boys finished second in photo finishes. In 1950, the Charleston area won its second national championship when Harold Williamson beat all challengers at Akron. In 1993, another boy from Kanawha County, Ryan Hoffman, won the All-American Soap Box Derby World Rally Championship. cn

BK

As Johnny Harris Won 1937 Local Soap Box Derby

Johnny Harris, Charleston, winner of the first annual Soap Box Derby, co-sponsored by The Gazette, is shown surrounded by spectators after his triumph. At the left is Bobbie Londeree, runner-up, finishing the finals at the Patrick Street Bridge course. (Gazette Photos)

Soap Box Derby

In 1937 *The Charleston Gazette* sponsored the first Soap Box Derby competition in Charleston. Fifteen-year-old Johnny Harris swept down "derby downs" on the Patrick Street bridge before 8,000 wet and cold spectators. His car, sponsored by Ideal Furniture, cost him $9.19. There were 98 other entrants with Bobby Londeree coming in second, eight lengths behind. Interviewed in the *Gazette*, Harris stated: "It cost me $9.19. It was money I saved from carrying papers for *The Gazette*. And let me tell you that as soon as I come back from Akron, I'm going to try to get another route. Do you think they'll give one to the soap box champion?" Harris went to Akron to represent Southern West Virginia but did not come back as the national champion. John Boone Harris went on to be a B-17 crew chief in World War Two and was a prominent member of the West Virginia Air National Guard.

BUFFALO RANCH WILD WEST

AND

TRAINED WILD ANIMAL EXHIBITION.

TENTH TRANS-CONTINENTAL TOUR.

THE LARGEST WILD WEST SHOW ON EARTH

COMING DIRECT ON THEIR OWN SPECIAL TRAINS
OF DOUBLE LENGTH RAILROAD CARS FROM
THE BIGGEST RANCH IN THE WORLD.

Menagerie of Trained Wild Animals

From all parts of the Globe. Daring and death defying acts almost
beyond the realms of lucid imagination.

COSMOPOLITAN COLLECTION OF COWBOYS AND GIRLS, VANQUEROS
SENORITAS, GUARDIS RURALES, CHAMPIONS OF THE LARIAT,
ROUGH RIDERS PONY EXPRESS VETERANS, DARING
ATHLETES COMICAL CLOWNS, THRILLING
INDIAN FIGHTS AND WAR DANCES.

PRINCE BOTLOINE'S TROUPE OF RUSSIAN COSSACKS,

The most daring Horsemen in the World.

BANDS of SIOUX, CHEYENNE and COMANCHE INDIANS

Fresh from the Camp-fire and Council, making their first acquaintance
with pale face civilisation.

The Grand Ethnological Performance concludes with the Super
Spectacular, Dramatic, Historical Fantasy,

'The Battle of Wounded Knee

Introducing a vast and motley horde of Indians, Scouts, Trappers and Soldiers
that actually took active part in the last brave stand and hopeless
struggle the noble redskin made for his freedom and rights.

TWO PERFORMANCES DAILY, RAIN OR SHINE

Afternoon at 2. Evening at 8. Doors open One Hour earlier.

WATER PROOF CANVAS. CANNOT LEAK.

Grand, Gold Glittering Free Street Parade

TWO MILES LONG at 11 a. m. daily on the main thoroughfares.

BIG FREE EXHIBITIONS on Show Grounds Immediately after the Parade

BRING IN YOUR BAD HORSES AND MULES

Our Cowboys will ride them FREE OF CHARGE.

CHARLESTON

AFTERNOON and NIGHT

MONDAY, APRIL 20.

Note this ad includes the invitation to "Bring in your
bad horses and mules - our cowboys will ride them
free of charge!"

A 1907 circus parade in Charleston, believed to be on
Capitol Street in front of the state capitol. RAA

Ad at left from 1914.

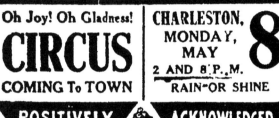

Oh Joy! Oh Gladness!

CIRCUS
COMING To TOWN

CHARLESTON, MONDAY, MAY 8

2 AND 8 P. M.
RAIN-OR SHINE

POSITIVELY THE HIGHEST CLASS CIRCUS IN THE WORLD

ACKNOWLEDGED GREATEST EXHIBITION TRAINED WILD BEASTS ON THE EARTH.

The Circus De Luxe
World's Greatest
Circus Organization!

3 RINGS
Colossal Steel-Girted Arena.
Royal Roman Hippodrome.
2 STAGES

3——Great Herds of Performing Elephants——3

48 CHAMPION EQUESTRIANS, the Greatest Bare-
back Riders the World Has
Ever Seen, Including **4 CONNORS**

1,000 People 1,000	11 Acres of Tents 11
500 Horses 500	87 R. R. Cars 87
387 Performers 387	87,000 Daily Expense
400 Wild Animals 400	$3,000,000 Capital Invested.

More Acts, More Features and More Thrills Than
Any Circus on Earth. Never Divides or Splits

1907

-317-

Circus setting up on West Side, circa 1916.
H. FIELD COLL.

West Virginia's "Great Free Fair"

by James R. Cavitt

The 27th annual West Virginia Great Free Fair will be presented at the 4-H fairgrounds at Dunbar beginning August 31 and continuing through September 8th. It is interesting in comparing the attendance figures at this annual state event to note that in 1939 there were 37,000 persons present each day, while latest reports say that the Golden Gate Exposition this year averages only 38,000 and the New York World's Fair 89,000 persons daily. So it would seem that West Virginia's Free Fair, during its course, has a drawing power equal to the San Francisco Fair and almost half that of the one in New York.

Directors of the Fair this year have arranged a program of streamlined and up-to-the minute entertainment, and in order to transport the great crowds a great variety of facilities have been provided. Automobile and busses, as usual, will afford the major means of travel, but those who desire can go round-trip by motor boat or

plane from Charleston to the fairgrounds at Dunbar, these means of travel to be provided by Glenn T. Clark of the Kanawha Flying Club.

In addition, there will be a skywriter over Charleston each day of the Fair, to advertise it in letters of smoke a half-mile high.

Each day during the Fair those in attendance will receive war bulletins and the latest news through a system of loud speakers, and radio stations WCHS and WGKV will have engineers and announcers on hand for frequent broadcasts of the program highlights.

The usual fair fare will be provided for the entertainment of visitors, and leading attractions for this year will be the performances nightly before the grandstand of fireworks exhibits, and the Kaus Brothers Carnival with an endless variety of amusements, rides and shows. On opening night, the Renfro Valley Barn Dance entertainers, who have be-

come so popular for their performances over WLW, in Cincinnati, will make personal appearances in an old-time show packed with fun, music, songs and dances.

The Army, Navy and Marine Corps have been invited to have exhibits, and there will be 42 commercial booths of merchants exhibits. The exhibit of the Kanawha Board of Education will be under the direction of Superintendent Virgil L. Flinn.

For followers of the Sport of Kings, there will be horse racing, both harness and running, during four days. The Little theatre, as in the past, will present dramatic entertainment with a variety of well-known entertainers, drawn from the Old Farm Hour of WCHS.

The West Virginia Great Free Fair is operated by the Kanawha State Park association, under the direction of President S.C. Savage, and Director T.H. "Pat" McGovran.

From the August 1940, *West Virginia Review*

Circa early 1950s. This edition of Ringling Brothers Circus was about the same time the Cecil B. DeMille film "The Greatest Show on Earth" was made. The circus had to unload in St. Albans and move by road to Dunbar - a long walk for the animals. Note the old half-mile track (see page 508, motorcycle racing) and the later smaller quarter-mile circuit.

This caption appeared in a July 1954 issue of the *Charleston Daily Mail*. The photos are not shown. "Today is Circus Day in Charleston and the populous stretches of the broad Kanawha valley, and the Greatest Show on Earth has brought its countless miracles of the world of entertainment to the Dunbar Fairgrounds. There will be an afternoon show at 2:15 and an evening performance at 8:15. The doors will open at 1 and 7 p.m. in the big top seating 10,000. The show began arriving at the St. Albans yards of the Chesapeake and Ohio railroad shortly after midnight today in three special trains following an appearance in Huntington. At dawn almost 1,000 persons, dominated by children but with a heavy count of adults, were at the yards to watch the circus unload and move over 5 miles of highway to the fairgrounds. The largest privately owned herd of elephants in the world - perhaps excluding some Indian prince - moved with majestic dignity across the St. Albans-Nitro bridge while all traffic was halted by state troopers.

"Doc" Folden was a prominent racer from Kanawha City. He was killed in a plane crash at Kanawha Airport.. Ad dated May 29, 1953.

A 1900 view of a circus parade near the corner of Virginia and Morris streets.

Amazingly the houses shown in these happy scenes still exist after a century. The parade is moving north on Morris from Virginia. Take a few minutes to see these houses today.

At right: The John Robinson and the Hagenbeck-Wallace Circuses were frequent visitors to Charleston after 1900. These circuses together with the Buffalo Bill Wild West Show usually came in on the K&M tracks and unloaded at the end of Capitol Street where Smith and Dryden streets meet it. The circus wagons would then go up Smith Street to Brooks Street and out to Washington Street where they turned up Washington and continued to the show grounds which were about where Ruffner Avenue and Beauregard Street are now.

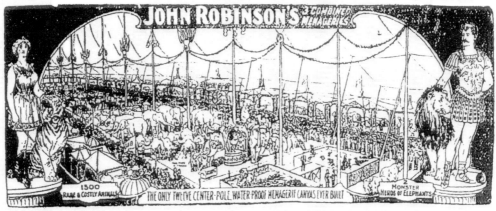
1906

Radio Log For Local Listening

WCHS CBS—580	WKNA ABC—950	WTIP MBS—1240	WCAW 1400	WGKV NBC—1490
MONDAY NIGHT				
5:00—Rhythm Varieties	Challenge	Superman	News, Music	News & Jive
5:15—Rhythm Varieties	of Yukon	Superman	Daily Mail Funnies	Portia
5:30— Amber Room	Sky King	Story Lady	Rem, Rhythm	Teen-Age News
5:45—Herb Shriner	Sky King	Tom Mix	Scores; O'Brien	Memorable Music
6:00—News	Provence Sports	News	News	Farris, Sports
6:15—Saunders, Sport Page	Good Fellowship	Starlight Roof	Waite Hoyt	Here's to Vets
6:30—Korn Koblers	RPM Time	Passing Parade	Townsend Sports	News-Richards
6:45—Lowell Thomas	RPM Time	Music	Jan Garber	Album Portraits
7:00—Beulah	Dateline W. Va.	Fulton Lewis	Cote Glee Club	Supper Club
7:15—Jack Smith	Elmer Davis	News	Mike Mysteries	World News
7:30—Club 15	Lone Ranger	Wood Jamboree	Public Health	Sports Tips
7:45—Edw. Murrow	Lone Ranger	Wood Jamboree	Salon Serenade	H. V. Kaltenborn
8:00—Inner Sanctum	Railroad Hour	Straight Arrow	Meet the Band	Cav. of America
8:15—Inner Sanctum	Railroad Hour	Straight Arrow	Meet the Band	Cav. of America
8:30—Arthur Godfrey	Railroad Hour	Sherlock Holmes	Eddie LeMar	Barlow Concert
8:45—Arthur Godfrey	Henry Taylor	Sherlock Holmes	Land of Free	Barlow Concert
9:00—Radio Theater	Cancer Society	Gabriel Heatter	News, Music	Telephone Hour
9:15—Radio Theater	Cancer Society	Newsreel	Off the Record	Telephone Hour
9:30—Radio Theater	Child's World	Fish & Hunt Club	Off the Record	Dr. I. Q.
9:45—Radio Theater	String Ensemble	News B. Henry	Off the Record	Dr. I. Q.
10:00—My Friend Irma	Morris Harvey	American Forum	Wrestling Match	Contented Hour
10:15—My Friend Irma	Morris Harvey	American Forum	Wrestling Match	Contented Hour
10:30—Bob Hawk Show	On Trial	Honey & Sonny	Pipes of Melody	Radio City
10:45—Bob Hawk Show	On Trial	The Davis Twins	Melody, News	Playhouse
11:00—News, Music to 1	News, Sports, Music	Honey & Sonny	News, Music to 1	News, Music to 1
TUESDAY MORNING				
5:30—Texas Slim				
6:00—Uncle Si	News, Jamboree	Coffee With Coman		Ham 'n Eggs
6:15—Uncle Si	News, Jamboree	Coffee With Coman		Ham 'n Eggs
6:30—Uncle Si	Folk Songs	Coffee With Coman		Ham 'n Eggs
6:45—Eddy Arnold	Country Church	Coffee With Coman		Ham 'n Eggs
7:00—News	Mountain Mis.	Coffee With Coman	News Roundup	Ham 'n Eggs
7:15—Cap-Andy-Milt	Church Bulletin	Coffee With Coman	Rhythm Ranch	With
7:30—Cap-Andy-Milt	Church Bulletin	Coffee With Coman	Sunrise Serenade	Don
7:45—Top O' Morning	Shepherd's Call	Coffee With Coman	Sunrise Serenade	Evans
8:00—News	Hopkins News	Coffee With Coman	Clock Watcher	News
8:15—Uncle Si	Moods & Music	Coffee With Coman	Clock Watcher	Ham 'n Eggs
8:30—580 Club	Rhythm Rambles	Chapel Hour	Clock Watcher	Ham 'n Eggs
8:45—580 Club	Mary Jordan	Morning Reveries	Clock Watcher	News
9:00—News	Breakfast Club	Devotional Hour	News, 4 Knights	Ham 'n Eggs
9:15—Church in Wildwood	Breakfast Club	Tell Neighbor	Sacred Heart	Ham 'n Eggs
9:30—Friendly Four	Breakfast Club	Bob Poole	Pan Americanos	Annie B.
9:45—Community Reporter	Breakfast Club	Bob Poole, News	Variety Time	Devotions
10:00—Music for You	My True Story	Magic Jamboree	Homemaker Holiday	Fred Waring
10:15—Dr. Crane	My True Story	Magic Jamboree	Homemaker Holiday	Fred Waring
10:30—Arthur Godfrey	Betty Crocker	Magic Jamboree	Musical Horizons	Road of Life
10:45—Arthur Godfrey	Side Saddle Sue	Magic Jamboree	Musical Horizons	Brighter Day
11:00—Arthur Godfrey	Kay Nay	Magic Jamboree	News, Music	Dr. Paul
11:15—Arthur Godfrey	Music for Moderns	Magic Jamboree	Pianorama	Love & Learn
11:30—Variety Gang	Ted Malone	Gabriel Heatter	Myrt & Marge	Jack Berch
11:45—Public Service Pgm.	Galen Drake	Easy Rhythm	Unity Program	Lora Lawton
TUES. AFTERNOON				
12:00—Wendy Warren	Provence News	Kate Smith	Song in My Heart	Bandwagon
12:15—Aunt Jenny	Stork Club	Kate Smith	Midday News	News, Hilites
12:30—News	Swap Shop	Daily Mail News	Luncheonaires	Vogel News
12:45—Hilltop House	Swap Shop	Melodies	Luncheonaires	Marine Band
1:00—Big Sister	Baukhage	Cedric Foster	Concert Hall	Tropic Echoes
1:15—Ma Perkins	Radioland Express	Happy Gang	Concert Hall	Holy Week Program
1:30—Dr. Malone	Recordings	Happy Gang	Feature News	R. McCormack
1:45—Guiding Light	Charles Greybill	Claude Thornhill	Rhythm Lullaby	R. Leibert
2:00—News	Breakfast in	Queen for a Day	Jukebox Revue	Double or Nothing
2:15—Perry Mason	Hollywood	Queen for a Day	Jukebox Revue	Double or Nothing
2:30—Editors Daughter	Scotlite	Anniversary Club	Jukebox Revue	Today's Children
2:45—Matinee Melodies	Dorothy Dix	Anniversary Club	Jukebox Revue	George Wright
3:00—Linda's First Love	Ladies Be	Magic Jamboree	Jukebox Revue	Life Beautiful
3:15—Hearts in Harmony	Seated	Magic Jamboree	Jukebox Revue	Ma Perkins
3:30—Robert Lewis	House Party	Magic Jamboree	Jukebox Revue	Pepper Young
3:45—Robert Lewis	House Party	Magic Jamboree	Jukebox Revue	Right to Happiness
4:00—Hint Hunt	Kay Kyser Kollege	Magic Jamboree	Jukebox Revue	Backstage Wife
4:15—Hint Hunt	Kay Kyser Kollege	Magic Jamboree	Jukebox Revue	Stella Dallas
4:30—Winner Take All	Provence News	Magic Jamboree	Jukebox Revue	Lorenzo Jones

Ernie Saunders and sports go together. It's always been that way, for this is a man who realized his dreams. What began as childhood flights of fancy evolved into a long career in sports broadcasting, mostly on WCHS radio and television in Charleston. When Ernie retired in 1980, sports columnist A.L. "Shorty" Hardman called him "the dean of West Virginia sportscasters." Nobody questioned that. Ernie had put in his time. He came to the state as a young graduate of New York's NBC School of Broadcasting in the early '40s, and took his first radio job with the old West Virginia Network. In the years that followed, Ernie left West Virginia twice, living briefly in Phoenix and then in New Hampshire for five years. By 1960 he was back in the Mountain State to stay. He retired 20 years later on August 1, his birthday, signing off the air with the 11,266th edition of the "Sport Page of the Air," his nightly program. *Interview by Debby Sonis, Saunders' niece.*

- LUNA PARK -

Beautiful Luna Park was Charleston's most popular amusement site from 1912 until May 1923 when it was destroyed by fire. Located on the city's West Side and bounded by present-day Park and Glenwood avenues - Park Drive, Grant Street and the river - its main attraction was the elaborate roller coaster seen here in 1916. Among other features there was a dance pavilion and a roller skating rink where races were often held. Streetcars provided access from all over the valley and steamboat excursions to Luna Park were popular. On one long ago fourth of July over 10,000 people paid fifteen cents each to take in the delights of the tree shaded park.

It is interesting to note that almost all prosperous towns like Charleston had their amusement parks including Parkersburg's "Terrapin Park" and, of course, Cincinnati's "Coney Island." After the 1923 fire the owners wanted to rebuild but could not raise the money. The walkways were eventually paved over and the old park became a residential area. The outlines of the park can be seen by the odd arrangement of streets in the neighborhood.

Record-Breaking Crowds Visiting Luna Park

(By James F. Lee)

As an old settler who has lived all his life in the vicinity of Luna park, told it yesterday afternoon to a party of visitors, one year ago yesterday the 4th of July, on the ground where Luna now stands, there was a party of twenty persons enjoying themselves as a small picnic party, while yesterday, one year later, on the grounds of this popular amusement park in the afternoon there was 15,000 and last night. 16,000 making a total for the day of 31,000. If this had been predicted one year ago by any person in Charleston, they would have been told they were fit for a sanatarium. However, it only goes to show that Luna park was wanted by the amusement going public, and when a statement can be hung up in the manager's office showing 31,000 paid admissions for one day, it is quite a sure fact it will take a long time for any place of amusement in Charleston to break this record.

The Cog City Band will be on hand this afternoon and tonight, playing the usual daily concert and the merry whirl will be going this afternoon and the big concessions will be wide open to care for the public wants.

Commander, the night owl monkey was one of the big hits among the visiting strangers yesterday. This pet will be photographed tomorrow and every visitor to the park will receive one of Commander's photographs. Jocko the fighting monkey, who escaped ten days ago from the cage, is still at large and yesterday afternoon attacked a dog that strayed into the grounds. In one minute Jocko made it so unpleasant for the dog that he left the grounds yelping in the usual howl of a whipped canine. Jocko lives now on the top of one of the big trees and nothing can induce him to come down and go back to his original monkey quarters.

There were no accidents yesterday to mar the enjoyment of the thousands on Luna Grounds and at no time was there anything undesirable seen. The forty special police officers engaged for that purpose, did their duty well.

July 1913

1913. BK

The Skating Rink At Beautiful Luna Park

Is One of the Great Drawing Cards at Charleston's Beautiful Summer Resort---The Dancing Hall is Nearing Completion

(By James Fenimore Cooper.)

Luna park will open its gates this morning at 10 o'clock, as it will do every morning this week. Nin p. nicking parties will be on hand to day from Montgomery, and the management has set tables and benches for them in part of the grounds under the shade of the big trees. Hundreds of those who go to the celebration show grounds in the afternoon finish the day by spending the evening at Luna. Charles Leonard McGuire, the world's champion fancy skater of twenty five years ago was a visitor to Luna Park skating rink, and although it has been twenty years since he has skated he could not resist the temptation last night. The management extended to him an invitation to try the new floor out as he would like to have McGuire's opinion of it, and after half an hour on the floor he had to quit, saying he was not as young as he used to be, and was positive he was not such a fancy skater as well. However, he said he had skated on the floors of all the best skating rinks in the world, but he never skated on a better floor than the rink at Luna park. This will give persons an idea what a great floor this rink has. McGuire is here attending the celebra-

tion, and leaves next Saturday for his home at Mount Pleasant, Pa. It was a banner crowd last night as well as yesterday afternoon, and every day Luna is breaking its old records with new ones. Forty special police has been added to the grounds, for every night this week to keep order, and no one need fear of being molested at any time while they are in Luna park. Last night the crowds came in automobiles, taxicabs, motorcycles, bicycles and buggies and every kind of a vehicle obtainable. The cars were crowded to their utmost capacity, and hauled passengers at the rate of twelve hundred an hour, so one can judge what the crowd was last night at this popular amusement resort. Judging from the crowds, Luna is in its infancy as a drawing power. There is no telling as yet how many thousands will be the total at the end of this week. The management will announce through these columns next Sunday just how many people attended Luna from Monday this week until next Saturday night, and those who will read it will be astonished when they learn the number of persons who paid admission to see the prettiest park in the state of West Virginia.

1913. BK

1922

BK

1943

1943

The Casa Loma located on McCorkle Avenue at Mission Hollow Road, was Charleston's leading night spot for many years before, during and after the war. An open air dance pavillion was one of its features. It closed in the 1950s and the site is now next to the Watt Powell Park. Photos circa 1946.

Dance at the American Legion Armory Post 20 at the corner of Lee and Goshorn streets, circa 1930s.

John Brawley Post 20 American Legion drum and bugle corps in front of the public library in the old capitol annex, 1920s.

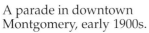

An early 1900s band at Kelleys Creek.

A parade in downtown Montgomery, early 1900s.

Sheet music, 1921. Jones and Hamilton did not rival Irving Berlin but at least they tried.

Charleston High School's band on the steps of the new school, 1929. Mr. J. Henry Francis was the music director. The band's first uniforms were obtained from the U.S. Naval Academy.

The Ferguson Theatre was of course segregated and for Blacks only.
Cap Ferguson was a very successful Black entrepreneur. Ad from 1922.

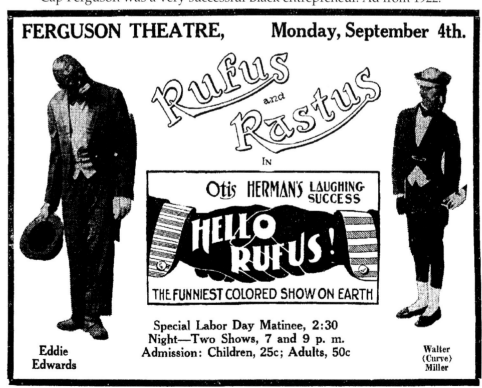

The Charleston News.

RACE ON ROLLER SKATES

WILL BE GIVEN SOON AT THE NEW RINK AT THE CORNER OF DICKINSON AND LEE STREETS

Three Crack Racers From Ohio Have Arrived in City and Will Skate Matched Race.

Mr. H. W. Johnson, proprietor of the new skating rink arrived in Charleston last night accompanied by three crack skaters from Ohio. Two are young men, who have bested the fastest products of the Buckeye state on the rollers, while the third is a youngster who will be matched against some of the local speeders. Kendricks, one of the men, has skated all over the state of Ohio, and holds the record for the distance of one mile He has defeated all comers and his race against Sowers, the champion of Cincinnati, at the big Music Rink at Cincinnati was witnessed by nearly ten thousand people, that big hall being packed to the very doors by Cincinnatians who came to witness the cracks race Kendrick defeated Sowers by two laps and while there s no championship in this line of sport, he is conceded to be able to take the measure of anything in Ohio The match race will be pulled off some time in the near future

The *Charleston News*, July 19, 1906.

Ads from 1906.

BURLEU
CHARLESTON, W. VA., THURSDAY, MAY 31, 1906

FAREWELL APPEARANCE

MME. SARAH

BERNHARDT

IN

CAMILLE

Sarah Bernhardt (1844-1923) was the leading actress of France and recognized as one of the greatest actresses of her time. She was best-known for her performance in *Camille*. Her appearance at the Burlew Opera House, however, was cancelled when she broke her leg on the boat bringing her to New York for her American tour. BK

This Penny Arcade was located somewhere in downtown Charleston probably on Capitol Street, photo circa 1910. Admission was free but you had to feed the various viewing machines with pennies.

B.E. Andre's first business, a shooting gallery on Capitol street, 1907. The dome of the capitol annex can be faintly seen in the top background. Andre's shooting gallery career ended when a drunk shot a window out of the Capitol Annex.

Williams would die the next year (1952) in Oak Hill, West Virginia, on his way to a concert in Ohio. Although many have tried to immitate him there will never be another Hank Williams.

This 1930 ad for Laidley Field indicates a sham battle where National Guard troops would stage a great fight with blank cartridges. The Amerian Legion often sponsored these exciting shows.

An ice skating rink was located at the lower side of the Kanawha City bridge for a few years but was unprofitable so it was turned into a roller rink by the Barlows. It burned later in the 1940s.

1935

-330-

ROCK LAKE SWIMMING POOL
THE LARGEST AND MOST BEAUTIFUL POOL IN THE EAST
OPENS MAY 30, 1941

	Admis- sion Plus Checking	All Tax
Children to Age 14....$	.20	.01
Adults	.35	.05
Season Tickets to Age 14	2.00	.24
Adults	4.00	.48
Checking Only	.10	.01

FREE DANCING

to

LLOYD NEELY'S ORCHESTRA
Each Wednesday Night
8 to 11 P. M.

BOB ROSE'S ORCHESTRA
Each Thursday Night
8 to 11 P. M.

SPECIAL RATES FOR 25 OR MORE, WEEK DAYS ONLY
20c A PERSON, ALL AGES

"SWIM AND DANCE SAFELY WITH THE CROWD YOU LIKE"

Old-time valley residents will fondly remember Rock Lake Pool in a former Spring Hill rock quarry. At 400 by 200 feet, it was one of the largest concrete-bottom swimming pools in the country. It was opened in the 1930s by C.A French and George Caldwell and purchased by Joe Wilan in 1942. Joe and his brothers, Dave and Sam, had operated a swimming business at Lower Falls Beach on Coal River but the Depression put an end to that business. Rock Lake Pool in its heyday had slides, a spraying fountain, trapeze and miniature churning sternwheel. It was the summer recreation mecca for decades but also was involved in the 1960s civil rights demonstrations which eventually contributed to its demise along with many other government-subsidized pools constructed in the valley. Sam Wilan closed the pool in 1985 and Mike Haynes bought it in 1992 and turned it into a Putt-Putt golf complex. SAM WILAN COLL.

We can all remember the intrepid ("show offs") fellows who would climb up on the cliffs and dive into the depths. A juke box was usually blaring from the dance pavillion where teenagers over several generations gyrated to everything from the boogie-woogie to the twist.

1950

Greyhound Races
AMERICA'S NEWEST SPORT

Opens Wednesday Evening

SEPTEMBER 15th
CHARLESTON PARK
Kanawha City, W. Va.

Under the Auspices of the International Greyhound Racing Association

8 RACES NIGHTLY 8

Take Dana Ferry, Kanawha City, or Cabin Creek Cars Direct to Grounds

STOP No. 2

Admission Including War Tax 99c.

1926

This night club was located in the old General Early house (see page 258). Ad circa 1929.

1949

1930s

ROBERT YOUNG

DU PONT
CAVALCADE OF AMERICA

presents

ROBERT YOUNG

in

"Under The Big Top"

MONDAY, MAY 26, 1947

NATIONAL BROADCASTING COMPANY

FROM THE
MUNICIPAL AUDITORIUM,
CHARLESTON, W. VA.

BROADCAST No. 525

BETTER THINGS FOR BETTER LIVING . . . *THROUGH CHEMISTRY*

Cavalcade Visits Charleston

CHARLESTON, West Virginia, from which this DU PONT CAVALCADE has come to you, is an unusual and inspiring city in several respects; a pleasant place in which to live, bright with rhododendrons and roses, circled by green hills—Daniel Boone walked these very hills. And Charleston has also proved to be a convenient location for industry.

But this is only the beginning. Although Charleston is by no means a big city, with a "big city" budget, it has achieved a cultural level of which many a larger place might well be proud — very proud indeed!

A unique advertisement appeared some time ago, for instance, in the *Chemical and Engineering News.* "Wanted"—it read—"Chemical engineers and chemists who are also symphony musicians."

Who wanted these scientists who were also symphony musicians? The industrial plants of Charleston, and the townspeople!

Today, as a result, Charleston has its own symphony orchestra. Several of the symphony artists are in our CAVALCADE orchestra this evening. Some of our actors, too, are Charleston men and women from the Kanawha Players. The works of Charleston painters and sculptors are on exhibit in Charleston's own art gallery.

Accomplishments of this stature do not come by accident. They are achieved only through imagination, planning and enterprise—and lots of hard, hard work.

The DU PONT COMPANY is represented in this Charleston community by a plant devoted to what is known technically as high pressure synthesis. In this plant pressures up to 15,000 pounds to the square inch, and extremes of temperature ranging from 350 degrees below zero Fahrenheit to 2,400 degrees above are used as tools in the manufacture of chemical compounds such as the DU PONT "Zerone" and "Zerex" anti-freeze you use in the radiator of your car in the wintertime, and the nylon chemicals which after further processing become nylon yarns and nylon plastics.

Plants are nothing without people, however. It is the men and women of the DU PONT COMPANY and of this Charleston community, with their chemical "know-how", with their good-will, with their friendly spirit of cooperation and service, who are responsible for these DU PONT

In May 1947 the DuPont Company and NBC brought their national radio show, *DuPont Cavalcade of America* to Charleston for a performance at the Municipal Auditorium. It featured well-known movie actor, Robert Young.

Hope Captivates Overflow Crowd

Municipal auditorium overflowed last night with Bob Hope fans who were hilariously entertained with the comic's two-and-a-half hour variety show.

Veteran entertainment promoters estimated that it was the biggest attraction - from a money standpoint - ever to play a one-night stand in Charleston. Orchestra and messenaine seats ranged in price from $5 to $6 and every one of the 3,000 was filled. Less desirable ones were occupied at $3 a seat.

And the whole audience was with Hope for every minute of the show. They laughed and whistled at his stock stories, gave loud applause for The Titans, an acrobatic team that performed amazing stunts with muscle coordination.

Doris Day, blonde singing star of stage and screen, with Les Brown's popular orchestra, obliged with half a dozen encores and the fans still clamored for more.

But Hope, as usual, was the favorite. His fans howled when he quipped that "I wouldn't have made this trip, but the government needed the money - what with Truman's salary raise and Margaret taking singing lessons - that costs money."

Thousands of fans lined the route from Kanawha airport to the Daniel Boone Hotel to wave and yell a welcome to the famed radio, stage and screen comedians, as he arrived.

The troupe will leave Charleston this morning in the DC-6 "Bob Hope Special" for a matinee and evening show today in Washington, D.C. - (ELG)

Parade Planned For Hope Cast

Both Gov. Patteson and Mayor Andrews will be at Kanawha Airport Wednesday at 6:45 p. m. to meet Bob Hope and his company when the nation's No. 1 comedian and his troupe alight and head by special motorcade for a performance at Municipal auditorium.

The wise-cracking entertainer with Doris Day and Les B r o w n, singer and bandleader, will go down Washington street to Broad, out Broad to the boulevard, on the boulevard to Capitol street, a n d up Capitol to the Daniel Boone hotel, where the troupe will be quartered during its overnight stay.

The performance is scheduled for 8:30 p. m. at Municipal auditorium, with Hope, Day a n d Brown, Irene Ryan, the ailing comedienne, and all the others of the regular Hope show cast on stage for the performance, including a tumbling act.

Tickets for the performance are on sale at Galperins box office Tuesday and will be on sale at the auditorium box office all day Wednesday, Harry Lashinsky, Charleston manager, said.

The well-known Lashinsky family of Kanawha City is still sponsoring entertainment shows around the country.

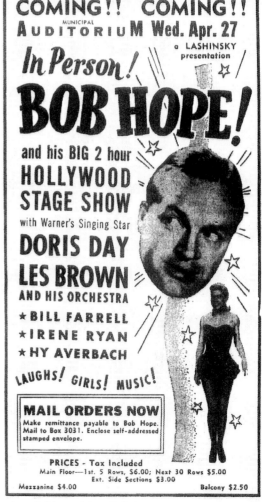

As of this writing Bob Hope is still with us - who else can you think of that has made you laugh all of your life.

OF LOCAL NEWS EVENTS   -:-   -:-   By VINTROUX

Vintroux touched on just about every subject, both comical and controversial, including elected officials, businessmen and current events in the city and surrounding areas.

1950

The Municipal Auditorium, a PWA project was dedicated on Nov. 5, 1939. The $500,000 building was opened to a packed 3,000-person audience. On hand were Mayor D. Boone Dawson, Gov. Homer Holt and other city dignitaries. A four-hour dedication program was held in the new auditorium.

In 1938 Walt Disney asked Donald Duck to write a note of congratulations to Kanawha County on its 150th anniversary. Not bad, huh? You can't do much better than Donald Duck!

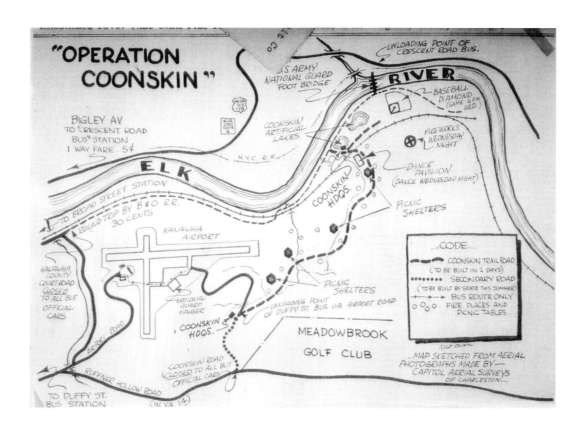

The Spirit Is Still Here

THE W. VA. PIONEER MOUNTAINEER

"OPERATION COONSKIN"

June 27, 1950

The greatest concentrated movement of construction machinery in West Virginia gathered in Charleston in June 1950 for "Operation Coonskin." For two days - June 27 and 28 - hundreds of pieces of equipment and hundreds of volunteer workers built a public park that we know today as Coonskin Park near Yeager Airport. The project was sponsored by the *Charleston Gazette*, the Associated General Contractors of West Virginia, Inc., Kanawha County members of the West Virginia Contractors Assoc., Associated Equipment Dealers, the Charleston Building Contractors Assoc., and many other business and civic organizations in the area. A two-mile long parade was held in Charleston on June 25 and over 25,000 people helped dedicate the park on the 28th. Paul Anderson, president of Anderson's Inc. stated: "We humbly hope that the people of Kanawha County get as much fun from Coonskin Park as we the contractors, equipment people, and workers had in building it."

Enjoying the Good Life in 1939

The *West Virginia Review* made a survey for their magazine in August 1939.

GOLF: The Meadowbrook Golf Club, the first course open to the public in Charleston was located three milesup Ruffner Hollow from Washington Street (near the location of Capitol High). It had 18 holes and cost $1.00 to $1.50 greens fees. A nine-hole course, Capitol View Golf Club, was located at South Ruffner. Greens fees were 35 to 50 cents.

BOATING: Motorboating was available at the Kanawha Flying and Boat Service at the City Levee (now the Haddad Riverfront Park). Guthrie's boat-house at the foot of Greenbrier Street and Beller's, a short distance east of the C&O bridge rented canoes for 50 cents an hour. The Charleston Boat Club on the south end of the Kanawha City bridge was a new establishment that offered private boat dockage and clubhouse activities.

TENNIS: Fine public clay courts were opened at Laidley Field at 15 cents an hour per person. You could rent a private court from Mrs. Oscar H. Lindon across the street from her home at 619 Greenbrier Street at 10 cents per hour per person.

FLYING: It cost one dollar to fly with Glenn Clark in one of his Aeronca seaplanes taking off from the Kanawha River. He gave flying lessons at $3.75 a lesson. West Virginia Airways operated out of Wertz Field and gave sightseeing flights for one dollar..

BATHING: Miss Sally K. Sattes owned the beach at Lower Falls on Coal River, one-and-a-half miles up the river from St. Albans. She charged 25 cents for persons over 12 and served a chicken diner for $1.00. For 25 cents one could spend all day swimming at Rock Lake Pool in the Spring Hill area.

SHOOTING: The Charleston Gun Club was located on Route 119, east of the Kanawha City bridge.

RIDING: One-and-a-half miles east of the C&O bridge at South Ruffner was located the Wewanna Riding Club. The Young Brothers Riding Academy at Lick Branch and at the south end of the Kanawha City bridge were the Kanawha Stables where most of the privately owned horses were kept.

MISCELLANEOUS SPORTS: Lake Chaweva at Cross Lanes offered fishing, boating, swimming, tennis, picnicking, and ice skating in the winter. The YWCA was and still is located at 1114 Quarrier Street. The YMCA was located at facing Capitol Street between Lee and Washington streets.

The Bill Garten Orchestra played beautiful swing-type music in Charleston and surrounding communities from 1935 to 1948. The photo was taken in The Club Charlban on Route 60 just east of St. Albans. Bill was born in Prince, West Virginia, lived in Hinton and moved to Charleston about 1923. He worked at Appalachian Electric Power Co. for 47 years. He organized the band about 1935 and they practiced in a storage room in the basement of the AEP office building. Garten was a self-educated musician and studied the history of jazz music and its musicians. If you mentioned a particular band, band leader or member, he could tell you the accomplishments and/or contributions to music of that group or person. He was interviewed several times on radio by Hugh McPherson on WTIP on his nighttime radio program. Hugh would draw on Bill's vast knowledge and memories of the Big Band era. Remember Hugh's pet mynah bird who would say when prompted, "I'm a cowboy, bang, bang."

THE SILVER SCREEN

The motion picture has had perhaps more influence on our society than any other single medium. Mary Pickford was America's Sweetheart, Douglas Fairbanks swashbuckled his way across the silent screen, Tom Mix and his horse, Tony, galloped into the hearts of millions of adoring fans, and John Wayne stormed the sands of Iwo Jima.

Mr. Edison changed the world with his marvelous flickering moving pictures and Charleston boasted of several early movie theaters. If one were to argue as to which was the first movie shown in Charleston, technically the answer would be a film of the heavyweight championship fight between Gentleman Jim Corbett and Herb Fitzsimmons shown at the Burlew Opera House on Capitol Street in 1897. The Burlew was built as an opera house and films were only occasionally shown.

The first actual movie theater was the Wonderland of 1904 which stood on Capitol Street where the K.B. & T. Building is now next to the library. The Wonderland was a nickelodeon, which meant that admission cost a nickel. In 1907, the Dreamland was listed in the City Directory at the same location so apparently the name was changed. In 1909 a man named Abe Cassis operated the Eagle Theatre across Capitol Street from the Dreamland. It was at the Eagle that one of the first attempts at talking pictures was made. The Royal Theatre was operated by Mr. J.C. Adler in 1911-12, but evidently didn't last long.

Since phonograph records could reproduce sound, it was a foregone conclusion that some would-be inventor would try to mate the moving picture with the photograph. The film was a comedy that involved a goat. Unfortunately, according to witnesses the lack of synchronization caused the actors to bleat like a goat and of course, the goat occasionally talked, so it must have been quite a sight and perhaps more of a laugh than the producers intended.

As movies gained in popularity it was inevitable that theaters would gain in opulence and perhaps the first real quality theater was the Colonial at 213 Capitol Street. There was also the Hippodrome at 211 Capitol which was operated by Timothy Kearse who later built the grand Kearse Theatre on Summers Street. The Hippodrome fell on hard times and in its later years lapsed into a girlie show house. The Strand was a popular theater on the corner of Lee and Summers, where the One Valley Square Building now stands. In later years the Strand was renamed the Greenbrier. The Rialto will be remembered by many in the Morrison Building on Quarrier Street. What is today known as the West Virginia State College Capitol Center Theatre on Summers Street started out as the Plaza Theatre. It was operated by Mr. Charles A. Midelburg, who was also the Hudson automobile dealer.

No story of Charleston's cinemas would be complete without note of the fine old Virginian on Lee Street (State Street) which was erected in 1912. The Virginian was a Warner Brothers First Class House so it ran the Cagney and Bogart classics.

Located on Summers Street.

Ads from 1939.

The Custer was located on West Washington Street, the State on East Washington Street.

The site of the Kearse Theatre on Summers Street is now a parking lot. Built in 1922 in the era of silent films for half a million dollars, the Kearse was billed as the largest and finest theater in the state. The Kearse was named for its owner, Timothy Kearse. The grand old showplace was familiar to Charlestonians for more than 60 years. In its early years, the Kearse was often host to the still popular vaudeville shows that featured live entertainment. In 1929, movies with sound arrived. With its luxurious design, the Kearse was Charleston's only true picture palace. The Kearse was a 20th Century Fox franchise while the Virginian was Warner Bros. and the Capitol was Metro-Goldwyn-Mayer. Thus we know that, for example, "Gone With the Wind" first played Charleston at the Capitol, and "Casablanca," the Virginian. The Rialto theater near Hale Street on Quarrier Street was what was known as a second-run theater, where you got to see two pictures. Those were the films that had had their first local showing at one of the finer theaters a few months earlier. A weekly ritual of kids growing up was the Saturday matinee, anticipated all week long. Only the Capitol theater remains to remind us of the way it was.

Crowd in front of the Kearse Theater in 1939. This could have been a Halloween event. The movie, "The Human Monster," starred famous movie monster, Bela Lugosi, who made movies from 1930 through 1956. ③64

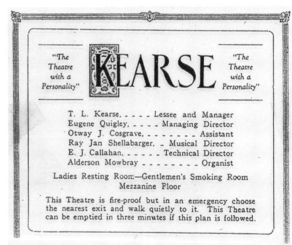

1922

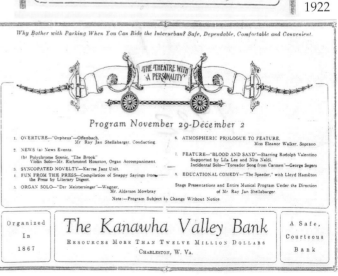

Grand opening, Nov. 29, 1922.

PLAZA THEATRE

Opening of Amusement Palace a Big Local Event Tomorrow Night

Curiosity on the part of the Charleston public will tomorrow night be satisfied, so far as concerns the New Plaza Theater, what it looks like on the inside and what sort of attractions have been booked for the gratification of those who promise to become patrons of the finest vaudeville house in West Virginia, and one of the finest in the country.

For the opening bill, Manager Gus Bartram has provided a real treat for those who wish to take advantage of the chance to see the initial performance. There will be five attractions. Each number on the program is one that will appeal to every one who likes first-class and sparkling acts of the vaudeville nature.

The premier attraction is the Bobker Troupe of Arabian Whirlwinds, which is composed of twelve of the best acrobats that have ever been produced, and whose exceptional work has made them in great demand. They are working the Keith Circuit now, and because of the furore they have created in the East, being the best of their kind on the road, they have been engaged for the first three days of this week at a surprisingly big figure to assist in welcoming the first audiences that will see the Plaza in all its glory on the opening night. This troupe is coming direct to Charlestson from Keith's Fifth Avenue house in New York City, where they have been the sensation for the past two weeks. Leaving here they will go to oLuisville to open an engagement the latter part of this week.

But this troupe is not all, by any means, that has been arranged for the

Plaza patrons, 126 of whom have already reserved box seats.

There will be Hunter and Davenport, an expensive team of comedians, male and female, who have a splendid skit that is sure to bring smiles to every one who sees them.

Then there are Hallen and Hayes, eccentric comedians and singers, who can tip the fantastic just a little better that the other fellow can. Their offering is one of the neatest in the line that has been produced this season.

Agnes Carlton and Company will be on the bill, too. They have a whole show themselves, but it goes as only one of the five splendid ones. They are presenting at this time a playlet, known all over the East, "The Thoroughbred." It has all the elements of a first-class theatrical offering, and comes highly recommended.

Three Bohemians, who have as clever an act as has ever been sent this far

Even after mentioning all those designated in the foregoing, there are the West and South. It comes as a hummer, and is guarnteed to please every man, woman and child who goes to the theater.

It has required some rapid work to get the new amusement palace in readiness for the opening as per schedule, but all the work is completed, except the few finishing touches necessary in getting every item perfected. The stage is been put in readiness; the seats—1400 in number—are in place; the heating and lighting, as well as the ventilating plants, are in working order; the lobby and foyer are being nfiished. The decorators have completed their contract and did themselves proud.

After the opening day, there will be three shows daily. Matinee, 3 o'clock; night performances, 7:45 and 9 o'clock.

Prices for the matinees will be 20 cents for the whole lower flor, except Mondays, Thursdays, Saturdays, and Holidays.

Every lady attending the shows,

Monday night, will be presented with a souvenir.   380

1912

1929

In the days of vaudeville just imagine the downtown hotels full of entertainers - must have been pretty lively! ③64

SUNDAY, DECEMBER 22, 1912.   THE CHARLESTON GAZETTE.   PAGE SEVENTEEN

PLAZA THEATRE

"THE HOUSE BEAUTIFUL

Will open its doors to the Charleston Public Monday Night for the first time for which a Great Feature Bill has been booked.

The show for the first half of the week is as follows:
Monday, Tuesday and Wednesday

12 People   Bobker Troupe   12 People
The most elaborate Arabian whirlwind act, positively the greatest of its kind in the world.

Three Bohemians, Singing Comedians & Instrumentalists.

Agnes Carlton & Company
Presenting an exceptional clever one act playlett entitled "The Thoroughbred."

Hallen &Hayes, Eccentric Comedians, Singers & Dancers.
Hunter and Davenport, In a corking good Comedy Singing, talking and Dancing offering.
Gaumont Weekly, The Worlds Current Events.
Plaza Orchestra, Overture: Selections from the operetta "Naughty Marrietta" by Victor Herbert.
Orchestra composed of the following artists: Harry Bekenstein, leader; Harry Froehlich, pianist; Willy Shultze, celloist; Emery McClure, cornetist; Cam Mathews, drums.
Monday performances: 7.45 and 9 o'clock. After Monday their will be three shows daily, 3, 7.45 and 9 o'clock.

The show for the last half of the week is as follows:
Thursday, Friday and Saturday

"Sweet Sixteen Girls", Those classy girls in their big Broadway song review.

"Kipp and Kippy" Those clever juggling comedians.

"O'Donnell Brothers", Surprise supreme, Irish character comedians in a one act playlett entitled In Dear Old Ireland.

"Youno Brothers", A riot in China Town, introducing acrobatic in a new and novel way.

"Georgia Trio", Those clever entertainers from the Sunny South. Harmony in abundance.

Gaumont Weekly, Worlds current events.
Plaza Orchestra, Overture.

THREE SHOWS DAILY: 3, 7:45, 9 O'CLOCK

Prices:

Matinees, 10c and 20c, Except Mon., Thurs., Sat. and Holidays
Night, 10c, 20c and 30c.

The Plaza Theatre eventually became the Capitol Theatre and is now operated by West Virginia State College as The Capitol Center Theatre.

1912

Audience Stampeded At the Plaza Theatre; No One Was Injured

Moving Picture Film Caught Fire and Created a Panic Among the Timid--Bob Williams Proves Himself a Hero in Putting Out the Blaze

Last night, when the Plaza theatre on Summers street, was packed with hundreds of women and children, a moving picture film, which was being shown, caught fire and created a panic, and if it had not been for the heroic work of Bob Williams of the Globe Furniture Co., of Kanawha street, who rushed in to the steel cage in which the picture machine is operated, and at the risk of his life put the fire out, and the prevalence of cooler heads among the audience, no doubt numbers of women and children would have been trampled to death in the mad rush to leave the building.

The operator, who was running the picture machine when the film caught fire, made a hurried exit and left the audience to the mercy of the flames. The management of the theatre, assisted by a number of men in the audience, quieted the women and children and by this probably saved their lives.

This rather humorous but potentially tragic story from 1913 was probably repeated in other theaters across the country as motion picture film used at the time was made of highly flammable nitrate material.

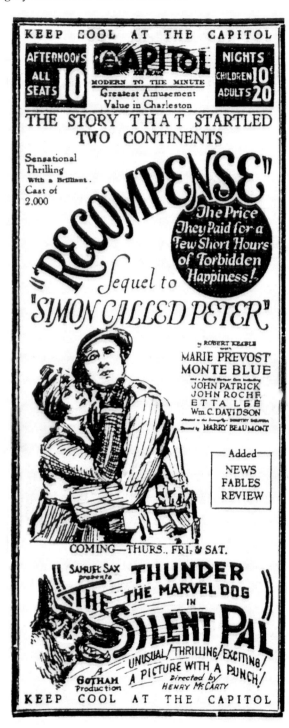

By 1929 the Plaza had become the Capitol Theatre and was now showing sound movies.

One of the greatest motion pictures of all time was
presented at the Captiol Theatre on Jan. 25, 1940.

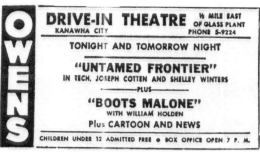

The Owens was in
East Kanawha City
where the K-Mart
store is today.

Ads from 1952.

The major drive-in in the upper Kanawha Valley was the
Trail Drive-In on U.S. Route 60 near Belle. This view is
from 1954.

The Gallagher Theater on Paint Creek looks little more
than a barn but in the 1940s and '50s heyday of Hollywood, it must have been a popular place. Photo circa
1957. JERRY SMITH COLL.

Hundreds Attend Opening of New Play House and Praise Beauties

Yesterday was the opening day for West Virginia's finest motion picture house, the Virginian, located on State street opposite the Y. M. C. A. building. Large audiences were in attendance throughout the afternoon and evening, and all who visited the new establishment were enthuiastic in their praise of the excellence of the arangements for the comfort of patrons. Four films were shown, all new in this city and all of a quality that speaks for the character of the entertainment patrons of the house may expect.

The Virginian is the most handsomely and comfortably arranged show house in the state, and cost complete $20,000. The house seats seven hundred spectators, and is so designed that every seat affords an excellent view of the screen.

October 20, 1912

1952

1925

The Virginian, although smaller than the Kearse, was none the less, one of Charleston's premier theatres. A Warner Brothers first run operation, many of the most memorable films were shown there. *Casablanca* with Humphrey Bogart and of course, the Jimmy Cagney greats took Charlestonian's minds off the worries of the everyday world. As we look at what passes for entertainment today we can only wonder, as the Statler Brothers song declared: "Whatever Happened to Randolph Scott Ridin the Trail Alone?"

HAS LARGEST LOBBY

With the announcement of the formal opening of the Grand theater for tomorrow evening at 6.30, another cinema palace has been added to the list of Charleston's amusement palaces.

The Grand, located in the new Knights of Pythias building at Charleston street and Bigley avenue, the West Side has provided a long-felt want in one of the finest and most up-to-date movie palaces in the city.

While several different movie houses have been located at various times on the West Side, they have all been small houses, in the second or third-class, and nothing has ever been attempted on the scale of the Grand. The Grand theater is on a par with the leading theaters of Charleston and will offer its patrons the highest class attractions obtainable. The finest and most up-to-ate equipment has been installed, assuring everyone that the programs offered will be presented in the most pleasing manner, especial attention being paid to projection and to the ventilation of the main auditorium. The Grand will seat 625 persons on its main floor, no balcony being used, and suitable ladies' rest rooms have been provided. Large reversible exhaust and blower fans have been installed, which will change the air in the entire theater every four minutes, not only assuring coolness in hot weather, but a continual flow of fresh air into the main auditorium. Patrons will not be bothered with that stuffy feeling so common in most theaters.

The Raven half-tone screen, the same as used in the world's largest theater, the Capitol of New York, has been provided, being so constructed that eye tiredness, due to glare and distortion, has been entirely done away with. Only one other theater in Charleston has this screen, it being the Eastern, which is also owned and operated by the Washington Amusement company, which also operates the Grand.

The largest lobby of any theater in the city has been made a feature of the new Grand, this lobby leading into the main auditorium directly from where Bigley avenue joins Charleston street, and is 18 feet wide, 60 feet long and a vaulted ceiling 20 feet high. Vogel Gettier, managing director of the Washington Amusement company, will have the management of the Grand under his direct supervision, as he now has the Eastern, and will give all of his time to seeing that the wants of his patrons are properly taken care of.

Mr. Gettier has instituted something new into the movie fields of the city. All of the super pictures that have been booked by him will have simultaneous showings in both the Eastern and Grand theaters. This will mean that both houses, the Eastern and the Grand, will have the same program on the same day and date.

On the regular program pictures these will be shown one day at the Eastern and on the following day at the Grand. This assures the patrons of the Grand of the same high-class features, comedies and novelties that have made the Eastern one of the most popular playhouses in the city.

The opening program for the Grand, which will also be featured at the Eastern theater on Monday, Tuesday and Wednesday, is announced in other columns of this paper.

The Grand Theatre on Charleston Street (West Washington Street) at Bigley Avenue was opened on Aug. 14, 1922.. Amazingly thousands pass by this old landmark building every day little knowing it started out as a theatre, once housed an A&P Store on the street level and ended up as Statts Hospital.

William T. Aldrich's Remarkable Entertainmen

A TRIP TO THE HAWAIIAN ISLANDS

WITH

IMPERIAL HAWAIIAN SINGERS

in Stage and Screen

Presented in Conjunction with

SATURDAY, MAY 28—

Tom Mix and Tony the Wonder Horse in "THE GREAT K. & A. TRAIN ROBBERY." The greatest western thriller of the greatest western star.

"A TRIP TO THE HAWAIIAN ISLANDS" on stage and screen.

Juvenile comedy, "EXCESS BAGGAGE," with Big Boy.

GRAND THEATRE   1927

CHARLESTON ST. AT BIGLEY AVE.

Mayor William W. Wertz

1944

William W. Wertz was the Republican mayor of Charleston for two terms, 1923-1931. Wertz Field was named in his honor. He was born in 1879 "up Elk" where his parents had migrated from Pennsylvania. He moved to Charleston in 1897 to teach school and graduated from the West Virginia University law school in 1900. He began his political career the next year with his election as city recorder. He was also elected city collector, police judge, five terms as a city councilman, three terms in the state legislature and 10 years on the Board of Education. His farm "up Elk" was known as "Dare Manor" and his home in Charleston was at 1422 Lee Street. Wertz was also a noted writer of short stories under a pseudonym. He died in 1956.

Mayor D. Boone Dawson

One of Charleston's greatest periods of expansion occurred during the three-term regime of Republican Mayor D. Boone Dawson, 1935-1947. During this time the South Side bridge was built, the largest Public Works Administration project in the country up to that time. The massive Kanawha Boulevard project was completed, the Municipal Auditorium was built, Littlepage Terrace and Washington Manor provided over 400 low-income housing units, and many other street, sewer, fire stations and recreational projects were completed. Dawson also held office through the turbulent years of the war and continued to have a presence in the community into the 1970s. He died in 1975.

Soliciting YOUR Vote

NOVEMBER 5, 1940

Is a
FARMER
MINER
LAWYER
JUDGE
MAYOR

Member of
BAPTIST CHURCH
AMERICAN LEGION
ELKS, MOOSE
EAGLES, K. of P.
LIONS

Daniel Boone Dawson

Republican Candidate for Governor

Boone Dawson's life has been a series of accomplishments.

From the time of his birth in 1897 on a farm near Sissonville, W. Va., BOONE DAWSON'S life has been a series of accomplishments. While doing his work on the Dawson farm he found time to complete the schooling offered at Sissonville. His father having been a country school teacher for 25 years, the governor-to-be recognized the value of more education, and came to Charleston to attend high school. Upon graduation he enlisted in the U. S. Army for World War service. Having faithfully served his country for the duration of the war, he worked in the Logan County coal fields and saved money to pay his way through law school. In 1921 he "hung out his shingle" in Charleston. The year 1931 found him serving as Municipal Judge, and in 1935 he was elected mayor of your capital city, to which post he was re-elected in 1939. In those five years Charleston has built the five mile long Kanawha Boulevard, one of the finest city auditoriums in the country, four new bridges, a new incinerator, new fire stations and many miles of new streets.

DANIEL BOONE DAWSON OFFERS YOU
Achievement, Vision, Executive Ability and Proven Administration

Let DAWSON Take

Schools Out of Politics

Cities Out of the Red

Farmers Out of the Mud

1968

Mayor John T. Copenhaver

Another charismatic mayor presided over the city for eight years, 1951-1959. John Thomas Copenhaver was known locally as "Jumping John." His campaign slogan was "The Man Who Gets Things Done" and he lived up to it. The Civic Center was built, annexation made Charleston the state's largest city and over 100 miles of streets were paved. But Copenhaver was a very controversial leader and led the fight to end vice in the city. He even banned the novel *Peyton Place* from city newsstands although admitting that he never read the book, but depended on the advice of others. He ran for governor twice on the Republican ticket but was defeated each time - 1952 and 1956. On Aug. 13, 1959, "Jumping John" finally met his match and died while still in office.

We invite you to meet

SENATOR JOHN F. KENNEDY
PRESIDENTIAL CANDIDATE

Wednesday, March 16

30

at

11:~~00~~ A.M. at Hotel Kanawha

West Virginians for Kennedy

Senator Kennedy won the West Virginia primary in 1960 which gave him the Democratic presidential nomination and eventually the presidency. He held his victory celebration at the Kanawha Hotel. BK

FOR PRESIDENT

☒ **JOHN F. KENNEDY**

BOSTON, MASSACHUSETTS

Mayor Copenhaver and a suppporter on Lee Street, April 19, 1959. The mayor had only a few months to live. CN

To Continue the Most Constructive Administration in the History of Charleston - Vote for -

ROY H. PIERSON
for City Treasurer

D. BOONE DAWSON
for Mayor

HAROLD H. NEFF
for Municipal Judge

for Councilmen at Large

1944

Franklin D. Roosevelt defeated President Herbert Hoover in a landslide victory in 1932.

Oct. 25, 1932

PRESTON - LAWSON FUNERAL HOME

A Courteous Efficient And Sympathetic Service

Ambulance

Day Night

Phone 30-221

MERRILL H. PRESTON

ROY A. LAWSON

116 Shrewsbury Street

Charleston, West Virginia

The Founders of Preston-Lawson Funeral Home, 1940.

Boy Scout Troop 110, sponsored by Simpson Memorial United Methodist Church, 1937.

Mattie V. Lee, M.D. - The Mattie V. Lee Home was named in her honor. She was West Virginia's first Black woman physician (M.D., Howard University, 1911). She labored untiringly among the people of Charleston for social betterment.

E.T. DuMetz, owner/operator of DuMetz Studio of Photography, 1918-1961. Mr. DuMetz also was a staff photographer for the *Charleston Gazette* from the early '40s until his retirement in 1961.

J.F.J. Clark Sr., second principal of Garnet High School, 1908-1946.

Garnet High School newspaper, 1917.

Carter G. Woodson Junior High School in 1938, located on Pennsylvania Avenue, St. Albans. The school was moved to Stop 16 in 1943. The building now houses the American Legion.

The Charleston Business and professional Men's Club of 1940 visits the National Youth Administration Training Center which was located in South Charleston. From left to right: Mr. Johnson, James C. Campbell, Marsden Cabell, Thomas Posey, Andrew Calloway, Atty. T.G. Nutter, C.W. Boyd, Atty. Wm. Lonesome, Dr. Wm. Hall, Dr. Wm. Morris, Atty. Julius Love, Atty. C.W. Dickerson, Atty. Willard Brown, Atty. W. Ambrose, Dr. Robert Jones, J.C. Evans, Dr. Charles Payne, unknown, unknown, J.F.J. Clark, Dr. Andrew Brown, Edward James Sr., Mr. Murphy, Kermit Hall, A.H. Brown, and in the doorway, Charles King Price.

Mr. Desper's ice truck and employee, Billy Anderson, late 1930s.

Children's Christmas party sponsored by the Les Chercheuses Club at the K of P Hall, 1936. Club members from left to right: Elizabeth Burke, Hazel Brownley, Nan Louise Thompson, Thelma White (McDaniel), Alice Diamond, Gladys Mitchell, Virginia Cooley, Agatha Starling (Lowe) and Anna Gardner (Barnett).

A graduating class of the West Virginia Institute of Beauty Culture. The founder, Mrs. Carrie Jackson stands at left front. Her sister, Mrs. Lillian Tinsley is at right front.

Members of the Charleston Improvement League, 1984. Left to right, front row: Miss Elizabeth Burks, Mrs. Lottie Morris, Mrs. Susan Mitchell, Mrs. Ruth Norman. Second row: Mrs. Mona Robinson, Mrs. Alfrelene Armstrong, Mrs. Martha Haynes, Mrs. Phyliss Curry, Mrs. Thelma McDaniel. Third row: Mrs. JoAnn Manns, Mrs. Frances Hale, Mrs. Katherine Gaines, Mrs. Daisy Alston. Fourth row: Mrs. Alice Dexter, Mrs. Mary Dews, Mrs. Rosa Bradford, Mrs. Mary Cook. Fifth row: Mrs. Daisy Sweeney, Mrs. Alice Clark, Mrs. Betty Tate. Sixth row: Mrs. Marian Jones, Mrs. Josephine Moore, Mrs. Jane Dunlap and Mrs. Frances Haston.

Intermediate Troop #78 of Simpson United Methodist Church in 1961.

Child Care Center and Simpson Church joined together for Daily Vacation Bible School, circa 1953.

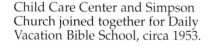

This West Virginia National Guard camp was established at Pratt in 1912 in response to strife in the coal fields. The big house in the center is still standing. swv

After martial law was declared in the southern coal fields in September 1912, these arms and ammunition boxes were seized from miners and coal operators, brought to Charleston and stacked on the Capitol lawn. Note the Colt

machine guns owned by the operators and national guardsmen guarding the seized arms. Ammunition belonging to the National Guard was also stored in the attic of the Capitol building when it caught fire on January 3, 1921. The resulting fire caused bullets to explode in all directions. View at the rear of the building looking north with Dickinson Street to the right. (146) swv

20ᵀᴴ Century Military Affairs in the County

Two military camps were established in Charleston during the short Spanish-American War. Camp Atkinson, which was named for West Virginia's governor at the time, George Atkinson (1897-1901), was located in the west end of Charleston, near what is now the Patrick Street Plaza. The first troops of the state national guard set up camp on June 27, 1898. The Second West Virginia Infantry Regiment, comprising 1,322 men left the camp on Aug. 19 for Pennsylvania and then South Carolina. An article in the Aug. 20, 1898, issue of the *Charleston Daily Gazette* stated:

"Camp Atkinson is now part of the history of Charleston, and one of the prides of the past... On those who, no doubt out of habit, drove to Glenwood yesterday evening, the scene that met them at the end of their drive must have produced a strange impression. Where, 20 hours before, had been visible the bustle of a thousand men, lay only a wreck - a field of mud strewn with rubbish - a deserted village- the remains of what had been pretty Camp Atkinson."

A second camp was established in the flatlands of Kanawha City and named Camp Lee. Here the First Regiment West Virginia Infantry was formed.

It left the camp on May 20, 1898, for Tennessee and eventually Georgia where it was mustered out of service in February 1899.

Camp Lee (later Camp Kanawha) continued to be used by the National Guard up through the First World War. In 1921, U.S. Army Air Service bombers landed here at the request of the governor to possibly do battle with striking coal miners. The planes were commanded by well-known aviator, Maj. Gen. Billy Mitchell. Fortunately, the planes were not needed in a combat role and soon returned to their Virginia base.

In the summer of 1916 the Second West Virginia Infantry Regiment was mustered into federal service at Camp Lee and sent to Texas to patrol the border with Mexico.

In 1925 Camp Lee was renamed Camp Charnock in honor of Brig. Gen. John Hobbs Charnock who died Dec. 29, 1924, while serving as the eighth adjutant general of West Virginia. Because it would cost less to conduct training for the West Virginia National Guard closer to home, the camp was used in 1925 and '26. Approximately 900 troops of the 150ᵗʰ Infantry, commanded by Col. W.E. Eubank, used the area.

National Guardsman in front of his bell tent at Camp Lee in Kanawha City, 1908.

CAMP KANAWHA

This photo is thought to be of state guard troops camped in Kanawha City in 1915 or '16. The rifles are Model 1903 Springfield 30-0-6, standard issue to troops at this time. TODD HANSON COLL.

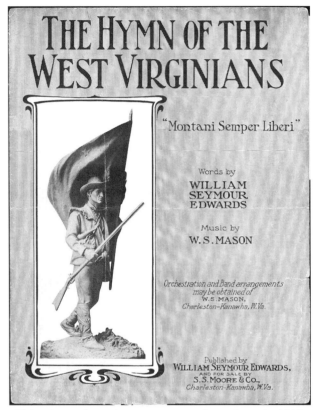

This piece of music was apparently written in 1912 by the well-known owner of the Mason School of Music, Sandy Mason.

This photo and the following pages show national guard troops in camp from 1915 to 1917 in Kanawha City, just east of the Kanawha City bridge. Troops from this camp were federalized and sent to the Texas-Mexican border to protect it from Pancho Villa's rebels.

The state guard band, 1915.

Incredibly the troops were kept waiting in 1916 at the Kanawha City Camp for four long months before departure for Texas and the Pancho Villa expedition. Morale became very low and A.W.O.L. (going back home) was not uncommon. Visiting the "boys" in Kanawha City became such a regular habit that steamboats were scheduled from the levee to the camp.

1916

This escort wagon is similar to ones used in the Civil War but in 1878 its size was reduced to facilitate ease of control. The army at this time was still dependent on horsepower for a big part of its transportation needs.

This extremely rare view of officers on horseback leading marching soldiers down State Street (Lee Street) at Capitol Street is undated but it is certainly of the World War One era. The building visible on the left still stands and houses the Winter Floral Shop. For speculation we can note these troops are pretty sharp and could be General Bandholtz's Regulars who were ordered to Charleston from Columbus, Ohio, in 1921 to put down the miner's strike.

Unfinished latrine, 1917.

We now live in an age of the 21st century when we may no longer have months to prepare for war.
Thomas Jefferson - that wisest of the founding fathers said: "The price of liberty is eternal vigilance!"
We must never forget that!

Throughout the 20th century Americans have almost always been unprepared for war - being a peace-loving people. The soldiers of World War One drilled with broomsticks and made do with Spanish-American War (1898) leftovers.

Sunday was the biggest day yet passed at the state mobilization camp. Thousands of visitors thronged the streets of the city of tents, and witnessed the drills and parades put on by the men in kahki. Street cars, taxis and launches were taxed to capacity throughout the afternoon, and hundreds of cameras were trained on the moving troops for snapshots for album and press.

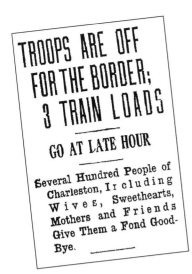

TROOPS ARE OFF FOR THE BORDER; 3 TRAIN LOADS

GO AT LATE HOUR

Several Hundred People of Charleston, Including Wives, Sweethearts, Mothers and Friends Give Them a Fond Good-Bye.

West Virginia National Guard troops and their vehicles depart Charleston in 1916 to join General Pershing on the Mexican border to participate in the expedition against Pancho Villa.

MARINES ARRIVE TO GUARD MAILS

Three Come to Charleston From Quantico, Va., and Will Ride on Trucks

DAY AND NIGHT PROTECTION

Three United States marines arrived here this morning from the marine base at Quantico, Va., to guard the mails between the Charleston post office and the railroad stations in accordance with Postmaster General New's order to "shoot to kill."

The soldiers of that branch of the regular army are being assigned to this duty at post offices in the more important cities throughout the nation to stop the operations of bandits in mail robberies.

The three marines sent to Charleston will go on duty at once and will operate in three shifts, both day and night.

Their duty will be to ride the motor trucks carrying mail from stations to the post office and from post office to the stations. They also will stand guard over mails at the railroad stations until loaded on trains, and likewise at the post office while loading and unloading are in progress.

November 10, 1926,
Charleston Daily Mail

- *Sham Battle* -

AERIAL BOMBS TO PRECEDE PROGRAM

Airplane Also Will Take Part in Armistice Day Event in Laidley Field

Plans for the biggest local celebration of Armistice day since 1918 have been completed by the American legion and the National guard.

A big fireworks display, followed by a realistic sham battle, will take place tomorrow night in Laidley field, commencing at 8 o'clock. At 6 o'clock, however, aerial bombs will be sent up to draw attention to the celebration. Four will be sent up until 7 o'clock, and thereafter until the program begins the bombs will be exploded at intervals of 10 minutes.

The fireworks will be the preliminary to the chief feature of the observance, the reproduction of a battle scene to represent the attack upon a German "pillbox," in which different units of the guard will participate.

The "pillbox" will conceal three machine guns. Infantry and artillery will attack the "enemy" and an airplane will add another touch to the make-believe battle. The artillery and airplane will cover the advance of the infantry with fire and bombs. Hand grenades will be used.

The fireworks display was arranged first so that the smokescreen of the sham battle will not interfere.

Salvation army officers will be at the gates to collect an admission fee of 25 cents. The surplus above the expenses will be turned into the neediest families' fund. A large crowd is expected, and the gates will be open shortly after seven o'clock, it was said, to accommodate the early comers. The gates on the New York Central side of the field will be used, the other side to be closed for the display.

Buglers tomorrow morning at 11 o'clock will stand on the steps of the federal building and sound "cease firing." One minute later "taps" will be sounded.

From November 10, 1926 issue, *Charleston Daily Mail*

Standing second from left, a youthful Cramer Bollinger was an officer in the West Virginia National Guard. This September 1924 scene of machine gun practice was likely in the Kanawha City area. Note the water-cooled barrels.

West Virginia State Guard

The West Virginia State Guard was organized on Feb. 6, 1942, to replace state National Guard troops called to Federal service. Headquarters was in Charleston with an authorized strength of 1,282 officers and men. Companies were established around the state. They performed emergency services at mine disasters, guarded downed military aircraft, fought forest fires, helped with floods along the Ohio River and other duties. The guard was disbanded by July 31, 1947, with the thanks of the State for the "self-sacrificing manner in which the Guardsmen met all demands and responded to all calls of duty."

Men in the State Guard were able-bodied but usually a bit too old or were for some reason not called up for regular service. The principle was simple - while millions of soldiers were overseas fighting the Germans and Japanese - someone had to watch over the security of the home front and that was the State Guard.

The Salvation Army clubhouse for military personnel was located at the corner of Kanawha Boulevard and Broad Street during the war. The USO or United Service Organization was established on Feb. 4, 1941. It included the YMCA, the YWCA, the Salvation Army, the National Jewish Welfare Board, the National Catholic Community Service and Travelers Aid International. At the peak of World War Two there were a total of 3,035 USO operations and USO camp shows gave more than 438,000 performances to military audiences.

MILITARY CLUB OPENS MONDAY

Salvation Army Seeks House Furnishings

Although not completely furnished, the Salvation Army's Military and Navy clubhouse at Kanawha boulevard and Broad street is expected to open Monday to members of the armed forces, Major Hal Hughes said Friday.

Headed by Major Hughes, the Salvation Army's personnel took over the vacant house this week "to clean it and put it in shape for a club." Major Hughes said about 10 inmates of the city jail had been "loaned" by Mayor Dawson to help with the cleaning of the house, and that Sheriff N.R. Henderson has offered the services of several county jail prisoners.

The service club will accommodate about 30 men, Major Hughes said, but in case of emergencies "we will be able to take care of 75 or 100 men if we can obtain the necessary furnishings."

Comfortable chairs and blankets are needed for the club, he said, in urging that Charlestonians make any possible donations to help furnish the club. "We will have enough mattresses for the cots," he added.

Labor unions of the building trades council, Major Hughes said, have volunteered to do necessary plumbing, carpentry, glazing and all other repair work incidental to putting the house in order. Signs will be placed at entrance points to the city to direct men on furlough to the clubhouse, which will be the downtown center of hospitality, Major Hughes said.

FDR's Visit to the Kanawha Valley
- Sept. 3, 1940 -

President Franklin D. Roosevelt visited the Kanawha Valley on Sept. 3, 1940, to inspect the newly reconditioned naval ordnance plant in South Charleston. He was assistant secretary of the navy in 1917 when the plant was constructed. The president and first lady, Eleanor, arrived at the South Charleston railroad station and along with Senator Matthew Neely and Governor Homer Holt were taken on a 50-minute tour of the plant. Then the entourage drove in a five-mile parade over the Patrick Street bridge down the newly opened Kanawha Boulevard over the South Side bridge to the C&O depot. More than 50,000 local citizens turned out to cheer the president who boarded an eastbound train for Washington. Mrs. Roosevelt left later in the day by plane.

F.D.R.'s train leaves the C&O station after his visit. DOUG NEALE COLL.

This rather poor amateur photo shows F.D.R. proceeding through South Charleston heading for the Patrick Street bridge. 301

INFORMAL REMARKS OF THE PRESIDENT
OVER THE RADIO,
Charleston, West Virginia,
September 3, 1940.

I am very glad to have this chance to say "How do you do?" to you good people of West Virginia. I have had a most interesting drive with Senator Neely and with the Governor.

In a way this is a sentimental journey for me because I have seen an old plant that was started by the Navy when I was Assistant Secretary in 1917, an armour plant which I am glad to say last summer we have put back into business. And we are also changing over the old shell plant to make more guns for the Navy and probably for the Army too. Since then we have come up past many other plants that are turning out munitions for the Government over a very wonderful new highway, new boulevard, that I was delighted to see.

And so I have come to the end of this sentimental journey and the idea that was started twenty-three years ago is now bearing full fruit.

F.D.R. on Kanawha Boulevard after his tour of the Naval Ordnance plant. With him are Governor Holt and Sen. Matthew Neely. Thousands of people lined the parade route to get a look at one of America's most memorable presidents. F.D.R. is looking to the side in the rear. SWV, HARRY BRAWLEY COLL.

Eleanor Roosevelt visited the South Hills home of Arthur Koontz. She stayed after F.D.R. departed for Washington, D.C. The naval officer is believed to be Arthur Koontz, Jr., who was killed in World War Two.

Eleanor Roosevelt and Arthur Koontz leave his home in South Hills. DOUG NEALE COLL.

America was not at war in 1940 and 1941 but as this newspaper article shows, American military personnel were being killed on the high seas.

2 Charleston Boys on Reuben James

Former Junior High Grid Star, Lick Branch Youth Aboard Destroyer

Two Charleston youths, one a former star athlete, were among the six West Virginians believed to have been aboard the U.S. destroyer *Reuben James* which was sunk near Iceland Thursday night.

Joe Settle, 17, son of Mrs. Emma J. Settle of 1317-A Crescent road and Harry Settle of Quarrier street, was a graduate of Lincoln junior high school where he was a star all-round athlete, excelling at football. As fullback for Lincoln he was named on the Gazette's all-city junior high team in 1938. He also played on the basketball and track teams there. In 1939, he was a member of the Charleston high school "B" football team. He transferred to Stonewall Jackson high school last year and left school in January to join the navy.

The other Charlestonian is Clarence F. Robinson, 21, who made his home with a brother, Ivan Robinson of Lick Branch. He wrote his brother recently telling him that he was being sent to Iceland aboard the *Reuben James* and that he was rated as a first class seaman serving as a cook.

Young Settle had recently written his mother and two brothers, H. Paul and H. Cameron Settle, that he and seven mates of a gun crew had their bunks on the topside where there was little chance of being trapped in the event of a mishap.

What Were Their Names?

Folk singer Woody Guthrie once wrote a ballad whose refrain went: "Tell me, what were their names;/ Tell me, what were their names;/ Did you have a friend on the good *Reuben James?*" Guthrie's lament was for some of the men who served and died almost unsung during America's undeclared war against Germany in the Atlantic in 1941. For it was war in all but the legalistic sense of the word. Ships of the United States Navy escorted convoys through cold northern seas; American vessels were torpedoed, American lives lost. The situation had come about by degrees as Roosevelt moved carefully to aid Britain without arousing the nation's isolationist sentiment. There had been the destroyers-for-bases agreement, and then Lend-Lease, and in July of 1941 the sending of American troops to Iceland to relieve British forces already there to defend that strategic island against possible Nazi seizure.

Then, in a step barely short of war, American naval units went on convoy duty. Roosevelt and Churchill had divided the Atlantic between them. The ocean west of the dividing line was declared part of the American defense zone, and through its waters the American Navy shepherded the convoys; east of the line the Royal Navy was responsible. There could have been war at any time Hitler wanted it, but he actually tried to avoid it. Even so, on Sept. 4, 1941, the destroyer *Greer* exchanged torpedoes for depth charges with a submarine; both vessels were unharmed, but Roosevelt ordered the Navy to shoot German warships in the west Atlantic on sight. In mid-October, the *Kearny* was torpedoed with 11 killed but did not sink, and just after dawn on Oct. 31, the *Reuben James* was hit and sank at once; 115 men, more than two thirds of all aboard, perished. Robert E. Sherwood, a Roosevelt adviser, observed that the public seemed more interested in the Army-Notre Dame football game.

Sunny Joe Settle was lost on the *U.S.S. Reuben James.*

USS Reuben James
U.S. NAVAL INSTITUTE

To say that World War II was the biggest thing that ever happened to Charleston and the Kanawha Valley would be an understatement because never before and never since has the valley played so important a role on the world scene.

It was during the worlds greatest war that it received its boastful name - "The Magic Valley."

The second World War was fueled by the chemicals and synthetics that Kanawha magically distilled from the rich natural resource treasure chest that is West Virginia.

German prisoners of war often saw Charleston and the Valley from the C&O train windows as they passed through on their way to prisoner of war camps and locals who stood at the station could attest to their wide-eyed faces peering through the coach windows - doubtless wondering why the Führer chose this great land with its endless expanse to make war on.

From the alloy metals plant upriver, to the vast production cornucopia of the middle valley, even on to the yards of the Marietta Manufacturing Plant in Point Pleasant which built minesweepers that served across the world's oceans, the great Kanawha Valley played a big part in driving a stake into the Nazi heart. As long as noble history shall be celebrated, West Virginians and the people of Kanawha County in particular, will take pride in standing up to the best the tyrants wrath could summon and winning the V for Victory!

Needless to say that victory was not without cost and their memory will live forever.

ANTI-AIRCRAFT UNITS SOUGHT

Kanawha, Ohio Valleys Named as Sites

Establishment of anti-aircraft batteries in the Kanawha and Ohio valleys to protect railroads and vital defense industries was proposed Wednesday, Kanawha County Co-ordinator Virgil F. Frizzell learned.

Cabell County Prosecutor J.J.N. Quinlan said he will recommend the batteries' establishment to governmental agencies and Huntington's civilian defense committee.

Mr. Frizzell on Wednesday announced at his headquarters in the courthouse basement that plans for Thursday's meeting of mayors, fire chiefs and police chiefs of 12 Kanawha county towns in the intermediate courtroom were nearly completed.

"We'll get the county defense ball really rolling at tomorrow's meeting," he added. "There is a tremendous defense job in our vital county and we will require the co-operation of every available man and woman in the work. As soon as possible, we will take registrations of persons desiring to co-operate and they will be classified as to their capabilities.

Several score went to the defense headquarters Wednesday to offer their aid but were told to await the registration setup.

Meanwhile, Mayor Dawson met at city hall with City Manager Carl B. Early, Police Chief W.A. Tully and Sam Richard, chairman of the city council police committee, to consider immediate purchase of needed equipment, including motor vehicles and weapons, to co-ordinate the city's defense plans with those of the county.

Use of uniformed police to augment of the plainclothes squad has been suggested.

Mr. Frizzell conferred with Sam Montgomery, executive director of the Charleston American Red Cross chapter, to set up a medical staff for emergencies.

Dec. 10, 1941

FRANK HASTIE, CIVILIAN MURDERED BY JAPS

Frank Hastie, a former Belle Works employee has been reported killed at Wake Island in a communique from the Navy Department to his mother and father, Mr. and Mrs. J.J. Hastie of Noyes Avenue.

Frank was one of the many civilian workers who were captured by the Japs. He was in a group that was lined up on the beaches and machine gunned.

Frank was active in Charleston High School athletics and had attended Bowling Green Business College. He was a well-known boxer. Hastie was 27 at the time of his death.

February 1946

December 7, 1941 - Pearl Harbor Attack

Like all Americans, people in Kanawha County were going about their business on Sunday morning, December 7, 1941. Christmas was only a few short weeks away and the thought of war was not uppermost on the minds of citizens.

As articles in local newspapers stated, citizens responded immediately to the attack on the United States.

West Virginia Plant Guards Placed on 'Alert' in Crisis

Orders to "tighten up security" at the vital naval ordnance plant at South Charleston were received Monday by Capt. Roy Pfaff, officer in charge.

Increased vigilance also is in effect at Kanawha valley's other vast chemical and industrial plants, which supply materials for munitions.

C.H.Doherty Jr., manager of the Belle plant of the du Pont company, called his guard "ample for the time being."

Compulsory fingerprinting for employees at the Carbide and Carbon Chemicals corporation is in effect. S.W. Pickering II, personnel director said. The huge South Charleston plant has 60 regular guards and the state police have offered their services at a "moment's notice."

"We have our regular guard on duty at the ordnance plant units as we have had all along." Captain Pfaff said. "As far as I am concerned we have been at war all the time, and the regular guard will protect the ordnance plant against any measures of sabotage."

The Carnegie-Illinois Steel company has a contract to manufacture armor plate at the ordnance plant, while the General Machinery Ordnance company is making guns up to six-inch capacity in other units.

Practically every plant in the valley is turning out material for navy orders, R.G. Rau, resident navy inspector of materials said.

Plant Superintendent R.K. Turner announced regulations aimed at sabotage and espionage at the Carbide plant will be "revitalized." Longer hours for guards there may soon go into effect, as at other valley plants.

Plants filling defense orders in other areas, including Huntington, Morgantown, Point Pleasant, Parkersburg and Martinsburg, placed their guards on alert.

The sudden outbreak of Pacific hostilities brought to end plans for a welders' strike at the huge Morgantown du Pont ammonia plant, which would have called an estimated 75,000 welders from their jobs in the nation's shipyards and defense construction areas.

Jesse V. Sullivan, executive secretary of the West Virginia Coal association, said Monday the state's mines already have set "adequate guard," including conservators of the peace. They include justices of the peace constables and state police protection.

Mr. Sullivan, who served as secretary of the state defense council in the World war, added that there were only a few suspicions of sabotage of coal mines in 1917-18.

West Virginia Starts Girding For Full Defense Activities

Northern West Virginia cities considered banding together Friday for comprehensive civilian defense and air raid precautions, while in Charleston a second suggestion was heard that anti-aircraft guns and fighter planes be obtained to protect vital spots.

Chairman George Hunt of the Marion county civilian defense office said officials of northern state cities will be asked to meet in Fairmont next week with Miss Helen Ludwig, field worker for Region 5 of the United States civilian defense office.

David Giltinan of Charleston, secretary of the state board of aeronautics, made public a letter to U. S. Senator Harley M. Kilgore suggesting that both anti-aircraft units and fighter planes be stationed in the state, to safeguard such places as the industry-rich Kanawha valley.

He declared that enemy bombers could start at Gauley Bridge—if they reached that point—and bomb the industries through the valley's entire length "with nothing to stop them."

Cut Age Limits

While state selective service headquarters received instructions for reclassification of all men deferred because of previous military service, the West Virginia Recruiting district announced a lessening of restrictions on ordinary enlistments.

The maximum age limit for original enlistments was increased

sity school of agriculture announced that because of the war, certain research work at the university's experimental station would be abandoned and other work important to the nation's effort increased.

Adjutant General Carleton C. Pierce, who is executive director of civilian defense, announced he would notify all sheriffs to help check for any violations of the order banning the sale of tires and tubes.

Cabell Women to Aid

HUNTINGTON, Dec. 12 (AP).—Huntington women—more than 400 of them—have volunteered to help meet any local emergency the war might bring, by learning to repair a motor, operate a switchboard, read a military map or help curb a panic. The women, among them 200 Marshall college students, heard from Miss Lee Fairchild Bacon, president of the American Women's Voluntary Services unit, an outline of courses which will be offered in defense and emergency training.

from 28 to 35 years, and hereafter applications will be accepted from married men whose wives and children have independent means of support. Each married man must sign an affidavit that his enlistment will not leave his wife and children without support.

In addition, enlistment of selective service registrants already called for examination is permitted. They formerly had to wait for the draft boards' call if they had been examined.

Meantime, state departments moved toward a war-time footing.

Wants More Crops

Commissioner of Agriculture J. B. McLaughlin said his department

SPECIAL ALIEN TRIBUNAL DUE

West Virginia Hearings Set Before Group

A special tribunal to try aliens arrested by FBI agents due to the outbreak of the war is being established in West Virginia, Charles M. Love, Jr., assistant U. S. attorney, told Charleston Civitans Friday.

The special board, composed of three prominent Charlestonians and two Huntington residents, will have the power to determine whether the aliens on trial shall be confined in prison or freed. He did not disclose the names of the board members.

Speaking at the club's weekly luncheon at the Daniel Boone hotel, Mr. Love explained the proposed setup of the civilian defense committee and urged all to do their part in safeguarding the Kanawha valley.

"It is not beyond the realm of possibility that Charleston and the Kanawha valley may be bombed—although I hope and pray it will not be—but it is inevitable that we will be, attacked by sabotage and confronted with accidents due to the rush in defense production," he said, adding "We must be so organized to meet with any emergency."

Aside from being prepared, he said in conclusion, "we must remember that a democracy cannot exist without Christianity."

Dec. 12, 1941

As one can see from these newspaper articles a few days after the Pearl Harbor attack, war hysteria had struck the state with good reason. Not only the Kanawha Valley but other industrialized areas of the state were vulnerable to possible enemy attack or sabotage. The war would eventually affect every man, woman and child in the United States but luckily America was spared the massive destruction that occurred in Europe and Asia.

NAVY, MARINE STAFFS TAXED

Patriotism Is Credited for Enlistment Rush

Scores of Charleston young men Monday flocked into West Virginia district recruiting stations of the army, navy and marine corps in an effort to enlist in one of the armed services.

Recruiters attributed the spurt in enlistments to a wave of patriotism resulting from the development of war between the United States and Japan.

"We have had more applications for enlistment in the United States army this morning than in any one week for the past three months," said Master Sergeant Lloyd Williams.

He said candidates flocked into the recruiting station at 11 Capitol street all morning and that no let up was in sight.

"None of the appliants was seeking assignment to any special department in the army," according to the recruiter. "They did not seem interested in promotions. They just wanted in the army and to get to the front as soon as possible, if and when a front is established," he said.

Navy and marine recruiting stations also reported sharp increases in recruiting activity Monday.

Twenty candidates flocked into the U.S. navy recruiting station on the second floor of the Arcade in a wave of patriotism Sunday night, but only seven were accepted as applicants.

D.J. Parr, petty officer in charge of the station pending the arrival Monday of Lieutenant W.A. Saunders, who will be officer in charge of the West Virginia navy recruiting district, said he had received orders from Richmond to keep on 24-hour recruiting duty until orders to the contrary are issued.

The marine corps recruiting district will remain open from 7 a.m. to 7 p.m. daily, according to First Sergeant Leon W. Little, who said his instructions had been received from area headquarters at Philadelphia.

Sergeant Little said five candidates had applied for enlistment in the marine corps immediately after the office in the basement of the Kanawha hotel opened Monday. One was a former marine, who had walked 18 miles from his home on Paint Creek to re-enlist after learning of the situation. He was James F. Thompson, who was honorably discharged in 1925.

Lieutenant Edmund C. Stone, adjutant of the West Virginia army recruiting office, 10 Capitol street, said he had received no new orders as an outgrowth of the war development.

Headquarters of the West Virginia military area also had received no orders involving a change in policy, according to Colonel George W. Price, executive officer. He said last week's action designed to increase the strength of the army from 1.5-2 million men would involve the calling of a large number of West Virginia reserve officers to active duty, "but it takes time to work those things out."

All recruiters said they anticipated a lowering of the qualifications for enlistment, as in the last war. The marine corps and navy, especially, has set high mental and physical standards for recruits.

Chief Parr said he had one call from a young lady who wanted to know if applications were being received for yeomanettes - girl stenographers and clerks to take over office work in recruiting stations, thereby releasing sailors for duty at sea.

Six hundred men were enlisted in the navy through the Charleston office during the past fiscal year. Chief Parr said 15 boys would be ready to be sworn in Friday of this week.

December 1941

Guarding the Kanawha River

In April 1942, the U.S. Coast Guard stationed several 36-foot patrol boats at Charleston to patrol the Kanawha River from Marmet to Winfield. The purpose was to check all river craft operated by private owners to ascertain if they were properly licensed and also to protect the vital chemical plants and coal shipping depots along the river. At this time there was a great fear of possible sabotage of American industrial areas. The boats were armed with .50 caliber machine guns ready for any emergency. They were based at Clark's Kanawha Flying Club seaplane base on the city levee where fuel, repair service and communications were available. These boats were to supplement various Civil Defense and industrial plant patrol boats and other civilian craft authorized to protect the river. No acts of sabotage were ever recorded in the valley during the war.

2 Mosquito Boats Assigned to City

Coast Guard Plans Inland Network—Will Check Boats, Plants

A coast guard network of armed speedboats is being organized for inland waters, and two assigned to the Charleston area as a starter, it was learned yesterday. One is to patrol the local basin and another the Marmet basin with particular duty of watching the water side of the industrial plants.

The boats also will check all river craft operated by private owners to ascertain if they are properly licensed as provided by a 1917 statute recently revived. A coast guard mission which recently visited Charleston to receive applications will soon be back here, it was said, and properly qualified owners will get their identification cards by May 1.

Mount Machine Guns

Many of these, already members of a boat pool tied in with civilian defense activities, will cooperate with the coast guard in patrol work. Charleston base will be the Kanawha Flying club seaplane base on the city levee where fuel, repair service and communications will be available, it was said.

The C-47 from the Marine Corps Air Station Quantico.

Crashed Marine Plane Is Being Dismantled

The two-motored Douglas transport plane that crashed last Saturday at municipal airport with 13 marines aboard is being dismantled and will be sent by railway to Quantico, Va., within a few days.

Airport Manager Fred Alley said yesterday that three marine mechanics were sent here from Quantico to complete the work.

None of the marines was injured when the big plane made a crash landing near the U.S. Rubber Co. property.

Many people know that the World War II synthetic rubber plant at Institute was built on the site of Charleston's old municipal airport, Wertz Field. In July 1943, a Marine Corps C-47 transport had engine trouble and needed an airport to set down on. Quickly looking at his maps, the pilot saw that Wertz Field had a 4,500-foot runway, more than enough for his big twin-eingine craft, known as the DC-3 in peacetime. Unfortunately, the map was just a year or so out of date. What

should have been a routine landing turned into white-knuckle terror as about halfway down the formerly long runway, the huge yellow brick administration building loomed where the runway used to be. In a tribute to great flying skills and a virtual miracle, pilot Lt. Paul Nones skidded the plane with its cargo of 13 Marines into a ground loop striking a car. The two occupants had jumped from the car just seconds before its roof was cut off by the aircraft wing. Incredibly, everyone walked away from what could have been a disaster. The rubber plant was crucial to the Allied war effort. Hitler surely would have been pleased if the C-47 had plunged into the big plant. The adminstration building stands today virtually unchanged and - oh, yes - the C-47 had to be disassembled and loaded onto a railroad train to get back home.

The Charleston Gazette, Monday, April 12, 1943.

Army B-25 Bomber Lands Safely On City Airport's Short Runway

An army B-25 bomber—one of those huge double-finned jobs that are supposed to need 4,000 feet to land—did it in 1,500 feet at Wertz field yesterday afternoon. One tire blew out as the pilot "stood" on the brakes, an air field observer reported, but the giant ship settled down safely within about 15 feet of the administration building.

Capt. B. W. Fridge was in command of the party and told field attendants that it was still listed on his maps as accessible, as it was to the big American Airline and PCA liners before the adjacent synthetic rubber plant was built thereby reducing runway space.

The B-25 was an early World War Two medium bomber. It is the type that took off from the *USS Hornet* (16 aircraft) on April 18, 1942, to bomb Tokyo. It was one of the most daring air raids of the war.

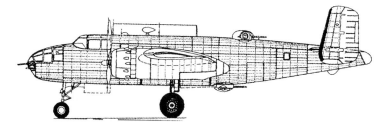

The B-25 in this story was stripped of all extra weight and successfully took off from the 1,500-foot runway emulating the Doolittle Raiders take off from the *U.S.S. Hornet.*

Army Day, April 1942 with John Brawley Post 20 American Legion parading in front of the C&P Telephone Company building on Lee Street. Photo was used as cover of 1943 state road map. ④06

America's New Vacation Land would have to wait two more years before people had the luxury of vacationing without wartime restrictions.

Legion Will Hear National Officer

Homer Chaillaux, national Americanization director for the American Legion, will speak at a public meeting of John Brawley post here Friday, June 9 at 7:30 p.m. at Charleston high school.

C. Paul Heavener, post commander, said special invitations have been extended to all past department commanders. W. Elliott Nefflen, present department commander, and others will speak.

The meeting will celebrate the post's achievement in securing 1,018 members this year, surpassing the 1,000-member goal which had been set for it. The local unit is one of only 33 posts, out of the total of 11,558 in the nation, which have a membership of 1,000 or more.

1939 newspaper article

25,000 Watch 3-Mile Parade

Record-Smashing Assembly Shows High Patriotism On Army Day

(Gazette Photos on Page 2.)

A 3-mile parade before more than 25,000 spectators here yesterday gave the U. S. army a rousing Kanawha county testimonial. It was the second record-smashing gathering within four days to show the solidarity of all community sections in backing the war effort, as some 3,000 pairs of marching feet beat a rhythm of unity.

Soldier and sailor, farmer and craftsman, men, women and children passed in review before the big, bunting-draped stands in which Maj. John P. West, the parade marshal, was flanked by high military and civil dignitaries.

Governor, Mayor Afoot

From 9:30 a. m. until noon practically all business activity, except that allied with the war industrial effort, lulled. Downtown traffic paused as the long line started down Virginia street. Gov. Neely was afoot with Mayor Dawson and W. Elliott Nefflen, parade chairman, behind 32 massed flags, as Mrs. Neely and daughter Corrine marched with the Red Cross units.

Said State's Biggest

Officially it was Army day—a date selected in remembrance of the time we entered World war I—but more than that, Nefflen said, it was a slap in the face to Axis spies among us attempting to spread dissension.

So far as could be learned from wire dispatches, it was the biggest observance in the state. Every band in Kanawha county was marshaled to provide music for the steppers. Their variegated uniforms, with those of sailors, soldiers, marines, Civilian Defense

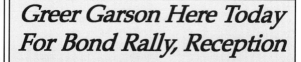

Greer Garson Here Today For Bond Rally, Reception

Lovely Greer Garson, Hollywood actress lately of "Mrs. Miniver" fame, will arrive in Charleston at 6 p.m. today on the first day of her two-day tour of the state--doing her share to help West Virginia move up from its present position of 49th among the states in the sale of war bonds and stamps.

Emphasizing that this is not an emotional thing, and that she, as all civilian soldiers are, is only doing her part to preserve the liberty of a freedom-loving people. Greer Garson personally greeted thousands of Charlestonians at a $500-war bond reception in the Daniel Boone hotel, followed by a gigantic public rally at Laidley Field.

"Thrilled" With Capitol

Wearing a powder blue suit with frilly blouse, and carrying a handsome deep green handbag, gloves and hat, the famed "Mrs. Miniver" was beautiful as she chatted gaily with the governor and others in the party. "Did you really kill that moose?" she asked Gov. Neely when she spied the giant mounted animal on the wall in his office.

She was "thrilled with the spaciousness of the state capitol and the beautiful gold dome."

Mayor and Mrs. Dawson extended her a welcome to the city when she arrived at the hotel.

Definitely Irish, with her blue-green eyes and red hair, Miss Garson appeared at the reception in a slender-cut black dress, wearing a bouquet of orchids. She insisted on shaking the hand of each guest, and gave special attention to all service men.

There will be a pre-rally parade moving east on Kanawha boulevard from Truslow street to Capitol street, north to Washington street, east to Ruffner avenue and north on Hansford street to Laidley Field. A mass formation of bands playing "God Bless America" will open the rally.

All Boy Scouts have been requested to report to Laidley field at 7 p.m. today to serve as ushers and assist with handling the crowd at the bond rally. Executive Director M.H.F. Kinsey said last night.

The program, prior to Miss Garson's appearance, includes an array of local talent. Sid Katz, in charge of acts, said last night. Included are Miss Frances Williams, personality singer; Dora Mazelli, violinist; Bobby Keadle, dancer; Ralph Thomas, accordionist; Helen Cox Schrader, dance chorus; Jimmy and David Stower, winners on a recent Major Bowes radio show; Slim and his Sunshine Boys, radio teams, Nancy and Margaret Whitehair, roller skaters, and many others.

Photo in front of Kearse Theatre.

Friday, September 4, 1942

More Bonds For More Tanks

$1,000 in Bonds Wins Ride in Tank

The purchase of $1,000 in war bonds won a free ride yesteray for S.D. Kirk of the Charleston Maytag company in the "Kanawha Valley Copperhead" (above), giant armored tank brought here through efforts of Charleston theater men and *The Gazette* for the bond rally at Laidley field tonight which will feature the personal appearance of Greer Garson, film actress. Others will get an opportunity to ride in the tank if they show $1,000 in bonds purchased today. The crew will meet all $1,000 purchasers at Broad and Kanawha at 3:30 p.m.On the tank with Kirk, left to right, Sgt. Alfred O'Brien, Sgt. William Earley, Sgt. James Dickenson, Kirk and Lt. George Brent. Peeking out of the gun turret is Sgt. Paul Danino.

Sept. 4, 1942

Eighty airmen in 16 B-25 medium bombers, led by Lt. Col. Jimmy Doolittle flew off the aircraft carrier *Hornet* on April 18, 1942, to bomb Japan's capital, Tokyo. It was America's first attack of Japan's homeland and helped boost the morale of the American people after the attack on Pearl Harbor and the loss of the Philippines, Guam and Wake Island. To keep the Japanese from knowing that the bombers left from a carrier, 650 miles from Tokyo, President Roosevelt announced that the raiders had left from Shangri-La (an imaginary place). Of the 80 airmen, the Japanese captured nine and executed five of them.

The Kanawha Valley was a major center of wartime manufacturing and manpower shortages were always prevalent. Women would take the place of the thousands of men called to service in the valley and throughout the country. The War Manpower Commission regulated all employment during the war. Ads from April 1945.

Civilian automobile production was curtailed in early 1942 and the supply of new and used cars dried up across the nation. "B" and "C" gas cards were issued for essential driving plus additional gasoline. The ad at right is from 1942 and the others are from 1943.

1942

SEE TOKIO'S 2-MAN
SUICIDE SUB

CAPTURED at PEARL HARBOR

CHARLESTON, WED., JUNE 23

CAPITOL ST. BETWEEN WASHINGTON & LEE—1 P. M. TO 10 P. M.

TOUR UNDER DIRECTION OF U. S. TREASURY DEPARTMENT

ADMISSION:

Adults-$1.00 in War Stamps
Children-1-25c War Stamp

Do your part for Uncle Sam. You buy the stamps and retain them.

SEE IT! Make this Jap sub pay for its treachery in U. S. War Stamps!

See with your own eyes the Jap submarine captured in the sneak attack on Pearl Harbor! 80,000 pounds of Jap treachery on exhibition! See, through cut out panels, what few ever see -- the secret equipment inside a sub that brings murder and tragedy to the high seas.

This space contributed by the
AMERICAN OIL COMPANY

Maker of **AMOCO** *Products*

The American Oil Company has dedicated all of its great facilities without stint so that men in the front fighting lines and men and women far back in the supply lines march to certain Victory.

The Japanese two-man midget submarine was one of five that attempted to penetrate Pearl Harbor before the December 7 attack. Two did get into the harbor and one supposedly managed to launch a torpedo that hit the battleship *West Virginia*. The sub pictured had gyro problems and sailed clear around the island of Oahu and beached near Bellows Field on the island's east side. One of the two crewmen was captured and became the first Japanese prisoner-of-war. His sub was brought to the mainland and toured the country to promote the sale of war bonds. It is now on permanent display at the Admiral Nimitz Museum in Fredericksburg, Texas. Over 51,000 people viewed it in a one-day display in Charleston on June 23, 1943, on Capitol Street opposite the YMCA and subscribed more than $102,000 in war bonds and stamps.

Charleston's Biggest Parade

On May 13, 1942, an unbelievable 90 to 100,000 people lined the streets of Charleston for a victory parade and to view famous movie actress, Dorothy Lamour. She was Uncle Sam's No. 1 bond saleswoman and stood on the reviewing stand at Capitol and Lee streets to promote the sale of war bonds. Chairman Fred W. Smith stated that in excess of $4 million was pledged that day. It was so crowded that seven people fainted around the reviewing stand. The parade contained bands, floats and, at least, 10,000 marchers. America's military fortunes at this time were in desperate straits. The last outpost in the Philippines had fallen with thousands of American's taken prisoner and the Japanese navy was the master of the Pacific Ocean. three weeks later the country's fortunes reversed when the Battle of Midway resulted in an American victory and Japanese forces were turned back. Lamour also visited Governor Neely at the Capitol and Mayor Dawson at City Hall.

The Home Front

Weekly Service Edition of The Charleston Daily Mail

Sponsored by Woodrum Home Outfitting Company

VOL. I   CHARLESTON, W. VA., SUNDAY, JUNE 27, 1943   No. 24

ARMY MANEUVERS

Many native sons of West Virginia may have an opportunity to pay an official visit to their home state under a plan for army maneuvers announced by the war department.

The West Virginia mountains will serve in the near future as the site for battle drills with live ammunition— The maneuver area is located mostly in Monongahela National forest, including parts of Preston, Tucker, Grant, Randolph, Pendleton, Webster, Nicholas and Greenbrier counties.

Army officials said they were negotiating now for rights of access in a small amount of private property not included in the forest area. The maneuvers will be the first to be held in the state since the start of World War II, and will be under direction of the 13th army corps. Adding realism to the maneuvers, "overhead fire, with live ammunition, will be used during the exercise on that portion of the area which is government-owned," the army said.

* * *

CUT GAS' USE

Mayor Dawson announced that city hall department heads have agreed on a 25 per cent curtailment of gasoline for municipally operated motor vehicles.

The slash will be on a voluntary basis in the beginning, and some machines owned by the city already are being maintained under the new order. The police department soon will experiment with non-use of squad cars for the first shift—7:30 a. m. to 3:30 p. m., the mayor said.

* * *

PERRY SUCCUMBS

Funeral services were held this week for Joseph E. Perry, 44, manager and secretary-treasurer of the T. E. Perry and Sons Awning Co., who died in a local hospital after a brief illness. He was a Democratic member of the 1941 legislature.

Mr. Tojo of Tokyo's own "little" instrument of destruction—a two-man Jap sub, shown above—while on exhibition in Charleston Wednesday may have netted the cost of several block-busters and other weapons to blast the little yellow men back to their ancestors. To see the sub, captured at Pearl Harbor on December 7, 1941, Kanawha countians subscribed more than $102,000 in war bonds and stamps. Some 51,204 persons viewed the pigboat while it was on exhibition here.

WINS $50 BOND

For submitting a prize winning poster slogan in a recent contest, Ida Lopez, 10, daughter of Generene Lipez, a Koppers Coal timberman at Powellton No. 6 mine, has received a $50 war bond from the Koppers Coal Co.

"A shortage of 50,000 tons may cost the lives of 10,000 sons. Mine More Coal," Miss Lopez's slogan read. A special poster bearing the slogan will be made by Koppers Coal and distributed to all its mines and Koppers stores.

DIES OF BURNS

Manuel Terry, 55-year-old mine worker, died this week in a Rainelle hospital of burns suffered June when he became entangled in high tension wires at a mine near Charmco where he was employed.

VICTORY GARDENS

West Virginians are expected to exceed by several thousand the 150,000 Victory gardens planted last year if present indications of the increasing number of cultivated areas hold true, the state agriculture department reported.

The increase has resulted largely in industrial and suburban areas while farm gardens are about the same as in 1942. The Kanawha county farm agent estimated 10,000 gardens alone in the city limits of Charleston.

* * *

LOVINS ELECTED

Judge W. T. Lovins, state supreme court judge from Huntington, was re-elected chairman of the state judiciary council. The council sets up roles, methods and procedure in the state judicial system.

WEIGHTS BUREAU

Mayor Dawson reported that a petition from the Kanawha Valley Central Labor union, asking for a revival of the city's checking system on weights and measures, has been referred to the financial committee for consideration as an item in next year's budget.

The union men, in a formal resolution, asked the city to take preventive steps in regard to short weighing practices in local stores which were said to be especially serious now because of high prices and rationing.

* * *

C. L. SMITH DIES

Claude L. Smith, prominent in West Virginia American Legion affairs during the past several years, died unexpectedly at his home in St. Albans of a heart ailment.

GETS SUSPENSION

The Kendall Greyhound filling station, 35th street and Noyes avenue, Charleston, was suspended from dealing in gasoline for 15 days after a hearing before OPA Hearing Commissioner Fred S. Glover, Jr., The station operator, Charles Durfee, was suspended from acquiring or dealing in rationed gasoline until Sept. 1, 1944.

The Kendall company, according to OPA officials, admitted that loose "T" coupons had been accepted, but contended that all such sales were made without prior knowledge of the company and contrary to instructions given all station managers.

* * *

DONATE BLOOD

County OCD Director Virgil F. Frizzell was elated with the "splendid" response of Ford, Bacon and Davis employees in donating to the Kanawha county civilian defense blood plasma bank.

Arrangements have been worked out with Dr. Walter Putschar, director of the blood bank, for getting blood from a large group of the company's employees. This plan was worked out through the co-operation of C. C. Whittelsey, superintendent of the company, and G. O. Phillips, another official.

* * *

EXCHANGE HEAD

Virgil W. O'Dell, cashier of the Kanawha Valley bank, has been elected president of the Charleston Exchange club. Other officers are Robert E. Witschey, vice president; Charles Hall, treasurer, and Dr. C. J. Moore, Cline Jackson, Ray Tincher and Nicholas Trivillian, board of control members.

* * *

TAGS EXTENDED

The state road commission announced that the life of 1942-43 automobile licenses would be extended beyond July 1 because of a delay in shipment of supplies needed for the new 1943-44 tags.

Turn the Page

Silk and nylon hose became non-existent during the war. Many everyday household items such as electric fans were not available until the war was over. Cohen Drug Company was the largest drug chain in West Virginia for many years. Notice the ad for pour yourself a pair hose, wherein the buyer painted her legs to simulate hose.

June 1943

The first table food to be rationed was sugar, beginning in April 1942. The first item rationed was rubber, a critical material for war production. Coffee was rationed in November 1942, but removed from the ration list in July 1943. Gasoline was rationed first in the east and later in the west as well. Ration books were issued to every household in America and rationing became a way of life for most essential items for the duration of the war. The notice above is from June 1943.

In 1943, the U.S. Army took over the Greenbrier Resort in White Sulphur Springs and converted it into one of the largest hospitals in the United States for the treatment of wounded soldiers. The resort did not open again until 1948 after extensive remodeling.

The WASP (Women's Air Force Service Pilots) commanded by Jacqueline Cochran worked with the U.S. Army Air Forces Ferry Command to release men for combat duty. Between September 1942 and December 1944, over 1,000 women flew nearly every type of military aircraft from factories to air bases throughout the United States along with other aviation duties. The WAFS was formed in September 1942 by Nancy Love and was shut down on May 6, 1943. It performed similar duties as the WASP. Ad from 1943.

School kids buying war stamps in an Institute school. WEST VIRGINIA STATE COLLEGE LIBRARY

Bonds and stamps being sold from a victory booth at West Virginia State College in Institute.
WEST VIRGINIA STATE COLLEGE LIBRARY

Real German Messerschmitt Raises Funds for U.S. Sailors

by Mark Camp

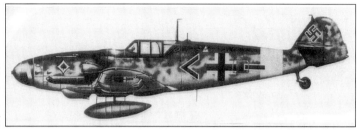

Wow! A real Messerschmitt!

Although slightly demolished by anti-aircraft gun fire, British Air Minister and U.S. Custom Officials, a real German Messerschmitt 109 E airplane was to be seen on exhibit at the corner of Capitol and Washington streets last week.

Still wearing its original paint job, the plane was a dull grey color with a yellow spinner and rudder to show that the pilot was an ace.

On both sides of the wing and on each side of the fuselage was painted the respected German Iron Cross, while the despised Nazi swastika was on the rudder. Near the swastika were eight white marks, the pilots official record of planes shot down. Other markings on the plane were a large numeral five on each side just behind the pilot, denoting the position of the plane in the squadron. and a small yellow triangle with 87 in it telling the fuel capacity.

For a ship having been shot down by anti-aircraft guns, it seemed in very good condition. It only had six large shrapnel holes, about eight inches in diameter, plus some smaller machine gun holes. However, one of the shell bursts knocked out the liquid cooling system.

Having removed the instruments for inspection, the British Air Ministry then sent it to Canada to boost the Bundles for Britain Campaign. The Naval Aid Society picked it up there and brought it to the United States to raise funds for needy sailors and their families.

U.S. Custom officials removed the three 23 mm cannon and the four 303 machine guns before they would admit it into this country because of its danger as a weapon. They also required a $50,000 bond for its safe exit.

On display with the Messerschmitt were self sealing gas and oil tanks and the oxygen tank removed from the plane. The eighty-seven gallon tank seemed almost as large as the plane itself but closer inspection showed that it fit rather snugly in the space just behind the pilot. REPRINTED FROM DEC. 18, 1942 ISSUE STONEWALL JACKSON HIGH SCHOOL NEWSPAPER

Women Civil Defense workers, Charleston 1943. Mayor D. Boone Dawson's administration created a municipal defense council several months before Pearl Harbor. It was the second city in the country to pass such an ordinance. More than 7,000 local citizens took part in civil defense activities.

Your Opportunity To Take A Crack At The Enemy

MORE GUNS AND SHELLS FOR THE AXIS

SCRAP DRIVE

HOW TO PREPARE TIN CANS FOR COLLECTION

1 After emptying contents, wash the can *thoroughly.*

2 Cut off bottom, as well as top of can, or cut open, so that can may be flattened.

3 Step heavily on can to flatten—but do not flatten by hammering. Now tear off paper label, which is loosened by flattening. Labels printed on can need not be removed.

4 Save your cans for tin can collection. Keep separate from other scrap. If collection has not yet started, save your prepared cans in a dry place —do not throw them out!

This message approved by WAR PRODUCTION BOARD

Cans to Be Collected Tomorrow

Urging all Charleston housewive to cooperate to the fullest extent in an effort to collect at least two carloads of tin cans, Robert W. Chidester, chairman of the drive, said yesterday that city trucks will start picking up cans at 7 a. m. tomorrow and emphasized that containers should be placed on the curb tonight or not later than 7 a. m. in the morning.

The first city-wide pickup was Oct. 24, when one carload was collected. Chidester said he hoped to double that amount tomorrow. Truckloads are dumped directly into freight cars on the Virginia street siding, and shipped to Pittsburgh detinning plants.

The illustration above shows the four important steps in the preparation of salvage cans. Milk cans are not usable, neither are oil cans, beer cans or other oblong-shaped tin containers. Fruit and vegetable cans supply the great majority of those suitable for salvage.

Members of American Legion Post 20 posed in front of the old Capitol Annex (Library) with a German World War One 77mm cannon destined for the local scrap drive. It formerly was on display at the Lee Street triangle. Johnnie E. Andre sits on the cannon.

Charleston Shows Its Metal a

★ ★ ★ ★ ★ ★ ★

This Is the Largest Pile of Scra

Panoramic view (in two sections) showing how   worked until midnight to fill it. The top p
the scrap lot at Virginia street and Elk river   shows the western half, the second picture

rap Half-Holiday Is Observed

★　　★　★　★　★　★　★

Any One Lot in West Virginia

d. Join the pictures and the full lot is in view. tremendous task was accomplished through

of workers in the outlying districts. Fifteen thousand persons gathered along the streets watch the trucks arrive and to view the scen

Rayon was a vital material for tires, which kept the military moving. American Viscose Corporation was a major supplier of this product, 1943.

A.W. Cox, Jr., Dies in Dunbar Airplane Crash

Arch Clemens, Theater Owner at Montgomery Is Second Victim

A. Ward Cox, Jr., 20, son of the Charleston department store owner, and a companion, Arch Clemens, about 32, Montgomery, chair theater operator, were killed about 4:30 p.m. yesterday when the Culver Cadet light plane they were flying crashed in a lawn on the western edge of Dunbar. The plane belonged to Glenn Clark of the Kanawha Flying School and is one of the landtype ships he uses at his private field in Putnam county.

An additional tragedy was narrowly averted. The diving plane missed by inches the small cottage of W.J. Schruhl, Evans Lead Co. machinist, in which were his wife and son, Arthur, and buried its nose in the yard not 20 feet from where Schruhl was working. Clemens, Schruhl said, was thrown clear but Cox remained in his place. Both were dead when Schruhl reached them a moment later. A crowd soon jammed 21st St. about the scene, and state police put a guard over the wreck pending arrival of a federal inspector expected today.

The plane which took off from the municipal airport a short time earlier, seemed to stall during a turn, Maj. Hubert Stark of the state aeronautics department said he was told by eye-witnesses. Clemens seemed to be the pilot by his position in the smashed ship. Stark began an immediate investigation.

There was no fire. The Dunbar fire department was called and assisted in extricating the crushed bodies from the plane.

Both Qualified Pilots

Both were qualified, licensed private fliers, it was said, with Clemens additionally licensed as a commercial pilot and young Cox ready to take that examination.

The bodies were first removed to the Mays-Parsons mortuary at Dunbar, and later the body of young Cox was taken to the Scales mortuary in Charleston.

Clemens, a CAP member and active in aviation for six or seven years, leaves a wife and no children, Montgomery friends said. He owns and operates a chain of motion picture theaters in the coal fields.

Cox, a Charleston high school graduate and then a student at Morris Harvey college, had dropped his classes to concentrate on his flying and had hoped to get into the army air corps, it was said. He was on the verge of going up for his commercial pilot's license.

June 27, 1943

Well-known ex-baseball player and manager Gabby Street took time off from his bond selling duties at Frankenberger's on Feb. 12, 1944, to repeat a stunt he performed when he was 25 years old in 1908. That stunt was catching a baseball thrown from the top of the Washington monument, a distance of 555 feet. Gabby defied the wind and snow to catch the ball thrown by Watt B. Powell from the top of the Kanawha Valley building. The ball he caught was auctioned off and the glove he made the catch with was given to the highest purchaser of war bonds.

The Civil Air Patrol parades down Kanawha Boulevard by the Union Building. The CAP was created on Dec. 1, 1941, under the Office of Civilian Defense. It consisted of over 75,000 volunteers who flew many different types of domestic aviation missions during the war. The CAP was transferred to the War Department in 1943 as an auxiliary of the U.S. Army Air Forces.

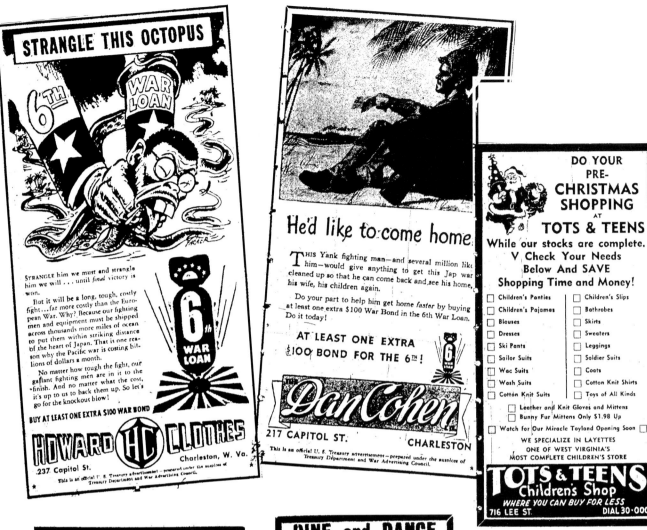

The Barlow Skating rink started as an ice skating rink at the lower side of the Kanawha City bridge for a few years and then the Barlows bought it and turned it into a roller skating rink. The building eventually burned down.

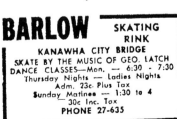

By 1944 the enemy was on the run and life went on in the country.

All Ads from 1944.

Note the address - an old building behind Young's Diner off Quarrier Street.

HEADS UP—
CHARLESTON!
Here Comes the Great American Orchestra
MUSIC THAT MAKES YOUR HEART THROB YOUR FEET DANCE
THE IDOL of the Airlanes
M. C. A. PRESENTS
In Person

JAN GARBER and his ORCHESTRA

WCHS AUDITORIUM
WED., DEC. 29th
9 to 1
Tables Reserved, Call 28-145

ADMISSION, $3.00 COUPLE
PLUS TAX .36
$3.36 TOTAL

★ THE NEW ★
GYPSY VILLAGE

★
★ SPEND ★
THIS EVENING IN COOL COMFORT
★
4 ALL STAR ACTS FLOOR SHOW
★
DANCE
TO THE MUSIC OF
NED GUTHRIE
and his CHARLESTONIANS
★
LEE HOTEL BLDG. - DUNBAR ST

The WCHS Auditorium was the former Midelburg Auditorium which formerly housed the Butler Chevrolet dealership on Lee Street

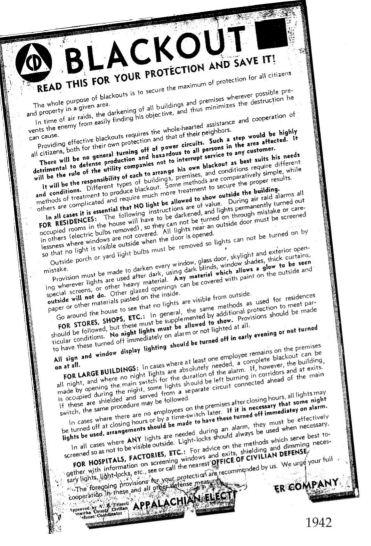

BLACKOUT

READ THIS FOR YOUR PROTECTION AND SAVE IT!

The whole purpose of blackouts is to secure the maximum of protection for all citizens and property in a given area.

In time of air raids, the darkening of all buildings and premises wherever possible prevents the enemy from easily finding his objective, and thus minimizes the destruction he can cause.

Providing effective blackouts requires the whole-hearted assistance and cooperation of all citizens, both for their own protection and that of their neighbors. Such a step would be highly

There will be no general turning off of power circuits. Such a step would be highly detrimental to defense production and hazardous to all persons in the area affected. It will be the rule of the utility companies not to interrupt service to any customer.

It will be the responsibility of each to arrange his own blackout as best suits his needs and conditions. Different types of buildings, premises, and conditions require different methods of treatment to produce blackout. Some methods are comparatively simple, while others are complicated and require much more treatment to secure the proper results.

In all cases it is essential that NO light be allowed to show outside the building.

FOR RESIDENCES: The following instructions are of value. During air raid alarms all occupied rooms in the house will have to be darkened, and lights permanently turned out in others (electric bulbs removed), so they can not be turned on through mistake or carelessness where windows are not covered. All lights near an outside door must be screened so that no light is visible outside when the door is opened.

Outside porch or yard light bulbs must be removed so lights can not be turned on by mistake.

Provision must be made to darken every window, glass door, skylight and exterior opening wherever lights are used after dark, using dark blinds, window shades, thick curtains, special screens, or other heavy material. Any material which allows a glow to be seen outside will not do. Other glazed openings can be covered with paint on the outside and paper or other materials pasted on the inside.

Go around the house to see that no lights are visible from outside.

FOR STORES, SHOPS, ETC.: In general, the same methods as used for residences should be followed, but these must be supplemented by additional protection to meet particular conditions. No night lights must be allowed to show. Provisions should be made to have these turned off immediately on alarm or not lighted at all.

All sign and window display lighting should be turned off in early evening or not turned on at all.

FOR LARGE BUILDINGS: In cases where at least one employee remains on the premises all night, and where no night lights are absolutely needed, a complete blackout can be made by opening the main switch for the duration of the alarm. If, however, the building is occupied during the night, some lights should be left burning in corridors and at exits. If these are shielded and served from a separate circuit connected ahead of the main switch, the same procedure may be followed.

In cases where there are no employees on the premises after closing hours, all lights may be turned off at closing hours or by a time-switch later. If it is necessary that some night lights be used, arrangements should be made to have these turned off immediately on alarm.

In all cases where ANY lights are needed during an alarm, they must be effectively screened so as not to be visible outside. Light-locks should always be used when necessary.

FOR HOSPITALS, FACTORIES, ETC.: For advice on the methods which serve best together with information on screening windows and exits, shielding and dimming necessary lights, light-locks, etc., see or call the nearest OFFICE OF CIVILIAN DEFENSE.

The foregoing provisions for your protection are recommended by us. We urge your full cooperation in these and all other defense measures.

APPALACHIAN ELECTRIC... ER COMPANY

Approved by V. H. Frissel
...awha County Civilian
...fense Coordinator

1942

City Churches
Draw Crowds

The daily routine of Charlestonians was broken Tuesday as news of D-Day led groups of heavy-hearted citizens through the open doors of the city's churches.

As the liberation of Europe began, anxious parents experienced mingled feelings of hope and fear and relief after the long period of waiting.

A new seriousness was evident everywhere, as crowds gathered around radios and poured over newspapers. But the real concern and uneasiness was expressed on the faces of those who fled to the sanctity of the churches for silent prayers and short services.

Almost every church in the city remained open all day and members as well as non-members fell to their knees to ask protection for America's sons and victory for the cause of freedom. The largest groups of worshipers entered the sanctuaries after working hours and paused for a few moments of private meditation.

Several special services were held throughout the city and all were well attended. Some ministers conducted prayer meetings Wednesday morning and others are preparing special liberation messages for their mid-week services Wednesday evening. Prayers by local pastors were heard at intervals Tuesday over the broadcasting stations and were followed by hymns and the national anthem.

As the long-awaited D-day came to an end, the voice of the President quieted Charleston crowds in public places as the commander-in-chief asked Allies all over the world to join in his prayer for the success of the invasion and a peaceful world to come.

1944

The chance that enemy planes might appear over Charleston was really never even a remote possibility, but the government apparently believed the "blackouts" for Charleston would emphasize the fact that America was in a desperate world war.

D-Day

June 6, 1944 was the beginning of the end of German occupation of Europe.

THE WEATHER

The Charleston Daily Mail

FINAL EDITION

VOLUME 192 — No. 156 — CHARLESTON, WEST VIRGINIA, TUESDAY EVENING, JUNE 6, 1944 — 14 PAGES — FIVE CENTS

Invaders Surge 10 Miles Into France
Crushing Sky Onslaught Sets Stage for Infantry

11,000 Planes Soften Coast For Invasion

Troops, Tanks Land In Wake of 96-Hour Aerial Bombardment

Nazi Resistance Fails to Develop; Hitler, Rommel Reported at Front; Paratroopers Flank Atlantic Wall

FDR Calls For Prayer

Desires World Unity And a 'Sure Peace'

Allies Reported on Channel Isles

Although the war curtailed many activities for Americans to keep up morale theaters, dance halls, roller rinks and other recreational activities were allowed to continue. Most of the movies made during the war had somewhat of a war or patriotic theme. Many Hollywood stars had joined the armed forces such as Clark Gable and Tyrone Power. The circus was apparently allowed to travel around the country, also to boost morale. According to the April 29, 1945, *Sunday Gazette*, the Clyde Beatty Circus was "late in arriving due to transportation difficulties, but the huge crowd was unusually patient and a good time was had by all."

This movie ad is interesting as the theater located on West Washington Street near Stockton Street stayed open past midnight to accommodate shift workers at area plants.

Even with men and women stationed at outposts all over the world, Americans were still able to cast their ballots for local and national elections. This is part of what these men and women were fighting for.

OFFICIAL WEST VIRGINIA WAR BALLOT --- VIA AIR MAIL

(Complete Military or Naval Address)

To THE CLERK OF THE CIRCUIT COURT,
KANAWHA COUNTY,
CHARLESTON, WEST VIRGINIA

1942

Help a fighting man enjoy his precious leave

Give *your* Holiday trip to a man in uniform! That doesn't mean buying him a ticket — it just means saving him a bus seat during the pre-Christmas rush when he wants to go home on leave. It's simple — just take your trip before the crowds are heaviest or wait until the New Year. You'll help, too, by traveling on mid-week days whenever possible—and traveling light!

GREYHOUND TERMINAL
155 Summers Street
Phone Capitol 28-121

GREYHOUND
LINES

1942

It seems that every action a citizen did would help the war effort as is evident by this ad for the Charleston Transit Company. All forms of transportation in the United States were using old, outdated equipment especially inter-city modes. Greyhound was a vital part of wartime activities as attested to in this ad.

"We Fought A Good Fight, Dad . . .

WE BOYS ON THE BATTLEFRONT . . . AND YOU DADS ON THE HOME FRONT! Our combined efforts brought about the Victory that is ours today. But our job isn't finished. There's another bunch of Little so-called Supermen that must be taught a lesson, too! They must be taught—ONCE AND FOR ALL—not to meddle with Uncle Sam and his allies. We must turn our full strength on these blood-thirsty devils and bring them to their knees . . . never to rise again . . . never to attempt to enslave other nations . . . never to massacre innocent women and children of other nations. Yes, we must FINISH the Job This Time!

Goodbye, Berlin!
HAIL—With Bullets and Bombs—TOKYO!

SCHOOLFIELD-HARVEY
Electric Company

1016 Quarrier   Dial 23-187

State Will Pay Tribute To Memory of President

West Virginians will pay tribute to President Roosevelt today in "mourning prayer and rededication to duty" under a proclamation issued yesterday by Gov. Meadows, who urged that people work even harder for victory rather than take a holiday.

Instead of taking time off from "the paramount task of winning this war," the governor called upon state citizens to pause at their work, in their homes and in public places for at least one minute at 4 p. m., the hour of funeral services for the President "so that we may with bowed heads and reverent hearts pay our individual and collective tribute to the memory of him who has meant so much to us and to all humanity."

Statehouse offices regularly close at noon on Saturday and it was indicated that this routine would be followed today with isolated exceptions.

The state supreme court announced its offices would be closed all day while the Office of Price Administration, the War Production Board, the War Manpower Commission and similar federal agencies with offices in West Virginia said they would be closed in respect to Mr. Roosevelt.

All courts in Charleston adjourned yesterday and will not be in session again until Monday morning.

Meadows To Pay Respects

Gov. Meadows will serve as the official representative of the people of West Virginia at funeral services today for President Roosevelt.

The governor left for Washington last night after receiving a telegram from Secretary of State Stettinius notifying him that reservations had been made for his attendance at the private services.

Offices at city hall and the court house also will be closed throughout the day.

Charles E. Hodges, managing director of the Chamber of Commerce announced that most retail merchandise stores will close at 3:30 p. m. and remain closed.

President Roosevelt, who had visited the Kanawha Valley in 1940, died almost four months before V-J Day.

V-J (Victory over Japan) Day was celebrated all over America and the world on Aug. 14 1945. V-E (Victory in Europe) Day had been celebrated on May 8, 1945. After almost six years of war, Kanawha County and the world would return to peace.

Lights Focussed On Capitol Dome As V-E Symbol

The golden dome of West Virginia's capitol stood proudly in a flood of light last night, a silent reminder that victory had come to the battlefields of Europe.

It typified the way V-E day was received by the people, of Charleston, who observed the victory in Sunday-like quiet but whose faces wore brighter smiles.

Like the people who live around it and consider it their showplace for visitors, the dome had been in gloom since Pearl Harbor day and then suddenly brightened when one phase of the war reached a successful end.

As a way of celebrating, Building Supt. H. N. Martin planned to leave the floodlights on throughout the night before returning to the prewar practice of darkening the dome at midnight.

Along with the capitol lights, signboards, window displays, theater marquees, and other outdoor lighting went on again with the War Production Board's approval. These lights had been out only since Feb. 1 when the brown-out order went into effect as a fuel and power conservation move, but the capitol had been in darkness since the early war days of OCD blackouts and other precautions against bombing attacks.

Charleston yesterday resembled a Sunday afternoon, with most retail establishments closed and churches giving an open door invitation for people to come in and give thanks, and also a quiet Memorial Day with flags displayed and plenty of parking space in the downtown business district.

Churches throughout the city held services last night, and the combined bands of the Shrine Mosque and Charleston high school presented a V-E day concert on the steps of the old postoffice.

Families with men in the service received the official victory proclamation with mixed emotions— some happy in the hopes their loved ones soon would be home, others saddened by the reminder they never can return.

Typifying the reaction, Mrs. Lewis W. McQuain of Wellford, mother of nine servicemen, was too excited and nervous to talk, and Mrs. L. A. Wilson, 521 Main St. mother of three sons in Europe, "just felt numb" but said mothers can't get too excited because w still have the Pacific war to face

These notices are from local papers in 1944 and 1945.

War is all too often portrayed as glorious but here is its grim reality. Life ended for these fine, young Americans long ago. The misery of war is not only in the deaths but the broken hearts of family members who are left with only memories. These are but a few of the brave young people of Kanawha who did not return.

Killed in Germany

Pfc. Cecil V. McShurley, husband of Mrs. Zella McShurley of RFD 2, was killed in action in Germany April 8. the War Department has announced. He was the son of Mrs. Kate Pearson of St. Albans. Pfc. McShurley entered the Army in 1943, and was assigned to overseas duty last June. Before entering the service he was employed at Carbide and Carbon.

Killed on Luzon

1st Lt. James M. Cummings, son of Mrs. Ora Cummings of Mink Shoals, was killed Feb. 24 while fighting on Luzon in the Philippines, the War Department has announced. He served with an infantry unit and had been overseas since March, 1944.

Lt. Cummings was a graduate of Charleston high school, and prior to enlisting in the Army was employed by the Nelson Transfer Co. Other survivors include one brother, Robert Cummings stationed with the state police in Wheeling, and two sisters, Mrs. Julia Mac-Queen of Mink Shoals and Miss Margaret Cummings at home.

Killed in Action

Mrs. Mary F. Cale of 2308 Pennsylvania Av. was notified recently by the War Department that her husband, Pfc. Hamilton N. Cale, 24, was killed in action April 5 in Germany. A former employe of the Appalachian Electric Power Co., he entered the service in June, 1944, and had been serving overseas since November with an infantry unit of the 7th Army. He was the son of Ernest Cale of Chesapeake and Mrs. Stella Cale of Elkton Md. Also surviving are a daughter, Patricia Ann, and his grandmother Mrs. Edna Crookshanks of Charleston.

Missing Since April 9

2d Lt. Harry B. Shafer, son of Mr. and Mrs. Roy C. Shafer of North Charleston, has been missing in action since April 9 his parents have been notified. Lt. Shafer piloted a fighter plane with the 12th tactical air force in France. He was reported missing over Germany. Prior to entering the service, Lt. Shafer was employed at the Carnegie-Illinois Steel Co. He has been overseas eight months.

Anna Marie Fisher, a 1939 Charleston High graduate was a 1st Lieutenant in the U.S. Army Women's Corp. (WAC). She was killed in an airplane crash in Italy on April 20, 1945. Her brother, Steve, a 1943 CHS graduate was shot down over Europe and survived a German POW camp. He became a well-known Charleston real estate executive.

Capt. Jack Baker Dies in Aleutians

Mr. and Mrs. Ben F. Baker of 1711 Virginia St., E., have been notified by the war department that their son, Capt. Jack Baker, met his death in the line of duty Aug. 16 when his plane crashed in the Aleutians.

Capt. Baker was born in Bluefield in 1916 and attended schools there and in Charleston. He was graduated from Georgia School of Technology in 1937. He enlisted in the army in February 1942, and spent 14 months in England before being assigned to the Aleutians. Before entering the army he was associated with the Westvaco Chlorine Products Corp. His parents and a sister, Miss Anita Baker, survive. Capt. Baker will be buried in the Jewish Section of Spring Hill Cemetery.

- Lest We Forget -

Sunday, December 5, 1948

DEDICATED TO THE 359 MEN WHO GAVE THEIR LIVES IN WORLD WAR II FROM THE CITY OF CHARLESTON

☆

MEMORIAL SERVICES FOR THOSE WHO DIED BY THOSE WHO LIVED!!
City Churches having Services in their Memory:

First Presbyterian Church .... 11:00 AM—Rev. George Vick, Pastor
Liberty Baptist .... 11:00 AM—Rev. J. C. Tyree, Pastor
Bream Memorial Presbyterian .... 11:00 AM—Rev. J. B. Overmyer, Pastor
Allen's Chapel Methodist .... 11:90 AM—Rev. R. L. Nance, Pastor
Union Mission .... 7:30 PM—Rev. Pat Withrow, Pastor
Sacred Heart .... 10.30 AM—Rev. Father Boniface Weckman, Pastor
Wesley Methodist .... 11:00 AM—Rev. C. S. Thompson

"Peace"

A strong America means a Peaceful America.

The thought that is foremost in the minds of all Americans and peoples of other democratic countries today is Peace.

History reveals that from time to time the world becomes a chaos of strife and turmoil in the form of war. All because a few people have yet to taste the fruits of a free democracy and are held in a world of darkness, dispute and misunderstandings. Now that the big guns of World War II are a dying echo, our job is to see that those guns remain silent for all time. We have won the war. Now we must do our utmost to reach the ultimate goal—PEACE FOR THE WORLD.

Much thought has been given to the subject of peace through preparedness. Military leaders and civilians alike agree that permanent peace can be achieved only through a strong America. This peace will never be gained by physical means. We must, through the development of the intelligent minds of free thinkers, profit by the mistakes of our predecessors.

Therefore, all Americans must lead the way in striving for one common goal everlasting peace—and a mutual understanding among all patriotic citizens of our great democracy, of the aims and hopes expressed by this statewide observance of PEACE WEEK.

KANAWHA VALLEY MILITARY MANPOWER COMMITTEE—WEST VIRGINIA RECRUITING HEADQUARTERS

VETERANS' DAY

MONDAY, DECEMBER 6, 1948

"Dedicated to those who so gallantly defended America in War and returned home to continue their fight for a lasting peace"

A Banquet and Military Ball
in
HOTEL RUFFNER BALLROOM

Toastmaster: C. S. Collier, Jr., Asst. Director of Dept. of Veterans Affairs State of West Virginia

7:00 PM—Banquet
8:30 PM—"Communism in China", Address by Colonel Walter C. Phillips, US ARMY (Ret) who was Chief of Staff for Lt. Gen. Walter C. Short at the time of the Japanese Attack on Pearl Harbor, December 7, 1941.

Committee in Charge of Arrangements:
E. D. Hardman, V Comdr American Legion Post No. 20
Colonel Benjamin W. Venable, US Army (Ret) Member National Defense Advisory Committee
R. B. Greene, Chaplain, Veterans of Foreign Wars Post No. 3466

10:00 PM—The Military Ball. Music for Dancing by Billy Williams and his Orchestra. This performance is given gratis under the auspices of the AFM, James C. Petrillo, President, and the Charleston Musicians Union Local No. 136 of Charleston. They are being paid from their share of the Recording and Transcription Fund allocated for this area.

TO THE VETERANS ORGANIZATION OF THE CITY OF CHARLESTON:

We salute you on your day, Veterans Day of Peace Week. We wish to congratulate you on your fine Civic, Patriotic and Veterans Programs.

We wish to thank you for your help on the Committee's program the past six months. You have always answered our call for assistance and we hope in the many months to come, to be able to repay you for your splendid cooperation.

We want you to feel free to call on us at anytime.

THE KANAWHA COUNTY MILITARY MANPOWER COMMITTEE

KANAWHA VALLEY MILITARY MANPOWER COMMITTEE—WEST VIRGINIA RECRUITING HEADQUARTERS

"PEARL HARBOR DAY"
TUESDAY, DECEMBER 7, 1948
Committee: Gordon Hamill and Sgt. Regis Cole

We Welcome West Virginia's Favorite Son!

Captain "Chuck" Yeager

Captain Charles E. Yeager, 25 year old Hamlin Ace, is the only living pilot who has flown faster than the speed of sound. He shot down 12 German Fighters during the War and is reputed to have more jet and rocket flying time than any man living.

The top speed he has flown has not been announced but Air Force Officials said, that he had exceeded the speed of sound by many hundred of miles an hour. This would place his highest speed at well beyond a thousand miles an hour.

Welcome home Chuck!

☆

PEARL HARBOR DAY CEREMONY

LEE TRIANGLE — 1:15 PM

1:15 PM—"THE UNITED STATES AIR FORCE BAND" from Bolling Air Force Base, Washington, D. C., under the direction of Major George S. Howard.
1:30 PM—Ceremony. John S. Phillips, Master of Ceremonies
Rev. Ralph Kipp, First Presbyterian Church
United States Senator Harley Kilgore
United States Senator Chapman Revercomb
Mayor Carl Andrews
Governor Clarence W. Meadows
1:50 PM—Governor Meadows pulls switch that lights Community Christmas Tree
Arrival of B36, B29's and P51's over the Triangle
Captain Charles Yeager
Broadcast from B36 to Ground
The South Charleston Mothersingers will sing Christmas Carols and the US Air Force Band will play the Musical Selections during the Program
7:00 PM—Christmas Carols at the Community Christmas Tree by the Youth Choir of the Calvary Baptist Church. The Choir has 35 members and under the direction of Mrs. Lee Shane.

KANAWHA VALLEY MILITARY MANPOWER COMMITTEE—WEST VIRGINIA RECRUITING HEADQUARTERS

"Preparedness Day", Saturday, December 11, 1948
Committee: Ruth Sarles and James Brown

Welcome to Charleston
Major General Anthony C. McAuliffe
Hero of Bastogne

Anthony C. McAuliffe was born in Washington, D. C., on July 2, 1898. He was appointed to the United States Military Academy, West Point, New York from the State of West Virginia on November 1, 1918.

One of the United States Army's outstanding General's, he became famous in December 1944, when he commanded the 101st Airborne Division and the attached troops in defense of the key road center of Bastogne during the battle of the Bulge.

He commanded the 103rd Infantry Division in the attack of March 1945 from Alsace when the Division broke through the Siegfried Line and later raced through Germany and Austria to capture Innsbruck and the Brenner Pass and make the historic link up with the American Fifth Army Troops from Italy.

In June 1945, General McAuliffe returned to the United States and assumed command at Fort Bragg, North Carolina.

In January 1946 he became Ground Forces Adviser to the Joint Army and Navy Task Force One, for Operations Crossroads . . . the tests of the Atomic Bomb.

In December 1947 he was designated Deputy Director for Research and Development, Logistics Division, General Staff, United States Army, which position he now holds.

☆

1:30 PM—Welcome to General Anthony C. McAuliffe at Kanawha Airport
2:00 PM—Preparedness Day Parade. The Parade Forms on Broad St. and Kanawha Blvd., to Capitol, Down Capitol to Lee and right on Lee and disband at WCHS Auditorium
5:00 PM—Reception for General McAuliffe and Distinguished Guests at The Army-Navy Club
7:00 PM—Banquet and Ball at the West Side Women's Club
8:30 PM—Main Address of the Evening, "Preparedness" General McAuliffe

KANAWHA VALLEY MILITARY MANPOWER COMMITTEE—WEST VIRGINIA RECRUITING HEADQUARTERS

Although World War II ended in 1945, the echo's have reverberated through the years.

The legendary Douglas DC-3 served Charleston throughout its long life from Wertz Field to Kanawha Airport. First flown in 1936, it is certainly one of the five most famous aircraft of all time. It served in all theaters of World War Two and Korea, and in Vietnam as the C-47. This gleaming silver Eastern Airlines DC-3 is seen here at Kanawha Airport, circa 1950. A virtually identical DC-3 is on display at the National Air & Space Museum in Washington, D.C. where it is in perpetual flight suspended from the ceiling. It is not unusual to see a DC-3 still soldiering on, ignoring the passage of time. JUNIOR MEADOWS COLL.

WINGS

George Bumbaugh came to Charleston as a tight-rope walker but found a full-time job with the gas company. In 1905 he built this lemon-shaped propeller-driven airship and on a windy summer day, he flew it around the dome of the 1885 Capitol then across the Kanawha River where he lost his rudder and crash landed on Louden Heights. He attempted another trip in July 1906 to circle around the post office but a stiff east wind proved too much for the balloon and he landed safely at a ballpark after dark. This apparently ended Bumbaugh's adventures with his airship. This was not the first balloon to either fly over or land in the Charleston area. So the story goes that in 1835, a man named Richard Clayton, an amateur balloonist, ascended in his balloon in Cincinnati. The flight was to be purely for exhibition and entertainment and was to stay in the area. However, he was caught in an air current and carried eastward over 300 miles, going up the Ohio River Valley, then up the Kanawha Valley, passing over Charleston, up the New River Valley to a point in Summers County where the flight ended unceremoniously in a tree. Passing over Malden at night Clayton could see lighted salt furnaces. After some difficult arrangements, Clayton and his balloon were apparently taken to the Kanawha River somewhere west of present-day Montgomery so he could get a salt boat to take him back to Cincinnati. SWV, HARRY BRAWLEY COLL.

This view and the top two on the opposite page show either Oscar Brindley or Eugene Heth in a Wright biplane. They participated in an airshow on June 26, 1912, on a ballfield (note grandstand pillars) about where the Carbide plant in South Charleston is now located. (192)

Note: the aircraft below has a rotary motor while the others at the show had in-line cylinders.

This is Paul Peck's Columbia biplane, the first aircraft to take off from a West Virginia landing field. Col. Paul Peck (he was appointed a colonel by Gov. William G. Glascock) was originally from Lewisburg and carried the first air mail in the United States from Coney Island near Cincinnati to California, Ohio. He also held the endurance record of more than four continuous hours in the air above Boston. His pusher-type craft with a rotary motor was at the old baseball grounds at South Charleston with the above aircraft on June 26, 1912. Peck was killed soon after his appearance here in an exhibition flight in Chicago. (192)

The Union Building is in the background.

This rare Boeing B-1 seaplane landed on the Kanawha River in 1918. It is shown tied up at the city levee and taking off from the river. It was probably the first seaplane on the Kanawha. The B-1 was popular for carrying mail. GA

Taking off opposite Ward Boiler Works.

1925

Local children get the thrill of their lives sitting in the cockpit.

Front and rear views of U.S. Air Service Martin MB-2 bombers at the Kanawha City field in August 1921. Brig. Gen. Billy Mitchell was sent to Charleston in command of 13 aircraft to back up Federal troops who were sent in to restore order in the southern coal fields.
(149)

This MB-2 sits about where the City National Bank is today. In 1921, this aircraft was the height of technology and the equal of a B-1 jet today.

The plane on the left is one of the big twin engined bombers but all the rest in the line are single engine and considerably smaller. Gen. Mitchell flew one of the single engine craft. Although they were prepared to drop tear gas on the striking coal miners luckily this drastic action was not needed.

On Sept. 3, 1921, the bombers were ordered back to their base at Langley, Virginia. Plane No. 5 and two others took off but ran into a severe storm over Nicholas County. The storm caused No. 5 to roll over and crash into the dense forest below. Of the five crewmen, four died. The fifth died months later of his injuries. The author's father, B.E. Andre, one of the Red Cross searchers salvaged one of the huge V-12 motors. The plane was a total wreck. Bomber No. 5 had the distinction two months before of sinking the captured German warship "Ostfriesland" in Chesapeake Bay bombing trials. Those trials forever changed the thinking of naval commanders that warships were unsinkable by aircraft. The top photo shows one of the balloon tires in the foreground. BEA

All decked out in aviator's garb including leather boots and helmet, Ruth Miller Bonham is shown refueling a plane for duty with the Civil Air Patrol. Bonham learned to fly with Glenn Clark in the 1940s and helped organize the local C.A.P. in 1941. SWV STARK COLL.

Bollinger Field - present site of Southridge Shopping Center in South Charleston.

Closer the Better

We are told that the new Kansas City airport, skirted on two sides by the Missouri river, is to be 687 acres and is within five minutes drive of the postoffice. Charleston officials would do well to consider this last feature of proximity in selecting a flying field here. Unless we are mistaken, the only ones thus far proposed here have been pretty far outside the city limits. Of course it is well understood that the farther from town you get, the cheaper is the land to be bought. There are also quite definite limitations to the city's ability to pay for an expensive landing field because of the depleted condition of our exchecquer. Time, however, being the essence of aeroplane service, we must get our field as close as possible to the city proper so that delivery of mail and passengers will not be delayed any longer than necessary. The delay of half an hour or more in getting from the landing field into the city might sometimes obviate the necessity of sending merchandise by aeroplane here from all except distant points. Ready and quick access to the postoffice and downtown districts from our air field, that would render the fastest service possible, should be the first aim of those interesting themselves in this matter. Not until all possible sites within or closer to Charleston have been proven absolutely unfeasible, should we contemplate sites which would delay our service here any inconvenient length of time. A field close-in would probably be in the long run more popular and a better paying proposition than one half-an-hour's distance from the city, but can we afford to pay the necessary difference in price at this time?

The article at left appeared in *The Charleston Gazette* on Dec. 26, 1928. Wertz Field at Institute would open a year and a half later. This editorial would be somewhat timely today.

View of Wertz Field, named after Charleston mayor William Wertz, which opened for business as the valley's main airport in July 1930. The buildings and water tower of West Virginia State College are in the background. They are still easily recognizable today. SWV STARK COLL.

1930

Come Out and See Charleston's Airport!

The people of Charleston and vicinity have a new source of civic pride, and center of interesting activities, in the city's municipal Airport, Wertz Field, located just below Institute. Here, just a short distance from Charleston, reached by auto or by trolley and motor coach service, there has been laid out a thoroughly modern landing field for commercial aviation, with all the up-to-date equipment that mark the best present-day airports.

Exhibition Flying
by
U.S. Army
and
U.S. Navy
Ships and Flyers

Daily Program
of Thrilling
Aerobatics and Stunts,
Races and
Parachute Jumping

A Wonderful time and place
to spend your holiday.

Admission Free!

Ample Parking Space for
Automobiles.

Street Car Bus Service to
Field Every 20 Minutes.

Roadway Through Dunbar
Marked—Drive Down!

OPENING and DEDICATION
JULY 4-5-6

After months of preparation Wertz Field is ready for opening, and a gala three-day program has been arranged in which Army and Navy flyers will participate along with many of the most capable and expert aviators and pilots in this section of the country.

On each of the three days there will be thrilling air races over a charted course, a program of aerial acrobatics, parachute jumping and the like. Also, there will be on display scores of the newest and finest flying equipment representing the product of leading manufacturers throughout the country.

The Municipal Airport is your airport—you are cordially invited to visit Wertz Field on July 4-5 and 6. Admission free. Parking space for 50,000 automobiles.

WEST VIRGINIA
AIRWAYS INC.

Operated by Charlestonians!

1930

Army-Navy Fliers

IN ACTION TODAY AT
Airport Opening
WERTZ FIELD-INSTITUTE
TODAY and TOMORROW

A GREAT PROGRAM OF
AEROBATICS, AIR RACES
PARACHUTE JUMPING,
ETC.

Parking Space for Approximately 10,000 Cars Inside
Airport Grounds. 25c per car Including Passengers.

Street Car -- Bus Service Direct to
Field Every 20 Minutes. Take
Dunbar Cars.

Ride In a Plane -- See Charleston From The Air

1930

Pioneer aviator Wiley Post visited Wertz Field in his famous Lockheed 5-B Vega *Winnie Mae* in 1934. Post was the first person to fly around the world alone and would die in a crash in Alaska with Will Rogers in 1935. (194) EAGLE AVIATION

American Airlines used Stinson A Tri-Motor airplanes for commercial service in the late 1930s. The airline started passenger service in 1933. Pennsylvania Central Airlines started service in 1935.

Giant Airplane To Visit Wertz Field

Ford Tri-Motored Ship to Fly Here Three Days Next Week

Charlestonians will have an opportunity to ride in one of the largest airplanes in the country during the three-day celebration of the opening of Wertz field, the city's new municipal flying field, on July 4, 5 and 6.

A giant tri-motored Ford plane, under the command of Capt. O. M. Goodsell, World war ace and night airmail pilot, will land here July 3. From eight until nine o'clock that night those who wish to ride in the plane will have an opportunity to do so. A charge for trips will be made, however.

The airplane will be illuminated during its night flights and will circle over the city. The Ford motor company also will have a five passenger Stinson plane here during the opening of the field.

Activity at the new airport is concentrated on putting the field in shape for the celebration. Large steam rollers are packing the newly scraped ground and the large airplane hangar is nearly completed. The front doors of the structure were being hung yesterday.

The sign "Wertz Field, Charleston" is being painted on the roof of the hangar.

Practically every day airplanes passing through West Virginia land at the new field for service. Yesterday a Barling plane, owned by J. B. Rich of Huntington and piloted by Louis Stone, landed at the field. A record of each visiting plane is kept at the field office.

1930

Henry Ford's famous airplane the Ford Tri-Motor landed at Wertz Field during its dedication ceremony on July 4, 1930. From 1926 to 1933, 199 of these airplanes were built. They became the first monoplane airliner to be used by the fledgling airline business in the United States. Several Ford Tri-Motors are still flying today. In the background is a Curtiss "Condor," the last U.S. biplane airliner and the first sleeper plane in the world. SWV STARK COLL.

The West Virginia Air Tour Association was an early organization to promote flying in the state, which was photographed at Wertz Field on May 16, 1932. The aircraft behind the group is a Howard Model SN-8A, operated by West Virginia Airways. Two Wacos are to the left. At the extreme right foreground is Hubert Stark's stunt plane, a Great Lakes 2T-1A. Other aircraft in the background include a Waco, Stinson, Great Lakes trainer, Curtiss Wright pusher type and a high-wing Barling. A 15 passenger Bellanca is in the extreme background, the largest single-engine plane in the world in 1932. COURTESY JERRY WATERS

Hubert Stark, better known as the "Duke," is flanked in front of a Stinson by state troopers and an unidentified man (in hat) at Wertz Field. Stark was the governor's pilot and inspector for the State Board of Aeronautics in the 1930s. Who this other person is and why he rated a police escort is unknown but the vintage 1940 Plymouth tells us about when the photo was taken. SWV STARK COLL.

West Virginia's
Greatest

AIR CARNIVAL

WERTZ FIELD
TUESDAY, JUNE 21

PARACHUTE JUMPS
AIR RACES -- STUNTS
ARMY PLANES -- AUTOGIROS
West Virginia's State Air Tour Meet

Death Defying
OUTSIDE LOOP
First Time Done In West Virginia

Capitol Dedication
Air Show

1932

Freddie Lund was famous enough to have his name painted on the wing but all we can tell you is that he was a barnstormer.

Barnstormers toured the country in the 1930s promoting the new world of aviation. These views are at Wertz Field with a Curtiss Hawk coming in for a landing in the lower photo. The hangar was located at the present site of the plant garage and the background building was formerly the West Virginia School for Colored Deaf and Blind, and is now part of the West Virginia Rehabilitation Center. The hangar is said to still exist at the South Charleston plant of Dow (Union Carbide) next to the railroad overpass. It was disassembled and moved to South Charleston.

CHARLESTON HAS WINGS

This week Charleston will be host to visiting Aviators from all parts of the country who have come here to assist at the Dedication of our Municipal Airport.

We want these men to leave Charleston with the belief firmly planted that we have here a progressive city and a desirable place to live and ask your cooperation in making pleasant their brief visit.

Toward this end you are cordially invited to attend

A Dinner In Honor Of
Visiting Pilots

SATURDAY, JULY 5, 1930 AT THE DANIEL BOONE HOTEL 7 P. M.
TICKETS $2.50 EACH   LIMIT 250 PLATES

Tickets on sale at Daniel Boone Hotel, Automobile Club, at the Field Office at the Airport and by members of the Entertainment Committee.

West Virginia Airways, Inc.

This Space Contributed by:

ESKEW SMITH & CANNON

Manufacturers and Distributors
"We Believe in Aviation as a Major Form of Transportation"

1930

Harold Moore's collection of photographs is an example of the type of images that the authors tried to obtain for inclusion in this volume. Not only do they add a personal touch but Harold Moore himself had a very interesting story and was an outstanding citizen of the area.

Moore's great-great-grandfather Clement Moore wrote the famous story, "Twas the Night Before Christmas." Harold was a flying officer in the U.S. Air Service during World War One and was awarded the Legion of Merit. In 1913, he moved to Charleston and was a pioneer aviator in the Kanawha Valley and even attempted an air transport service at Wertz Field. In 1929-30 he was commander of John Brawley Post No. 20 of the American Legion.

For over 50 years Moore was well-known in auto and truck sales in the Charleston area. He died in 1984.

HAROLD MOORE COLL.

West Virginia Airways, Inc. was formed by a group of local businessmen in 1930 to operate a commercial airport on a leased tract of land at Institute. It operated the field (Wertz Field) for the next 12 years.

World War One service photo.

His later years.

Moore, second from left, by a Curtiss Hawk Biplane at the old Kanawha City Airfield, circa 1930.

Moore on the left as a Ford salesman, 1934

An All American Airways aircraft picks up mail at the old Bollinger Field in 1946. A wire was stretched between two poles and a hook on the aircraft snatched up the mail bag. BENNY MALLORY COLL.

With very mountainous terrain it is obvious that aviation facilities lagged in development in the state. In 1939, West Virginia had only 23 airports and only two were served by scheduled airlines. In the late 1930s the Air Pick-up system was developed to pick up from the ground by airplane in flight, air mail and air express. By 1944, 34 state cities and towns had this service. There were no established airports in the county during the war so this method of pick-up and delivery was essential, especially for the many defense plants in the Kanawha Valley. On May 12, 1939, the first air mail dispatches and delivery of incoming mail from Pittsburgh, the terminal point, occurred at Nitro, Dunbar and Charleston. With the building of many new airports after the war, including the Kanawha Airport, this service was discontinued.

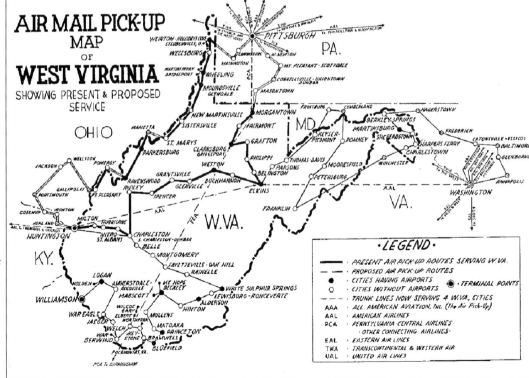

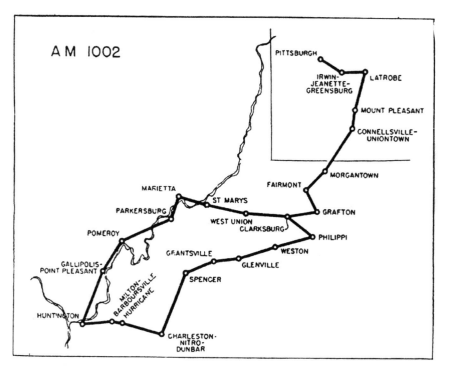

Route 1002 left for Pittsburgh each morning for West Virginia. After arriving at Clarksburg, the plane made a large counterclockwise loop around the state, traveling south through the Ohio River valley to Huntington, then turning northward to Clarksburg where it retraced its route back to Pittsburgh by evening. The communities between Pittsburgh and Clarksburg had southbound and northbound service. The communities on the "loop" had service in one direction only.

Glenn T. Clark

Glenn T. Clark, a native of West Virginia, returned to Charleston in 1931 after flying on the West Coast and in Hawaii, and established a seaplane base at the city levee. He was the pioneer seaplane pilot in the state. He was using Aeronca seaplanes and had one of the busiest flying services in the country. In 1939, the National Youth Administration built Clark a new floating hangar. Clark stated in 1939, "Seaplane flying gives one the combined thrill of piloting an airplane and of handling a fast motor boat, and yet the seaplane is safer than the land plane because you always have a larger landing area." Sometime after the war Clark moved to a landing field in Putnam County, where the John Amos Power Plant is now located. He was later killed at his field when a plane landed on his plane.

A Pennsylvania Central Airlines Boeing 247 aircraft at Wertz Field in 1939.

Even seaplanes were subject to accidents and in a bizarre twist of fate a young South Hills pilot, Miles V. Dixson was killed in 1935 when his seaplane lost a wing over Spring Hill Cemetery and he crashed near the old mausoleum.

On April 16, 1941, a 10-passenger Boeing 247 Pennsylvania Central airliner took off from Wertz Field heading for Pittsburgh. At 4:30 p.m. the plane lost an engine and crashed a few miles south of the airport coming to rest in a grove of trees, its wings and tail section torn away. The six passengers and three crewmen were not seriously injured. The crash occurred up Green Valley Drive on Dry Ridge near St. Albans. ⑲③

KANAWHA AIRPORT

Grading the Coonskin Ridge was a massive undertaking. More than nine million cubic yards of earth and rock were moved requiring two million pounds of explosives.⑲⑥

Officials view the first earth moved for the new airport on Oct. 18, 1944. Long-time airport director, Fred C. Alley is fourth from left, Charles E. Hodges, long-time head of the Charleston Chamber of Commerce is on the extreme right.

An April 5, 1945, aerial view of airport construction from the northern approach.⑲⑥

By late summer 1945 grading covered an extensive area.

Famous World War One ace and president of Eastern Airlines, Eddie Rickenbacker came to Charleston for the dedication of the airport on Nov. 3, 1947. At the time Eastern flew between New York and St. Louis with a stop in Charleston, and between Detroit and Miami with a stop in Charleston. Other airlines servicing Charleston in 1947 were American, Capital, Piedmont and All-American Airways. Rickenbacker returned to Charleston many times. In June 1950, Eastern bought a fleet of Martin 404 passenger airplanes to service smaller airports such as Charleston's.

Bumper to bumper buses as thousands arrived for the 1947 airport dedication. It would be 1950 before the terminal building was opened.

Sailors in abundance showed up along with civilians for the dedication. The Charleston High School band furnished the music.

All-American Aviation, Inc., made the first commercial flight into the still-uncompleted Kanawha Airport on Oct. 2, 1947. On hand to meet the plane were from the left: Col. H.C. Fry of Pittsburgh, the oldest licensed pilot in the United States; Norman Rintune, pilot of the plane; Fred C. Alley, airport manager; R.L. Woody, the airlines air-mail manager; Maj. Hal Bayley, vice-president of the airline; H.H. Stark, Director of the State Board of Aeronautics; Carl Andrews, mayor of Charleston; Carl C. Calvert, president of the Kanawha County Court; Carl Hodges, president of the Charleston Chamber of Commerce; Julius W. Singleton, Charleston postmaster; Fred E. Wiseman, assistant postmaster; John Graham, field representative of the airline; Dale G. Casto, county attorney; M. Bullock, Railway Express Co. agent and T.T. Jackson, assistant agent. SWV STARK COLL.

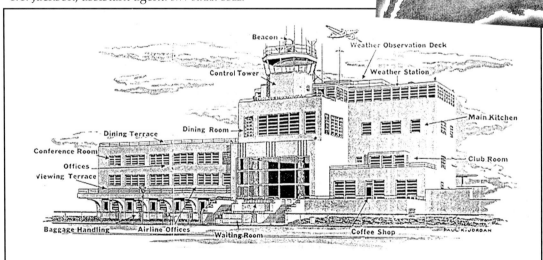

The present terminal was constructed in 1950. It has gone through several expansions in the past 50 years.

Captain Yeager Lands Jet 'Shooting Star' at Kanawha Airport

Capt. Charles E. Yeager, famed Army Air Force pilot and the first man ever to fly into the mystery land beyond the "sonic wall," dropped into Kanawha Airport at noon yesterday in the newest jet F-80-C (pictured above) built by Lockheed and put into use only about a month ago.

The new "Shooting Star" travels at a speed in excess of 600 miles per hour, has a service ceiling of more than 45,000 feet, wing span of 38 feet, 10-1/2 inches and is equipped with 50 calibre machine gun.

Capt. Yeager flew the ship from his base in Muroc, Cal., to Day-ton, O., Friday. He decided shortly before noon yesterday to visit his parents, Mr. and Mrs. A Hal Yeager of Hamlin, and in a matter of minutes was over Kanawha Airport. He experienced no trouble letting the ship down here. Capt. Yeager will return to Muroc today.

Capt. Chuck Yeager.

Believed to be the first jet ever to land at Kanawha Airport this beautiful F-80 Lockheed "Shooting Star" sits on the unfinished runway Oct. 11, 1948.

Piloted by the world's fastest human being, Capt. Charles "Chuck" Yeager of Hamlin, the F-80 was flown to Charleston to make an aerobatic exhibition at the annual boat races on the Kanawha River.

In his exuberance to impress his home folks, Yeager flew under the South Side Bridge, a stunt that was not on the schedule and almost landed the world renowned flier in trouble.

The stunningly sleek "Shooting Star" was developed at the end of World War Two but was too late to see combat. The standard U.S. Air Force fighter of the postwar decade, it saw much service in Korea until superceded by swept wing aircraft.

Although Kanawha Airport opened for use in 1947, it was not really completed until 1950. The steel runway mats, visible in this photo, were for temporary use in World War Two but were obviously used for parts of Kanawha Airport in the early years. (198)

An incoming Capital Airlines Constellation with 44 persons aboard ground-looped from a rain-drenched runway and plunged over an embankment at Kanawha Airport on May 12, 1959. Two were killed and 28 injured, the first commercial airline deaths at the airport since its opening in 1947. The plane was en route from the north to Atlanta with a stop in Charleston. CN.

On August 10, 1968, a Piedmont Airlines, Fairchild-Hiller 227 twin engine prop jet slammed into the hillside overlooking Coonskin Park. The plane was en route from Cincinnati to Roanoke. Thirty-two passengers were killed and five injured, the worst plane crash in the state up to that time. CN

WCHS-TV news department at the airport in 1954 with the governor's Aero-Commander airplane in the hangar. Left to right: Ross Edwards, news director, WCHS-Radio; Bob Boaz, TV news director; Dick Johnson; Phil Smith; Neil Boggs; Nilo Olin and Bill Kelly. COURTESY BILL KELLY

Passengers getting ready to board a plane in 1957, years before jetways and security changed procedures for boarding. An Eastern Airlines Constellation is in the background. CN

By Wilma Dodson

The Kanawha flying club celebrated its third birthday yesterday. Since its organization in the spring of 1932 by Glenn T. Clark and others interested in sportsman flying. 64 student pilots have soloed, of which 20 have received private pilot's licenses. One holds an amateur pilot's license and one holds a limited commercial pilot's license.

The club owns three seaplanes, one of which is a Savoy-Marchetti. The other two planes are Aeroncas.

FROM *THE CHARLESTON GAZETTE*, FEB. 17, 1935

An Aeronca Champ seaplane over Charleston, circa 1950. Note Elk River Boulevard Bridge.

Bellanca Aircraft Engineering at Scott Depot unveiled their new single engine Fiberglass aluminum honeycomb airplane in 1975. Henry Payne III of Charleston was the managing director of the West Virginia Bellanca project. The plane was funded by a group of local investors but production never got started. John Harris broke speed records for light piston aircraft and still flys it. The project was sold in 1980.

By the late 1930s, Wertz Field proved to be inadequate for the DC-3 aircraft but city officials persuaded American Airlines to continue service with the smaller DC-2 aircraft shown above.

Pennsylvania Central Airlines (later Capital Airlines) established a branch route for passenger service between Pittsburgh and Charleston in 1935.

An American Airlines Convair CV-240 at Kanawha Airport, circa 1950s.

The Supreme Sacrifice

General McLaughlin participated in the raid on Schweinfurt, Germany (the ball bearing works) on Aug. 17, 1943. He was also on the second raid known as "Black Thursday" on Oct. 14, 1943 which turned out to be the greatest aerial battle of the war. The 220 American bombers were under constant attack from the European coast to the target and halfway back to the coast, for about five hours. McLaughlin described the raid in a 1944 *True Magazine* issue:

The 167th Fighter Squadron of the West Virginia Air National Guard was established in January 1947 at Kanawha Airport. The first commander was Lt. Col. J. Kemp McLaughlin. When this photo was taken in 1947, the squadron consisted of 27 World War Two P-47 fighters and 353 personnel. (199)

West Virginia Air National Guard P-47s.

"Maj. George Ott, of South Dakota, our deputy leader, was flying on my right wing. Suddenly, while we were under an attack from the right by two 110s, an Me-109 came down out of the sun like a flash and knocked out one and possibly two of Major Ott's engines. Immediately he began having trouble and could not keep up. He fell back and down. Nine chutes were counted to come from his ship as he went down under control.

"Two Ju-88s came in at ten o'clock high. I called them out to Sergeant Edison in the top turret in time for him to send home some good shots that made them break off the attack. Harry yelled, 'My God, Mac, take some evasive action!' This I promptly did, as two rocket shells exploded off our nose.

"By this time we were getting our heaviest attacks. Almost every type of enemy fighter they had was there, including night fighters and fighter bombers. The low group ahead of us had now lost more than half of their ships, most of them exploding or burning in the air. Just then Staff Sergeant Van Horne in the ball turret said that Lieutenant Clough, leading the second element of our squadron, had been badly hit and was afire. Then he reported that an explosion in the left wing of Clough's ship had blown the wing off, and two chutes were reported coming from it. All the time we were being pounded by the German twin-engine fighters. These ships, attacking in groups of two to four and carrying two rocket guns each, were closing to about five hundred or six hundred yards from us and then letting go with a double salvo from each gun, leaving twin clouds of black smoke all around us. The single-engine fighters were making close frontal attacks, attempting to break up our formation, and finding plenty of 'easy meat' in the many stragglers left crippled by the rocket ships.

"After we had gotten well into France on our return flight, the fighters broke off their attack, having accounted for three more of our bombers. We let down over the south coast of England and started home.

"No sooner had we touched the ground than Lieutenant O'Grady raised our flag from the astro-hatch. O'Grady's aunt had given him this American flag before his coming overseas. The flag had been blessed by his parish priest, we'd always flown with it, and we had come to consider it our good luck charm. As the flag came up, Colonel Peaslee let out a cheer. You know how hearing the Star Spangled Banner can send chills up your spine; well, as we taxied around the perimeter of our airfield the various ground crews came to attention and smoothly saluted our flag. The scene gave me a strange thrill, and I felt that they were not only paying tribute to their flag but also to the men who had made the supreme sacrifice that day."

A P-47 on display to the public.

Later the 167th received World War Two P-51 fighters. This one, piloted by Capt. Jess Burchett crashed at the Kanawha Airport near the end of the short runway in 1951. He was uninjured but pinned beneath the wreckage and dirt had to be dug out from underneath the cockpit to free him. He was extremely fortunate as 100 octane fuel had soaked his flight suit.

Loading .50 calibre ammunition for gunnery practice with a P-51, 1948. Jim Keeler on left, Louis Price, third from left. WILLIAM GUTHRIE COLL.

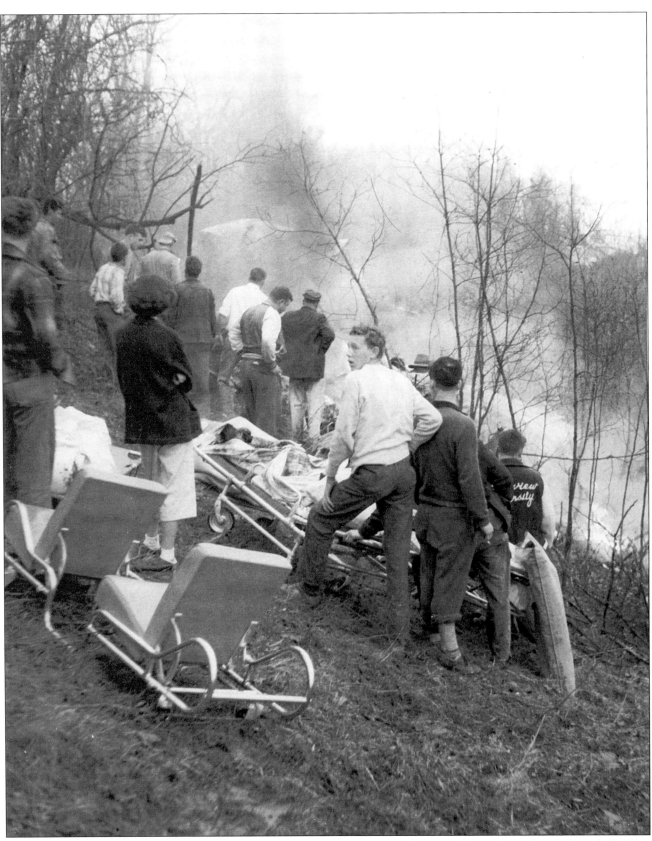

The worst accident in West Virginia Air National Guard history occurred on April 19, 1951, when a Guard C-47 aircraft attempting to make a landing at Kanawha Airport crashed into a nearby mountain killing a total of 21 guardsmen. The plane was coming to Charleston to attend the funeral of Major Sutherland. For a community the size of Charleston and Kanawha County, the sudden loss of 21 native sons was an unspeakable tragedy. CN (199)

Looking ready for aerial combat, Lt. Harlow D. Sheets was a P-51 pilot with the air guard when this photo was taken. He was killed on duty in an SA-16 crash in Virginia in the 1960s. His family owned well-known Sheets Bakery.

Gov. William Marland with pilots of the 167th Fighter-Bomber Squadron of the West Virginia Air National Guard, circa 1950s. WILLIAM GUTHRIE COLL.

A C-119 cargo plane unloading an Air Force spotter plane at Kanawha Airport, circa 1960s.

Of all of mankind's machines the steam railroad locomotive is perhaps the most fascinating and awesome.

This westbound L-2 Hudson class passenger engine seen here at the Charleston station in 1948 was one of the swift race horses that powered the legendary Chessie name trains—the George Washington, the F.F.V. and the Sportsman.

If only our book could bring you the vivid sounds of hissing steam—thumping air pumps—bells and of course the unforgettable whistle.

One can almost hear the conductor shouting, "All aboard."

Steam engines are gone now of course—victims of abundant Middle East oil, but there was a day when they were king—burning West Virginia coal.

AUGUST THIEME COLL. RICHMOND, VIRGINIA

RAILS

Although it is a fact that the first C&O Railroad train to pass through Charleston was Jan. 29, 1873, the tracks were laid in Charleston in 1871 and it was possible to ride from Charleston to Huntington over a year before the grand completion in 1873.

On Feb. 1, 1873, several carloads of West Virginia coal arrived in Richmond and on that same train a bottle of Ohio River water was carried for a grand ceremony where in the water was poured into the James River to symbolize the linking of the east and west.

The early years of the rugged mountain route were plagued by frequent landslides.

This is the oldest known photo of Hansford taken in 1879. The Hansford house is to the left of the tracks. Note covered railroad bridge over Paint Creek. CET COLL.

These are "Buck Jimmys," wooden cars built in the 1870s and used to transport coal from the mines to a railhead.

"Westward Ho" was built in 1857 and survived the Civil War. Shown here at Winifrede Junction in 1870. It had been transported by water up the Mississippi, Ohio and Kanawha rivers for use in building the C&O from the western end.

BK

W. Va. & S.R.R.
40 Trip Ticket
BETWEEN
MARMET
AND
HERNSHAW
This Check is worthless if detached or presented by any person other than the original Purchaser.
142

One of the world's pioneer railroad men passed away in 1896 at age 90. Rev. Ralph Swinburn of Davis Creek ran the first steam locomotive ever operated and was the superintendent of the first steam railroad ever constructed. He was associated with George Stephenson, the inventor of the first successful locomotive. Swinburn was born in England in 1805 and came to the U.S. in 1850 and was employed by the Winifrede Mining Company to locate their first railroad on Fields Creek, the first railroad in the Kanawha Valley. He also located the Paint Creek Railway and the inclines of the Lovebury, Old Dominion and Armstrong Creek mines. He retired in 1850 to become a Baptist minister.

A very rare view of the Hernshaw depot in 1896. GA

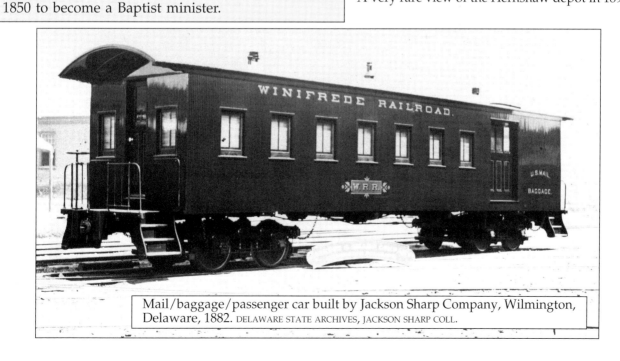

Mail/baggage/passenger car built by Jackson Sharp Company, Wilmington, Delaware, 1882. DELAWARE STATE ARCHIVES, JACKSON SHARP COLL.

Circa turn of the century, this scene shows the steel replacement of the original wooden C&O bridge over Paint Creek at Hansford. JERRY SMITH COLL.

A huge Heisler-type shay locomotive on Cabin Creek. JERRY SMITH COLL.

One of the earliest photos of a main line passenger train—this C&O Flyer is seen near Pratt about 1900. Note the single main line track. The engine is a ten wheel F-4 class consolidation. JERRY SMITH COLL.

Posing for the camera this passenger train is believed to be on Coal River, circa 1910.

A Coal River Railroad passenger train at the Indian Creek flag stop with the water tank in the background. W.O. Wintz, the engineer, in center foreground.
ORA WINTZ MCDERMIT COLL (125)

A C&O carpenter crew and their motor car on the Coal River Division about 1920.
LAYTON WILLIAM COLL.

COAL RIVER RAILROAD ENTERPRISE.

WEST VIRGINIA.

The chief points about this enterprise are as follows:

(1) The Coal river basin contains an area of one thousand square miles, or 640,000 acres of land, well timbered and abounding in Splint, Cannel and Bituminous Coal, Black Band Iron Ore, Carbonate Iron Ore, Fire Clay, &c., &c.,

(2) From four to ten workable veins of Superior Coal are found in the Coal river hills and mountains above the Forks of Coal. Cannel Coal of the very best quality and workable veins of good Iron Ore are found within six miles of the Forks of Coal, which is twelve miles distant, by railroad route, from the Chesapeake & Ohio Railroad and Kanawha river, at St. Albans, Kanawha County, West Virginia.

(3) A narrow gauge railroad (3 feet) can be constructed to these lands at a cost of $10,000 per mile. Distance, 18 miles.

(4) The Coal river lands are 250 miles nearer to Cincinnati than the Monongahela and Youghiogheny coal lands are.

(5) Cincinnati requires one hundred million bushels of Coal annually, of which Pittsburgh supplies about eighty millions, and Kanawha only about five million bushels per annum.

(6) The quantity of Superior Cannel Coal on Little Coal river is greater than all other known Cannel Coal deposits in the Great Kanawha Coal Field, which coal field embraces the lands drained by the Great Kanawha and its tributaries: New river, Gauley river, Elk river, Coal river and Pocatalico river.

For forty miles on Little Coal river, workable veins of Superior Cannel Coal crop out here and there on the hill and mountain sides.

(7) Cannel Coal brings from 40 to 50 per cent. more in market than the Bituminous or Splint Coal does. In New York ten million bushels of the Coal River Cannel Coal can be sold every year, and in Cincinnati and other Western cities five million bushels can be sold every year.

(8) Coal from the Great Kanawha Coal Field should supply the Cincinnati demand for Coal (100 million bushels per annum). But how is this to be accomplished? Only by the formation of a company sufficiently strong to mine and place that quantity of Coal every year in Cincinnati, and this can be accomplished through the Coal River Railroad Enterprise.

(9) The quantity of land on Big and Little Coal rivers thus far subscribed to the Coal River Railroad Company on the terms and conditions set forth in the printed circular of April, 1879, is 100,000 acres. The construction of the railroad must be commenced by July 1st, 1880, to make these subscriptions continue valid beyond July 1st, next. Certainly there never was a more liberal offer made to secure the building of a railroad than the Coal River land-owners are now making.

(10) Coalboating stages on the Kanawha are more frequent from St. Albans up Coal river than they are on the Ohio from Pittsburgh. Hence, a railroad from St. Albans up Coal river would make these lands more accessible to the Cincinnati market than the Monongahela and Youghiogheny lands are. From St. Albans the Cannel Coal can be sent to New York over the Chesapeake & Ohio Railroad.

(11) The construction of Lock and Dam No. 7 by the United States Government on the Great Kanawha just below St. Albans, will create an excellent harbour in Coal river at and near its mouth, and it is said that this work will soon commence.

(12) The Coal River Railroad charter contains many very liberal provisions, and is perpetual in its duration. The Coal on Coal river is practically inexhaustible, and the demand in Cincinnati and other Western cities and towns for the Superior Coals of this region is at present at least one hundred million bushels per annum, and this demand is increasing every year with the rapid growth of the Ohio and Mississippi valleys.

(13) The Board of Directors will assign the charter and land subscriptions, subject, however, to the present liabilities of the Company, to nine responsible parties who will construct and equip the railroad from St. Albans to Forks of Coal, (12 miles), thence up either Big or Little Coal river for a distance of 25 miles.

For further information address,

April 17, 1880.

COAL RIVER RAILROAD COMPANY,
Charleston, Kanawha County,
West Virginia.

$36,000.00   No. 4 $36,000.00

UNITED STATES OF AMERICA

Coal River Railway Company

TEMPORARY OBLIGATION

EXCHANGEABLE FOR FIRST MORTGAGE FOUR PER CENT. GOLD BONDS

COAL RIVER RAILWAY COMPANY, a corporation existing under the laws of the State of West Virginia, acknowledges itself to be

indebted unto *Richard Wetherill*

in the sum of *Thirty Six Thousand* Dollars in gold coin of the United States of, or equal to, the present standard of weight and fineness, with interest at the rate of four per centum per annum, payable semi-annually on the first days of October and April, in like gold coin at the office of The Chesapeake and Ohio Railway Company, in the City of Richmond, State of Virginia; but this obligation is issued and received, or transferred, solely upon the condition that the same shall be by the holder thereof, upon ten days' notice given, either personally or by United States mail, or by publication in some newspaper published in the City of Richmond, by Coal River Railway Company, surrendered to the Coal River Railway Company at the office of The Chesapeake and Ohio Railway Company, in the City of Richmond, Virginia, for cancellation and exchange into a like amount of First Mortgage Four Per Cent. Gold Bonds of the Coal River Railway Company, to be guaranteed, principal and interest, by The Chesapeake and Ohio Railway Company, secured under the terms and conditions of a deed of trust or mortgage to bear date the first day of April, 1905. It is expressly understood and agreed that all interest on this obligation shall cease at the succeeding due date of coupon of said First Mortgage Gold Bond after the notice above referred to has been given as above provided.

In Witness Whereof, the Coal River Railway Company has caused this obligation to be duly executed under its corporate seal as of the first day of April, 1905.

_____ President.

_____ Secretary.

Ex-president Teddy Roosevelt stopped at the C&O depot for six minutes on April 3, 1912. He can be seen on the right on the back of his private car "Convoy." About 2,500 gathered to hear him speak as he was running for president again, this time as a third party candidate on the Progressive or "Bull Moose" party ticket. Woodrow Wilson won the election and Roosevelt died six years later. (298)

William Jennings Bryan stopped in Montgomery in 1912 to promote the presidential candidacy of Woodrow Wilson, who later won the election. Bryan ran for president in 1896, 1900 and 1908. He was an orator, politician, lawyer and newspaperman and one of the most notable Americans in history.

Teddy Roosevelt speaks at Montgomery in 1912.

Campbell's Creek Railroad Co.
DECLARATION OF VALUE
The value of the property covered by check Nos.
is not more than { $100.00 for each shipment of one or more pieces.
{ $.
Date 191
Signed
Shipper.

BK

Rail and river tipple at Cedar Grove. (121)

Coal & Coke Railroad trestle on Blue Creek, 1913. Note the Frankenberger & Co. sign in background. (163)

Shops of the Winifrede Railroad. RAA

C&O Engine #423 with train crew at Cabin Creek Junction, circa 1915. C&OHS #7584

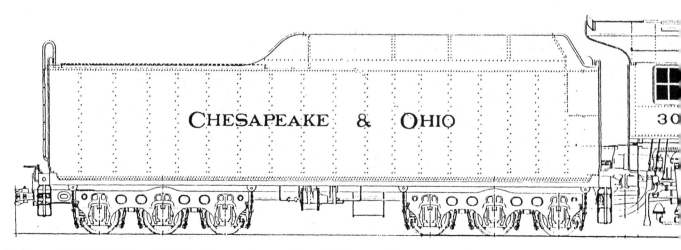

Delivered in 1930 the huge T-1 class locomotive could pull 160 car—13,500-ton coal trains.

Sproul railroad yard in May 1929. Big Coal River to the left and Little Coal River to the right. H.R. HEREFORD COLL

Posing for posterity, a group of ladies at the Sproul depot on the Coal River Railroad, circa 1910.

Culvert being constructed under the C&O Railroad at Washington Street in St. Albans, circa 1918, near the present K-Mart store. ST. ALBANS HISTORICAL SOCIETY ⑪

Columbus Train Leaves on Final Journey Today

Fifty years of passenger train service between the capital cities of West Virginia and Ohio by the New York Central railroad will end Friday when the final train leaves the Broad street station here at 3:40 p. m. for Columbus.

The train, formerly known as The Charlestonian, has made the round trip daily for the past year.

The public service commissions of West Virginia and Ohio approved discontinuance of the passenger run when it was shown that the train was being operated at a large loss to the railroad.

The discontinuance of two daily trips was approved last year.

1950

The Charlestonian
to COLUMBUS
connecting for Buffalo and Chicago

Lv Charleston	....	4:50 p.m.
Ar Columbus	....	10:35 p.m.
Lv Columbus	....	12:01 a.m.
Ar Toledo (Union Sta.)		3:25 a.m.
Ar Chicago NYC (C.T.)		8:05 a.m.
Ar Detroit	....	7:50 a.m.
Lv Columbus (Big 4)		10:50 a.m.
Ar Buffalo (NYC)	....	6:45 a.m.

Parlor Car (Broiler Buffet) Charleston to Columbus, Sleepers Columbus to Detroit, Chicago to Buffalo.
Returning Charlestonian leaves Columbus at 3:20 p.m.
All Schedules Standard Time

Here's the fine, efficient train that superbly meets the busy Charleston man's needs ... equally praised by the ladies! A distinctive, comfortable trip ... You change at Columbus without leaving the station —for East or West—over the famous water level route.

Ohio Central Lines
NEW YORK CENTRAL

1931

—SPOILS OF WAR—

When World War One ended on Nov. 11, 1918 there was a feeling that "To the Victor Belongs the Spoils" and so it was that each state received at least several railroad cars of captured German war equipment.

As hard as it is to believe today—German machine guns (presumably made inoperative by the removal of the breechblock) were given to patriotic organizations such as the American Legion and Mauser rifles were sold to the public for 50¢.

These extremely rare photos show the arrival of the German equipment in the K&M Railroad yards near Capitol Street.

The artillery piece was placed on the capitol (1885) lawn on Capitol Street and after the Capitol burned in 1921 it was displayed on the Lee Street triangle until about 1942 when it was donated to the World

War Two scrap drive to be melted down and fired back at the Germans. (See pages 380-81—WWII)

When World War Two ended victoriously the federal government perhaps recognizing an obligation sent captured Japanese and Nazi cannons to replace those donated in the scrap drives.

At least three Japanese cannons were displayed after World War Two in Nitro, South Charleston and Charleston.

The Charleston cannon at this writing is in Montgomery at West Virginia Tech. The Nitro cannon is still on display in Nitro.

Assigned the prestigious task of pulling the flagship of the C&O Line this F-17 Pacific is seen here at Montgomery in the 1930s. The image of George Washington is mounted on the front of the engine proclaiming to all that this is no ordinary train. A crewman uses the stop to apply grease to the rods. The roof of the Montgomery Station is seen on the right and a movie theatre is on the left. C&OHS

1932

SLEEPER ON VIEW

George Washington Pullman on Display at C. & O. Station

An air-cooled sleeping car, The Ferry Farm, typical of the kind that will make up the Chesapeake and Ohio's new fast passenger train, The George Washington, went on exhibition at the station here Saturday morning. The car will be open for inspection until Saturday night at 10 o'clock, during which time a committee of road officials will receive visitors.

The George Washington, which is said to be the country's first long-distance air-cooled sleeping car train, will begin operations on Sunday, between Cincinnati and New York.

The George Washington will be entirely new in equipment but is, in reality, a substitution for the West Virginian, a name which has been used to designate No. 1 and No. 2, for many years.

(1935)

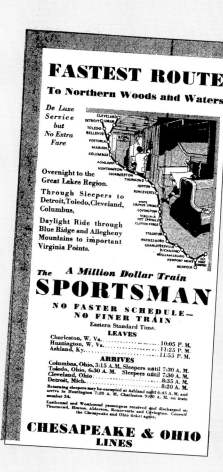

The food was simple, one didn't have to dress up for dinner, and the waiters were apt to engage the patrons in friendly conversation in deep Virginia accents. It was this folksiness, and at the same time the style, the courtesy, the desire for excellence of service, and the pride, which combined with the superb food to make the C&O's diners legend. When "The George" went into service the diners were named "restaurant cars" and, as has been recounted, were named for ancient hostelries of Colonial Virginia.

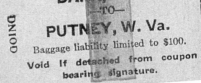

Kelley's Creek Railroad #12, circa 1940.

Station workers mugging for the camera at St. Albans C&O Railroad depot ticket office, circa 1930s.
PHOTO COURTESY OF GUY COTTRELL, J.W. (BILL) WILLIAMS COLL. (117)

When we see the diesel locomotives of the Norfolk-Southern thunder through the heart of Charleston, it's hard to recall the days of steam when railroaders wore striped caps and cinders could ruin a clothesline of fresh laundry. These photographs, circa 1941, were rescued from a trash bin, but it brings back a time when the New York Central yards in Charleston were busy 24 hours a day. These photographs were taken near the Ruffner Avenue crossing. The building on the right is still recognizable after 60 years. Originally opened in 1884, the railroad through the capital city has seen several owners and the century-old railroad bridge across the Elk River still stands, although not used since 1939. The Institute of Industrial Archaeology at West Virginia University recognizes it as a historic structure worth saving, photos circa 1941.

For many years students and fans from East Bank took the train to Charleston to attend the Charleston High-East Bank High football game at Laidley Field. These photos are from 1939.

ALL PHOTOS BOB CRAIGO COLL.

Football banquet after East Bank's victory over Charleston.

Yard shifters near Capitol Street. The Kanawha Valley Bank building is in the background.

Turntable and roundhouse New York Central B&O yards near Capitol Street, circa 1941. Greens Feed and Seed store is now on this site. ⟨215⟩

View toward Elk River showing the B&O yards near Court Street, circa 1941. Stone apartment building on right still stands.

One of the fabled C&O K-4 Kanawha Class 2-8-4 engines pulls through Charleston just west of the depot, circa 1948. Adept at handling either freight or passenger service, this class was one of the most successful of all Chessie's locomotives. For years Number 2700-K4 was on display in Coonskin Park but it was vandalized and neglected and finally removed.
RAY SHAMBLEN COLL.

C&O mainline tracks run right through the town of Montgomery, circa 1940. Two trains are passing.
BILL SPARKMON COLL.

This motorized New York Central "Budd Car" ran up the Elk River tracks from Charleston's Broad Street yards. Photo at old Broad Street Depot. Note brick paving on walk, circa 1960. RAY SHAMBLEN PHOTO

Rare winter scene of a C&O mainline train eastbound in Charleston, circa 1940s.
RAY SHAMBLEN PHOTO

A G-9 Consolidation near Cabin Creek. This class of engine, built before World War One, survived until the 1950s.

A K-2 Mikado. A virtual trademark of the C&O was the mounting of air pumps on the front of the boiler.

A C&O switcher pausing at the east end of the Charleston depot, circa 1940s.

A 2-66-2 Mallet at Handley.

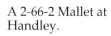

Winifrede Railroad #8, 2-8-0, (ex C&O G class) shifting hopper's in yard at Winifrede Junction, summer 1954.
OFFICIAL C&O RAILWAY PHOTO. C&OHS #10072.04

This engine servicing facility was at the South Charleston end of the old Kanawha River railroad bridge. A yard switcher awaits coal and water.
RAY SHAMBLEN PHOTO

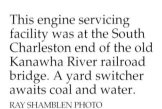

A classic 4-8-4 Greenbrier Class engine at Handley. Once the queen of the late 1940s passenger fleet, they were relegated to freight service in the power shortage of 1956 and then scrapped.

C&O H-5 Mallet #1529 on summit of Scary Hill, Teays, May 1949. The engine was based at St. Albans and used as a pusher for the long trains over the hill. C&OHS GENE HUDDLESTON PHOTO #1354

The huge H-8 Class. One of these engines exploded near Hinton in the mid-1950s killing three crewmen. One of these monsters is on display at the Henry Ford Museum, Dearborn, Michigan. Photo at Montgomery, 1956. C&OHS #1719 GENE HUDDLESTON PHOTO

Cabin Creek Junction, 1940s.

Kelley's Creek Coal Railroad 2-8-2 with hopper drag. C&OHS #4664

An early diesel switch engine in South Charleston, 1950s. (111)

The infinite fascination of a steam engine's working parts. New York Central switcher at the Charleston yard, 1950.

The last B&O steam engine on the Elk River route, 1956. This was one of the last steam engines to run to Charleston. CN (116)

Ross Rowland was a millionaire railroad buff who in the mid 1980s resurrected a 1940s vintage C&O steam engine hoping to prove that steam could return. Shown here at the Charleston depot, number 614, a splendid J-3 Greenbrier class, being admired by fans—many who had never seen a steam engine. Rowland's experiment failed but it gave the upper Kanawha Valley a déjàvu thrill that will be long remembered.

This handsome little Atlantic class has just pulled into St. Albans from its run up Coal River with a local. Built in 1902 these little workhorses served into the 1950s. (111)

Poised at Charleston near Broad Street this Virginian Railway passenger locomotive prepares to depart for Roanoke, circa 1948. This Virginian train shared trackage rights over the N.Y.C. from Deepwater to the capital city and was a familiar sight until its demise in the early 1950s. DOUGLAS ANDRE COLL. (118)

TRAIN WRECKS

Believed to be about 1907 this wreck is somewhere in Kanawha County but little is known except that it speaks for itself.

The crew cab has been totally ripped away—probably with fatal results.

Rockslides often resulted in scenes like this—hopefully there were no deaths.

A rockslide caused this C&O wreck on Coal River near tunnel to St. Albans, 1950s.

The August 1916 Cabin Creek flood was devastating as this photo of a wrecked railroad locomotive attests. A close examination will reveal that it is of the "Shay" type which was gear driven. A few of the men standing on the wreck are in uniform - apparently National Guardsmen with one holding a rifle. Two children have made their way near the front wheels, doubtless enjoying one of the most memorable experiences of their young lives.

The eastbound train No. 2, the George Washington, consisting of seven Pullman cars, four coaches and a mail car, was derailed in the western limits of Marmet, about two miles from the Marmet Locks on Dec. 30, 1938. The coach train, crowded almost to capacity with holiday travelers, was running an hour late prior to the wreck at 11:33 p.m. Nineteen passengers were injured. A crowd estimated at 2,000 persons were attracted to the scene within a few minutes after word spread around town. Soon after daylight another crowd, seemingly indifferent to the penetrating cold, assembled at the scene to watch the operations of the wrecking crews.

ALL PHOTOS BILL SPARKMON COLL.

In April 1956 the St. Albans terminal was heavily damaged when another fast freight swept by dragging a derailed car. Sections of the terminal were torn away. CHESTER HAWES PHOTO, BILL WILLIAMS COLL. (117)

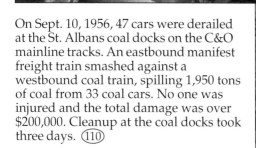

On Sept. 10, 1956, 47 cars were derailed at the St. Albans coal docks on the C&O mainline tracks. An eastbound manifest freight train smashed against a westbound coal train, spilling 1,950 tons of coal from 33 coal cars. No one was injured and the total damage was over $200,000. Cleanup at the coal docks took three days. (110)

DEPOTS

C&O depot at Winifrede Junction, circa 1900. Trackside view, Kanawha subdivision. C&OHS #7581

C&O depot at Cabin Creek, trackside view, circa 1925. C&OHS #7585

Hansford depot, circa 1934. C&OHS #7588

"ALL ABOARD"

The C&O Passenger Stations of Charleston, West Virginia

The C&O Railroad did not reach Charleston until 1873 and Wheeling became the first capital largely because the B&O mainline had arrived there in 1852.

Located too far north, Wheeling was not well suited to remain the capital and in 1870 a group of Charleston politicians and businessmen led by Dr. John P. Hale succeeded in having Charleston replace Wheeling as the seat of government.

Rare view of original 1873 station later used for freight only.

Dr. Hale and the other city fathers knew that the arrival of the "C&O" line would make their town accessible and remove one of the greatest obstacles for Charleston as the capital city. The first through "C&O" trains were eagerly anticipated.

Up until 1873 steamboats provided the major transportation link with the rest of the nation—especially Ohio where the meat packers of Cincinnati welcomed the millions of barrels of salt produced in the Charleston area. Before refrigeration salt was a crucial need for meat preservation.

The scene was set for the progression of the "C&O" passenger stations in Charleston from the first to the last.

To understand the history of Charleston's "C&O" depots we must remember that they have always been located on the south side of the great Kanawha River. Passengers have always had to cross the river to reach the city and from 1873 to 1891 it had to be by ferry.

A circa 1876 map clearly indicates the "passenger depot" several hundred yards west of the present station. The map outlines a long narrow structure and it is probable that the building was a combination passenger-freight facility.

The *"1901 City Illustrated"* includes a photo of a two story "C&O" building titled "C&O Freight Depot" which is almost certainly the original Charleston passenger depot.

When the second station was built circa 1890 the original was relegated to purely freight status and demolished sometime after the turn of the century.

It is interesting to note that nearby St. Albans had a very similar structure that survived into the post World War Two era.

In 1873 when the original station was apparently built there was no bridge to dictate its location and it was logically located across from the county courthouse.

In 1890-91 the construction of the new bridge further east caused the second or circa 1890 depot to be built adjoining the bridge for convenience.

The best photos we have of the second station are not very clear, however it is easily recognizable as a rather typical mainline "C&O" station of the 1900 era.

The existing station at Alderson, West Virginia is very similar and it can be seen that the Charleston building had small extensions on each end, probably baggage facilities.

Charleston was growing by leaps and bounds. It

Distant view of original two story 1873 station in center of photo.

was not only the capital city but also the business and financial center of a vast natural resource area, including coal—oil—gas—timber and salt, although the salt industry was in steady decline.

The virtual "boomtown" status of Charleston

soon dictated the need for a bigger and more ornate station and it came in 1905.

Truly a Charleston landmark, the 1905 station is still very much in existence although the main structure is occupied by a fine restaurant and office combination. As of this writing "Amtrak" is housed in the remodeled baggage room to serve the "Cardinal."

Over the last 20 or 30 years our grand old depot has dodged man's "bullets" and we are indeed fortunate to have this classic building that has seen so much history pass by its doors.

From the drama of 1917-18 when West Virginia boys boarded "C&O" trains to go and fight "the war to end all wars" to the 1920s and 30s halcyon years with the glistening "C&O" flagships the "F.F.V."— "the George Washington" and of course "the Sportsman."

Then came World War Two with the sons of the first World War veterans leaving from the same platform bound to places with strange sounding names like Iwo Jima—Anzio—Normandy or Guadalcanal.

Most of them came home but too many arrived in flag draped coffins borne on baggage carts to waiting hearses.

By 1946 the 1905 station was growing weary and as we all know there is a sad almost compulsive desire among some people to destroy classic architecture.

Robert Young—president of the postwar "C&O" had grandiose plans for a revival of passenger train service and a part of that plan was the construction of a new ultramodern station at Charleston. The artists rendition shown can only be described as "ghastly" and we may thank our lucky stars that it died in the planning stage. Incidentally the present station at Prince, West Virginia, bears some resemblance.

In 1930 the railroad in cooperation with the city built a highway ramp between the station and the tracks to alleviate the problem of traffic tie-ups while trains sat in the station.

Second C&O depot 1890 to 1905.

To fill out the rail history of Charleston we can tell you that it was not until 1884 that we welcomed our second railroad—the Ohio Central on the north side of the river, later renamed the "K&M" provided a good route to the Columbus, Ohio area among others.

The "K&M" was absorbed by the New York Central.

Although never as busy as the mainline "C&O" it was connected with the "Virginian" which ran to Roanoke and Norfolk. The old K&M is today the Norfolk-Southern.

The "K&M" depot was at the north end of Broad Street and was an attractive typically "Victorian" steepled structure—now long gone, a victim of highway construction.

The "K&M" had the advantage of arriving in the downtown rather than across the river.

The "B&O" also had access to Charleston along the Elk River from the north.

And so there you have it—today one hundred car coal trains roar by the 1905 "C&O" depot and three times a week the "Amtrak Cardinal" makes a brief stop.

For over 125 years the "C&O" stations of Charleston have been a focal point of history.

In 1873 partly to inaugurate the new railroad and partly to attend the wedding of a niece, President U.S. Grant arrived here.

Teddy Roosevelt spoke from the platform of an observation car in the campaign of 1912 and another Roosevelt—Franklin D. visited in 1940. Many recall the somber passing of the Eisenhower funeral train on a gray predawn morning in 1968.

For years rail fans have been thrilled by the fall "New River Train" which brought back a taste of long ago when the aroma of sweet steam and coal smoke drifted around the old station.

We assume locomotives have no feelings but one must wonder if somehow in her heart of steel— Greenbrier 614 sensed an old friend as she paused by the Charleston depot with the "New River Train."

RICHARD ANDRE

Photo circa 1930.

A Vintroux cartoon—*Charleston Gazette*, 1930

IF I GET OVER WITH THIS WAGON SHE'S SAFE.

YOU WOULDN'T KETCH ME ON THAT RAMP,

FLEM HANNA, OWNER OF THE JORDAN TAXI CO., WAS THE FIRST TO DRIVE OVER THE C.&O. RAMP. HE TESTED IT WITH HIS BIG 12 PASSENGER PACKARD SIGHT-SEEING SEDAN AND PRONOUNCED IT SAFE. THE RAMP IS NOW BEING USED BY THE PUBLIC.

Views of the C&O Depot
in the 1940s.
PHOTOS ON THESE PAGES COURTESY
C&OHS AND TOM DIXON

Ground floor interior west end of
general waiting room, showing ticket
windows and Union News Company
stand where travelers could get candy,
magazines, souvenirs—even a few small
toys to keep restless children happy.

Top floor interior east end of general
waiting room, showing stairway to
highway bridge level. Looking east.

Ground floor interior east end of
station building, showing steps to
second floor. Looking east.

Railway Express Agency facilities, Ward Engineering Company building and highway just west of station facilities. Looking west, circa 1930s. Now all gone.

The news stand offered travelers an opportunity to step off the train during a brief stop and buy a wide variety of newspapers—magazines—tobacco. Recall that in those long gone days it was not unusual to have a fellow passenger puffing on a cigar, 1947.

Before the airlines came into vogue the train station was a beehive of activity. We can only wonder about the travel plans of these people over half a century ago. Station platform opposite Union News Company stand. Night scene just before arrival of train 47, June 26, 1947.

CHARLESTON GAZETTE 1946

Here are architects drawings of the new passenger station which the Chesapeake and Ohio Railway will build 250 yards west of its present Charleston station as soon as details are completed for a new South Side river-front boulevard and other necessary highway changes. At left is an exterior view showing one of the "picture" windows

through which passengers may look out over the new boulevard, the Kanawha River and the Charleston business section. At right is an interior view showing the concourse, looking north toward the city. The latest architectural thought will be embodied in the building for the Railway Express Agency just west of the passenger station.

(This depot was never constructed.)

1985 excursion seen eastbound at Charleston depot. Engine is a powerful 2-8-4 of 1940s vintage. One of the many steam train excursions that were enjoyed by young and old alike in the 1980s called "The New River Train," they made a round trip from Huntington to Hinton in the fall when the leaves were at their height of colorful beauty. Insurance liability problems doomed the excursions.

Early 1900s photo of the railroad facilities and the K&M terminal at Dickinson east of Charleston.
JERRY SMITH PHOTO

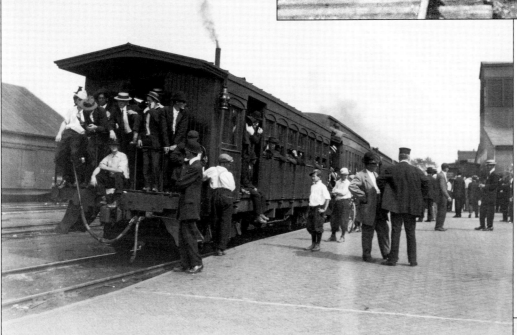

Excursion train about to leave the Kanawha & Michigan Broad Street depot, heading east. Note last car is very old—possibly Civil War vintage, circa 1907. RAA COLL.

118

Rare 1915 photo of the station at Pinch. Note old manual signal semaphore.

Cabin Creek Junction. STAN COHEN COLL. (402)

This panoramic view is of special interest because it depicts an entire railway junction and related structures, as well as housing a large industry. Therefore, many elements needed to portray railroading of the era are captured in a single portrait.

1950s

The most prominent structure found in the photo is the massive, coal-fired electric generating plant owned by the Virginia Power Company. In fact, this photograph may have been commissioned to commemorate the completion of the plant in 1914.

Next, the viewer's eye may be drawn to CA Cabin, a standard rectangular telegraph tower, resplendent in its original 1890s appearance. To its rear stands a concrete bridge carrying eastbound trains onto the branch. Above looms a wooden water tank constructed

The same scene today.

with steel support legs. To the far right stands a boiler house with its twin stacks plainly visible.

Adjacent to the main line is the depot with its obligatory baggage wagons. The design for this building is almost unique; the only other known example is at St. Albans.

All of the rail structures except the concrete bridge have long since passed into history. In the early 1950s CA Cabin was replaced by a yellow brick building, devoid of any architectural value.

Time grinds along, yielding to no man. However, pictures like this allow one to capture a tiny segment of the ever-fleeting past. As human memories recede into darkness, photographs preserve images of long ago for generations to come.

COURTESY C&O HISTORICAL MAGAZINE, JUNE 1994, DOUGLAS ANDRE

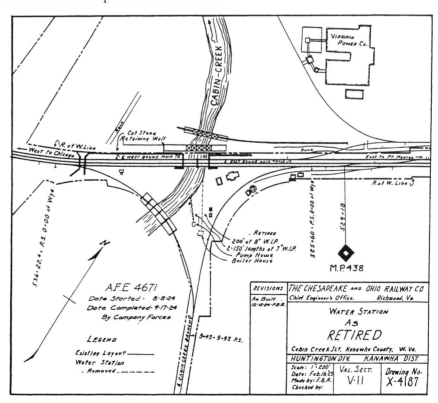

These gentlemen who drove the "Iron Horse" were highly skilled and the job of locomotive engineer was an esteemed goal requiring exceptional reliability, truly a vanished part of Americana.

C&O engine crew standing beside K-4 Kanawha, #2789 with the Friendship Train at the Charleston station, winter 1947. The Friendship train was taking carloads of donated food to the starving people of war ravaged Europe.
PHOTO BY T.L. WISE. C&OHS #10808 (111)

C&O K-4 #2789, left 3/4 view, circa 1947, seen at C&O Depot, Charleston.
PHOTO BY T.L. WISE
C&OHS #10805

The 2700 class was considered one of the all around best steam engines ever built and although intended for freight use they often pulled passenger trains with ease.

1890

K&M engine #577, 4-4-0 on the turntable
at Gauley Bridge. BOB CRAIGO COLL.

Early 1900s view of a wrecked K&M Railroad steam engine at the Quincy depot. Crew cab has been torn off.

Kanawha and Michigan #552 was built by Brooks in 1914, builders no. 54532. New York Central class was G461.

New York Central Lines (T&OC) #9661 was built by Schenectady in 1912, builders no. 51228. New York Central class was G46e. BOB CRAIGO COLL.

Both of these engines were familiar to Kanawha countians of long ago. BOB CRAIGO COLL.

Kanawha and Michigan #666 was built by Richmond in 1911, builders no. 49874, and is shown in a flood at Charleston. New York Central class was B98e. PAUL B. DUNN COLL.

A maintenance crew gets together for a group photo on the K&M. Young fellow with a banjo near center was probably the only entertainment they had in 1920.

STREET CARS

Beside cave on Edgewood Dr., circa 1910.

Scene in Charleston's east end showing middle loop car coming over some rebuilt track, circa 1920s.

In September 1906 a new park was opened in the new suburb of Edgewood in Charleston's west side. It was serviced by trolley cars of the Kanawha Valley Traction Company. As a local newspaper reported, "The new line is bound to become immensely popular with the public, being not only substantially constructed, but being an ideal scenic route, presenting a pleasing succession of changing views from the time the city limits are passed until the park is reached, to say nothing of the relief from the heat and dust of the city.

Typical Charleston trolley cars that were built for in-town service along narrow streets and sharp corners. They were usually smaller than the big interurban cars that ran all the way from town to town, circa 1915.

THE C. I. R. R. CO.
CABIN CREEK DIVISION
HAT CHECK
East Bound

BK

The last Charleston streetcar ran in 1939 but this photo was taken long before that.

CABIN C.	★
DICKINSON	★
CHES. P. O.	★
WALL ST.	★
RUSH CR.	★
FRY HOLLOW	★

		2
Jan.	1	
Feb.	3	4
Mar.	5	6
	7	8
	9	10
May	11	12
June	13	14
July	15	16
Aug.	17	18
Sept.	19	20
Oct.	21	22
Nov.	23	24
Dec.	25	26
	27	28
	29	30
		31

Globe Ticket Co., Phila., Pa.

Rebuilding track for the Charleston Interurban Railroad Co. Top: On Summers Street, note the Kearse Theater sign. Bottom: On the Lovell Street (Washington Street) Bridge over Elk River looking west, circa mid 1920s.

Top: Laying heavier track along the 1100 block of Virginia Street by the First Presbyterian Church, circa mid 1920s. Bottom: The Charleston Interurban Railroad Co. trolley at the Malden siding looking west. Many of the old streetcar tracks still lie beneath decades of asphalt under Charleston streets.SWV ROY SMALL PHOTOGRAPHER #1585 13, 1589 09

Mrs. Myrtle Bryan in front of a street car at the old St. Albans armory, circa 1930. CLIFFORD BRYAN COLL. ⑱⓪

Corner of Washington and Capitol streets, 1937. In the left background is the I.O.O.F. building on Lee Street. On the right is Howards Fruit Stand and Hennegans News Stand and Shoe Shine Parlor. The Diamond Department Store is just out of photo on left.

The Bigley Avenue car is about to turn east up Washington Street where it ran a few blocks before heading west towards the Elk River and its Bigley Avenue destination. ㉕⑤

The Kanawha City Bridge was originally built in 1915 to service the streetcar line. The 1920s photo shows two cars coupled together to handle bigger crowds, many of whom were glass plant workers.

Souvenir hunters virtually stripped the last car on that day in 1939 when the familiar sound of steel wheels on steel rails was stilled forever.

On the Kanawha City Bridge, 1939.
CHUCK HIGGINS COLL.

The last Charleston streetcar, 1939. On Duffy Street with the Capitol in background.
CHUCK HIGGINS COLL.

Corner of Summers and Lee streets, 1936. With three years left before the trolleys passed into history, these pedestrians little suspected that the end of an era was at hand. It is ironic that the rubber tired bus killed the trolley car and the Greyhound Depot is visible in the lower left of this photo.
JIM BARTH COLL.

CHARLESTON STOCKTON AND PATRICK STREETS

THE TREND IS TO TRANSIT

Same view today.

Wheels

A 1914 motorcycle tour by some Charleston cyclists. B.E. Andre is on the far right. Note sign on bike—1914 was the first year for electric lights and starters.

A fancy buggy and a curious horse in front of 1516 Kanawha Street (Boulevard), circa 1910. These buggies would soon be overtaken by the Model T. The house is unchanged today. ANN BIRD COLL.

Mr. and Mrs. Howard S. Johnson, their nurse and baby Charles L. in their 1905 "Merry" Oldsmobile. ⑱⑨

This is a page out of a 1915 auto tour guide on the route from White Sulphur Springs to Charleston. It appears the route, not a road by today's standards, followed the Midland Trail to some extent until the Kanawha River was crossed at Cannelton near Montgomery. It then followed the south side until recrossing the river on the South Side bridge. Notice the number of creek fords the traveler had to make. (191)

1913

Interior of
Wm. Hoferer &
Son garage, 1910.

Wm. Hoferer & Son auto
repair shop was on
Dickinson Street where the
main U.S. Post Office is now
located, 1914.

A very early truck owned by Elk
Furniture Co. of Montgomery.

1906

Bernard E. Andre (1886-1963) on one of his first jobs driving a delivery truck for the Gates Paint Company, circa 1907. Note oil lamp light on truck.

An ambulance for the Sheltering Arms Hospital which was located at Hansford. The hospital was organized in 1886 to provide care for people in the Kanawha/New River coal fields and the C&O Railway. It was closed in 1922. (324)

The Capitol Garage was located on the north side of Washington Street near Duffy Street and the State Capitol, circa 1925.

In the 1940s a Kroger Store occupied this building and up until the 1960s the West Virginia Library Commission—the building was demolished in 1970 and the site is now near the Veteran's Memorial.

Some type of event at the Kanawha City airfield, 1921. Could possibly be connected with the Miner's Strike of that year.

Baird Hardware's mule drawn wagon, circa 1918. Floyd Baird is seated. The store was located on the corner of Ohio Avenue and Washington Street West. The sign reads: 3300 rolls of wallpaper furnished for U.S. Government probably ordered for the Nitro plant houses. DED

The Summers/Quarrier family of Glenwood in a Reo model automobile at Cross Lanes, 1915. This area is now one of the county's most populous and a far cry from this country scene 86 years ago. GA

This photo was taken to publicize the first DeSoto automobile in 1929. The DeSoto, a Chrysler product was familiar to motorists until its demise in 1961. Harold A. Moore is at the wheel of a shiny new 1929 DeSoto Six in front of Sterratt Motor Co. at the corner of Dunbar and Virginia streets.

Sears founder Roy O. Sears beside the new International truck, circa 1920. Certainly one of the oldest businesses in Charleston, 1911 to the present. Note power winch on bed to handle heavy monuments.

A 1920 vintage oil tanker truck taken in front of the Standard Oil plant in Charleston just west of the C&O depot. The truck is a Mack with solid tires. Operator is Andrew J. Guthrie.
WILLIAM GUTHRIE COLL.

American Legion campout convention, circa 1920s. B.E. Andre is on the hood. He was the commander of John Brawley Post 20 in Charleston in 1925.
BEA (294)

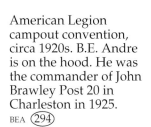

This may look like a runaway locomotive but it was really a rubber tired parade vehicle to celebrate the 40 and 8 sections of the American Legion. In World War One the French boxcars would hold 40 men or 8 horses and the American doughboys were hauled to battle in these boxcars. After the war the Legion 40/8 adopted the strange boxcar as their symbol. Seen here on Dickinson Street between Lee and Quarrier boyscouts are distributing food for Christmas 1937.

Virginia Street at McFarland Street circa 1918. The lined up cars may have something to do with World War One, perhaps a war bond sale. The *Charleston Mail* and the Y.W.C.A. were on Virginia Street at this time. CN

Winfield Scott Chapman's Pennzoil station on the southeast corner of MacCorkle Avenue and 35th Street, 1931. A gas station still occupies this site. DANNY CHAPMAN COLL. ④16

Removing old gas tanks at the corner of Court and Lee streets by the Walter Clark Company, 1940. DED

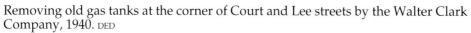

They made them out of "real steel" but it still bent—

A car wreck in 1938 at the corner of Thompson and Washington streets in Charleston's East End. The house on right looks much the same today. Note streetcar tracks which were very dangerous for motorcyclists.

Thumm's Garage tow truck hauls away a terrible wreck, circa 1935.

A 1937 Ford sedan used by the Dunbar police department, photo taken June 30, 1939.

Town Tops Taxi Company used Packard automobiles in 1946. Photo in front of the state capitol.

Ford dealer, Capitol Motors on Broad Street just north of Washington Street, 1948. TH

The bus depot at the corner of Alderson (Laidley) and Virginia streets circa 1930. This facility served both the Charleston Interurban Railroad Co. streetcar line as well as the Atlantic Greyhound Lines. The building was torn down during urban renewal in 1962. The Hotel Kanawha is seen on the left background. The magic of photography is clear in this scene of life 70 years ago and the bright face of a little boy remains forever young.
PHOTO BY BOLLINGER (182)

Another view of the streetcar/bus terminal looking north on Alderson (Laidley) Street. Woodrums Furniture Store is across the street, circa 1927.
SWV ⑱⑤

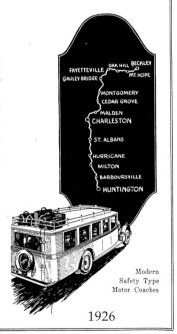

Top: Front view of the art deco Greyhound Bus Depot on Summers Street which opened in 1937 and was torn down in 1980, photo circa 1957. Bottom: Rear view of boarding area, circa 1940s. CN ⑱⑥

CHARLESTON'S TRANSPORTATION SYSTEM

The history of the Charleston Interurban Railroad Company dates back for more than 30 years. The company then known as the Kanawha Valley Traction Co., operated mule-drawn cars up to 1900. During 1900 the company purchased and put in service four electric cars. The folk of Charleston stood amazed when these cars went by. It was hard to believe that these cars could run from power fed them by that little wire overhead. One of these cars is still in service (as a lunch wagon) at the west end of the Kanawha City bridge.

It was in 1911 that the company purchased new cars. Again here was something to marvel at. . . they were equipped with air brakes, and all the motorman had to do was to turn a little lever and the brakes were set. No more did he have to twist and turn, click and clatter, to old hand brake. These cars were of the open type . . . . no complaint about not having plenty of fresh air then! In winter the crew put straw on the floor to keep snow from sticking to the floor, also to keep the passengers feet warm.

In 1901, the first trolley track was laid over the old Virginia Street bridge. thus connecting up the cities on both sides of the Elk River. This old bridge was a suspension bridge. It was later replaced by the present bridge.

The Charleston Interurban R. R. Co., now serves the city of Charleston with local trolley and bus service, as well as the suburban towns of Saint Albans, Dunbar, South Charleston, Kanawha City and Cabin Creek . . . . a transportation system that has grown with Charleston.

1930

Yellow coach model 740, bus No. 310, Charleston Transit Co. The roof duct was located to collect clean air for the diesel engine, which was, at that time, a new phenomenon as far as widespread use in buses was concerned. The headlights are not of the sealed beam type, and turn signals were still in the future. The colors were red, grey roof, and white belt. Photo circa 1940.

Circa mid 1950s

1938

BK

CHARLESTON INTERURBAN RAILROAD CO.

WEST CHARLESTON LINE

WESTBOUND.
Leave Capitol and Virginia Streets every 15 minutes from
6:07 A. M.
Until 11:52 P. M.

EASTBOUND.
Leaves 4th Avenue and Patrick Street every 15 minutes from
6:07 A. M.
Until 11:37 P. M.

Cars start 1 hour later on Sundays.

1917

BUSSES BEGIN URBAN RUN TUESDAY

First Cabin Creek Trolley's Passenger to Be on Last Car

"Just for the novelty of it," 23 years ago, Miss Ina Hoylman stepped aboard at Marmet and rode in to Charleston on the first Cabin Creek street car ever operated.

Again for the novelty, the same woman, now Mrs. Ina Vinyard of Wall street, Marmet, will ride on the final run of the cars late Monday night, just before they are replaced Tuesday morning with busses.

Mrs. Vinyard, who recalls that the new cars "just crept along" 23 years ago, plans to ride the 11 o'clock car Monday night from Marmet to the end of the line and return to Charleston on it as it completes its final journey about 1 a. m. Tuesday.

A number of persons have called Charleston Transit company officials about removal of the cars, with a view to taking the final ride. Among them are City Policeman Henry H. Clendenin and Mrs. Clendenin, who rode on the line on its first day and plan to make a final ride Monday.

When the busses begin running Tuesday morning, they will travel a slightly longer distance than did the street cars. Service on the line will be extended on to South Malden instead of stopping at Dana Ferry, company officials said.

End of the street car service Monday will mean much to D. T. Moore and M. O. Brotherton, veterans on the Cabin Creek run. Mr. Moore has been a street car employee since 1908; and Mr. Brotherton has been on the cars since 1916.

Both have been trained as bus operators and will take over that job Tuesday morning, continuing in the service of the company for which they have worked many years.

The first Cabin Creek car was operated Feb. 24, 1916. In charge of it were the late O. D. Darby and Harry Morrison.

Operating the second car on the run were O. A. VanDine, now dispatcher for the company, and Frank Whitt, who now lives at Bluefield.

1939

MIDLAND TRAIL TRANSIT CO.

Schedule Effective May 20, 1925.
CHARLESTON, HUNTINGTON AND INTERMEDIATE POINTS

Coaches leave Charleston hourly, on the even hour from 6 a. m. to 7 p. m. Last coach leaves Charleston at 9:30 p. m.

Coaches leave Huntington for Charleston hourly on the even hour from 6 a. m. to 7 p. m. Last coach leaves Huntington for Charleston at 10 p. m.

Mondays only, special coach leaves Charleston at 5 a. m., making connection at Barboursville with Guyan Valley train.

Coaches leave Charleston from Charleston Interurban Railroad Station, Virginia and Alderson Streets.

Coaches leave Huntington from Midland Trail Transit Station, Third Avenue, near Ninth Street.

CHARLESTON-CEDAR GROVE
(Schedule Effective August 25, 1925)

Coaches leave Charleston from the Charleston Interurban Station, Virginia and Alderson Streets, hourly on the exact hour from 6 a. m. to 9 p. m., last night coach leaving at 11:15. For the accommodation of those employed in the Charleston industrial district, special coaches are operated daily at morning and evening rush hours.

CHARLESTON-GAULEY BRIDGE
(Schedule Effective August 25, 1925)

Coaches leave Charleston Interurban Station at 6:00, 8:00 and 10:00 a. m., 12 M., 2:00, 4:00, 6:00 and 8:00 p. m., for Gauley Bridge and intermediate points, these coaches connecting at Kanawha Falls with Beckley coaches.

For the accommodation of those employed in the Charleston industrial district, between Gauley Bridge and Charleston, commuter rates are available.

CHARLESTON-BECKLEY

Via Midland Trail Transit Coaches, Charleston to Kanawha Falls, connecting with New River Transit Coaches.

Seven daily trips between Charleston, Beckley and intermediate points, coaches leaving Charleston Interurban Station at 6:00, 8:00 and 10:00 a. m., 12 M., 2:00, 4:00 and 6:00 p. m.

Round Trip Tickets at a Reduction of 10% from Agents.

FOR ADDITIONAL INFORMATION
Phone Capitol 3305. Call Phone 117
Charleston. Huntington.
Phone 4—St. Albans.

1925

Wayne all steel body, model 4360: Length—23' 9"   Width—95"   Inside Height—67"
Body installed on a Diamond T chassis model 412-B, 250" wheelbase. DENVER PUBLIC LIBRARY

NEW PASSENGER CAR REGISTRATIONS FOR WEST VIRGINIA
for Period January 1 to June 30, 1937. Figures supplied by Automobile Dealers Association of West Virginia

County	CHRYSLER	DeSOTO	DODGE	PLYMOUTH	FORD	LINCOLN ZEPHYR	BUICK	CADILLAC	CHEVROLET	LaSALLE	OLDSMOBILE	PONTIAC	TERRAPLANE	HUDSON	GRAHAM	NASH	NASH-LaFAYETTE	PACKARD	STUDEBAKER	WILLYS	TOTAL
Kanawha	96	49	133	544	791	16	138	11	696	20	125	125	51	11	7	4	16	107	93	42	3075

Kanawha County buyers preferred Ford in 1937.

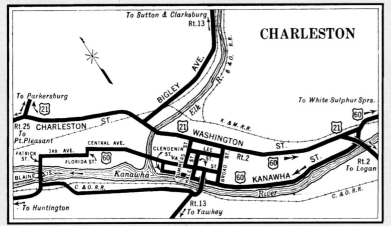

1933

John Lucenti driving a Jaguar XK-120 in a 1954 parade. Lucenti Motors was the premier foreign car dealer in the 1950s. Lucenti Motors was at the corner of Summers and Washington streets. CN

Before interstate construction, bumper to bumper traffic was common on Kanawha Boulevard, circa 1954. Note the first car, a Studebaker has the trunk lid removed and is hauling a refrigerator! CN

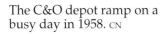

The C&O depot ramp on a busy day in 1958. CN

Midget Racing

There was standing room only at a 1946 midget car race at the Dunbar Fairgrounds. Charlie Stewart is on the left. (375)

"Doc" Folden in his "Nagasaki Nightmare" 101 at the Dunbar Fairgrounds, 1946. The midget car had a 74" Harley motor mounted sideways. Folden was killed in the crash of his private plane at Kanawha airport in 1954.

Midget racers at the Dunbar Fairgrounds, 1947.

Charlie Stewart in his racer
and Joe McCall on right pose
at the Kearse Theatre in 1949
in conjunction with the movie
"The Big Wheel" starring
Mickey Rooney. DED

Charlie Stewart was the state midget race car
champion of 1946-47, and he is shown here sitting
in his racer in the lobby of the Kearse Theatre.

Charlie and his friends—all also daredevils of
the speedway—are promoting the Mickey
Rooney racing film "The Big Wheel."

On the left is Charleston policeman "Smokey"
Stover, while "Speedy" Estep kneels in front. To
the far right, Joe McCall.

All of these men engaged in the dangerous
sport of midget racing mostly for the thrills
because their cars usually cost them more than
they won.

The name midget is rather misleading
because they were full-fledged racing automobiles. Many of today's racing stars, including Jeff Gordon, started out in the mighty
midgets.

Stewart's jet-black speedster was powered
by a Ford-V8 engine, which generated
plenty of action for the big crowds at the
Dunbar Fairgrounds' dirt track. A broken
neck was not unusual in those days, before
the safety feature of the roll bar. In fact,
Estep was killed in a race in Columbus,
Ohio.

McCall's Car Primed For Midget Feature

Joe McCall, who has done right well this season with a new car in the midget auto racing grind, was busy this week ironing out a few "bugs."

And when he's through, McCall's shiny maroon, "Zero" is expected to be primed to give some of the past dominating pilots a real run of their money.

MCCALL, WHOSE auto is powered with a Ferguson tractor engine, was timed for the first racing program at 18191—not bad, but not outstanding, either.

His efforts for that night consisted of a third in the fourth heat, a battle for early contention but failure in the 20-lap feature.

Last week, McCall qualified better with an 18.20 timing. Then, after pulling out with engine trouble in the first heat, he ran a good second in the third heat.

IT WAS in the third heat that McCall was bumped by Mac McCormick of St. Albans and later by Johnny Harris of Charleston. The first bump was in the early part of the rac eand really hurt and really hurt and McCall isn't very pleased with the incident.

"Wait until next week," he said. "I won't give those guys a chance to get close enough to me to give me a bump."

MEANTIME, AS the West Virginia Auto Speedways, Inc., officials prepared for Friday night's program at the 4-H fairgrounds below Dunbar, they posted this list of "best" times for events thus far this season:

One lap qualifying—Billy Miller of Los Angeles 17.13.

10-lap heat—Smokey Stover of Charleston with 2:56.42.

Australian pursuit—Chet Moody of Akron with 3:01.10.

20-lap feature — Moody with 6:11.48.

June 19, 1950

Called Smokey Joe because of his ever present cigar—Joe McCall owned and operated the Eastern Garage on Elizabeth Street in Charleston for many years.

A gregarious son of an immigrant, McCall had no children of his own but all the neighborhood kids were friends of Joe and loved to hang around the garage admiring the Zero Special. He died in 1979.

Joe McCall in his racer, "Zero" Special, 1948.

Midget racing was terribly dangerous as can be seen by the wreckage of this Ohio car that came to grief racing in the Charleston area. The fate of the driver is not known but he is believed to have survived.

Quite rare #97 was a six cylinder Studebaker powered car—seen here at Dunbar, circa 1948.

Stock Car Racing

Skyline Raceway in Charleston, 1956. Located where the Job Corps is today.

Owen Spradling in his stock car at Marietta, Ohio, May 13, 1956. He set a new track record at Marietta four consecutive weeks. Spradling is a South Charleston resident.

1953

Owen Spradling is shown with his V-8 Mercury (32 Ford body) stock car racer at the Skyline Raceway in Charleston, 1956. OWEN SPRADLING COLL.

Owen Spradling on left accepts the 50-lap championship race trophy at the Dunbar Fairgrounds, June 1955. Spradling won with a V-8 Mercury. Joe Border is in the middle and Al Carey, Kanawha County Sheriff is on the right. Flagman Border was himself a former race car driver.

Amos Wadell (head near steering wheel) built this little sports car out of Ford parts radically cut down. They are at the Dunbar Fairgrounds in 1956. Wadell was killed in an aircraft accident in the early 1970s.

Tommy Ringstaff's Mercury powered racer leads at Dunbar, 1956.

Charles Sigmon with his stock car sponsored by White's Garage, 1959.

Children examine Tommy Ringstaff's stock car racer at his garage near St. Albans, 1956. His car was a 34 Ford body with a modern Mercury V-8 engine. Ringstaff was killed in a seaplane accident near Dunbar in the 1970s.

STOCK CAR RACES
100 WRECK FILLED LAPS
Thrills! Excitement!
TODAY
Make Up of Friday Night Rainout
Phone 2-5425 for Box Seat Reservations
TIME TRIALS 2:30 P. M. — RACES 3:00 P. M.
Friday's Tickets Good Today Only!
DUNBAR FAIRGROUNDS
RACES EVERY FRIDAY NIGHT—7:30
If You Haven't Seen a Stock Car Race—You Haven't Lived

1953

MOTORCYCLES

Quick Time Made On a Motorcycle

Mr. William Barr of this city, state manager for the Pitner Lighting Co., of Chicago, and member of the American Federation of Motorcyclists, on last Friday rode his big twin Excelsior motorcycle to Huntington in 2 hours and 53 minutes although he says the roads were in a fearful condition, and he could have made much better time, but had to get off frequently and stop his engine on account of meeting horses or persons drivng buggies and on horse back and teamsters scaring at the machine, as the horses in West Virginia, although accustomed to the bicycle, have not become used to the chug, chug of the motorcycle. He therefore calls attention in these columns to the motorcyclist, that when they see a scary horse, when ridng the country roads this summer, it is better to dismount and stop their engine, and thereby save a runaway and perhaps somebody's life. Mr. Barr has the honor of building the first safety bicycle that was ever built in West Virginia, also he built the first automobile that was built in West Virginia, which was mentioned in the papers at the time. He says when a boy he drove his father, the late Dr. Barr who was pastor of the First Presbyterian church of this city for a number of years, to Huntington in a buggy to dedicate a church before the C. & O. railway was built, and there were only two or three houses in Huntington, and the small white church. It took them the best part of two days to make the trip.

1930 Indian 4

Motorcycle race, at the Dunbar fairgrounds, 1913. B. E. Andre on the right.

"Bee" Andre was perhaps the foremost person associated with really early motorcycling in the area. Opening his first shop in 1911 he became a racer of note riding his beloved "Indians" and all Charleston motorcyclists trace their ancient beginnings back to B.E. Andre.

Top: B.E. Andre in the middle on his Indian Twin Racer on the Dunbar Fairgrounds 1/4 mile track, circa 1913. RAA ㋟

Below: Andre nicknamed his racer "The Virginia Creeper" and is shown leading at the old Dunbar Fairgrounds 1/2 mile horsetrack, circa 1913. RAA

Hillclimb racing up Bridge Road in South Hills, 1914. The Presbyterian Church is virtually unchanged.

Crude but interesting scenes of what the "Roaring Twenties" were like in Charleston.
East and west on Virginia Street near Capitol Street, circa 1920. Note arcade on far right of left hand photo.

What a pothole!

West   East

A trade show display believed to be in the Scottish Rite Shrine building which was the National Guard Armory across from the Daniel Boone Hotel, 1916. Andre was a motorcyle dealer in Charleston for many years. In the foreground right is the innovative Smith Motor Wheel which could be bolted onto virtually any vehicle for power—usually bicycles but sometimes even a sled with snow chains. Yes, Indian once made a bicycle and they are almost priceless on the antique market. RAA ⑤⑤⑤

Cycle shop at 442 Virginia Street across from the courthouse, circa 1925. Mike Kelleher, third from right; B.E. Andre on far right. Kanawha County Courthouse annex stands here today.

B.E. Andre with what is believed to be the oldest motorcycle in the United States, the 50th motorcycle made by the famous cycle manufacturing company, Indian. This cycle was donated for display at the Smithsonian Institution in Washington D.C. in 1930 and can be seen there today. ʀᴀᴀ

John Grant Tompkins is seen in white shirt—Tompkins was the scion of the noted Tompkins family of Cedar Grove that was related to President Grant. (See President Grant's visit in the first chapter.)

Weekend excursion by Charleston cyclists, circa 1924. This old bridge across the Elk River at Elkview is still standing but abandoned. (190)

Early 1920s, Nitro.

New Harley-Davidson motorcycles for the West Virginia State Police. They were ridden from the factory in Milwaukee, Wisconsin to West Virginia, circa 1920.

Indian Summer All the Time
B.E. Andre, Charleston Motorcyclist

My father Bernard Andre was born in Charleston in 1886, on the eve of the gasoline age. His father was the godson of Edgar Allan Poe. The Andres had been musicians, from generation to generation, and one might have expected that Bernard would follow in their footsteps. Instead "Bee," as he came to be called, took after his Scotch-Irish grandfather, Samuel Robinson. Sam was a first class blacksmith who had settled in Charleston in the 1840s.

From the beginning Bee had an extraordinary love of anything mechanical, especially if it rolled. He must have been electrified by his first encounter with a horseless carriage. That may seem quaint today, with space flight becoming common. But space travel is too remote for most of us really to get a feel for. An automobile, on the other hand, was something you could get right up close to-into the clatter and smoke and the rich new aroma of gasoline and motor oil. And to think that it went by itself! From the first young Bernard took to internal combustion, although he later graduated from four wheels to two.

In the meantime, he had his growing up to do. As a youth, and throughout his life, he was thin and wiry and enjoyed athletics. An old photograph shows him knocked cold on the football field, his obliging teammates propping him up for the camera. Bee finished Charleston High later in 1907, the last formal education he had. He set out to make his fortune, working for four years in a variety of jobs. He drove a delivery van, worked at the old Kelly Axe Factory, and was circulation manager for the *Charleston Gazette*.

By 1911, at age 25, Bee Andre felt he had enough of both savings and experience to set up for himself. It didn't take him long to decide upon a line of business. Gasoline transportation still fascinated him and, as a lifelong bicyclist, he instinctively turned to motorcycles instead of automobiles. He found a Quarrier Street storeroom and had a sign painted. "B. E. Andre Motorcycles and Bicycles" was the place to go if you wanted to put two wheels under yourself.

Charleston's new motorcycle dealer settled on Indian for his main sales line. He recognized the quality of the bright red machines. Besides, as he used to say, "They had plenty of soup." The Andre customer could expect good times on a good machine and some of my father's early newspaper ads carried the upbeat motto, "Indian Summer All the Time."

Bee Andre was a born mechanic and he made a good living from his shop. A 1914 advertisement boasted that "74 of the 89 motorcycles in Charleston are Indians." It was inevitable that my father took up racing, with his competitive bent and direct access to parts and the finest motorcycles. He named each of his Indian racers the "Virginia Creeper," reflecting an ironic sense of humor.

The Indian racer got by without certain accessories. There were no fenders, as the rider noticed when his hindquarters slipped back onto a speeding rear tire. What the machine lacked in frills, it made up in speed. The big one could blister along at 100 miles per hour or better.

His racing accidents were numerous, breaking most of his limbs as well as his nose at one time or another. Still, the fearlessness propelled him to championship status and he brought home very few second-place ribbons.

As it happened, second place was dead last for him in one of his most celebrated early contests in Gallipolis, Ohio. That was the time he raced his Indian against one of the early flying machines. The pilot, Lincoln Beechey, made his living barnstorming the country to race autos and motorcycles-anybody, in fact, who wanted to take him on. Bee Andre lost, but he accused the bi-plane pilot of cutting corners and buzzing his motorcycle at no more than an arms reach. He told the story in good humor in later years, but never failed to call Beechey a "damn fool" for his flying practices. Those were strong words coming from a man not noted for his own cautiousness. They evidently were on the mark, however, for Beechey managed to kill himself a few years later in a San Francisco crash.

Andre never challenged another airplane and he never lost many more races, either. Old newspaper clippings document his success. In 1914 the Fayette Democrat reported that he ran "something like a mile a minute, which is good time on a small track," in winning the Oak Hill race celebrating the Fourth of July. A Harrisonburg, Virginia, paper noted that he "led the field . . . and finished a hundred yards or more ahead" in winning their county fair race in 1916. The *Bluefield Daily Telegraph* said he established a local track record there in June 1917.

As the teens progressed, larger affairs than cycle racing came to occupy the attention of young men. The European war loomed ever larger, and after his discharge from WWI he got himself back home to West Virginia. The 1920s promised to be good years for a hustling motorcycle man in the busy town of Charleston.

They were. The motorcycle reached peak popularity in the early part of the decade. Bee Andre got his share of the new business and the original location at 913 Quarrier Street was soon outgrown. He moved his dealership to Virginia Street, about where Kanawha County's new Courthouse Annex stands today. B.E. Andre Motorcycles and Bicycles remained in business there well into the 1930s.

He was proud to have left his mark on regional racing, and prouder still to leave a monument to early motorcycle days for the permanent enjoyment of the people of America.

That two-wheeled monument had to be a red Indian, of course. It had come into his sales shop back in the 1920s, brought by a customer with only an intuition of its significance. Bee had a clearer idea of its importance and checked the serial number to confirm that it was a very early model - in fact, the 50th Indian ever made. The little 1902 motorcycle had a single cylinder producing 1 3/4 horse power and weighed less than 100 pounds.

He kept the 1902 cycle in his shop for several years. Finally, he decided that it should be turned over to the Smithsonian Institution in Washington, which accepted it in the early 1930's. Curators there recognized it as one of the very earliest surviving American motorcycles and have kept it in the collection for 70 years now. It was still on exhibit the last I visited. I view it personally, of course, as a tribute to my father's youth, but I am glad that it can be shared, so that others may catch a glimpse of a time when motoring Americana had not yet decided in favor of four wheels over two.

by Richard Andre

Mike Kelleher and his Indian motorcycle on Kanawha Street near Brooks Street in 1924. The C&O depot is in the background. Kelleher was a native of Ireland. He was killed a few years later in a motorcycle accident.

Mike Kelleher on his Indian Scout at the Owens Bottle Works in Kanawha City.

1954

A tiny four wheeler powered by a detachable "Smith Motor Wheel" at the corner of Quarrier and Dickinson streets, 1914. Building in background still stands.

Two Wheeled Memories

Much of this book would not have been possible were it not for the talents and dedication of Daniel E. Davidson.

Over 20 years ago "Danny" discovered the lure of antique photographs and through largely self-taught technical work in his darkroom he has found

and preserved hundreds of images that would otherwise have been lost.

But Dan Davidson has other facets and he has lived a chapter of local history that we believe you will find interesting—probably no one living knows more about the story of motorcycling in the Kanawha Valley.

You might say Dan was not shy and he is shown here with his wife, the former Lorraine Lyons on Woodland Drive in the summer of 1952. The cycle is one of the most remarkable bikes of the era, a British Ariel "Square Four" which had four cylinders—two in front and two behind—thus the name "Square Four." Just returned from a stint in the 101st Airborne Division in Germany Danny was not content to leave the already lightning fast "Ariel" in stock form. Modified to burn methanol, this machine could leave any other motorcycle or automobile of the era in the dust from zero to sixty.

Retired but still active, Dan Davidson left his old house on Ohio Avenue on Charleston's west side for the plush Teays Valley suburbs. Any sunny afternoon you may see Danny enjoying a ride on one of his bikes—perhaps with a slight smile as he recalls the rides of a half century ago and the friends who have gone on.

Motorcycle friends on Bigley Avenue in Charleston, Jan. 1, 1952. Left to right: Hugh Jones, Dan Davidson, Bruce Perry, Bob Harder, Benny Marshall. The first cycle is a new British B.S.A. *Golden Flash.* This was a time when British motorcycles were just becoming popular. A short ten years later the Japanese motorcycle invasion vanquished most other foreign makes.

"Les" Parker will be remembered as the long time owner of "The Cycle Shop" that was located on Washington Street close to where the "Embassy Suites" is today. Les got his first job working for B.E. Andre in the 1920s.

Something big has attracted a crowd to the C&O Railroad depot in Montgomery in this lively scene about 1910. The makeshift awning and booth near the baggage carts seem to indicate a fair of some sort. Coal smoke and steam would have been a part of this moment in time and the ladies had to be careful of the flying cinders.

COMMUNITIES

The dedication of a new building attracted curious spectators in downtown Montgomery, circa 1920.

Ferry Street in
Montgomery,
early 1900s.

The Central Hotel in Montgomery catered to the many traveling salesmen who covered the coal fields, circa 1920.

If you were on Main Street in Montgomery in 1911 an automobile would be a rare sight because as we see the long-suffering horses still were a central part of American life.

Atlantic Greyhound Bus Depot in St. Albans at the corner of 3rd Street and 6th Avenue, early 1930s.

North side of Main Street near B Street in 1940. St. Albans featured an A&P Grocery and an A.W. Cox department store (see page 383 for death of A.W. Cox Jr.) Antique car buffs will recognize a streamlined Chrysler Airflow (middle) that was a failure because of its then radical styling.

This panoramic view of St. Albans in 1907 brings back a vanished time when the American Column and Lumber mill was beside the Kanawha River. The beautiful Victorian Mohler mansion is clearly visible and it along with buildings along Main Street survive to this day. CALVERT MCNEELY PHOTO 440

Aerial view of St. Albans, circa late 1940s.

Doubtless the same photographer took both of the photos on this page. Here we see the Coal River Bridge on Main Street, December 1950.

Christmas is coming along Main Street in St. Albans in 1950. The Korean War burdened the hearts of Americans but Gene Autry sang "Rudolph the Red Nosed Reindeer" and the children awaited the arrival of "Old Saint Nick."

The people of Ward celebrate their heritage each year with a popular reunion. This panoramic view is of the coal mining community in the early 1900s.

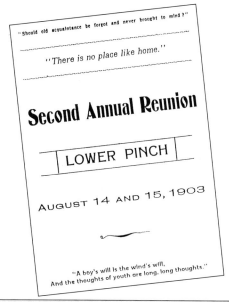

"Should old acquaintance be forgot and never brought to mind?"

"There is no place like home."

Second Annual Reunion

LOWER PINCH

AUGUST 14 AND 15, 1903

"A boy's will is the wind's will,
And the thoughts of youth are long, long thoughts."

Responding to the photographers request these residents of Pinch became a part of history in 1914. A shoe repairman was set up in a tent. The oil boom made Pinch a very busy place.
ED O'DELL COLL.

If you could walk in the door of Browns Theater at Chelyan in 1951 you might see Roy Rogers or Gene Autry vanquishing the bad guys. The good guys always won - remember?

7th Avenue in South Charleston has not changed much since this 1950 scene except the tiny Martin Theatre is long gone along with the "Bathtub" Nash and the Packard automobiles parked at the curb. CN

Two thousand years ago the mysterious Adena built the mound in South Charleston as a sacred place for the burial of their dead but in June 1951 the photographer thought it was a good place to stand for this picture of Main Street. CN

Groundbreaking for the U.S. Naval ordnance plant in South Charleston, August 1917. LIBRARY OF CONGRESS

This aerial view of South Charleston in the foreground and Dunbar across the river reminds us of the Fletcher Enamel plant in Dunbar (see page 155) and the auto junk yard in South Charleston, circa 1952.

The aircraft is now over Dunbar and the view is towards South Charleston.

Early view of Clendenin. The old flour mill was built by J.N. and Grant Copenhaver and J.M. Fleshman in 1904. It was sold to D.H. Stephenson and later to Jarrett, Givens and Naylor.

Clendenin High School in 1953. CN ⑨

Clendenin is a pretty little town in the Elk River Valley, perfect for a Sunday afternoon walk that will turn back the pages of time, photo circa early 1900s.

A century ago the Sissonville post office ran on horsepower and an undertaker was close by.

Hillbilly music was featured at the Roadside Inn near Slip Hill, Sissonville, 1959.

Opportunity
CONTRARY to general belief, opportunity is not a condition here today and gone tomorrow; it is ever present
SEE IT: GRASP IT!

COMMUNITY EVENTS

"The Press, the Voice of Progress—May It Never Be Tongue-Tied!"

Co-operation
THE principle of co-operation is one of the chief bulwarks on which civilization has its foundation; it is vitally essential to progress!

VOL. 1. NO. 2.   SOUTH SIDE-CHARLESTON, W. VA., SUNDAY, OCTOBER 28, 1923   PRICE 5 CENTS

MASS MEETING HELD ON TUESDAY NIGHT BY SOUTH HILLS ASSN.

Despite Inclement Weather Hardy Band of Citizens Hear Speakers Discuss Issues

MAYOR W. W. WERTZ IS PRESENT

Proposed Bond Issue Along With That of Water Question Explained To Voters

The called meeting of the South iHills Association last Tuesday evening held at the South Side Womans club house was well attended, despite the very inclement weather that prevailed.

Brooke Price, president of the association, who has just lately returned from a tour of Europe, opened the meeting by calling upon the chairman of the water committee to make a report. The committee, of which Major James I. Pratt is the chairman, was appointed at the last meeting of the association for that purpose of trying to get a better water supply for the South Side. Major Pratt, in reporting to the president the accomplishments of the committee, begged leave to allow Mayor Wertz, who was present to address the association on the merits of his proposed bond issue, to go into the water question in detail, he being better qualified to present to the association what had been done along that line, as he had worked with the committee and without the committee in the conferences with the water company. Mayor Wertz was then introduced, and after presenting his bond issue proposition, which was well received by those present, entered into the report of the water committee, supplementing Major Pratt's statements. He said the South Hills, by virtue of the new system would receive an abundant supply of water for both domestic and fire purposes. Also he stated the water company was installing a booster pump at the foot of the hill, and was enlarging the present water tank to a capacity to take care of the South Hills community for at least the next ten years. He closed by commending the committee upon their active and successful work in bringing to the South Hills this necesary and much needed improvement.

The South Side bridge committee report was received and filed, it being stated that the road commission would make a fuller and more detailed examination of the bridges' condition and safety, which report would probably be ready by the next meeting. The meeting then adjourned subject to the call of the president.

GYMNASIUM WORK PROGRESSES

It is with much satisfaction that progress is watched on the gymnasium at community center. It is still being rushed rapidly forward.

REPAIRS NEEDED ON PART OF BRIDGE AVE.

Has Become Difficult to Travel in Some Places and Growing Expense to People

With improvements going on on every hand, including the paving of new streets, the installation of a new water system, and various sewerage projects, throughout the city, and new roads being built in many sections adjoining there has been considerable speculation as to what is to be the final disposition of that stretch of Bridge avenue leading from the Odd Fellows' hall to St. Mathews church, and having its continuation on out through the Pine Grove section, (where it is known as Oakwood drive) thence on to its intersection with the Joplin and Ferry Branch roads. Widening, grading and resurfacing of the Ferry Branch portion has been in progress for sometime, and, it is understood, this portion of the improvement will extend to the city limits at Norwood and Bridge avenues, at which point it passes from the county's jurisdiction. This entire road, leading from the South Side bridge on up through the fifteenth ward, out through Pine Grove and thence back down Ferry Branch to the C. & O. railway, was built several years ago, and with the exception of that portion leading up Bridge avenue to Walnut avenue, has been allowed to get into such poor condition that it is very difficult to travel, for both vehicles and pedestrians, when it could have been kept in its former good condition at much less expense than it will now require to repair it. Residents of this community have watched this portion of Bridge avenue almost revert to its original almost impassable condition, and have waited for relief until patience has almost ceased to be a virtue, and feel that it is high time that measures be taken to remedy it.

NEW COLORED SCHOOL WILL BE ON SITE OF OLD

Latest reports as to the location of the proposed new South Hills Negro school are to the effect that the board of education entends to stick to their original proposition, that is to build on the old site, despite the objections of the citizen's committee.

This committee should be commended in review of their work on that issue. Their work was purely for the advancement of the community as a whole without prejudice or partiality. Their argument was just and should by all means be heeded. Whether or not it will remains to be seen.

WILL BUILD NEW HOME

It is understood that Russel Evans intends to soon build on the tract of land recently acquired on Hazel avenue between Neale and Oakmont avenues. The property was purchased from I. H. Johnson.

NEW THOMPSON HOME NEARLY COMPLETED

Will Add Greatly to Appearance of That Part of Bridge Avenue; Others Will Follow

The new residence being built by W. H. Thompson on Bridge avenue on the site of that destroyed by fire several months ago, is rapidly nearing completion, and will soon be ready for occupancy. This house is the first step in a project Mr. Thompson has had planned for some time, which plans are ascertained to call for the erection of several others on adjoining lots in the near future. The house is of frame construction, two stories, and makes quite a pleasing impression, and cost in the neighborhood of six thousand dollars. It is quite an addition to the section of Bridge avenue on which it is located, and bespeaks the future growth of the community.

REMODELING OF OLD DUNLAP HOME IS NEARLY COMPLETED

Improvements Will Convert Property Into Conparatively Modern and Pretentious Home.

Remodeling which has been in process for some time on the future home of W. Y. Johnson, on the corner of Walnut and Chestnut avenues, is just nearing completion, and will soon be ready for occupancy. This property which is being converted into a very originally built by Walter Dunlap a great many years ago, and being one of the very few houses of brick construction in the community at the time of its construction, it was considered one of the section's nicest homes. The house stands on property adjoining that of J. R. Thomas, and will, when completed, add another fine home to the great number in the South Hills.

The improvements on the property will, when completed, cost in the neighborhood of $10,000.00.

GROSSCUP DRIVE IS SOON TO BE PAVED

Street Said to Be in Worst Condition of Any in Community

Engineers have recently completed a survey preparatory to the paving of Grosscup drive, which has long been in need of repairs. This street runs through one of the finest restricted residence communities on the South Side and is surrounded on all sides by attractive homes. It has been said to be in the worst condition of any of the streets of the section, and the announcement of its improvement will be the cause of satisfaction to those having homes thereabouts .

ODD FELLOWS HALL TO BE REMOVED TO ANOTHER LOCATION

Building Will Be Removed to Rear Of Site Occupied At Present; Future Plans Unknown

LONG A COMMUNITY LANDMARK

Has In Turn Been Occupied At Various Times By Theater, Church Congregation and Store

Work will begin a few days on the removal from the lot on the corner of Bridge and Walnut avenues of the Odd Fellows' building to a lot in the rear located on the corner of Walnut and Chestnut avenues. The lot on which the building now stands, was sold about two years ago and at that time it was stated that the building would be allowed to remain in its original location for a period of two years, at which time it would be moved to a lot which the lodge retained in the rear of where it now stands. With the announcement of the removal of this building comes no information as to the plans of those who are now in possession of this property, but at the time of the transaction, it was stated that a modern business building and flat would be erected at some future date. While nothing can be learned at this time pertaining to such a project, it is highly probable that some not far distant date will witness the erection here of a fine business structure, as the location is situated ideally in what is sure to be the logical heart of the business district that is certain to come in this fast growing community. The removal of this building marks the passing from prominence of one of the community landmarks, and one which has long been a silent witness to many of the events which have marked the transformation of the community of which it has been so impirtant a part, from a small, country settlement of scattered houses and almost inaccessable dirt roads to one of the city's most attractive suburbs, with its several miles of well paved streets, lights, sewarage, water system, and, in fact, all of the things which go into the making of a bigger, better community. Could it but speak of the many incidents of which it has been a mute witness it could recount practically step by step the wonderful advancement of a community which, once considered in the backwoods, is now recognized the peer of and residence community in the city. A theater, with a drop curtain, scenery, footlights, dressing rooms, stage and all other requisites of this nature once occupied the lower floor, which in later years was converted into a store room, for which purpose it was used until about two years ago. It was also used by the congregation of the Methodist church, prior to the erection of Elizabeth Chapel at the corner of Bridge and Myrtle avenues.

Bibliography

Andre, Richard A., Stan Cohen, Bill Wintz, *Bullets and Steel, The Fight for the Great Kanawha Valley*, Pictorial Histories Publishing Co., Inc., Charleston, W.Va., 1993.

Cohen, Stan with Richard Andre, *Kanawha County Images, A Bicentennial History*, Pictorial Histories Publishing Co., Inc., Charleston, W.Va., 1987.

_____ and Richard Andre, *Roar Lions Roar, Charleston High School, A Pictorial History*, Pictorial Histories Publishing Co., Inc., Charleston, W.Va., 1988.

Denham, Charles J., *Sentimental Journey, The DuPont Belle Works, A 75 Year History (1926-2001)*, E.I. DuPont de Nemours and Co., Charleston, W.Va., 2002.

Kemp, Emory L., *The Great Kanawha Navigation*, University of Pittsburgh Press, Pittsburgh, Pa., 2000.

Morgan, John G. & Robert J. Byers, *Charleston 2000, The Charleston Gazette*, Charleston, W.Va., 2000.

Randall, James D. & Anna Evans Gilmer, *Black Past*, Charleston, W.Va., 1989.

Roper, Peter W., *Jedediah Hotchkiss, Rebel Mapmaker and Virginia Businessman*, White Mane Publishing Co., Inc., Shippensburg, Pa., 1992.

Stealey, John E., III, *The Antebellum Kanawha Salt Business & Western Markets*, The University of Kentucky Press, Lexington, Ky., 1993.

Sutphin, Gerald W. & Richard A. Andre, *Sternwheelers on the Great Kanawha River*, Pictorial Histories Publishing Co., Inc., Charleston, W.Va., 1991.

Tolley, Ova H., *History of Dunbar*, Dunbar Printing Co., Dunbar, W.Va., 2001.

Wintz, William D., *The Annals of the Great Kanawha*, Pictorial Histories Publishing Co., Inc., Charleston, W.Va., 1993.

_____, *Nitro, The World War One Boom Town*, Pictorial Histories Publishing Co., Inc., Charleston, W.Va., 1985.

Withrow, Dolly, *From the Grove to the Stars, West Virginia State College (1891-1991)*, Pictorial Histories Publishing Co., Inc., Charleston, W.Va., 1991.

Woomer, Warren J., *The Institute Site, From George Washington to the World of Chemicals*, Aventis Corporation, Institute, W.Va., 2000.

Index